RECREATION THEORY AND PRACTICE

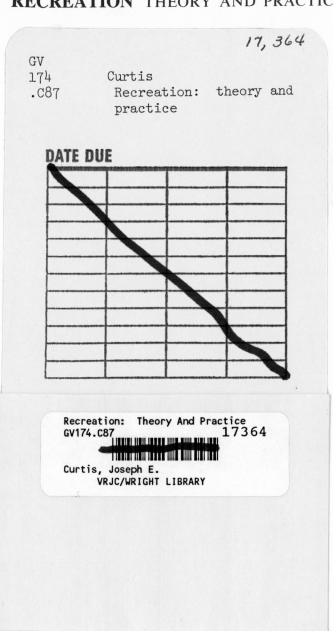

RECREATION
THEORY AND PRACTICE

JOSEPH E. CURTIS

Director of Parks and Recreation
New Rochelle, New York

The C. V. Mosby Company

ST. LOUIS • TORONTO • LONDON   1979

The C. V. Mosby Company
11830 Westline Industrial Drive, St. Louis, Missouri 63141

Library of Congress Cataloging in Publication Data

Curtis, Joseph E   1922-
  Recreation: theory and practice.

  Bibliography: p.
  Includes index.
  1. Recreation.   2. Recreation—Vocational guidance.
I. Title.
GV174.C87   796'.023   78-31266
ISBN 0-8016-1183-0

C/M/M 9 8 7 6 5 4 3 2 1   02/A/260

This book is dedicated to my wife Ruth, not simply because she typed and read and corrected every word of the text, but because she has borne the pressures, interruptions, late night phone calls, and last-minute schedule changes of thirty years marriage to a recreation professional. Loyally, she has packed and moved our clan and its household goods seven times to new jobs and new locations, governed by the peregrinations of her itinerant husband.

Ruth has given me eight lovely daughters, and each has received a full family recreation exposure. Four are presently employed in the recreational craft. Ruth is a recreation spouse, and the only real reason I have been able to keep body and soul together in this politically frustrating, unpredictable, energy-consuming, low-paying but marvelous field of recreation! Thanks, Ruth.

PREFACE

Why bother to teach play or recreation? This familiar query has been directed at enthusiasts since the beginning of the recreation movement. Questions concerning the need for recreation motivation and leadership have prompted politicians to slash recreation budgets, schools to cancel special skill classes, and apartment house builders to discard plans for new resident sports facilities. Worst of all, skepticism by parents and friends of young people who display high skill in sports and recreation has often discouraged promising talent from entering the field.

Despite this skepticism, however, recreation has boomed in myriad shapes and forms, and a profession has evolved. This profession provides an academic and technical framework within which men and women may generate, lead, teach, and administrate recreation services.

Still, many unanswered questions remain about recreation. Why is the desire for recreation spontaneous in some people, while it must be actively stimulated in others? Are all human appetites for recreation basically similar, and can these appetites be modulated from without? Can people suffer from too much leisure? Does recreation substantially help the mentally ill? So much remains to be learned about play and the quest for it.

While leisure and recreation represent one of America's major growth industries, they are identified almost exclusively through the personal experiences of the definer, leading many to hold contradictory attitudes about them. When asked about their leisure pursuits, many persons are quick to retort, "I have no hobby—who needs one? I love my work." And they are sincere, but they probably view hobbies and recreation in the stereotypes of golf, tennis, bridge, or playing with model railroad trains. Overlooked is the fact that these same cynics will devour a gripping mystery novel or trace with their eye the intricate lacework of a many-colored rose window in a great cathedral. The vulgar image of recreation has too often reflected the most obvious and conventional offerings of municipal recreation departments. The true picture would disclose a spectrum of recreation and leisure so vast as to be almost limitless. Such diversity would be in direct proportion to the numbers of people asked to express their interests. The glory of recreation is its boundless variety. Even so, recreation is more a state of mind, a conditioned attitude, than a finite listing of activities and schedules.

The advocacy of recreation interests is seemingly endless. High school and college students will find leisure studies and leisure education embroidered in and around their basic technical and liberal arts curricula.

Leisure counseling has arrived. Teachers, doctors, lawyers, family counselors, psychologists, and close friends all prescribe leisure recreation freely. Magazines, newspapers, and books are flooded with friendly advice on how readers should use their leisure hours. The very abundance of their suggestions may compel individuals to flee in search of a quiet place and time in which to analyze their own tastes, needs, and desires free from the well-intentioned flood of leisure advice.

The entry of business and industry into the realm of profit-making recreation and leisure makes it important for students from all educational sectors to obtain basic training in the roots of recreation. Recreation products and services are being mass-produced and sold in the marketplace, and this traffic in leisure is part of the contemporary cultural-social scene. Regardless of their career goals, young people must anticipate functioning within a leisure-oriented society. A knowledge of recreation and leisure philosophy and operations can enrich their personal lives and serve as a valuable tool in making their careers more relevant to the life styles and changing customs of the 1980s.

This book is intended as a practical working text for the recreation student and practitioner. From a brief introductory chapter on the history and early development of the recreation movement, the reader moves directly into the basic preparation, challenges, problems, and opportunities of the field. This text provides a valuable addition to the resource library of the student, leader, supervisor, or administrator. It can be most helpful as a ready reference on problems of personnel, training, unions, activity programs, and the variety of tasks that face all dedicated and ambitious recreation leaders.

The introductory section is brief and to the point, since the book's prime purpose is providing solutions and aids to contemporary problems and needs. Rather than placing heavy emphasis on history or philosophy, this text profiles the personal characteristics and necessary academic preparations so vital to the shaping of the recreator. In the next section, several subfields within recreation are reviewed and their distinguishing features and common elements are noted.

Thereafter, each major activity component is explored and categorized and a wealth of valuable resource information is provided. Personnel, finance, politics, public relations, and other pertinent elements are outlined. These are illustrated with actual occurrences from my own career and the experiences of other veteran recreation administrators. This authenticity, deriving directly from the rich experience of seasoned recreators, is one of the most positive features of the book.

Most chapters conclude with a series of pertinent questions for classroom assignment or for the reader's edification through problem solving. The final section of the book is a look at "Tomorrow's Leisure," an analysis of today's trends and tomorrow's possible developments. This is valuable information for both the recreation student and the mid-career practitioner.

In researching and preparing this book, I drew upon the talents, experience, and good natures of some of the profession's finest people. I wish to acknowledge the advice and assistance of Bill Lederer, Greenburgh, New York; Bob Crawford, Philadelphia; Suzanne Umphrey, Wichita, Kansas; "Chuck" Christiansen, Phoenix; Ruth Pike, Seattle; Joe Trapasso, Branford, Connecticut; John McGinn, Hewlett-Woodmere, New York; Nate Washington, Newark, New Jersey; Grover Keaton, Dallas; Frank Evans, Raleigh, North Carolina;

Bernie Guagnini, Harrison, New York; Dave Laidlaw, Detroit; Ken Smithee, Huron-Clinton Metropolitan District, Michigan; Bob Ruhe, Minneapolis; Frank Vaydik, Kansas City; and Bob Wilder, Seattle.

I received much information and direction from the campuses, especially from Dr. Edith Ball, Dr. Diana Dunne, Dr. Richard Kraus, Dr. Allan Sapora, Dr. Joseph Bannon, Dr. Jay Shivers, Dr. Bill Ridinger, Professor Frank Robinson, Dr. Bert Kessel, Dr. Doris Berryman, Dr. Don Bridgeman, Dr. Jackson Anderson, Dr. Larry Neal, and Dr. Dick Wall.

Many people, by the mere fact of their friendship, dynamism, and vision, provided priceless ideas and direction. Such people include these park and recreation entrepreneurs: John E. Hill, John Kroll, Herb Podell, John Vann, John E. Burke, Claude Aarons, Paul Aarons, Bill Hope, Don Rhuda, Bob Wormser, and Don Howig.

I thank them all sincerely.

Joseph E. Curtis

CONTENTS

10   Children and recreation, 150

11   Programming and special events, 166

12   Legal aspects of recreation, 182

13   Facilities, 198

14   Politics and minorities, 218

RECREATION THEORY AND PRACTICE

1

HISTORY

DEFINITIONS

The word "recreation" has many meanings. *Webster's New International Dictionary* defines it as "refreshment of the strength and spirits after toil; amusement; diversion." William Shakespeare asks in his play *Much Ado About Nothing,* "What revels are in hand? Is there no play to ease the anguish of a torturing hour?" Others would dissect the word, prefix from root, as in "re–creation"—the restoring of newness, zest, a replenishing of the vitality of birth.

Generally, recreation is that effort or activity in which one indulges solely for the resulting pleasure, fun, satisfaction, or relaxation. It is not normally induced by monetary gain or authoritative order, as from a boss or military officer. A wife may "demand" that her husband take her to the movies or to the horse races, but this is usually more an influence than an order. Presumably, once they arrive at the movie or track, the husband forgets the wifely coercion and lapses into a pleasurable recreational frame of mind. Office workers, on the other hand, when ordered by a health-minded boss to join in the lunchtime calisthenics program, are participating, but not recreating.

George D. Butler, one of the greatest recreation thinkers and writers of modern times, identifies recreation as "any form of experience or activity in which an individual engages from choice because of the personal enjoyment and satisfaction which it brings directly to him/her."

The late Dr. Gerald B. Fitzgerald of the University of Minnesota stated that recreation activities, to be such, must be "voluntarily motivated and provide a sense of pleasure and achievement."

Definitions and meanings abound, but the following are the most common characteristics of recreation: (1) voluntarily entered, (2) generally wholesome, with some positive results, (3) no financial reward sought, and (4) no immediately perceived career or personal advancement involved. Additional characteristics might include: fun-filled, social interaction, free of prohibitive costs, open to all races and both sexes, but these are variable and many legitimate recreation pursuits lack one or more of them. The four basic characteristics mentioned above represent a reliable profile under almost all conditions.

Kraus[4] provides some interesting comments and philosophical views on recreation and leisure. According to Kraus, Dr. H. Douglas Sessoms believes that the public image of the recreator is one of the major stumbling blocks to understanding the meaning of recreation. "Short pants, knee socks and an Alpine hat" seem a likely uniform for the overly gregarious recreation leader, according to Sessoms. de Grazia,[1] noted leisure philosopher, sees free time as not necessarily leisure. Anyone can have free time, but not everyone is wise enough to digest the concept of leisure. He sees spiritual and mental involvement in leisure, an attitude of nonaction, inward calm, silence, contemplation, serenity, and openness—all very suggestive of the yoga mood. He sees recreation as purposeful and restorative for future work, thus not truly leisure. He views, somewhat sadly, the frantic pace at which people struggle to fill their "free time" with hobbies, crafts, chores, education, travel, and voluntarism. He regards this animation as totally devoid of leisure.

Some definitions of recreation given by a group of current practitioners should be of interest. It is important to note that these people have been dealing administratively with the subject of recreation for several decades.

Dave Laidlaw, Huron-Clinton Metropolitan District in Michigan, says "Recreation is activity undertaken during leisure time that provides or gives the feeling of enjoyment, gratification, and pleasure or achievement."

Nate Washington, Newark, N.J., partly defines recreation as the "formulation of comprehensive and coordinated programs of cultural and physical activities. It answers the need of all parties seeking a basic floor on which leisure time can be expressed."

Bob Ruhe, Minneapolis, describes recreation as "An attitude of mind contributing to the physical, social, and emotional growth of the individual."

Beverly Sheffield, Austin, Texas, views recreation as "What one does in his free time—leisure—that refreshes and renews the body or mind and/or the spirit, or all three by the same activity."

Al Howard, Miami, Fla., states "When an individual has the opportunity to participate in an activity of his choice or his own volition and his own time, and when the outcome is positive or you have fun—that's recreation."

Ken Smithee, Genesee County, Michigan, calls recreation "a voluntary activity, active or passive, engaged in for the enjoyment received from it."

Grover Keaton, Dallas, Texas, sees recreation as "renewal of life and the quality of living through leisure time activity."

Jack Hoxsey of Pomona, Calif., says "Recreation is what you do when you don't have to."

A unique feature of recreation is the fact that a specific recreation for one person may be drudgery or hard work for another. The professional baseball player, after a tense, exciting game, tosses his glove and uniform into his locker, showers, dresses, and heads for his favorite recreation—bowling and a cold beer. The bowling proprietor, meanwhile, puts his assistant in charge while he takes his wife to a baseball game to "relax." An old English proverb says, "One man's meat is another man's poison."

The precise differences between work and play are difficult to ascertain, and they change and diffuse even as they are studied. The same baseball player who normally leaves the ball park immediately after the game is over is delighted to remain one evening to play ball with a group of mentally retarded children. He was *asked* to do this by management, not *ordered*.

Recreation is rooted in man's darkest and most ancient history. Archeologists and historians of the most ancient periods have identified jumping rope, running, swimming, tag and chase games, painting, and craft works in these early periods. The late Dr. Jay B. Nash of New York University related humankind's primitive, "Fight or Flight" reflex to modern humans' social and recreational habits. American Indian culture is laced with hockey-like games, lacrosse, horseback competition, and many other familiar stunts and activities.

The men who replaced the Neanderthalers in Europe some 35,000 years ago are believed to have migrated from the Middle East. Intellectually and culturally superior to their predecessors, they gradually acquired sufficient leisure to produce the first art—sculptures, painting and stone engravings so powerfully conceived and executed as to rank among mankind's great artistic achievements.[5]

Ancient China, steeped in caste systems, produced a mandarin class whose education included archery, horsemanship, and music, yet these individuals never fought, rode, or sang for a living.[7] The cultures of Central Asia, the South American Inca, the Mexican Aztec and Toltec, the Australian aborigine, the Stone Age dweller of inner

New Guinea, all devoted time to hunting and fishing competition, as depicted in cave wall inscriptions, primitive books and cartoons, and swimming and canoeing jousts; clay and straw masks; wooden sculpture; ceramic bowls; and the mock combative use of sticks, poles, and hands (e.g., Japanese Kendo and Judo). The golden eras of Greek and Roman history, 461-431 B.C. for Greece, 200 B.C.–200 A.D. for Rome, are replete with chariot races, sports arenas, boxing, dueling, wrestling, and swordplay, as well as painting, dancing, singing, poetry, sewing, tilework, gardening, fishing, and summer camping. Human beings have, in all periods of history, sought that change, release, escape, we call "recreation."

One significant difference, however, between the life styles of ancient and medieval peoples from that of modern people must be noted. In ancient times and through the Middle Ages, men and women did not compartmentalize their lives as so many people do today. Consequently, they did not stop "work" to go and "play" or finish "playing" so that they might return to "working." The simplicity of the ancient world and its primitive pressures to survive saw a man's daily activities fusing one into the other. Arising, he might head for a nearby stream to catch his breakfast (work or recreation?). Satisfied, he walks through the forest seeking firewood. In the process, he throws small stones in the air and whacks them with large pieces of firewood (work or recreation?). Returning to his abode, he spends some time with crude lapidary tools, shaping arrowheads, or doing leatherwork (work or recreation?). Suddenly bored, he drops his tools and jogs along the river bank, stretching his legs and searching for signs of fur-bearing animals to be hunted later (work or recreation?). To-

day, persons who function in a continuous, unbroken cycle of worklike activity are called "workaholics," and doctors and laypersons alike urge them to break their routine, change their pace, establish sharper separations between work and play. "Get away from it all," is often the prescription. The student of recreation should study this phenomenon carefully. Who is more fortunate, the compartmentalized modern man or the Leonardo Da Vinci total man of the past?

. . . The African bushman could not tell us—nor would be interested in telling us—which part of his activity is work and which is play. Our mental comfort depends strongly on our system of categorization: to be comfortable with an activity we must define it as either work or play . . . you would be shocked if I were to deliver this scientific paper while dancing the rock-and-roll, and you might fail to give it the serious consideration you now accord it.[2]

Man's need for recreation and diversion is evident in every walk of life. Bertrand Russell, English philosopher-mathematician, believes that, ". . . to be able to fill leisure intelligently is the last product of civilization." Population increases, social upheaval, fast-paced business and industry, frenetic urban life, and a perpetual struggle to maintain one's own identity are some of the reasons why men and women need and seek wholesome recreation on an unprecedented scale.

Simultaneously, forces are at work that bring not only more stimuli daily toward recreational pursuits, but include a seemingly endless variety of choices. Toffler[6] says, "Ironically, the people of the future may suffer not from absence of choice, but from a paralyzing surfeit of it. They may turn out to be victims of that peculiarly super-industrial dilemma: overchoice. . . .

Whether man is prepared to cope with the increased choice of material and cultural wares available to him is, however, a totally different question. For there comes a time, in short, when choice turns into overchoice and freedom into un-freedom.'' The forces, the lures, the releases, the ticklers are all there—shorter work weeks; increasing personal incomes; increasing flow of sports, games, and leisure devices; a mass communications system that preaches, like the proverbial Jewish mother inviting you to her sumptuous dinner table, ''Enjoy, enjoy!'' A leisure growth industry is also present that is devoted totally to stimulating recreation appetites to capitalize on them financially—''Travel now, pay later''; ''You've seen Europe? Try it again, it's changed!''; ''You've seen Europe? Now try the Orient—another world!''; ''Family problems over the car? Get a second (or third) car so all can have their own wheels.''; personalized surf boards; ''Go skiing even if you hate the slopes—the apres-ski action is worth it!''; ''Make your own ice cream with your own freezer just like the ice cream shops use''; wigs, bras, bars, and sports cars for your Barbie and Ken dolls.

Despite this commercial glut, the need for wholesome recreational diversion is evident everywhere. Bored prisoners in tightly enclosed courtyards; bed-ridden patients in hospitals; assembly line workers performing the same repetitive tasks all day long; soldiers with short-term work assignments and lengthy off-duty periods; office workers hemmed in by paperwork pressure; young wives at home when children have gone off to school—all have a common hunger, a need for change, release, challenge, an opportunity to sing, run, leap, shout, write, swim, jog, or indulge in some form of positive, satisfying diversion. Recreation is a basic ingredient for healthful living in modern times.

ANCIENT HISTORY

The ancient Greeks had one word for leisure, meaning serious activity without the pressure of necessity, and another word meaning playful amusement to pass the time. Both were excellent things for man, so the Greeks believed.

No race, culture, or society of the past is without its rituals and dances, its music and its painting, its games of pursuit and coquetry, its hunting, fishing, beadwork, leatherwork, and wood carving, or their counterparts.

Easy Street might be something like ancient Rome at the time of the rise of the plebs urbana. The workers were a dedicated and skilled few—administrators, lawyers, artisans, merchants, inventors and military officers. The PLEBS were those who had free time and the vote to insure their bread and circuses. The circuses, like TV, went on at all times of the day. ''We are the Romans of the modern world,'' boasted Oliver Wendell Holmes.[1]

As indicated earlier, the roots of today's recreational pursuits emanate from the earliest recorded histories and cultures. Modern history, however, provides a more discernible and directly related base.

MODERN HISTORY
Colonial era

The American colonials were not thorough-going prudes; they did have their bundling boards, cock fights, horse races, and kissing games. Recreation, however, was not held in high esteem in the puritanical Calvinistic culture of the times. In addition to religious edicts against most play, the movement was hampered by lack of usable open space. In the rocky country of the northeast where farmland had to be chopped out of forests, and stumps and boulders carted off by horses, there were few of the luxurious grassy meadows and lawns that we know today.

Public opinion and church activists in Massachusetts, Connecticut, New York, and Pennsylvania railed against leisure and play, demanding laws to control "such foolishness." The Continental Congress discouraged horse racing, cock fighting, gambling, and boxing. Pennsylvania passed "blue laws" which, even today, suppress certain forms of amusement on the Sabbath. A more tolerant attitude was displayed toward the English game of cricket, played at Dartmouth College, along with the new game of golf from Scotland. The southern region of American was distinctly more favorable to leisure pursuits than the north. Poetry, singing, needlepoint, pastry cooking, painting, and card games were highlights of holiday and family gatherings in the warmer climates and mellower living of large estates and plantations. Nevertheless, the colonial era must be characterized, generally, as restrained where fun and games were concerned.

Expansion

Plunging south, southwest, west, and northwest, men and women of the early 1800s shed much of the religious and social restraints that were part of the colonial world. Rum, guns, prostitutes, primitive surroundings, and the predatory hope for sudden riches through gold, furs, timber, land, and trade brought on a lust for fun and diversion that became part of the legend of the "Wild West."

Explorers, fur traders and missionaries to the Indians did much to open America's Far West in the early 1800's. . . . The 1849 Gold Rush to California was followed 10 years later by an almost equally exciting rush to Colorado. Then came Nevada's Virginia City, built on the Com-

stock Lode, a fabulous desposit of gold and silver. Mark Twain described the town with its mansions, banks, saloons, gambling houses and dance halls. A series of gold and silver discoveries next attracted thousands of prospectors to Montana, Idaho and the Black Hills of South Dakota.[8]

The flow of recreation interests included social and ballroom dancing in the east and square and round dancing in the west. The waltz, polka, and quadrille flourished although many thought that the placing of a young man's arm around the waist of a young woman was immoral. There were sleigh rides and ice skating in the winter and excursions to beaches in the summer. Some of the early winners of the West's bonanza of natural resources now began return trips to Europe as "dirty rich barbarian Americans," and gentlemen's clubs began forming in the major cities of the east. Legitimate theatres and music halls began in Boston, New York, and Philadelphia, as did minstrels and amateur theatres in the smaller hamlets. That "den of iniquity"—the pool room and billiard parlor—surfaced and seduced young men on every Main Street in eastern America. Hunting and fishing flourished in the seemingly endless American wilderness. Buffalo hunts, fish fries, turkey shoots, mountain lion slaughters, and eagle kills were considered manly recreation, great fun, and also part of "ridding the territory of vermin."

During the middle of the nineteenth century, many of our modern professional sports came into formal existence. The National Professional Baseball League was organized in 1876, with football appearing on college campuses about the same time. The great American bicycle in its crudest wooden-wheeled form emerged at this time, and the nation discovered the fun of pedalling for recreation as well as transportation. Approximate birth dates for many well-known sports are: baseball—1845, basketball—1891, billiards—1845, gliding—1885, field hockey—1875, rodeo—1850, softball—1887, table tennis—1895, and volleyball—1893.

Civil War

The period from the Civil War to today gives a good profile of the birth and growth of recreation and leisure in this country. In the earliest stages of this ultimately devastating war, residents of Washington, D.C., according to John Jakes in his Bicentennial series on American history, drove wagons and buggies to the rolling hills south of the capitol city. There, comfortably seated on the heights, they opened luncheon hampers and picnicked as they observed the blue and gray forces skirmishing in the nearby valleys. Shades of the Roman arena!

Soldiers of the Civil War saw little of the familiar U.S.O. amenities of World War II. Commanders of that era, like their predecessors for centuries before, believed that a fighting man, off-duty, should be free to find his own recreation. This usually meant women and liquor in copious quantities. A few zealous volunteers moved through military encampments when permitted, exhorting the young soldiers to shun the camp followers and "demon rum" and give their free time to Bible reading, psalm singing, healthful exercise, and all the sleep they could get. They were blessed with little or no success for their efforts.

Barracks and camps were drab, austere settings. There was no radio or television and very few books or magazines. A few of the young soldiers managed to keep themselves occupied with wrestling, boxing, and other physical competitions. A small minority, risking the label "queer" or "freak," would spend their idle moments in sketching, writing, poetry, or wood-carving.

Large numbers of young men were moving over vast distances, breaking home ties, meeting new people, hearing new accents, tasting new foods, and experiencing new social customs. Some of these men would take home new customs, both from the citizens they had met and from their comrades-in-arms. Others would quietly vow to return later to a certain windy hilltop or lush meadow, there to buy land, settle, and grow. Cultures were mixing and recreation interests were being fed.

The Spanish-American War of 1898 saw more of this social intermingling of young troops and foreign cultures—Spanish, Tagalog, Pangasinan, and Moro in Cuba, and the Philippine Islands. Their tastes, games, and music became more varied. The unsophisticated American soldier—city dweller or farmboy—returned home changed and broadened despite the harshness of the war. He would never view his hometown or nation in quite the same way he did on embarkation. His recreation tastes and perspectives were expanding.

Industrial Revolution

With post–Civil War reconstruction, a profound change began in American industry. Small, male-oriented shops, forges, small farms and factory workrooms became larger, more mechanized, and more centralized. Huge knitting and clothing mills, giant shoe factories, steel works, and corporation farms employed hundreds of thousands of workers. Home crafts waned and many people took jobs that were long distances from their homes. A glut of veterans flooded the industrial scene as the growing nation shifted from its prewar agrarian society to that of a heavily industrialized producer of goods—an irreversible trend. The social structure of factory life emerged, and new games, strains, heartaches, and opportunities developed with it. Most significant, however, was the fact that now great numbers of young women were going to work in these factories. This revolutionized American home life and, in effect, triggered the liberation of the American woman. Women now spent 60 to 70 hours per week in the factory, merely sleeping and eating at home. Although little time remained for recreation, what little existed was related to the factory and to co-workers. The basis was being laid for industrial recreation as we know it today.

World War I

When the United States entered World War I in 1917 and the number of uniformed troops grew sharply, social upheaval was being experienced by every city and town in the nation. Especially impacted were those communities adjacent to army camps, naval bases, airfields, and the areas in which war industries were being expanded. Soldier villages and industrial boom towns took on the riotous atmosphere of the earlier mining and railroad settlements of the west. This provoked a demand for adequate off-duty recreation facilities and opportunities for soldier and production worker alike. The War Camp Community Service (WCCS), the first of its kind, was organized in 1917 and was led by personnel of the Playground and Recreation Association of America. The PRAA was founded in Boston in 1906 by Joseph Lee and a small group of visionary volunteer recreation leaders. This, in turn, had been the result of a burst of interest in city parks and playgrounds during the latter part of the nineteenth century. Central Park in New York City, 843 acres, was begun in 1857 and was designed by the legendary landscape architect Frederick Law Olmsted. Fairmont Park in Philadelphia, 2,816 acres, was begun in 1867, followed by Boston's Franklin Park, 527 acres, in 1883.

During World War I, WCCS organized more than 650 communities adjacent to military posts and industrial centers. The program employed about 2700 leaders, and 60,000 volunteers rendered services of all kinds. This program only slightly resembled the public recreation operation of today, and depended heavily on the involvement of private agencies such as the Young Men's Christian Association, Knights of Columbus, Salvation Army, the Friends Service Committee of the Quakers, and the National Travelers Aid Association. These programs were not totally recreational in nature, but included religious, health, and social instruction, with recreation and sports serving as a bridge or stimulus for joining. Nevertheless, this represented the first major growth period for recreational services as we know them, and the period also contributed substantially to the development of the Y's, Catholic and Protestant social service wings, the urban settlement houses, and other units devoted to uplifting men's and women's activities during off-duty or off-the-job hours.

Following World War I, the Roaring Twenties were, in many ways, an hysterical period of leisure and diversion. The onward march of the Industrial Revolution brought more and more mass-produced goods, more workers earned more dollars faster, and there was the national relief of the end of the war. A sharp rise of interest was evidenced in sports, in books, in the recently introduced game of contract bridge, and in the new talking motion pictures. Americans also began drinking large quantities of bootleg liquor and experienced a zest for fast, noisy, flashy automobiles and flashier clothing, increased gambling and betting on sports events (mostly illegal), and a rash of exotic fads, stunts, and attention-getters that amazed people around the world. Dance marathons, flagpole sitting contests, bathing beauty contests, beer-guzzling competitions, and countless other zany stunts and capers characterized the leisure and recreation tastes and pursuits of a nation that had not yet matured beyond the adolescent stage.

The Depression

The colossal financial crash of the Stock Market in 1929 resulted from the brashest of credit buying policies in the nation's history. Banks, corporations, and individuals had, for a decade, been buying stocks, bonds, and commodities on the barest of cash margins, 10% or lower, assuming that the post-war boom would never end. It did, and I.O.U.'s of all kinds were called in simultaneously, plunging the nation into the deepest financial crisis in its history. Production, industry, and progress all came to a halt and one fourth of the nation's working population received dismissal slips with no prospect of new jobs or unemployment compensation. Gloom prevailed and the easy-money, flashy flapper era ended abruptly.

Ironically, the Depression (1929-1939) saw the greatest single boost to the growing recreation movement. Under the eagle-emblazoned banner of the National Recovery Act of 1933, President Franklin D. Roosevelt, less than 1 year in office, established a host of task forces and projects to stimulate the sagging economy. One of the best known of these, the Works Projects Administration (WPA), was often ridiculed in song and prose as a giant boondoggle or waste of money. The aim of the WPA was to pump federal dollars into the almost lifeless industrial and business economy in the form of construction projects and to provide leadership for intellectual, educational, and recreational pursuits.

Hundreds of parks, playgrounds, swimming pools, lakes, beaches, and sports fields were designed and constructed in cities, counties, and towns throughout America. Manpower, by the hundreds of thousands, was drawn from the millions of unemployed white-collar and blue-collar workers. Cost-benefit ratios were ignored in the WPA. Personnel were "poured" into the job sites. Gedney Field, a small park in White Plains, N.Y., was built in 1934 utilizing several hundred laborers. The laborers marched single file from rock piles to the areas to be filled, each man carrying a single stone or small boulder. Even with primitive machinery, this same project could have been completed using one fourth the manpower in half the time. But the aim was to "get them working," and so it did. Very few communities over 50 years of age exist today that do not boast one park, bridge, stadium, sports field, or artificial lake built by the WPA.

Prior to the WPA, there were less than 3000 paid recreation workers in the United States. What leadership existed was almost entirely volunteer. By 1936, however, 3 years after federal entry into the field, more than 45,000 WPA recreation workers and leaders were busily developing art centers, sports programs, music, crafts, dance, outdoor recreation, and a host of similar activities. Participants in 1938 numbered more than 5 million, and this included many unemployed men and women as well as adolescents and teenagers.

With the rapid construction of new recreation facilities, public demand arose for trained people to operate them. The WPA recreation leader training program was a most intense effort to produce top-flight talent. The majority of the 45,000 paid recreation leaders received a minimum of 2 hours weekly training. WPA recreation leaders worked under the supervision of local tax-supported units such as recreation departments, park boards, planning boards, departments of education, private social agencies, and welfare boards. This Depression–WPA era will always represent the largest single professional leap forward for the recreation movement, ironically during a time when America was steeped in the gloomiest and most discouraged mental state of the century. This is an interesting commentary on the basic value and strength of recreation services and when they are needed most.

In this same period other federal and state agencies experienced activity and growth and had an influence on recreation for the first time.

Civilian Conservation Corps (CCC). This organization, which provided employment and vocational training to unemployed young men, was created by President Roosevelt in 1933. The Corps consisted of young men between 17 and 28 years of age, including several thousand American Indians and a few thousand older men chosen for their leadership, technical skills, and experience. Between 1933 and 1942, the year of disbandment, close to 4 million men cut dead timber, planted seedlings, cleared fire breaks (and fought forest fires), and did major reforestation in every large woodland of the nation. A trip today to a dam site or a national or state park anywhere in the United States will reveal vast stands of 35-year-old pine trees, silent tributes to the CCC and its work to restore the sylvan beauty earlier generations had destroyed.

The CCC also built roads, picnic areas, camp grounds, cabins, hiking and riding trails, and swimming and boating sites throughout hundreds of smaller wooded reservations. While on duty in this quasi-military organization, Corps members received instruction in nature study, folklore, crafts, drama and music, athletics, social activities, games, and physical fitness techniques. These millions of young men returned to their homes and their later civil-

ians jobs with a definite taste for and understanding of recreation's important social contribution to our culture and country.

National Youth Administration (NYA). This agency was established by Roosevelt in June, 1935 within the WPA. It offered part-time employment to needy youths in recreation programs and in the construction of community recreation facilities. It also assisted in organizing local recreation training institutes. The Division of Student Aid gave grants-in-aid to schools to establish and operate recreation projects.

Public Works Administration (PWA). Limited entirely to construction, this agency concentrated on building large recreational facilities such as swimming complexes and regional parks and beaches.

World War II

The Japanese attack on the U.S. Naval base at Pearl Harbor, Hawaii, on Sunday morning, December 7, 1941, plunged America into the largest, costliest, and most debilitating war of all time. World War II was destined to have a major impact on American recreation as well. An unprecedented mobilization of every aspect of American life followed: education, production, manpower, energy, even social services and programs. Military and naval manpower mobilization, of course, was the most visible. The Army, Navy, Marine Corps, Coast Guard, and Merchant Marine totalled less than 2 million at the time of the attack on Pearl Harbor and now faced a flood of recruits that would number over 15 million by the end of the war.

The Army's Special Services Branch, largest of all military recreation units, acquired 12,000 officers and 50,000 enlisted men to guide the off-duty hours of its millions of troops at thousands of U.S. and worldwide locations. A Welfare and Recreation Section, Bureau of Personnel, served the U.S. Navy in the same manner aboard warships and at naval bases, air stations, and dockside facilities. Massive assistance was given these basic programs by the United Service Organizations (USO), formed in 1941 from the following member units Jewish Welfare Board, Salvation Army, Catholic Community Services, YMCA, YWCA and the National Travelers Aid. The USO became an off-duty beacon for lonely service personnel, at least those who were stationed in the United States. Overseas was another matter. Except for the Amercian National Red Cross, which operated around the world, most volunteer agencies had limited impact in the European theatre of operations and even less in the China-Burma-India theatre or the Southwest Pacific, land of islands, jungle, and endless ocean distances.

I personally experienced the quest for recreation, even the simplest kind, under a variety of wartime circumstances. While zigzagging across the war-zone Pacific Ocean during 1944 on a totally blacked-out troop ship for 2 straight weeks, every imaginable game and party idea, stunt and diversion was dug out and used to amuse and occupy the troops. Card, checker, and chess games, dancing (the personnel on board were a mixture of soldiers, marines, nurses, WAC's and Red Cross staffers), deck tennis, volleyball, boxing, wrestling, a ship's newspaper, language classes (Japanese and Filipino), dramatics, gymnastics and painting classes—these and many more were tried. Much of the movement came directly from the military passengers themselves, with minimal stimulation by the ship's staff. The activity played a role in dispelling the feeling of naked exposure to submarines and torpedoes that all felt as the ship moved across an empty sea. I was later stationed on a small, isolated Army Air Corps base near Port Moresby,

New Guinea. Jackson Airstrip was an insignificant metal ramp in a hot, insect-filled jungle. There was only a modest amount of air activity, and we had 150 men to do the work of 25. Morale was low. Fist fights, heavy drinking of home-brewed liquor, petty thievery, insolence to officers, and a general state of unrest pervaded. There was no recreation program except for occasional reruns of a limited selection of movies. GIs would travel 5 miles at night by truck over corduroy roads to sit amid dampness and mosquitoes and watch for the sixth or seventh time, Barbara Stanwyck and Fred MacMurray in *Double Indemnity*.

Finally, in desperation, a group of concerned officers and enlisted men began an off-duty recreation schedule that included nightly softball games, volleyball, and horseshoe pitching. A nearby river provided periodic swimming and diving, and target ranges were set up for archery and rifle shooting. For the more studious, weekly classes in painting and sketching, public speaking, and Spanish were initiated. Various other programs and special events were added from time to time. No miraculous change occurred, but after several weeks of these activities, there was a lessening of officer–enlisted men tensions and a perceptible drop in the incidents of violence, thievery, and heavy drinking. It was a most vivid illustration of the positive values of recreation experienced years before I considered it as a career.

Not all military recreation, however, was so primitive. On Army and Navy bases and at military airfields in the U.S.A. and abroad, vast play facilities were developed. Football and soccer fields, basketball courts by the dozen, swimming pools, jogging tracks, obstacle courses, golf courses, volleyball courts, movie theatres, gymnasiums, and craft centers became as much a part of military architecture as classrooms, drill fields, and firing ranges. Millions of American men and women who had not planned to go to college were exposed to the same sport and play complexes and programs they might have enjoyed at college, and they liked it.

To the civilian at home during World War II, many of these phenomena worked in reverse. Cities and towns lost most of their young men as they were stationed elsewhere in the nation or world. Conversely, huge drafts of strange, khaki-clad young men from outside poured into these same cities, there to seek their own off-duty diversion. Many young women, doing war work in large cities such as New York, Washington, D.C., Detroit, and San Francisco, had difficulty in finding dates among the limited field of young men they knew. To meet this recreation-social need, the USO Service Centers were set up in every sizeable city, town, and village in America for local service personnel and civilians to meet in a wholesome recreational atmosphere. Parties, dancing, fashion shows, picnics, bus and boat rides, musical concerts, and holiday events made up the schedule at most of these centers. Again, as in earlier wars, a worldwide mix of cultures, languages, tastes, ethics, and habits was being developed that would leave an indelible mark on the recreation patterns of the era following the war.

After World War II ended, some of the most visible effects of this wartime recreation concentration were:
1. Over 12 million American men and women came home with a strong new taste for sports, crafts, the outdoors, and better play facilities.
2. Hundreds of large sports and recreation complexes were scattered across the nation at military and naval bases, soon to be absorbed by neighboring municipalities.
3. Many cities, towns, counties, and villages began building new parks and recreation areas, or rehabilitating old ones, and dedicating them as living memorials to some wartime individual or to the war itself.

Korea and Viet Nam

The Korean War of the 1950s and the Viet Nam War of the 1960s and 1970s were more sophisticated reruns of World War II, as far as recreation was concerned. Fighting men spent shorter periods overseas or at the fighting front. The supply of reading and craft materials, sports and game supplies, movies, TV and radio, and hobby kits was richer, deeper, and faster flowing. In addition, the recreation profession had advanced rapidly. Now, personnel handling military recreation programs could often boast completion of full undergraduate training and preparation in the field, something almost unheard of in World War II. Again, discharged service personnel came home with increased appetites for sports, recreation, open spaces, travel, and the "better life."

In addition, a new method had been developed in military-civilian relations. Close involvement and cooperation between military base staff and program with their civilian counterparts in the surrounding community had become official Pentagon policy and was being strongly advocated. Interaction between the two was encouraged. Joint athletic tournaments, cosponsored events, and exchange of drama, hobby, and entertainment groups enabled both sectors to avail themselves of much larger and broader programming.

MISCELLANEOUS INFLUENCES

The period of the 1950s to the 1970s abounded in new inventions, sales pitches, technological advances, cultural warps, and recreation stimuli. Events and changes occurred at such a rate that Toffler[6] commented:

In our lifetimes the boundaries have burst. Today the network of social ties is so tightly woven that the consequences of contemporary events radiate instantaneously around the world. A war in Viet Nam alters basic policy alignments in Peking, Moscow and Washington, touches off protests in Stockholm, affects financial transactions in Zurich, triggers secret diplomatic moves in Algiers. . . . For the past is doubling back on us. We are caught in what might be called a "time skip". . . .

Television

Invented in the 1930s, crude and primitive in the 1940s, it blossomed in the 1950s and erupted in all its variety and impact in the 1960s. No single invention has had such subtle and powerful influence on public tastes, appetites, desires, and recreational pursuits. In addition to occupying a vast amount of people's free time, television programs have taught golf, tennis, swimming, bridge, fly-casting and an infinite number and variety of diversions from around the world. Television programs have conveyed the circus atmosphere of a Super Bowl half-time program, the sweaty countenance of a hat-trick scorer in the hockey dressing room minutes after the achievement, the fingers of a Heifetz on the strings of his violin, and the splashy vigor of a lifeguard team as they attempt to save a drowning swimmer in Miami. Television programs have introduced art, noise, films, sports, hobbies, competitions, and new pursuits to more people than lived on the earth 50 years ago.

Automobiles

Cheaper, flashier, faster, and molded in hundreds of patterns, the auto became Americans' magic carpet to recreational places. Whether jeeps, trailers, station wagons, vans, dune buggies, drag racers, fastbacks, scatbacks, sedans—the federal government reported in 1970 that Americans' No. 1 favorite recreation was automobile driving. The Recreational Vehicle Institute reports total annual sales now run into the billions of dollars.

Rock 'n' roll

In the early 1950s culture-hungry young Americans seized on a hip-swinging, guitar-strumming Tennesseean named Elvis Presley and the hundreds of his imitators, devouring the strange mixture of swing, bop, jazz, and country music they performed. Rock 'n' roll was born. The "Merseyside Sound" of Beatlemania followed in the 1960s, and this evolved into hard rock, acid rock, punk rock, and the other growling, aggressive strains and beats of contemporary music. Light-years separated this music from the Glenn Miller–Tommy Dorsey–Guy Lombardo, highly orchestrated, big band sound of pre–World War II. Presley died at 42 years of age in 1977, but he had attained such stature and had become so god-like that it is not likely that any successor or movement will challenge his place as the very source of modern rock music. Ironically, Guy Lombardo, aged 75, died within months of Presley, as did crooner Bing Crosby, aged 74, but the music of Crosby and Lombardo was a generation and a half earlier than Presley's. Recreational music had changed almost beyond recognition.

Student militancy

In 1964, at the University of California, Berkeley, a campus dropout set up a card table on the central quad, covered it with obscenities and pornography, and the "filthy speech movement" was born. In the middle and latter 1960s there was a growing student anger over the divisive and unpopular war in Viet Nam and an unprecedented rash of violence and brutality throughout the nation's colleges and universities. Very few higher education campuses did not experience the rock-throwing, burning of the college president in effigy, strikes, sit-ins, lockouts, chain-ins, auto burnings, and in some cases, violent campus war, including deaths, with the local police and National Guard troops.

As Commissioner of Parks and Recreation for the City of Boston, I experienced firsthand the student mood following the deaths at Kent State University. In May, 1970, over 110,000 students from Harvard, Tufts, Brandeis, MIT, Lesley, Emerson, Boston University, Boston College, Northeastern, University of Massachusetts, Holy Cross, Grahm, Chamberlayne, and a dozen other smaller colleges paraded in tense, stony silence onto the jampacked Boston Common. They carried coffins, black flags, presidential effigies, and a host of sombre fetishes. City officials and 500 helmeted police held their breaths, expecting the group to explode at any minute and destroy Boston. Instead, after a long series of angry, provocative, threatening speeches, the huge crowd began moving quietly off the park grounds. It appeared to be over. One hour later, a rump detachment of 3,000 students marched across the Massachusetts Avenue bridge to Cambridge and burned and destroyed every store front, plate glass window, and parked automobile in Harvard Square, the ultimate costs running into millions of dollars.

Only the end of the Viet Nam War and the total withdrawal of American troops signalled the end of this campus guerrilla warfare. The effect on campus life was substantial, and this changed the old traditions of campus recreation. Colleges and dormitories that had formerly admitted only males or only females were now coeducational. Student government became very strong and independent. The selection of books and magazines, the choice of lecturers, guests, and speakers, the printing of campus newspapers, and the pattern of singers, musicians and campus entertainers became far more liberal. Many campuses opened cash liquor bars in student centers, and beer and wine were no longer prohibited in most dormitories. The entire pattern of campus recreation changed from a rigid, sports-oriented, conservative, intramural style to one of rock music, fun sports, celebrity guests, casual living arrangements. With it came a disturbingly sharp rise in the use of so-called "recreational drugs," and an extremely free form of self-expression on the part of both students and faculty. "Do your own thing," became the campus slogan—a most significant trend for recreation planners.

Other influences on recreation at that time included:

1. Substantially increased government assistance for the purchase and development of parks and for leadership in new and creative programs, triggered by the U.S. Department of the Interior, Outdoor Recreation Resources Review Commission of 1962.

2. Explosion of interest in the arts through book clubs, museums, schools of art, purchase of art goods, self-teaching courses, concert orchestras, purchase of musical instruments, and high fidelity and stereo equipment.

3. Increase of ethnic and race consciousness in the ghettos and slums of all cities, especially the large crowded Northeastern cities. Pride in being "me" emerged and with it a rich outpouring of ethnic tastes, dances, clothes, history, language, and games that have greatly enriched recreation programs and festivals. Blackness, Hispanicness, Jewishness, became something of which to be proud.

4. Campus education and training for

careers in recreation work grew rapidly, and the profession began to be recognized by other professions and the public as a substantial contributor to the health and well-being of Americans of all ages.

5. The substantial increase in the number of baseball, football, basketball, and ice hockey franchises in the 1960s and 1970s meant more positions for young players to try to attain. New professionalism in tennis, softball, soccer, track, and golf further expanded the room at the top. The television sponsorship of these expanded leagues brought every detail of the game into the living room. Young persons heard of the fabulous salaries that athletes were now earning and the hundreds of millions of dollars involved in sportscasting contracts. They responded with a burgeoning increase in sports participation.

IMMIGRATION

A quiet, unglamorous force, but a persistent and powerful force nonetheless, had been at work in America since the period following the Civil War. Immigration from Europe began to increase during the 1860s until the 1880s. Reaching its peak at the turn of the century, the flow brought hundreds of thousands every year into America, chiefly through New York City, Boston, and Philadelphia. Major flows were from England, Ireland, Germany, and Italy, with only slightly smaller contingents from Spain, Poland, Portugal, France, Scandinavia, and Russia. The immigrants brought their food, songs, dances, clothing, books, games, customs, and the mores of their ancient homelands—a veritable treasure chest of folklore and folkways delivered to Americans. Recreation in America is infinitely richer because of this inflow of immigrants, which diminished rapidly during the Depression and never again regained its former proportions.

PROFESSIONAL PROGRESS

The recreation movement of today had its formal beginnings in 1906 with the establishment of the Playground and Recreation Association of America. The Boys Clubs of America and the Young Womens Christian Association (YWCA) were also organized that same year. Less formal recreational areas had begun earlier with the establishment of Central Park in New York City in 1857, Fairmont Park in Philadelphia in 1867, and the first professionally led children's playground in Boston in 1886.

Increasing emphasis was placed on the need for professional training of recreation leaders and professional design for parks, playgrounds, and recreational facilities. Campuses offering undergraduate curricula and degrees in recreation education for leadership rose from 1 in 1930, to 38 in 1950, and to 227 in 1970.

The National Park Service of the U.S. Department of the Interior was established in 1916, and the first White House Conference on Outdoor Recreation was held in 1924. In 1926, the National Recreational School held its first classes, a curriculum that was to produce some of the finest recreation leaders of the movement. The Playground and Recreation Association of America changed its name in 1930 to the National Recreation Association.

North Carolina was the first state to establish a state recreation commission. Annual conferences of the National Recreation Association, called Congresses for Recreation, were held in major cities, and in 1950 the Congress published *A Mid-Century Declaration of Recreation Policy,* a statement in use today.

In 1956 the International Recreation Association was formed, and its first Congress was held in Philadelphia. A milestone in professionalization came in 1960 with the creation of the Federal Outdoor Recreation

Resources Review Commission, the source of most of the progressive federal and state recreation development of the 1960s and 1970s. One almost immediate result was the establishment of the Bureau of Outdoor Recreation in 1963. This Bureau distributed almost $2 billion of Land and Water Conservation Fund monies by 1976—monies enabling national parks, state parks, and municipal park and recreation departments to acquire and develop thousands of new recreation facilities.

In 1965, after 10 years of intense collaborative work, the National Recreation and Park Association was formed through a merger of the American Recreation Society, the American Institute of Park Executives, the National Recreation Association, National Conference of State Parks, and the American Association of Zoological Parks and Aquariums.

From 1950 to 1970, there was an unprecedented growth in the number of new departments of recreation opening in cities, counties, and other municipal units. From 2400 such departments in 1950, the number rose to over 4000 in 1966. A trend by municipalities to combine the formerly separate departments of parks and recreation into one governmental agency developed during the late 1950s. The rationale for this union was a closer integration of services, better cooperation, and greater productivity.

THINKERS, PHILOSOPHERS, LEADERS

At the turn of the century, the atmosphere around Boston seemed particularly fruitful for new ideas and movements in recreation. "Boston, then, was the fountainhead of the American playground movement."[3] At that time, the term "recreation" was closely identified with "playgrounds."

Joseph Lee

Joseph Lee, probably the most famous and best remembered of the prime movers in recreation, was born of a wealthy, aristocratic Boston family in 1862. After a happy childhood, a Harvard education, a law degree, and European travel, Lee launched his efforts to help people live better lives. Delinquency and youth intrigued him, and after his first book was published, *Constructive and Preventive Philanthropy,* he began to point up relationships between family life, neighborhood influences, education, recreation, and other factors that mold youthful development.

Lee took an increasingly active part in the playground movement in Boston. He studied sites, leaders, designs, and participants in programs throughout the region. Under his direction, an experimental playground was set up in Boston to determine the best types of leadership. He worked with a philanthropic organization known as Associated Charities Playgrounds, which continues to influence the funding of youth and recreation projects today.

Lee believed that recreation was of profound importance to all age groups, not simply children. He was the first person to express his concepts of and views on museums, art, school fields, parks, and all forms of recreation and leisure pursuits throughout the country—a courageous move at the time.

Joseph Lee is considered the father of the recreation movement, and his birthday is celebrated wherever community recreation agencies function. Displays, special events, art shows, contests, and many other activities that are clearly identified with early stages of community playgrounds and recreation are featured.

Joseph Lee would probably have had an even greater impact on national policies and trends had he not been so deeply involved in the recreation developments within his beloved city of Boston. Until his death in 1937, Lee advised directors and staff of the then National Recreation Association on the relationship of strong individuals to a healthy society and the basic qualities of wholesome recreation.

Joseph Lee's children, Joseph Lee Jr. and Susan, have carried on the Lee tradition by dedicating their lives to youth, education, and recreation in Boston.

Luther H. Gulick

Luther H. Gulick was born in Honolulu in 1865 and attended Springfield (Massachusetts) College where he pioneered the expansion of the YMCA program. Founder of the Parent-Teacher Association (PTA), he moved to New York City where he became a high school principal.

Gulick developed the famous Public Schools Athletic League and a series of new, progressive camp and physical education programs. A prime mover in the Playground Association of America (later the NRA and NRPA), Gulick became its president in 1906. Among his further accomplishments were the Boy Scouts of America, the Camp Fire Girls, Inc., and during World War I he helped the YMCA expand its recreational and physical activity centers in Europe.

Among his greatest contributions was his refined concepts of play. His *Philosophy of Play,* published posthumously, was clearly his philosophy of life. He lived and taught this refreshingly new concept and offered it as the way for modern man to survive in an age of automation.

Howard Braucher

Howard Braucher, already a skilled public service worker with the Associated Charities of Portland, Maine, started working for the Playground Association of America in 1909. This former New Yorker was to serve for 40 years and brought to his work the zeal and idealism of a clergyman, which he originally expected he would be. He saw the recreation movement as having a "religious significance" in the lives of all. Braucher was a warm, open person, despite his dynamism and enthusiasm.

Howard Braucher was one of the first supporters of the concept that government should play a major role in recreation planning and operation. He believed recreation planning, however, was a local prerogative and resisted efforts to create a national stereotype or a national plan. Braucher functioned as the first paid executive of PAA and later NRA and worked in an excellent teamwork arrangement with lay leader, Joseph Lee. By the time of Braucher's death, the recreation movement had experienced massive growth and change.

Henry S. Curtis

Henry Curtis, who had earned Ph. D. degrees from Yale and Clark Universities, was very curious about child development and recreational activities. In 1905, he was supervisor of New York City's East Side Manhattan school playgrounds.

When Luther Gulick suggested the creation of a national playground association, he consulted Curtis. Original letters went out to many organizations with both their signatures. Curtis laid the plans for the new organization, which he called the Playground Association of America (PAA). He moved his base to Washington and wrote the original constitution for the proposed PAA. Intensive work by Curtis and a small group of zealots brought the PAA into existence in April, 1906. The initial session included a reception at the White House, and its first officers included Luther Gulick,

President; Jane Addams and Joseph Lee, Vice-Presidents; Henry Curtis, Secretary; and Seth Steward, Chairman of the Executive Committee. Because the fledgling PAA had no funds, Henry Curtis personally wrote 3690 letters in response to queries, at the same time vigorously soliciting contributions for the organization. He was already preparing for a even larger play congress in 1907.

With a small financial base and the beginnings of national membership, Curtis and Gulick began displaying playground and recreation exhibits at shows, conventions, and fairs. Curtis' enthusiasm and vigor seemed endless.

Henry Curtis was the force behind the most successful play conference in New York in 1908. With full approval of President Roosevelt, honorary president of the PAA, Curtis sent out letters with Roosevelt's signature, inviting mayors of municipalities to send delegates. Curtis' vigor, combined with Gulick's imagination and resourcefulness, made it a success.

In 1909, a rift grew between Gulick and Curtis that eventually forced the leaders' groups to oust Henry Curtis. Ironically, one of his many proposals that drew the leaders' opposition was his plan to establish a southern regional office of the PAA in Washington, D.C., the present site of the headquarters for its successor, the NRPA. When Gulick hired Howard Braucher as Executive Secretary of PAA, Curtis was passed over for a full-time, salaried position in the organization he helped create. Indignantly, he quit as secretary and accepted a far less important position as second vice-president.

SUMMARY

Recreation is any activity people do during leisure or free time for the fun, pleasure, or satisfaction it provides, with no compulsion by others, nor for purposes of salary, financial gain, or other reward. That which is recreation to one person may be work or drudgery to another. Generally, recreation is identified with the word "wholesome," but not always.

Recreation and leisure have been identified in some form or shape with every recorded civilization in every part of the world in every period of history. Man, ancient and modern, demonstrates a need for the diversion, the relief from the work of survival that only recreation provides. Even the tradition-bound and religiously inhibited colonials of America found outlets for their recreational needs, though society struggled to suppress such "foolishness."

The dynamism of America in the nineteenth century gave freedom and stimuli to the growth of recreation pursuits, though much of it was rough, tough, unscrupulous, and downright dangerous at that time. Despite the raucous quality of the period, this century also saw the explosive growth of theatres, concert orchestras, the first major city parks and the establishment of America's first professional sports leagues.

The Civil War period saw the crude beginnings of military recreation, though "recreation" was still thought by military commanders to be substantial drafts of liquor and women. The Civil War, and subsequent wars, brought wholesale movements of people, fighters and civilians, with the concomitant cultural mixes, a basis for the sharpened recreation appetites of the future.

The Industrial Revolution during the late nineteenth century caused massive flows of workers from farms and tiny villages to larger and larger urban factory settings. Mass recreation needs grew, and the

American woman first became aware of her numbers and her impact outside the home. Industrial recreation took its first halting steps.

World War I produced leaders who perceived the need for organized leisure leadership and programs for service personnel but it barely scratched the surface.

The financial and economic plunge of 1929 and the Depression years of the 1930s saw the largest measurable upswing it governmental interest in recreation. The WPA employed thousands of trained recreation workers to develop community recreation programs for unemployed men and women as well as for children of the poor. The recreation profession became aware of its growth and potential.

World War II plunged the nation into one of its most devastating wars and catapulted the recreation movement forward. Military recreation personnel established facilities and programs at bases around the world for the 12 million men and women in the military. These millions returned home seeking similar opportunities in civilian life. Frantic suburban homebuilding, the postwar marriage boom and its subsequent flood of babies insured a massive market for the expanding recreation profession and its services. The number of colleges and universities offering undergraduate and graduate training in professional recreation leadership grew sharply as municipalities rapidly established local departments of recreation or recreation and parks.

Influences and stimuli to the national taste and trend for leisure and recreation included the development of television, availability of the automobile, advent of rock 'n' roll, eruption of student militancy and youthful belligerence, government involvement in parks and recreation growth, ethnic and racial awareness and sensitivity, and the continued expansion of university training of leaders.

DISCUSSION QUESTIONS

1. Imagine you are an 18-year-old in the year 1877. What might a few of your social recreation activities be? What might three vigorous outdoor recreations be?
2. If the Civil War had not occurred, would the recreation and sports tastes of New Orleans and New York ever have mixed? How?
3. You are in a debate in 1917. The subject: Volunteer recreation leadership vs. paid professional leadership. Give five advantages of each of the two viewpoints.
4. Students of recreation maintain that recreational pursuits have had a profound influence on our history. Assemble a statement of your own that substantiates that position.
5. Name five recreational games or activities of modern times that have their roots or origins in some era of 100 or more years ago.
6. Select a recreation sport of modern times. Compare the equipment used in this sport several decades ago with that used in the same sport today.
7. Give your opinion of how American recreation has been influenced by the immigration from Europe during the eighteenth and nineteenth centuries.
8. As a youth center leader in a large northeastern city at the beginning of the twentieth century, what would be the basic outline of your activity program?
9. The earliest indoor recreation centers were often school buildings, since no other adequate buildings were available. Give six reasons why school buildings made good recreation centers during the early 1900s. Do all these reasons apply today?
10. Identify 10 parks and recreation facilities in your home region that were built during the WPA construction period of the 1930s.

BIBLIOGRAPHY

Beard, M.: A short history of the American labor movement, New York, 1968, Greenwood Press.

Hale, W. H.: Ancient Greece, New York, 1970, American Heritage Press.

National Recreation Association: Recreation and Park Yearbook, Washington, D.C., 1961, The Association.

National Recreation and Park Association: Employment—in the public sector, status and trends,

1966, Parks, Recreation & Leisure Services, Washington, D.C., 1977, The Association.

National Recreation and Park Association: Recreation and Park Yearbook, Washington, D.C., 1966, The Association.

National Recreation and Park Association: Special issue: Leisure—a new dawn in America, Parks Rec. 1971.

Sullivan, M.: Our times, 1900-1925, New York, 1953, Charles Scribner's Sons.

REFERENCES

1. de Grazia, S.: Of time, work and leisure, New York, 1962, Twentieth Century Fund.
2. Donohue, W.: Free time, Ann Arbor, Mich., 1958, University of Michigan Press.
3. Knapp, R. F.: The National Recreation Association—1906 to 1950, Parks Rec., August, 1972.
4. Kraus, R. G.: Recreation and leisure in modern society, New York, 1971, Appleton-Century-Crofts.
5. Life Nature Library: Early man, New York, 1971, Time-Life Productions.
6. Toffler, A.: Future shock, New York, 1970, Random House.
7. Wells, H. G.: The outline of history, vol. I, Garden City, N.Y., 1956, Garden City Books.
8. The World Book, vol. 19, Chicago, 1963, Field Enterprises Educational Corp.

2
COMMUNITY RECREATION

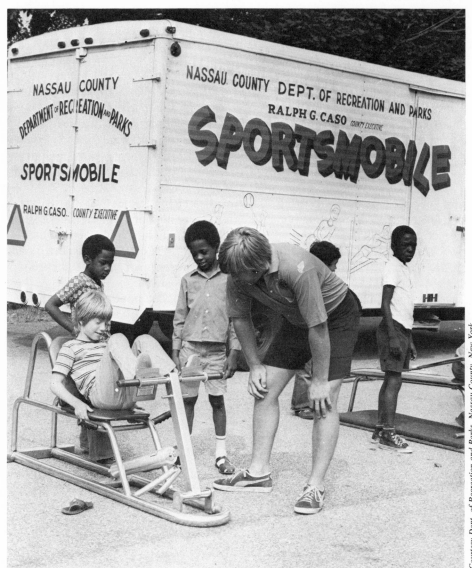

Community recreation is probably the best known segment of the entire recreation profession. Sometimes called municipal recreation or public recreation, community recreation seeks to provide the widest range of wholesome recreation and cultural and sport opportunities for the maximum number of municipal customers. It is a function of government, clearly and directly, and the stamp or seal of the local village, town, city, or county is plainly imprinted on the program and the facilities. At one time, perhaps 25 to 35 years ago, the providing of recreation programs by a municipality for its citizens was regarded as an option, a discretionary additional service that may or may not occur depending on the mood of government. No longer. From the status of a mere option, the providing of high quality recreation and park services has become as important and mandatory as the provision of pure drinking water, lighted streets, and police protection.

A prime reason community recreation is so well known to the public is its constant visibility and close proximity. Golfers using the local public course are aware of grass conditions, parking limitations, fees, locker rooms, food availability, and other perceivable operating conditions. The young mother who wishes to swim with her family in the local community pool will check on time schedules, costs, swimming lessons, bus routes, and the quality of lifeguard protection. Playing conditions, floodlighting, cleanliness, alertness of staff, and promptness of court assignments are all important matters to tennis players. Depending on the success or failure of the municipality to deliver, these citizens will communicate their pleasure or dissatisfaction to the local recreation agency. This makes community recreation a much more constituency-oriented situation than therapeutic recreation in a hospital or Armed Forces recreation at a military base. The users, or customers, in the latter two may be just as articulate and demanding in their quest for recreation outlets, but they are in a temporary, artificial setting and are transient as far as local geography is concerned. But because most people expect to remain in one area for a long time, the community recreation administrator is faced with both the advantage and burden of a permanent constituency.

BEFORE WORLD WAR II

Prior to World War II, this was not the picture, and community recreation was almost nonexistent as we know it today. True, municipalities were acknowledging some expansion of their responsibilities at the beginning of the twentieth century, but it was slow and on a small scale.

As indicated in Chapter 1, the early movements of recreation in cities such as Boston, New York, and Philadelphia were primarily in the setting aside of play and sports areas and the construction of small neighborhood parks. Highly structured programs of activity were almost nonexistent, and very few recreation facilities enjoyed the luxury of a trained, paid recreation leader. In many instances in which paid persons were provided, their roles were primarily to check out equipment and generally to maintain order. The assumption was that recreation-hungry children and adults would provide their own leadership.

Many of the programs and services later provided by community recreation were then part of the operation of private youth and family-serving agencies. It was the YMCAs, Red Shield Boys Clubs, CYO centers, Girls Clubs, Jewish Community Centers, and settlement houses of the urban population centers that offered gyms, pools, basketball leagues, workshops, and Saturday night dances for youth in the 1930s and 1940s. Some community recreation departments or divisions were functioning in a few cities and towns at this time, but their local role included little more than providing outdoor and indoor play areas. Some exceptions were New York, Philadelphia, Newark, Chicago, and Los Angeles where combinations of WPA funds and local school buildings provided substantial indoor, weeknight activity, staffed by the beginners of professional recreation leadership.

Some indications of early growth in community recreation include:

1. National Recreation Association Yearbook, 1930, reported that the number of employed recreation leaders in the United States increased from 10,218 in 1920 to 22,920 in 1929.
2. The National Recreation Association School for leaders was established in New York City in 1926. This 1-year graduate level course produced 300 dedicated new administrators prepared to take over top executive posts in the growing profession.
3. Cash expenditures for recreation rose from $7,199,430 in 1920 to $33,539,806 in 1929. Recreation expenditures were one of the few public services that consistently enjoyed annual budget increases during this period.

THE DEPRESSION

The Depression hit in 1929 and, inevitably, had its effect on community recreation. Surprisingly, however, it was not an adverse effect. In fact, recreation experienced its greatest growth stimulation during the 1930s. Public recreation facilities and programs suddenly felt the added burden of unemployed people or people with no money who had too much time and nothing to do. Unprecedented levels of attendance at indoor and outdoor local parks, playgrounds, gyms, pools, auditoriums, and shops created serious leadership problems for an unprepared profession. At first volunteers were asked to staff these programs and many did. The crush was simply too great, however, and the federal government's WPA program expanded its paid recreation leadership ranks accordingly. This began a trend that continued into the late 1930s.

Few cities dismissed their recreation executive or eliminated their program during the Depression; in fact, recreation budgets were soon fully or partly restored to pre-Depression levels in many cities. . . . Increased municipal revenues, resulting from greater employment and production due to the country's preparedness program, greatly accelerated the recovery of municipal recreation budgets and programs at the end of the decade.[1]

WORLD WAR II

Massive growth characterized the field of recreation during World War II, but it was federally dominated and placed great emphasis on physical plants and facilities. At home, professional recreation leadership became scarce since most skilled and capable people were absorbed by the armed forces. Some of the most pronounced effects of this national crisis were:

1. Hundreds of large, new sports and recreation plants were constructed in all parts of the nation and eventually throughout the world. Many new methods of design and construction were explored.
2. Millions of American youths experienced highly organized sports and recreation programs for the first time in their lives outside of school.
3. Homefront operations such as USO

and community settlement houses were forced to become creative and resourceful in providing recreation programs on limited budgets and staffs.

4. Industrial centers saw a particularly large growth of facilities and programs. Recreation centers for preschool and school-age children became a necessity as millions of women filled the jobs left vacant by men in the service.

The National Recreation Yearbook for 1946 revealed great forward strides in programs, leadership, and budget since 1941.

AFTER WORLD WAR II

If all this growth of the 1920s, the Depression era, and during World War II appears huge, it is nothing compared with what occurred in community recreation after World War II. A country relieved by the war's end, a backlog of spendable money, and a tremendous construction boom all broke loose in the late 1940s and early 1950s. In 1947 there were approximately 900 departments of recreation and/or parks in the United States, employing some 3500 full-time professional recreation leaders, and this rose sharply. Parks, playgrounds, swimming pools, tennis courts, ice rinks, and sports fields were designed and constructed at a breathtaking rate. The greatest majority of these new facilities were within the community recreation sector; that is, they were funded and produced by villages, towns, cities, counties, school districts, and special recreation and park districts.

The pace of new departments, construction, programs, and leadership continued escalating into the early 1970s and was only appreciably slowed by the worldwide financial recession of 1972-1975. During this phenomenal growth period, 1947 to 1972,

not even a series of recessions and small depressions (1950, 1956, 1962) nor the Korean and Viet Nam Wars, appreciably slowed the expansion of community recreation. Its continued advance appeared inexorable.

During this postwar period, the role of the individual states has expanded in helping local municipalities to develop and improve their community recreation programs. With greatly expanded federal and state financial assistance and grants during the 1960s and 1970s, local governments were able to expand and diversify their community recreation facilities and programs on an unprecedented scale. "Assisting local communities should be a key responsibility of State outdoor recreation agencies. Local governments often lack the funds, technical skills and manpower that the State can provide."[2]

STRENGTHS AND WEAKNESSES

Theoretically, community recreation is very close to the ideal vehicle for providing people with their recreational outlets and opportunities on a regular, day-to-day basis. Recreation should be optional, close by, low cost, and varied, and its quality and texture should be subject to the input and changing wishes of the user and participant. Community recreation comes out well on most of these, though it does have shortcomings.

The basic advantages of community recreation include the following:

1. Locally based: Usually, the main recreation office or operating center is no more than a mile or two from the home of the user, even in larger cities. Thus, a personal visit, discussion, interview, or complaint can easily be arranged or accommodated.

2. Locally financed: The greater portion of community recreation budget funds

comes from local taxation and from local fees and charges. This permits users to bring influence and pressure for greater or lesser expenditures and for program changes. Political leaders are directly available, and responsive.

3. Locally led: Leadership, even in larger cities, is locally oriented. Most paid personnel live either within the municipality or very close to it. Many have been raised in the very same community, own their own homes, and have wide family, social, religious, and political ties to the area. Obviously, such personnel are very interested in the healthy development of local recreation, sports, and cultural activities.

The basic disadvantages of community recreation include the following:

1. Budget limitations: Whether the local economy is healthy or not, the local government may place tight spending restrictions on the community recreation budget. This will be aggravated by economic slumps, budget and borrowing ceilings, and by the departure or closing down of local businesses and industrial plants.

2. Political pressures: Political pressures exist at all levels of government but are most evident and appear to have the greatest personal impact at the local community level. Such pressures can adversely affect or intimidate a community recreation administrator when an important decision on funds, playground construction, or hiring personnel is about to be made.

3. Limited scope: Except for the largest towns, cities, and counties, most municipalities have difficulty contemplating facilities as vast as the marina, year-round swimming pool, zoo, artificial ice rink, or lighted sports park. Still more difficult to accommodate are the ski slope, sports flying field, forest preserve, or mountain camp. It is simply a fact of life that modest-sized cities do not possess the geography, space, varied terrain, or the planning and operating staff to address such challenges. Compounding this problem, many citizens suffer a lack of such programs and facilities because the local municipality cannot, or will not, enter the necessary cooperating relationships with surrounding jurisdictions that might offer a solution to the problem.

COUNTY GROWTH

Because of the tremendous expansion of interest in community recreation by citizens and the inability of many cities and towns to fully satisfy this demand, a considerable growth in the role of county government in community recreation has developed.

The National Association of Counties in 1963 presented a series of guidelines to assist the county governments in promoting more effective community recreation programs and facilities. Based on the recommendations of Outdoor Recreation Resources Review Commission, the guidelines stated:

The special role of the county is to acquire, develop and maintain parks, and to administer public recreation programs that will serve the needs of communities broader than the local neighborhood or municipality, but less than statewide or national in scope. In addition, the county should plan and coordinate local neighborhood and community facilities with the cooperation of the cities, townships and other intra-county units, and should itself cooperate in state and federal planning and coordinative activities.[3]

The county government occupies a place in the structure of delivery of recreation services that is roughly between the local municipality and the state. Since World War II, a great increase in county government activity has been noted, and this is reflected in statistics from the National Recreation and Park Association Yearbook for 1966. The number of county park and recreation agencies increased during 1960-1966 from 290 to 358. Employed professional recreators rose from 7990 to 11,912, while budgets increased from $95.5 million to $195.7 million.

The county government has a number of major assets that make it capable of assuming increased responsibilities in community recreation. Among these are:

1. The county has been designated as the base for numerous federal and state financial grants and fund disposition programs in parks and recreation.
2. Most counties comprise substantial tracts of land (from 100 to 600 square miles on the average), which provides greater opportunities for new facilities and for the varied terrain sought by many recreational special activities.
3. Larger populations and the diversity they bring can be helpful in establishing new and unusual recreation programs.
4. Existing departments of county government can help in launching new community recreation programs and facilities. These include Highways, Public Works, Public Welfare, Police, Planning, and Health. Many local municipalities do not possess such department strength.
5. A strong and active professional organization, the National Association of Counties, has effectively promoted the cause of county government since World War II and has developed a most effective and influential lobby in 50 state governments and the national capital. This has become a major force for county recreation and park expansion.

The county's role in parks and recreation is, today, growing at a faster rate than that of local municipalties.

This must be watched with caution. The great value of community recreation being administered at the local level, in response to local tastes and needs, must not be overlooked in the rush to accept the power and efficiency of the county. The strengths of both county and local governments are needed if the important goals of wholesome recreation for the public are to be attained.

POLITICAL SIGNIFICANCE

Because of the relatively low profile of community recreation prior to 1950, it had little impact on the American sociopolitical scene. Except for the legendary Robert Moses, perennial Park Commissioner of New York City, 1938-1962, few people knew who their local park or recreation director was, or even if one existed. They knew little and cared less what their town or city appropriated annually for park maintenance or for recreation leadership. It simply was not an "in" subject. The recreation explosion of the 1950s and 1960s changed that. Now, political hopefuls on all levels of government do their homework on the current and future status of local and regional recreation programs and facilities. They make certain their platforms include specific popular items or issues such as "that long-awaited community swimming pool," "I can assure you that the lifeguard force at your beach will be expanded if I am elected," etc. Politicians are aware of the increasing popularity of community recreation and of the public's expanding knowledge of the subject.

Some of the citizen groups who can pressure politicians who lack knowledge on the subject of local recreation and parks include local recreation councils, Little League organizations, Pop Warner Football groups, Parent-Teacher Associations, garden clubs, urban beautification foundations, environmental protection committees, and groups identified with bicycling, forestry, golf, competitive swimming, sport flying, vegetable gardening, trail riding, and snowmobiling. Consider that in any one of these groups, an active, informed membership of 100, plus 100 spouses, plus 3 to 5 interested friends each, may result in 500 votes going either way on an issue or a candidate. It is not difficult to understand politicians' concern for community recreation when they speak publicly.

One month before the Presidential election of 1976, the following headline appeared on most of the major newspapers, "President Ford Promises $1.5 Billion More for Parks," a very timely announcement of his proposed expansion of the Land and Water Conservation Fund. Gubernatorial candidates in New York, Florida, Minnesota, California, Massachusetts, Connecticut, and Virginia, as well as mayoral candidates in Los Angeles, San Francisco, New York, Boston, Washington, Philadelphia, Phoenix, Dallas, and San

Diego must be especially sensitive and informed on the subject of recreation and parks if they are to be victorious because these states and cities have been among the national leaders in this field and their electorates are keenly aware of these particular issues.

STRUCTURE

The following charts show the typical community recreation structures for small cities or villages and large cities or counties.

QUALITY

To assess the quality, depth, and effectiveness of a community recreation agency normally takes days or weeks and a substantial amount of work and money by professional assessors or consultants. The following instrument, however, is provided so that recreation students and citizens may apply a simple measurement to the community recreation program or agency of their choice. It might be thought of as a kind of "litmus paper" test, rather than a highly

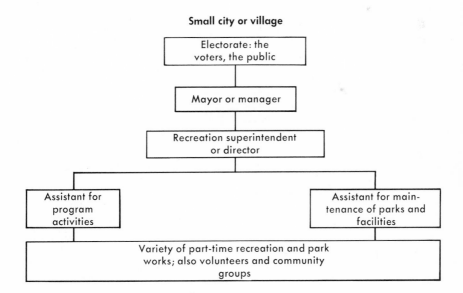

Small city or village

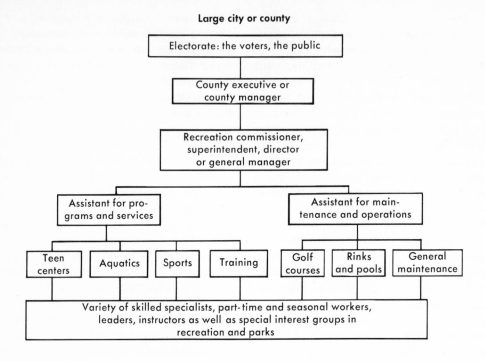

technical appraisal. It can give a general picture of the vigor or laxity of a recreation operation and should be followed by a more technical, extended study.

To the questions that follow, give a simple *yes* or *no*. Each *yes* has a value of 10; each *no* has a value of 0. Total value possible is 100. A score of 70 or higher is very good; 50 to 70 is fair; under 50 is poor.

_____ 1. Does the specific community have a clearly identified public agency providing community recreation (e.g., Department of Recreation)?

_____ 2. Does the recreation agency have a clearly identified director, superintendent, or similar person in charge who is well known to the public?

_____ 3. Does the director or agency head have a college degree and professional recreation training?

_____ 4. Is the recreation agency head a distinct member of the cabinet or staff of the Mayor or City Manager?

_____ 5. Is there an identified, appointed, and generally respected citizens group assisting the agency head in formulating policy for the recreation program (e.g., Recreation Board, Park and Recreation Advisory Committee)?

_____ 6. Does the community own and operate a substantial number of parks, playgrounds, and other recreation facilities for public use?

_____ 7. Is there a well-planned and varied program of sports, cultural activities, and recreation events available to all ages, both sexes, and all socioeconomic groups in the community?

_____ 8. Is the recreation program well publicized in schools, churches, clubs, and organizations, as well as in newspapers and on radio and television?

_____ 9. Does the general public express the feeling that it has direct input in the shaping of new recreation activities and in reshaping old ones?

_____10. Does the recreation agency director

make a general public annual report or statement on the work of the agency including a budget and financial report?

Chief executives in community recreation agencies generally carry one of the following titles: Director of Parks and Recreation, Superintendent of Recreation, Commissioner, or General Manager. Many of these top executives, especially in larger departments or agencies, occupy exempt positions, meaning that they are direct appointees of the current governmental administration and are not subject to competitive examination and selection. Most staff and employees beneath these executives, however, are civil servants with appropriate status, tenure, and benefits.

In summary, a community recreation agency that fully acknowledges its responsibility to the public will:

1. Establish a series of local ordinances and laws to provide a legal basis for sound operation.
2. Appoint a citizen board or commission to formulate policy and operating procedures for recreation and parks.
3. Employ a professional administrator and staff to carry out policy and operate the recreation agency.
4. Purchase appropriate supplies and equipment.
5. Set aside certain open lands for outdoor facilities and for the construction of indoor facilities.
6. Appropriate a budget for the total program and facility operation.

PROSPECTS FOR CAREERS

Community recreation saw its greatest growth pattern between 1955 and 1970, but modest growth continues. Some of the positions that are particularly receptive to young professionals moving into the recreation and parks field include recreation leader; playground leader; recreation supervisor; director, recreation for the developmentally disabled; and specialist (drama, dance, sports, etc.).

As indicated earlier, the new professional who wants a career in community recreation must be prepared for a broad and very changeable setting and must realize that service to the general public can be demanding and even frustrating. Growth opportunities are considerable because of the following:

1. The early wave of recreation professionals who opened the flood of new departments after World War II is now aging to the point of retirement and will thin their ranks considerably during the late 1970s and early 1980s. This will cause massive job-juggling as younger, lower-ranking people move upward and thousands of jobs become available at the bottom of the structure.

2. Federal involvement in recreation is steadily increasing, partly through the funding of hundreds of thousands of recreation and park positions at the local level.

3. Colleges and universities are doing a better job of advertising their recreation curricula and reminding government of the high quality represented by their graduating students.

4. Improved status of men and women in small, one-person recreation departments is enabling these people to expand their operations by adding one or two highly-trained, carefully selected assistants.

5. A continued, if moderate, increase in the number of new departments of recreation and parks on all levels of government.

NEXT DECADE

Community recreation will experience continued steady growth through the 1980s. An increasingly sophisticated public is asserting itself where new swimming pools, ice skating rinks, ski slopes, beaches, and tennis courts are concerned, and an increasingly responsible political machinery is giving them what they demand. Where it was once sufficient to build facilities and turn them over to the public, now trained professional recreation leaders are expected to staff and operate facilities and programs.

Many of the old, exhausted northeastern American cities are poised for total rehabilitative efforts, and many of these will succeed during the coming decade. An illustration of this is the huge rehabilitative project now underway for New York City's ravaged South Bronx community. A score of new and reconstructed parks and recreational facilities are in process, and hundreds of millions of dollars are committed to parks. There will be hundreds of new parks and recreation facilities nationwide and thousands of redesigned and improved old ones. Recreation leaders of all kinds will be needed. Simultaneously, the Sunbelt cities and counties of the south and southwest are building new and enlarged recreation facilities to accommodate their expanding populations. Relocating industries and retiring elderly account for much of this population boom. Here again, dynamic recreation leaders will be needed. Conservatively, some 125,000 to 150,000 new community recreation professionals will be needed nationwide during the next 10 years.

DISCUSSION QUESTIONS

1. As the recreation therapist in a large private hospital, you are asked to explore ways for co-sponsoring programs and activities with the nearby community recreation department of a medium-sized city. Where would you begin and whom would you contact? What are some advantages of such co-sponsorship and some disadvantages? Give three different ways that funding or budgeting of such a program might be arranged for mutual advantage.
2. The Parks and Recreation Department of a medium-sized industrial city is threatened with major budget cuts caused by economic slowdown. As Superintendent of Parks and Recreation you are expected to convince the City Council that severe cuts to your budget will do serious damage to successful community programs and facilities. Describe briefly what points you would make to accomplish this goal.
3. Fire departments, police departments, ambulance services and other emergency municipal services are often declared, "vital" to city life, while recreation services are labeled "desirable," but certainly not essential. Do you accept this position? Explain your answer.
4. When college graduates seek to enter the community recreation field, friends and relatives often try to discourage them because they regard recreation as such a nebulous, insecure kind of work. Give five sound arguments proving this position to be false and encouraging young professionals to enter community recreation as a career.
5. Communities differ as to the degree of involvement by their citizens in the role of volunteer workers in recreation activities. As a community recreation administrator you should encourage lay people to take an active role in the program as volunteer leaders, coaches, managers, door security guards, hiking guides, fund-raisers, speakers, and in dozens of other ways. Give several steps and techniques by which the administrator can get citizens to take this active role.

BIBLIOGRAPHY

Hjelte, G., and Shivers, J.: Public administration of recreational services, Philadelphia, 1972, Lea & Febiger.

Lutzin, S. G., and Storey, E. H.: Managing municipal leisure services, Chicago, 1973, The International City Managers Association.

Meyer, H. D., and Brightbill, C. K.: Community recreation, Englewood Cliffs, N.J., 1964, Prentice-Hall, Inc.

Meyer, H. D., and Brightbill, C. K.: Recreation administration, Englewood Cliffs, N.J., 1956, Prentice-Hall, Inc.

Rodney, L. S.: Administration of public recreation, New York, 1964, The Ronald Press.

REFERENCES

1. Butler, G. D.: Introduction to community recreation, New York, 1972, McGraw-Hill Book Co.
2. Outdoor Recreation Resources Review Commission: Outdoor recreation for America, A report to the President and the Congress, January 31, 1962.
3. Policy for county parks and recreation, Recreation Magazine 271-272, June, 1964.

3

OUTDOOR RECREATION

Courtesy Huron-Clinton Metropolitan Authority, Detroit, Mich.

The term "outdoor recreation" includes that sector of the recreation profession relating to large open spaces, mountains, lakes, forests, plains, and all the features and phenomena thought of as "wild, primitive, and natural." The people who work in outdoor recreation include foresters, nature lore specialists, zoologists, meteorologists and a wide range of wood and seashore oriented recreation and activity leaders. To some environmentalists, outdoor recreation identifies solely with hiking shoes, backpacks, and human beings pitted against the elements. On the other hand, outdoor recreation in today's culture can range from the wilderness camper atop a 6000-foot mountain, to a busy administrator struggling with garbage disposal in the crowded campgrounds of a national park. The spectrum of outdoor recreation is broad. Annually, over 50,000,000 Americans participate in some form of outdoor recreation.

During the nineteenth century and the first half of the twentieth century, the great outdoors was left to a comparative handful of Americans. It was civilized to live in cities, to sleep in beds with sturdy roofs overhead, and eat heavy, homecooked meals. Urban-oriented children and adults were rapidly filling the cities of the East and Northeast, many of them first or second generation immigrants from crowded, confined cities in England, Ireland, Germany, and Italy. They splashed and bathed at the beach during hot summers, and they sometimes enjoyed making tracks in fresh snow. Generally, though, they left the forests, lakes, mountains, and deserts to the hermits, cowboys, nature lovers, and construction gangs. Three things were happening, however, that would shape the coming field of outdoor recreation in America:

1. The increase in population was making life difficult in close, crowded cities.

2. The beginnings of recreation and leisure interests were stirring in ordinary citizens.

3. The United States, with no comprehensive plan, was acquiring vast tracts of virgin open space, so vast that it would take decades even to measure and evaluate.

LAND ACQUISITIONS

Through a series of wars, skirmishes, surveying expeditions, annexations, and outright purchases, the dynamic new nation of the United States was growing rapidly. Most of these acquisitions were to the west and southwest, and some were across many miles of open water. Illustrative of these colossal land deals were the following:

1. Louisiana Purchase: In 1803, the United States purchased 825,000 square miles of prime open space ranging from the Canadian border south to the Gulf of Mexico and from the Mississippi River west to the Rocky Mountains. The price— $15,000,000.

2. Oregon Territory: Through a treaty with Spain in 1819, the United States acquired what today are the states of Oregon, Washington, and Idaho and portions of Montana and Wyoming. The territory was rounded out by treaties with England in 1824 and Russia in 1825.

3. Florida Territory: 58,560 square miles of lush subtropics were transferred from Spain to the United States in 1821.

4. California: The Treaty of Guadalupe Hidalgo in 1848 required that Mexico cede 158,693 square miles of the far west to the United States.

5. Texas: In 1845, Texas joined the United States as the twenty-eighth state, bringing in an awesome 267,339 square miles.

6. At the conclusion of the Spanish-American War, Spain was required to cede Puerto Rico, with 3435 square miles, and the Philippine Islands, an archipelago of

115,707 square miles to the United States. In the same year, 1898, Spain gave up all claims to Cuba, 44,217 square miles, in the Treaty of Paris, while Hawaii, 6424 square miles, was annexed by the United States at the request of the Republic of Hawaii.

During the nineteenth century, the United States more than tripled its land size. This gargantuan growth in real estate was undoubtedly one of the prime causes of Americans' chronic cliché mentality, "our endless resources," "America's land without end," and "space to burn." In much the same thinking, Australians refer to the western half of their island continent as the Outback and regard it as a limitless supply of open space.

At the turn of the twentieth century, scarcely 5000 persons were employed in outdoor recreation. These dedicated men and women served as nature guides and interpretive leaders in regional, state, and national forest and park reservations. Because public interest in these parks was still very small, these recreation leaders and guides prepared themselves daily to receive small groups of 15 to 25 persons. Most guests were dressed comfortably but rather formally, and they were usually satisfied with modest, well-planned journeys on foot, on horseback, or in wagons, venturing only a few miles from the base lodge, and rarely after sunset. Most large government reservations consisted of rustic entrance facilities opening onto vast, relatively unexplored forest, lake, prairie, and desert beyond. No small wonder, then, that urban Americans of that era spoke of their forest, mountains, and plains as, "wild, trackless, unspoiled, endless." That's exactly what they appeared to be at that time, but the winds of change were stirring.

PERSONALITIES

Many courageous men and women were speaking out for the country and its re-sources. They were still a tiny minority and were characterized as "dreamers," "nature lovers," or "against progress," but they persisted. The following persons played prominent roles in the outdoor recreation history of America:

1. Theodore Roosevelt—twenty-sixth President of the United States, outdoorsman, cavalryman. He told Congress that "the forest and water problems are perhaps the most vital internal problems of the United States." To discourage the waste of natural resources, Roosevelt added more than 125,000,000 acres to the national forests and began vast irrigation and reclamation projects.

2. Gifford Pinchot—Governor of Pennsylvania. He favored planned conservation of United States forests. He became a member of the National Forest Commission in 1896 and was appointed chief of the Division of Forestry in 1898. This division became the Forest Service of the U.S. Department of Agriculture in 1905. Pinchot wrote "The Fight for Conservation" in 1910.

3. John Muir—explorer, naturalist, writer. He campaigned for forest conservation in the United States. He influenced Congress to pass the Yosemite National Park bill in 1890, establishing both Yosemite and Sequoia National Parks. He persuaded President Roosevelt to set aside 148,000,000 acres of forest reserves. A redwood forest in California's Coast Range near San Francisco was named Muir Woods in 1908 to honor this fighter for conservation.

4. Carl Schurz—American editor, soldier, political leader. He was Secretary of the Interior from 1877 to 1881. He worked to strengthen his department and to improve relations with the Indians.

MODERN TIMES

In 1969, sixteen federal agencies employed 20,000 persons in outdoor recreation services. These agencies included the U.S. Department of the Interior, U.S. Department of Agriculture, Army Corps of Engineers, Tennessee Valley Authority, and the U.S. Coast Guard. This level of operation (20% higher in the 1970s) resulted from a series of significant steps in the past two decades.

Outdoor Recreation Resources Review Commission

On June 28, 1958, the Congress enacted and President Eisenhower signed into law a document, PL 85-470, establishing the Outdoor Recreation Resources Review Commission (ORRRC). In his accompanying message President Eisenhower said:

Recreation promotes health, and health means strong people upon which the future of our nation depends. Our recreation resources are as much a part of our national resources as our minerals, our fuels and our forests. The increasing pressures of our population, our need for healthful exercise and recreation, necessarily call for an increase in our existing recreation facilities.[3]

This was one of the strongest support statements for recreation ever expressed by a President in office.

Goals. The new law set three goals:

1. To determine the outdoor recreation wants and needs of the American people now, and what they will be in the years 1976 and 2000.
2. To determine the recreation resources of the nation available to satisfy those needs now and in the years 1976 and 2000.
3. To determine what policies and programs should be recommended to ensure that the needs of present and future generations are adequately and efficiently met.

The establishment of the ORRRC was a particularly sound and timely move by government because something big had been happening for several years. Since the early 1950s, the American attitude toward outdoor recreation and open space had been changing, particularly among the young. Talk of diminishing space and resources had reached minds and souls and was becoming commonplace. Young people were beginning to hike and to seek lonely trails and campsites beside remote lakes and rivers. Indignation was kindling at the sight of ugly pollution smears curling across Lake Erie and the Hudson River. Voices were rising at the prospect of beaches and streambanks carpeted with beer and soft drink cans and at the $50 billion burgeoning federal highway system that was crossing and crisscrossing the nation's forests, prairies, and mountains, consuming millions of acres in the process. America was looking toward its wild lands for recreation and was frightened at the way civilization was threatening them.

Several causes aroused this interest and opened Americans' eyes.

1. Service men and women entering the military from the crowded coastal cities of the east and west had experienced real open space for the first time in their lives. The Army, Navy, and Marine Corps had sent these service people into the semi-wilderness of the Carolinas, Florida, Georgia, Texas, Arizona, New Mexico, and the northwest. Overseas, they tasted the limitless dimensions of the Pacific Ocean, had seen gorgeous Hawaii, the majestic mountains of Alaska and New Guinea. When they came home, they didn't forget. Philadelphia, Boston, Newark, and Rochester seemed small, confining, and stuffy. The open spaces beckoned.

2. Expanding industries and businesses enabled former urban dwellers to move to remote plant sites, many in raw, new, open country. The newcomers liked this easy access to open space.

3. Books by Rachel Carson *(Silent*

Spring, The Sea Around Us) and Captain Jacques Cousteau stimulated new thinking by urbanites who formerly regarded birds, fish, and wildlife as pests or as a hunter's endless bounty.

4. Boy Scouts, Girl Scouts, Campfire Girls, Future Farmers of America, and 4-H Clubs had been working diligently for half a century to bring their message across: *our country was not limitless.* Now they were succeeding. Former Boy Scouts and Girl Scouts were genuinely concerned about the conservation of our recreational resources.

5. The post–World War II baby boom made living in old city apartments and crowded neighborhoods increasingly difficult, and space-hungry parents began looking to the edges of the cities and beyond.

6. Twenty-five years of sound motion pictures, especially in technicolor and backed by the music of Andre Kostelanetz, glorified the soaring Rockies, the endless Great Plains, the purple steps of the Grand Canyon, and the snow-capped High Sierras as no book or radio personality could. Urban souls soared at the sound and color, and they headed west.

Whatever the cause or causes, Americans had been alerted and their appetites whetted for a better life in the rich outdoors that their ancestors had willed them.

ORRRC report. On January 31, 1962, after 3½ years work by a staff of 100, the ORRRC made its report to President Kennedy. The Chairman of the Commission was Laurance S. Rockefeller and the Executive Director was Francis W. Sargent, later to become Governor of Massachusetts. Both men were, and continue to be, dedicated leaders in the fight to preserve our outdoor resources. The ORRRC made five basic recommendations:

1. Formulate a national outdoor recreation policy.
2. Assemble guidelines for the management of outdoor recreation resources.

3. Expand, modify, and intensify present programs to meet increasing needs.
4. Establish a Bureau of Outdoor Recreation in the federal government.
5. Establish a federal grants-in-aid program to states.

These recommendations have been substantially carried out. The Bureau of Outdoor Recreation (BOR), U.S. Department of the Interior, was established in 1962. Additional significant legislative acts included:

1. Forest Service Multiple Use Act PL 86-517, June 1960. This law confirmed the recreational use of national forests.
2. Recreation Use of Fish and Wildlife Areas PL 87-714, September, 1962.
3. Wilderness Act PL 88-577, September, 1964.
4. Classification and Multiple Use Act PL 88-607, September, 1964. This law directed the classification of federal lands for outdoor recreation.
5. Federal Water Project Recreation Act PL 89-72, July, 1965.
6. Urban Open Space Land Program PL 87-70, June, 1961. This program authorized establishment of urban recreation areas in a fight against ugly urban sprawl.
7. Organic Act for the Bureau of Outdoor Recreation PL 88-29, May, 1963. This Act provided the authority for the BOR to serve as the focal point in the federal government for coordinating both public and private outdoor recreation programs. The Act authorized the following functions and activities to be directed toward that end: the preparation of a continuing inventory and evaluation of the nation's outdoor recreation needs and resources; preparation of a system for classifying outdoor recreation resources; formulation and maintenance of a comprehensive nationwide outdoor recreation plan; provision of technical assistance to states, political subdivisions, and private interests; encouragement of in-

terstate and regional cooperation in planning, acquiring, and developing outdoor recreation resources; sponsorship of studies and educational programs relating to outdoor recreation; and the coordination of outdoor recreation programs of all federal agencies.

8. Land and Water Conservation Fund Act PL 88-578, September, 1964. This Act is considered one of the most far-reaching conservation recreation measures enacted by the Congress. The Fund provides substantial financial assistance to the states and, through the states, to political subdivisions to meet the outdoor recreation needs of their citizens. Upon appropriation by the Congress, matching fund grants are made to the states for planning, acquisition, and development projects. Fund monies are also appropriated by the Congress to the Forest Service, National Park Service, and Bureau of Sport Fisheries and Wildlife to acquire land for outdoor recreation purposes and to protect endangered species of fish and wildlife.

9. Title VI Food and Agriculture Act of 1965 PL 89-321, November, 1965. This Act authorized the conversion of unused farmland to recreation land.

10. Wild and Scenic Rivers Act PL 90-542, October, 1968.

11. National Trails System Act PL 90-543, October, 1968.

12. River and Harbor Act Title I of PL 87-874, October, 1962.

Bureau of Outdoor Recreation

The Bureau of Outdoor Recreation (BOR) was created in April 1962 by the Secretary of the Interior as a direct outgrowth of the ORRRC report. The BOR became the recreation policy and planning agency for the Secretary of the Interior and "banker" for the Land and Water Conservation Fund, which provides recreation grants to states and finances acquisition of federal recreation areas. The BOR coordinates outdoor recreation programs and serves all federal agencies as well as state and local governments, private organizations, and individuals concerned with outdoor recreation.

The Land and Water Conservation Fund, administered by the BOR, was created in 1965 to help finance federal recreation land acquisition, state recreation planning, and state and local land acquisition and development. Since the Fund's inception, approximately $2 billion in matching grants have been given to states to purchase over 1 million acres of recreational lands and develop facilities at some 10,000 locations. In addition, nearly $1 billion has been divided among the principal federal land managing agencies for acquisition of 1.5 million acres. Fund revenues are derived from the sale of federal surplus property, the federal motorboat fuels tax, and outer continental shelf mineral drilling and mining receipts.

Responsibilities. The responsibility of the BOR is:

Department of the Interior has responsibility for most of our nationally owned public lands and natural resources. This includes fostering the wisest use of our land and water resources, protecting our fish and wildlife, preserving the environmental and cultural values of our national parks and historical places, and *providing for the enjoyment of life through outdoor recreation.*[2]

Additional functions of the BOR include:

1. Coordinator for the National Wild and Scenic River System and National Trails Program: The BOR studies rivers assigned to the Department under PL 90-542, to determine what steps are needed to preserve their free-flowing character and provide for maximum public use. The 1968 National Trails System Act, PL 90-543, established a

National Trails System of National Scenic Trails, National Recreation Trails, and connecting or side trails. The Act placed two "instant" National Scenic Trails in the System—the Appalachian and the Pacific Crest—and named 14 more routes for study. The BOR directs these studies of proposed trail routes and reviews applications for National Recreation Trail designation.

2. Planner of land and water resources: It accomplishes this function through its role in Statewide Comprehensive Outdoor Recreation Plans (SCORP), which are required of states for participation in the Land and Water Conservation Fund program. The BOR also serves as chairperson of the Department of the Interior's Land Planning Group, which reviews studies and proposals involving the federal portion of the Land and Water Conservation Fund.

3. Nationwide outdoor recreation planner: In December, 1973 the BOR published the first nationwide outdoor recreation plan, *Outdoor Recreation—A Legacy for America*. The plan is a mandate for action by the federal government to ensure better management of recreation resources and to increase the availability of these resources. It also presents actions for state and local governments and private interests to increase opportunities for outdoor enjoyment. By law, the plan must be updated every 5 years.

4. Coordinator of federal outdoor recreation programs: As the federal focal point for outdoor recreation operations, the BOR evaluates and monitors over 290 federal programs in 16 different agencies contributing to or affecting outdoor recreation.

5. Conveyor of federal surplus property for parks: Working with the Federal Property Council and the General Services Administration, the BOR transfers surplus federal real estate property to state and local governments for public park and recreation use.

6. Source of recreation technical assistance: The BOR provides broad-based technical assistance to recreation suppliers and users, publishes technical papers and booklets, maintains a clearinghouse of recreation-related information and a referral system to other sources of expertise, and conducts nationwide workshops and seminars on recreation problems and opportunities.

7. Environmental reviewer: The BOR prepares BOR environmental impact statements and reviews recreation-related statements of other federal agencies to ensure that proposed actions will not degrade or destroy existing or potential outdoor recreational opportunities.

Offices. The BOR is headquartered in the Department of the Interior building, Washington, D.C. 29240. Seven regional offices are located throughout the United States. Inquiries or requests for informational materials should be directed to the nearest regional office.

Northwest
Regional Director
915 Second Avenue, Room 990
Seattle, Washington 98174
   Area served: Alaska, Idaho, Oregon, Washington

Pacific Southwest
Regional Director
Box 36062
450 Golden Gate Avenue
San Francisco, California 94102
   Area served: American Samoa, Arizona, California, Guam, Hawaii, Nevada

Midcontinent
Regional Director
P.O. Box 25387
Denver Federal Center
Denver, Colorado 80225
   Area served: Colorado, Iowa, Kansas, Mis-

souri, Montana, Nebraska, North Dakota, South Dakota, Utah, Wyoming

South Central
Regional Director
5000 Marble Avenue, N. E.
Albuquerque, New Mexico 87110
    Area served: Arkansas, Louisiana, New Mexico, Oklahoma, Texas

Lake Central
Regional Director
3853 Research Park Drive
Ann Arbor, Michigan 48104
    Area served: Illinois, Indiana, Michigan, Minnesota, Ohio, Wisconsin

Southeast
Regional Director
418 Cain Street
Atlanta, Georgia 30303
    Area served: Alabama, Florida, Georgia, Kentucky, Mississippi, North Carolina, Puerto Rico, South Carolina, Tennessee, Virgin Islands

Northeast
Regional Director
Federal Office Building
600 Arch Street
Philadelphia, Pennyslvania 19106
    Area served: Connecticut, Delaware, Maine, Maryland, Massachusetts, New Hampshire, New Jersey, New York, Pennsylvania, Rhode Island, Vermont, Virginia, West Virginia, District of Columbia

In January, 1978, the Bureau of Outdoor Recreation was renamed the Heritage Conservation and Recreation Service (HCRS). Its emphasis on recreation continued, but a new dimension was added. Historic preservation of buildings, cultural centers, and other units relating to the nation's heritage and life style was to become a major concern of the agency. The changed title came by order of the Secretary of the Department of the Interior. The HCRS is now the focal point within the federal government for planning, evaluating, and coordinating the protection and preservation of the nation's

cultural and natural heritage and for assuring adequate recreational opportunities for all its people. It incorporates most of the responsibilities of the former Bureau of Outdoor Recreation as well as the National Landmarks Program and the Office of Archeology and Historic Preservation of the National Park Service.

FINDINGS

Extensive study of the outdoor recreational tastes, practices, and needs of Americans has disclosed some significant findings. The overwhelming majority of Americans, despite shrinking physical opportunities, participate in some form of outdoor recreation each year. Participation is increasing at the rate of 10% annually. Realistic projections indicate that, with rising income and more free time, participation will increase four-fold by the year 2000.

Seventy-five percent of all recreation occurs close to home in the after-work, after-school hours and on short one-day outings. Twelve percent occurs on overnight recreation trips, while 13% is enjoyed on vacation away from home.

Most people live in a relatively few large metropolitan areas, which keep getting larger. The resources for outdoor recreation, however, are not located where most of the people live. The total public recreation estate is 491 million acres. Yet, less than 3% of these lands are available for day use (within an hour's drive) to people living in major urban areas. Thus, severe inequities exist in the distribution of outdoor recreation resources and opportunities and they are steadily becoming more pressing.

The U.S. Department of the Interior reports that in 1974:

There was 1 tent camp space for every 330 Americans.

There was 1 trailer camp space for every 590 Americans.

Table 1
Volume of participation in selected outdoor recreation activities

Activity	1965		1980		2000	
	Number of occasions (millions)	Rank	Number of occasions (millions)	Rank	Number of occasions (millions)	Rank
Picnicking	798	7	1,127	7	1,715	8
Driving for pleasure	1,870	2	2,669	3	3,995	4
Swimming	1,664	3	2,752	2	4,800	1
Sightseeing	900	6	1,395	5	2,313	6
Walking activities	1,985	1	2,823	1	4,435	2
Attending outdoor spectator events	698	8	1,028	8	2,642	5
Playing outdoor games and sports	1,430	4	2,310	4	4,092	3
Boating activities	135	14	241	12	455	12
Fishing	570	9	740	9	1,020	9
Bicycling	984	5	1,344	6	2,040	7
Winter sports	312	10	474	10	816	10
Camping	175	11	315	11	595	11
Hunting	171	12	207	13	261	14
Horseback riding	144	13	207	14	333	13

Source: *The Recreation Imperative*, 1974, U.S. Dept. of the Interior.

There was 1 group camp space for every 370 Americans.

There was 1 acre of swimming beach for every 1450 Americans.

There was 1 swimming pool for every 5650 Americans.

There was 1 mile of horseback riding trail for every 1610 Americans.

There was 1 mile of hiking trail for every 1810 Americans.

There was 1 mile of bicycle trail for every 16,420 Americans.

There was 1 boat slip or mooring for every 450 Americans.

There was 1 picnic table for every 150 Americans.

There was 1 ski site for every 62,520 Americans.

There was 1 ice skating site for every 19,980 Americans.

There was 1 golf course for every 18,280 Americans.

A glance at these statistics demonstrates well the great gap that exists between supply and demand today.

Estimates as to the dollars needed to correct these outdoor recreation shortages range from $22 billion to $26 billion. The task ahead is colossal and will take the vision and efforts of our most brilliant and dedicated planners for decades to come. A federal action program now underway is directed toward:

1. A concentrated effort to provide recreation opportunity in the major metropolitan areas where the largest inequities now exist.

2. Cooperative federal-state efforts to identify outstanding resources, to plan for growth, and to preserve these resources for public enjoyment.

3. A coordinated effort to ensure that *all* public programs, both recreation and nonrecreation projects such as housing, transportation, and water resource development, are carried out in a way that preserves outdoor recreation resources, expands recreation opportunity, and enhances the quality of the environment.

Table 2

Public recreation land, total, and within day-use zones[1] of urban complexes, per 1000 persons, by section, 1965

	Population (millions)	Recreation acres (millions)	Recreation acres per 1000 persons
United States:			
Total	193.8	419.3	2,535
Urban complex day-use zones	90.3[2]	14.2	157
Northeast:			
Total	47.6	10.1	212
Urban complex day-use zones	27.9[2]	1.5	55
North Central:			
Total	54.1	30.9	571
Urban complex day-use zones	27.5[2]	1.4	51
South:			
Total	60.1	34.0	566
Urban complex day-use zones	16.3[2]	1.8	111
West:			
Total	32.0	416.3	13,010
Urban complex day-use zones	18.6[2]	9.5	506

[1]Within 40 miles of midpoint of central city of the urban complex.
[2]Population of the SMSA of 500,000 or more people at the center of the urban complex.
Source: *The Recreation Imperative,* 1974, U.S. Dept. of the Interior.

THE STATES' ROLE IN OUTDOOR RECREATION

The ORRRC of 1962 emphasized the key role of states and their political subdivisions in making available public outdoor recreation opportunities. Until 1965, however, states had to rely primarily on their own financial resources for park acquisition and development, and these funds were usually limited. With the establishment of the Land and Water Conservation Fund in that year, financial assistance was provided for planning, acquisition, and development. State outdoor recreation accelerated impressively thereafter. A few highlights of state actions for outdoor recreation follow:

Voters in at least 25 states approved bond issues of over $2 billion for recreation land acquisition and development. In addition, 30 state legislatures authorized bond issues totaling approximately $2 billion for outdoor recreation or other environmental quality programs affecting recreational values.

More that half of the states now have bond financing or authority to issue bonds to finance outdoor recreation programs.

At least 34 states have state recreation commissions, departments, councils, or boards to serve as focal points for statewide recreation efforts.

Legislatures in at least 16 states granted county and municipal governments greater responsibilities in establishing recreation organizations, districts, and commissions.

At least 21 states have established policies relating to highway beautification; all 50 states, the District of Columbia, Guam, Puerto Rico, and the Virgin Islands have developed water quality standards for interstate and coastal waters.

All 50 states, four territories, and the District of Columbia have designated liaison officers to work with the federal government on outdoor recreation matters. In 1967, the state liaison officers formed the National Association of State Outdoor Recreation Liaison Officers to represent state and local interests in the administration of the Land and Water Conservation Fund program.

Each state prepared a comprehensive outdoor recreation plan that was acceptable to the BOR as a basis for receiving matching grants from the Land and Water Conservation Fund. Since the establishment of the Land and Water Conservation Fund in 1965, matching grants totaling $252.7 million were approved in all states and territories as of December 31, 1969 for planning, acquisition, or development of recreation areas and facilities. Of this amount, $106.1 million in federal funds was matched by states to acquire 614.8 thousand recreation acres, and $141.4 million in matching funds was used to develop recreation facilities. In addition, $5.2 million in matching funds was used to prepare statewide outdoor recreation plans.

All states and territories examined their legal framework to assess their opportunities to participate in comprehensive federal outdoor recreation programs. At least 30 states clarified or strengthened their legal authority to participate, providing greater flexibility in acquiring and developing recreation resources.

LOCAL CONTRIBUTIONS

In communities—sprawling metropolitan areas, small towns, or rural counties—outdoor recreation became a community goal. Thousands of recreation areas were acquired or developed by local public agencies to meet everyday needs. A partial survey during the years 1960 to 1965 showed that nearly 5000 new park and recreational areas encompassing 300,000 acres were acquired by cities and counties. In subsequent years, federal assistance programs have contributed to further progress. Grants from the Land and Water Conservation Fund to local governments for acquisition and development of recreation areas totaled $111 million between the start of the program in 1965 and 1970. Local governments were often able to participate in federal programs because revenues from statewide bond issues were shared. Prompted by the availability of federal assistance, countless recreation bond issues were passed by local governments to match grants from other sources as well as to support independent local actions.

THE PRIVATE SECTOR IN OUTDOOR RECREATION

Concern with providing recreational opportunities has spread beyond public agencies throughout the private sector. Increasingly, individual families, garden clubs, civic clubs, small businesses, large corporations, and conservation organizations became involved in the recreational potential and environmental quality of the outdoors. The private sector, including both commercial and nonprofit interests, is the country's largest supplier of outdoor recreation resources and facilities. Its accomplishments have been many and varied.

The number of concessionaires serving visitors on lands under contractual arrangements with public agencies increased steadily. In 1968, some 2645 concessionaires on federal lands alone operated hotels, motels, trailer and other camping sites, restaurants, stores, service stations, marinas, and skiing areas, with an estimated total value of from $294 million to $324 million.

The donation of land, personnel, and equipment by industrial firms to help develop parks in local towns and cities throughout the nation became a frequent occurrence.

An ever increasing amount of land

owned, leased, or controlled by private forest industries was made available for public outdoor recreation. Also offered for public enjoyment are athletic fields, ice skating rinks, picnic, camping, and trailer park areas, and opportunities for hunting, fishing, hiking, swimming and boating.

Underground installation of new electric transmitter lines increased, reducing the need for space for transmitter towers.

New concepts were used by industry to prevent air and water pollution.

New trends in contracting housing projects to provide green and open spaces have been pursued.

Increasing numbers of grassroots conservationists wrote their congressmen or local public officials to make their interest known. Others joined growing numbers of organizations concerned with the use and management of our natural resources. These range from rural groups interested mainly in local environments and recreational opportunities to large professional and semipublic groups that support both local and national conservation efforts.

Although the conservation-minded public cannot be counted accurately and its accomplishments have not been comprehensively tabulated, there is no doubt that our grassroots conservationists and organizations are making their voices heard. As a result, this segment of the public has acquired new stature. It often serves as an innovator of conservation and recreational programs. Even more important in this age of conflicting interest in land use, it keeps in touch with the nation's lawmakers—in county seats, city halls, and state capitols across the country as well as in the Congress. The accomplishments between 1960 and 1970 are only part of the whole, but they indicate a continuous chain of events, specifically forged to enhance our environment by expanding our recreational resources.

BICYCLES

Perhaps the most dramatic example of recent expansion in outdoor recreation activity is bicycling. More than 25 million bicycles are pedaled along the streets, paths, and byways of America. Bicycling's enthusiasts are a constantly growing recreational group whose needs call for serious and careful planning. Bicycling enjoys its greatest popularity with young people, although it is certainly not without its middle-aged and elderly enthusiasts. Despite this enormous success, riding trails are in short supply. Of all trails constructed, only 6% lie east of the Mississippi River.

Most bicycling is done close to home. It is in the cities, however, that bicycle routes are most wanting. Bicycling calls for space with distance, a scarce commodity in the core area of many cities. Suburban residents have a distinct advantage here. In many instances, private enterprise and private initiative are finding ways to meet the demand. Roads with bicycle lanes, designation of roads as bikeways so that motorists will be alert to the presence of cyclists, development of bike trails on public lands, and rapid increases in bicycle rental facilities are bringing bicycling to more and more people.

Dr. Paul Dudley White, a Boston cardiologist, did more for the bicycle's return than any other person. He long and publicly extolled the healthy virtues of bicycling. With Dr. Bertram R. Kessel of Boston University, he helped develop the Charles River Wheelmen and bring about the construction of one of the finest urban bike paths in the country, circling the Charles River Basin in Boston and Cambridge, Mass.

In view of the difficulties most bicyclists face in asserting their rights of way, I have set down the material in the accompanying box in their defense.

A Magna Charta for the bicyclist

The following precepts are indisputable and are herewith set forth:

1. *The bicycle rider is legal.*

The bicycle rider has every legal right to travel our streets as much as any motor vehicle. There is no law, divine or civil, that says the motor vehicle should take precedence over the bicycle. Hence, all forcing of bicycle riders to the sides of and off the road by horn blowing, engine racing, or any other intimidation should cease at once.

2. *The bicycle rider is vulnerable.*

The sudden opening of the automobile door is one of the greatest hazards to the safety of the bicycle rider. Many bike riders are hurt when thoughtless persons suddenly swing their car doors wide out, cutting the bicycle rider off abruptly and subjecting the bicyclist to serious injury, as well as to possible damage to the bicycle. Hence, persons in automobiles should look all around for bicyclists and then open their doors slowly and cautiously. When possible, they should use the door opposite the bicyclist for exit.

3. *The bicycle rider pays taxes.*

Billions of dollars are spent on facilities for the automobile. Highways, parking structures, traffic lights, police patrols, and toll booths all represent a major portion of our nation's annual expenditures. Bicyclists by comparison, have received next to nothing by way of government investment of their dollar. Hence, bike routes, installation of bike racks, use of directional signs, benches, ramps, rest areas, and other accommodations to service the growing number of bicycle riders are long overdue and should be installed in the immediate future. To do any less is to discriminate unfairly against persons who are doing more to improve our environment than any automobile driver in the country.

4. *The bicycle rider is dignified.*

Most bicycle riders have a sense of humor. Nevertheless, they become weary of the pointed finger and the snickering catcall from every automobile that rides behind or beside them. Hence, the bicycle riders of America demand that they be permitted to ride with dignity and receive the same courtesy and respect as any other vehicle on the highway or street. Motorists should refrain from the glares, sneers, and strange gestures they so frequently use against "bikeys."

5. *The bicycle rider is using a legitimate form of transportation.*

In America's commercial, educational, recreational world, all travel plans, regardless of distance, are arranged, inevitably, to accommodate air, rail, ship, or automobile transportation. Now, bicycle riders demand that all travel plans for short and middle distances give equal competitive opportunity to the bicycle as a means for accomplishing the trip. People on business trips should be allowed to choose times, routes, and reimbursements in a manner to which the bicycle can be adapted, as long as the basic time and mission objectives can be met.

6. *The bicycle rider deserves protection.*

The bike owner receives little or no protection from municipalities, police, private industry, or the insurance/banking complex, and the result is staggering bicycle theft, no registration procedures, and a general official apathy toward the problem. Hence, the bicycle rider demands safe storage garages, bike service facilities, new locking devices, and other accommodations in proportion to similar services provided for automobiles, buses, and trucks. Further, bicycle manufacturers, dealers, and service agencies are encouraged to invest in and greatly expand, their facilities to provide necessary maintenance services.

These demands are not unreasonable. The bicycle is a piece of America's past and present and a major part of America's future. The bicyclists' Magna Charta asks only that their movements be given equal opportunity to grow and equal opportunity to serve alongside the other forms of transportation that have been greatly assisted and encouraged during the last half century.

Annual bicycle production is constantly expanding, with gross sales rising from $136.6 million in 1950 to $277 million in 1969.

Some bicycling statistics[7]

In 1965, 41 million Americans rode bicycles. By 1980, 56 million Americans will ride bicycles. By 2000, 85 million Americans will ride bicycles.

SWIMMING

In number of participants, swimming is the third most popular form of outdoor recreation. Swimming offers healthy activity to its enthusiasts at virtually every level of achievement. Swimming also merges well with other recreation activities, such as picnicking and boating, and is usually a consideration in vacation planning, particularly when children are involved. Spin-offs from swimming include AAU competition, ten million water skiers, three million scuba divers, and an estimated 600,000 surfers.

The encroachments of civilization have taken their toll on beaches, lakes, and rivers, but a tremendous expansion in swimming pools has compensated for the loss. New pool construction represents a more than $1 billion annual investment.

Some swimming statistics[3]

In 1965, 104 million Americans swam.

By 1980, 172 million Americans will swim.

By 2000, 300 million Americans will swim.

More men (52%) swim than women (46%). The adapted national financial profile of swimming is as follows (this includes swimsuits, beach toys, suntan lotions, local transportation, scuba and surfing gear, food, drink, and miscellaneous)[4]:

> 1960—$2,185,400,000
> 1965—$2,900,000,000

> 1980—$5,365,500,000 (est.)
> 2000—$9,040,000,000 (est.)

PICNICKING

Picnicking is America's most popular form of outdoor recreation, measured in number of participants. Over half of the nation's population picnics some time each year. Picnicking is particularly attractive to large families, and it usually involves some use of the family automobile. An event in themselves, picnics also play a large secondary role to other major events such as beach parties, sports events, and boat trips.

New product development has altered picnicking drastically in recent years, making picnicking more palatable, more pleasant, and more convenient. The industrial investment in selling the picnic is enormous, as even a cursory examination of the picnic goods counter of the supermarket or department store will show. Paper and fiber plates, paper cups, utensils, grills, fire starters, forks, charcoal, tablecloths, insect sprays, nets, lamps, candles, benches, tables, chairs, jugs, thermoses, baskets, dishes, pots, banners, aprons, caps, and trash bags and cans—the list goes on forever!

Some picnicking statistics[3]

In 1965, 114 million Americans picnicked.

By 1980, 161 million Americans will picnic.

By 2000, 245 million Americans will picnic.

A unique feature of picnicking is its appeal at all income levels. Only when the annual income dips below $3000 does picnicking suffer, and then not very much. A picnic can be so simple, so spontaneous, so primitive that it appears to be the least common denominator of American outdoor recreation.

BOATING

Boating in America has been companion to the booming prosperity of post–World War II. Following the war, America's pleasure boating fleet stood at 2¹/₂ million craft. Today, it numbers close to 10 million vessels of all sizes and shapes and represents an annual expenditure of $3 billion.

Boating's economic base is broad. Craft range from the skiff to the palatial yacht. Sailboats and canoes account for only 6% of the units, but they are growing faster than any other type of boat. Boat owners are no longer confined to a single body of water. Trailers and car-top racks make trips of 100 miles a relatively simple process. All types of new boat handling machinery and gear are available as are myriad plastics, fibers, aluminum, and combination materials for boat construction. Crowded waterways are an unfortunate but inevitable consequence of this boating explosion.

Some boating statistics[3]

In 1965, 52 million Americans took part in general boating.

By 1980, 93 million Americans will take part in general boating.

By 2000, 163 million Americans will take part in general boating.

Water skiing is a direct spinoff of boating, and annual water ski expenditures in America exceed $50 million.[1]

FISHING

The appeal of fishing continues to grow in the modern world. Fishing still attracts more men than women. Nearly one half of all men fish sometime in their lives; less than one quarter of all women do. Sport fishing has been encouraged for years by well-organized public and private groups. To ensure continued availability of fish, most states actively engage in fish conservation of one kind or another. Over two thirds of all fishermen are fresh water fishermen, so the menace of polluted inland waters is a major threat. The rapid growth of urban communities, a prime source of such pollution, runs headlong in the face of the serious fisherman's hopes.

Some fishing statistics[3]

In 1965, 57 million Americans went fishing.

By 1980, 74 million Americans will go fishing.

By 2000, 102 million Americans will go fishing.

Fishing expenditures in 1965 were approximately $3 billion. Almost as simple and low-budget as picnicking, fishing is within the range of most income levels. Only at the $3000 annual income is there some depression in fishing activity and then not much. The greatest number of fishing Americans is between income levels of $3000 and $6000. Fishing is one outdoor recreational activity that appears unaffected by the education level of the participant. Only the very young and elderly fail to participate in equal proportion to those of all other age groups, 12 to 65 years of age.

CAMPING

"Camping opens and cleanses man's senses, just as a warm bath opens and cleanses his pores."[5] Campers see more clearly in the woods beyond the cities and suburbs. Ears dulled by the endless clatter of machines pick up subtle and soothing sounds. The sense of smell, jaded by exhaust fumes, is awakened by the tingling odors of lakes, forests, and meadows. The skin gains a sharp awareness of warm sun, cold water, the soft pressure of wind.

Outdoor camps are thinking places too, but most people who try to explain their devotion to camping speak in terms of the senses. Crickets after dark, the crackling of the camp fire, the smell of frying bacon, the honk of lake fowl in the middle of the night,

the unmistakable aroma of canvas tenting—these are a few of the delights that capture and hold campers for life.

The pleasures of camping are luring the American public outdoors in increasing numbers, and campers are enjoying the activity with greater frequency despite the fact that more work is entailed in making camp than in most other outdoor recreational activities. In addition to publicly supported campgrounds, many private resorts and reservations are now in the business of renting campsites for the day, week, month, or season. Perhaps the best known of these proprietors is Kampgrounds of America (KOA).

Camping's increasing popularity reflects its dual role in the public's mind; campers may enjoy living outdoors—in the country, in the mountains, or by the sea—and at the same time they want to be immediately handy to picnicking, boating, hiking, swimming, mountain climbing, or fishing. These multiple pleasures accommodate individual members of a family who, because of increased enjoyment of the convenient special activities, wish to stay longer at the campsite.

Many campgrounds, including those in national parks and forests, are filled to overflowing. Some campers roll up in a blanket under the stars, but more bed down on a soft mattress in travel trailers or on folding cots in tents. Some campers invest in super-luxurious land cruisers and wheeled homes that are more like portable mansions, with television, baths, stuffed furniture, stereo, kitchens, bars, and shag carpeting topped off with wrap-around picture windows for enjoying sunsets. Such units retail for $20,000 to $50,000.

Most campgrounds are accessible by good roads and are laid out with pulloffs for automobiles or travel trailers convenient to water and to what are called "comfort facilities." Some very large campgrounds resemble villages. Core areas provide essential services, such as a grocery store, restaurant, gas station, and trailside museum. These are surrounded by acres and acres of tent and trailer sites. However, the quality of the environment is extremely important to the enjoyment of camping. Too much "urbanization" in the camp area will, if ignored, diminish camping satisfaction substantially.

One of camping's greatest attributes is its economy. Many families who do not feel they can afford motels and restaurants are able to take satisfying vacations with camping trailers. This is of great importance to the elderly retired couple, people who have waited lifetimes to be able to see the country. This age group is rapidly expanding.

Some camping statistics[3]

In 1965, 25 million Americans camped.

By 1980, 45 million Americans will camp.

By 2000, 85 million Americans will camp.

The income group between $3000 and $8000 (annually) accounts for 53% of all campers, an indication that camping need not be an expensive activity. Most campers go camping an average of about 7 days each year.

Some financial statistics on camping[6]

> *Travel trailers*
> 1960—$73,000,000
> 1968—$500,743,000
>
> *Coaches for trucks*
> 1960—$49,000,000
> 1968—$226,368,000
>
> *Camping trailers*
> 1960—$8,100,000
> 1968—$104,742,000
>
> *Camping gear*
> 1960—$79,400,000
> 1968—$140,800,000

THE CHANGE

Gradual though the change toward the outdoors and our natural resources, the movement seemed to surface and solidify at the beginning of the 1970s. The first Earth Day was held April 22, 1970. The greatest response occurred in Boston, Cambridge, Berkeley, Washington D.C., New York, and San Francisco. I was present on the Boston Common at that moment. Tens of thousands of students turned out with displays on bicycling, recycling, natural foods, gardening, physical fitness, home health care, arboriculture, fish and animal technology, yoga, transcendental meditation, and parapsychology. The atmosphere was tense because of the Viet Nam War and the frequent demonstrations being held in opposition to it. But Earth Day had been born, and millions of Americans were finally thinking and talking about Spaceship Earth. No longer was our soil, air, and water the concern solely of the agronomist, the outdoor freak, or the "flower child." Each year thereafter, preparations for and participation in Earth Day ceremonies and demonstrations have increased. The area of outdoor recreation owes much to the early pioneers, Roosevelt, Muir, Olmstead, and Pinchot. However, it owes much of its future potential to the zealous and articulate efforts of young people all over America who alerted us in the late 1960s and early 1970s to the ecological dangers at hand.

DISCUSSION QUESTIONS

1. Federal and state intervention in the acquisition and development of park lands may be interpreted as an intrusion on local prerogatives and a violation of home rule. Give five advantages and five disadvantages that arise from a local municipality accepting federal and state aid in acquiring and developing a local park.
2. Since the major portion of federally owned park acreage lies west of the Mississippi River, how would the typical eastern American dweller tend to regard a planned program of further park land acquisition? Is this position rational? Why?
3. When large forests and acreages are under consideration for acquisition and development as recreational areas, most citizens see little or no recreational programs or activities involved. Are they correct? How can their view be changed?
4. The outboard motorboat, the snowmobile, the light plane, the four-wheel drive vehicle, and the dune buggy all represent a threat to the serenity and primitive virginity that so many seek in their wilderness outdoor recreational areas. Should these machines be permanently banned from the major forest, mountain, desert, and seashore reservations? Explain your answer. Do these machines bring any good effects to the parks? How can these good effects be used to counteract the bad effects?
5. Should the federal government undertake a program whereby it eventually sells or gives away all or most of its vast forest, prairie, and seashore holdings to private organizations and businesses, as some have suggested? Explain your answer, in view of the fact that such sales could bring vast sums of new money into the U.S. Treasury.

BIBLIOGRAPHY

Appalachian Trail Conference, 1718 N Street, N.W., Washington, D.C.

Baranet, N. N.: Bicycling, New York, 1973, A. S. Barnes & Co.

Final Report to the President and Congress of the National Parks Centennial Commission, Washington, D.C., 1973.

Focus on the Hudson, Department of the Interior, Bureau of Outdoor Recreation, 1966.

The Hudson, Report of the Hudson River Valley Commission, New York, 1966.

Index of selected outdoor recreation literature, Department of the Interior, Bureau of Outdoor Recreation, Washington, D.C. 1969.

Lunn, A.: A century of mountaineering, 1857-1957, London, 1957, Geo. Allen & Unwin Ltd.

National Camping and Hiking Association, 7172 Transit Road, Buffalo, N.Y.

The national forests, U.S. Department of Agriculture, Washington, D.C.

The national park system, U.S. Department of the Interior, National Park Service, Washington, D.C.

National parks for the future, Task Force Reports, The Conservation Foundation, Washington, D.C., 1972.

The Nature Conservancy, Inc., 1522 K Street, N. W., Washington, D.C.

Open space preservation methods, Summary and Proceedings of First Professional Level Conference, Washington, D.C., 1963.

Outdoor Recreation Resources Review Commission: Outdoor recreation for America, A report to the President and the Congress, January 31, 1962.

The race for open space, Final report of the Park, Recreation and Open Space Project, Metropolitan Regional Council, Regional Plan Association, New York, 1960.

Recreational vehicle park guide, Mobile Home Manufacturers Association, 20 N. Wacker Drive, Chicago, Ill.

Riviere, B.: Backcountry camping, Garden City, N.Y., 1971, Doubleday & Co., Inc.

Riviere, B.: The complete guide to family camping, Garden City, N.Y., 1966, Doubleday & Co., Inc.

Rustrum, C.: The wilderness life, New York, 1975, The Macmillan Co.

Schwartz, A.: Going camping, New York, 1969, The Macmillan Co.

Sierra Club, 1050 Mills Tower, San Francisco, Calif.

Ullman, J. R.: The age of mountaineering, Philadelphia, 1941, J. B. Lippincott Co.

Wells, G., and Wells, I.: The handbook of wilderness travel, New York, 1956, Harper & Row.

For additional information, write to the Department of Environmental Affairs, the Department of State Parks, or individual state capitals.

REFERENCES

1. American Water Ski Association, Winter Haven, Fla.
2. Bureau of Outdoor Recreation: Focal point for outdoor America, Washington, D.C., 1975, Department of the Interior.
3. Eisenhower, D. D.: The recreation imperative, Nationwide Outdoor Recreation Plan, Department of the Interior, September, 1974.
4. Environmental Science Services Administration: Development potential of U.S. continental shelves, Department of Commerce, 1966; Skin Diver p. 12, 1975.
5. Miracle, L., and Decker, M.: The complete book of camping, New York, 1961, Harper & Row.
6. Mobile Home Manufacturers Association, Chicago, Ill., 1960-1966; Recreation Vehicle Institute, Des Plaines, Ill., 1968.
7. National Sporting Goods Association, Annual Bulletin, Chicago, Ill., 1977.

4
THERAPEUTIC RECREATION

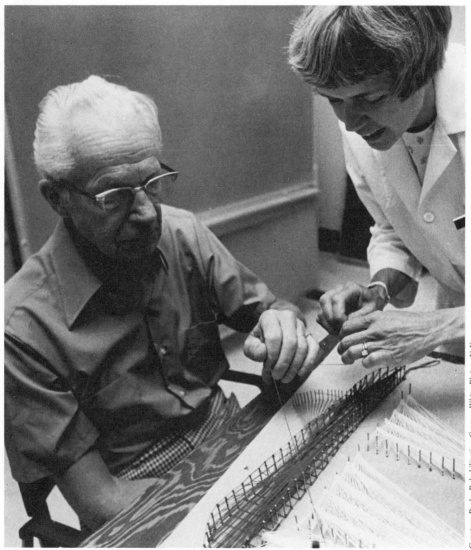

Courtesy Burke Rehabilitation Center, White Plains, N.Y.

Throughout history, human beings have demonstrated their awareness of the physical and mental good deriving from wholesome physical and mental activity. Ancient chronicles of Egypt, Greece, and Rome are replete with salutes to the value of dance, drumming, extension, gymnastics, weight training, running, swimming, and combat sports. Similarly, the cultures of Central and South America, the Aztecs, Mayans, and Toltecs of Mexico, and the Zulus, Basutos, and Swazis of Africa all record the therapeutic effects of music, aromas, the touch of sympathetic hands, the reading of ancestral testaments and the setting down of life's beauties and mysteries in picture and in word. They knew also that when the painter painted, he was painted; when the singer sang, she was sung, and when they danced, the dancers were drawn in and influenced as no watcher could ever be.

Avedon[2] states that in ancient Egypt ill persons were required to walk in beautiful temple gardens and to row boats on the Nile River. Excursions, dances, concerts, and shows were part of their prescribed treatment. Game boards, game tables, and other items related to mental challenge were found amid ancient ruins in Egypt, while Greek facilities included a sanatorium for patients connected to library, stadium, theater, and associated amenities. In China and India, games, puzzles, and mental gymnastics were evidently part of recovery programs. Many writers of the eighteenth and nineteenth centuries deplored the lack of provision in hospitals and sanatoriums of any exercise programs or equipment or even simple play activities for children. Avedon also tells us that even playing cards was absolutely forbidden.

Kraus[9] observes that the ancient Assyrians and Babylonians enjoyed many popular recreation activities such as boxing, wrestling, archery, and a variety of table games. Many of these same activities, in modified form, appeared as part of the social-medical treatment practices of the period.

Therapeutic recreation is the modern formalization and focus of this ancient awareness. It is not easy to define. Avedon[2] offers the following definition:

The phrase "therapeutic recreation" . . . was first coined to distinguish experiences and services offered to persons in special residential settings who are ill, impaired, or had some degree of disability that prevented them from using recreation resources, services and experiences offered to the public at large. Later, the phrase referred to services to persons who had special needs, regardless of their place of residence or limitation.

According to the U.S. Public Health Service,[14] therapeutic recreation is the specific use of recreational activity in the care, treatment and rehabilitation of ill, handicapped and aged persons with a directed program. Hayes[8] believes that "Therapeutic recreation services can be said to be services designated to assist or enable an ill, disabled or handicapped person to meet his basic need for recreative experiences."

HISTORY

As with many facets of the recreation profession, therapeutic recreation experienced its greatest advances during periods of national stress. During World War I, the International Red Cross provided recreation in military hospitals. After a slow period in the 1930s, the service burgeoned during World War II. For the first time, therapy in hospitals was used around the world, on both sides of the conflict, and involved professional staff and patients of both sexes and almost every conceivable ethnic background.

The U.S. Veterans Administration hospitals, by sheer size and number, performed a major leadership role during the 1950s and 1960s, although many state hospitals also expanded and modernized their programs. A significant year was 1950 when Beatrice H. Hill joined the staff of the then National Recreation Association as staff person for therapeutic recreation. Hill, a brilliant young professional, brought a new awareness and focus for the NRA in the field of patient recreation, and her 10 years service shaped the policy and concern for handicapped persons that guides today's National Recreation and Park Association.

Therapeutic recreation, as a professional jurisdiction, seeks to recruit, train, and motivate practitioners so that they may minister to the recreational needs of others, whether these be patients in a mental hospital, inmates in a prison, or long-term clients in a convalescent center for the aged. Therapeutic recreation differs from community, outdoor, industrial, and commercial recreation in that it utilizes the recreation experience more as a "means to an end." The desired end is the physical and mental improvement and recovery of the patient or inmate, his or her happiness, fun, or entertainment notwithstanding. In other areas of the recreation movement, the delight, joy, and satisfaction experienced by the participant is generally considered a sufficient goal or objective in itself.

Viewed academically, the therapeutic recreation cluster of services or practices constitutes one area of specialization within the generic field of professional recreation service. Men and women, after preparing themselves with a basic foundation in the history and philosophy of the modern recreation movement, will frequently choose one area of specialization in which to concentrate their study and work. Some choose the City Hall scene; others prefer to focus on the recreational needs and services of the industrial setting where they may operate among some 4000 to 5000 clerical workers or assembly line workers. Certain recreation professionals, however, will select the therapeutic sector for their study and performance. Skills, tools, and knowledge suited to people in confinement, the chronically ill, the recovering patient, the convalescing elderly patient, the embittered prisoner—these become the subject of intense study and learning by the therapeutic recreator.

Dr. Edith Ball, Professor Emeritus at New York University, is now a member of the faculty of the University of Arizona at Phoenix. Dr. Ball is a well-known and highly respected educational pioneer in the field. She reminds us that we must distinguish between the two words, "therapeutic," and "recreation." She believes "recreation" is the generic word, making recreation the constant in the formula, with "therapeutic" in the adjectival case. She also emphasizes that recreation is as much interested in maintaining and expanding the healthy parts of body and mind as it is desirous of consoling and ameliorating the pain and distress caused by disease or injury.

GOALS

The primary goals of therapeutic recreation include the following:

1. To promote and improve the health of the participant.
2. To prevent corollary breakdown or secondary breakdown arising from the primary disability.
3. To reduce and compensate for the incapacity, illness, or disability.
4. To enable the person to become a confident, fulfilled member of his or her environment or community,

granted the psychophysical limitation at hand.

SETTINGS

The following are the most common setting for therapeutic recreation:

1. State hospitals and schools: State hospitals for mentally ill persons and state services for mentally retarded persons offer organized therapeutic recreation and leisure services for patients and clients.

2. Federal hospitals, sanitaria, and convalescent centers: Veterans' Administration Hospitals, central drug addict rehabilitation institutions, and camps for the treatment of military service–connected disabilities place great emphasis on the values of therapeutic recreation.

3. Municipal and private hospitals, convalescent and rehabilitation centers: These include everything from the huge city hospitals, to the secluded rehabilitation center for alcoholics, to the small neighborhood convalescent center for elderly persons. Only the very short-term patient or the patient in the intensive care unit is excluded from comprehensive therapeutic recreation programming and activity. Every effort is made to humanize the treatment setting, build patient morale, provide amusement and diversion, and bridge the gap back to home and the community.

4. Community settings: A major portion of therapeutic recreation service is provided in the form of adapted and sheltered recreation and leisure activities within community or public settings. Municipal park and recreation agencies are the prime source of these services, guided and assisted by local therapeutic specialists, either inside or outside the departments. In addition, voluntary health agencies are major providers, including United Cerebral Palsy Association, Muscular Dystrophy Association of America, American Red Cross, Association for Retarded Persons, Multiple Sclerosis Society, American Heart Association, and the Easter Seal Society.

5. Sports for disabled persons: In recent years, there has been a surge of enthusiasm and support for sports, games, and athletics for the disabled. Foremost among these have been the Special Olympics for mentally retarded persons and Wheelchair Athletics for physically handicapped persons. The Joseph P. Kennedy, Jr. Foundation has been a prime source of support, encouragement, and publicity in these vigorous sports for handicapped athletes.

6. Camping for handicapped persons: Efforts in this area are aimed at providing participants with the same opportunities for experience and enjoyment in camping as afforded fully able, normal persons. Outdoor recreation, residential camps, day camps, camping hikes, canoe trips, and a variety of nature-related programs are included. Two examples of this service are Camp Liberty, Boston, Massachusetts; and Camp Joy, New Rochelle, New York. Both are day camps that include a broad range of sports, games, crafts, dramatics, and special events for mentally and physically handicapped children and young people in attractive urban park settings.

PROGRAMMING

The many varied factors that influence program planning in community recreation, outdoor recreation, or in voluntary agencies are present in planning therapeutic recreation. Physical location, equipment and supplies, tastes, interests and skills of participants, budget, and the leadership available are the basic elements. Obviously in an institutional setting, two additional points must be considered: physical and mental condition of the patients or inmates and the medical directives of the physician. In the hands of a creative therapeutic recreation professional, however, this situation still provides wide latitude for healthy, stimulating, fun-filled, recreational activity.

Some of the most reliable and satisfying events and activities for ward and institutional use are given below. Accomodation must be made in each, of course, for the special disabilities or handicaps of the people involved. A considerable supply of programming techniques and ideas is available through the National Recreation and Park Association.

> Wheelchair athletic games
> Bingo (used sparingly and with interesting modifications)
> One-act plays (classics and originals)
> Puppetry (extremely popular)
> Arts and crafts (should produce some small product early)
> Musical games, small orchestras
> Brain teasers, drawing and sketching games
> Trivia and nostalgia games
> Holiday festivals and birthday parties
> Amateur shows
> Photographic contests and displays
> Movie horse race night
> Las Vegas night
> Checkers and chess tournaments
> Cooking and baking (caution against fire)
> Woodworking
> Sewing
> Hobby collections and model kits
> Short story writing
> Monopoly and Parcheesi tournaments

Of course, patients and inmates are no different from other people in that they can spot a poor program quickly and will resent being served substandard activity fare. Frequent program conferences among staff and patients are helpful so that new patients, new ideas, and new treatment of old ideas can be accommodated. Questionnaires, question/answer sessions, and critiques after the event is over can help constantly improve the quality of the institutional program.

ACTIVITY

Therapeutic recreation is activity, both mental and physical. Wholesome recreation activity is good for patients. Recreators believe this but, surprisingly, many other professionals are either doubtful, skeptical, or downright negative. "A fad, a passing novelty," I was told recently by a doctor at the large hospital medical center in New Rochelle. "I've seen such fads come and go, this one will fade too." Incredibly, this is in the late 1970s and the spokesperson is a renowned and respected person in medicine.

Dr. Michael B. Miller, designer, builder, and operator of two very modern convalescent centers for the aged, both located in White Plains, N.Y., told me: "You recreators are so very important, but you are such poor image projectors. We medical people don't scorn you; we simply hardly ever realize you are there." Nevertheless, Dr. Miller pointed out that records indicate that, in most convalescent centers, and there are thousands of them, the doctor touches the patients 2% of their waking time, the nurses 12%, and the recreators over 70%. One may draw his or her own conclusions as to who has more contact with and the greatest responsibility for remolding the lives of these patients.

Dr. Miller's further research[11] showed that immobilization of patients for iatrogenic reasons (doctor-induced) and nurisgenic reasons (nurse-induced) caused the following symptoms:

1. Urinary and fecal calcium excretion increased (loss of bone matter).
2. Excretion of phosphorous, total sulphur, sodium, and potassium increased (valuable body chemicals).

3. The basic metabolic rate declined 6.9% on the average.
4. Posture suffered, fainting spells increased on tilt-table.
5. Venous engorgement and extravascular fluid increased, and there was capillary fragility and impaired venous or muscle tone.
6. Total blood volume decreased approximately 5.4% along with marked decreases in exercise tolerance.

Dr. Miller notes the uniformity of the effects in both sexes and many age groups. But, he points out, all symptoms were reversible just as soon as activity programs were restored. "Activity, mental and physical, is the answer," says Dr. Miller.

In addition to these findings by Dr. Miller, Gerald O'Morrow, Ed. D., Associate Professor, Department of Recreation, University of Georgia at Athens, sees activities as accomplishing the following:

1. Activities function as diagnostic and evaluative tool.
2. Activities increase the socialization of patients.
3. Activities increase growth and development.
4. Activities redirect attention from symptoms and problems and relate the patient to the world of reality.
5. Activities provide approved outlets for hostility, aggression, and other emotions.
6. Activities alter attitudes toward self, others, and the future.
7. Activities provide opportunities for creativeness, development of new skills and interests, and utilizing existing skills.
8. Activities provide opportunities for fun.
9. Activities prepare the patient for the activities of daily living.

Activity is the thing, and the therapeutic recreator can make it happen!

THE PROFESSIONALS

A branch of the National Recreation and Park Association is named the National Therapeutic Recreation Society (NTRS). Approximately 1000 professionally registered personnel make up this NTRS branch whose members work directly with ill and handicapped persons. This membership is drawn from public and private community agencies, residential facilities, hospitals, institutions, and voluntary agencies. Often, these members are known as "recreation therapists" although the professional term is "therapeutic recreation specialist."

The NTRS itself is the national professional organization for those concerned with providing recreation and leisure services to ill, handicapped, disabled, and other special populations in hospitals, institutions, and the community. Membership is open to all individuals working or concerned with those who are mentally retarded, physically handicapped, or blind, who have any other handicapping or disabling condition, or who are in correctional institutions or nursing homes. The NTRS bases its philosophy and ethics on the following:

1. Recreation is a basic human need—a necessary part of a well-balanced healthy life.
2. Physiological, psychological, and sociological limitations should not negate an individual's right to leisure pursuits.
3. Providing recreation services to ill, handicapped, or institutionalized individuals should mean a wide variety of activities and services within the institution, facility, and community.
4. Recreation for ill, disabled, and hand-

icapped persons should be both therapeutic and pleasurable.

For information and membership applications, contact: NTRS Branch Liaison, National Recreation and Park Association, 1601 North Kent Street, Arlington, VA 11109.

Membership in the NTRS includes membership in the parent body, NRPA, and makes available the following publications and services:

1. *Therapeutic Recreation Journal*—a quarterly publication containing articles on a wide range of therapeutic recreation topics.
2. *NTRS Newsletter*—a quarterly publication on news, meetings, new books, etc.
3. *Special publications* on various aspects of services to special populations, such as *Recreation in Nursing Homes, Recreation for Your Handicapped Child,* and symposiums on therapeutic recreation.
4. *NTRS Annual Institute*—held in conjunction with the NRPA Annual Congress for Recreation and Parks.
5. *Liaison and Coordination* with agencies and organizations related to the field or therapeutic recreation, such as Joint Commission on Hospital Accreditation, the Department of Health, Education, and Welfare, the President's Committee on Employment of the Handicapped, and the U.S. Bureau of Prisons.

Regional, state, and national conferences and workshops are held periodically by and for therapeutic recreation personnel. A glance at some of the printed programs and brochures from California, Texas, and New York gives a good idea of what subject areas are covered in the various sessions: *The Role of Creativity in Recreation Programs for the Aged, NRPA Adopts Revised Therapeutic Registration Standards (State of New York), Recreation as Therapy, The Vanishing Population* (retarded), *Let the Barriers Come Down* (architectural barriers), *A Scavenger Hunt for Architectural Barriers,* and *Barriers to Human Sexuality—Your Handicap or Ours?* Other training sessions cover subjects such as hospital staff organization, recreation for drug-withdrawal patients, vigorous sports within orthopedic hospitals, cooperation with communities outside the hospital, recreation for the homebound, and new game equipment for use in hospitals.

JOB TITLES
Professional job titles

A variety of titles exists for the therapeutic recreator in various settings and in different parts of the country. Following is the official list of registered titles adopted in February, 1977 by the National Therapeutic Recreation Society and is similar to titles used in most states.

Therapeutic recreation assistant. This requires 2 years of successful full-time experience in the therapeutic recreation field, *or* two hundred clock hours in-service training in the therapeutic recreation field, *or* a combination of these two.

Therapeutic recreation technician I. This requires successful completion of NTRS-approved 750 hours training program for Therapeutic Recreation Technician I.

Therapeutic recreation technician II. This requires an associate of arts degree from an accredited college or university with an emphasis in therapeutic recreation, *or* certification of satisfactory completion of 2 academic years of study in recreation with an emphasis or option in therapeutic recreation and current employment in therapeutic recreation, *or* certification of satisfactory completion of 2 academic years of study in a skills area (physical education, drama, arts and crafts, art, dance, music) and 2 years of professional work experience in therapeutic recreation.

Therapeutic recreation leader. This requires a baccalaureate degree from an accredited college or university with a major in recreation, *or* a baccalaureate degree from an accredited college or university with a major in therapeutic recreation or a major in recreation with an option or emphasis in therapeutic recreation, *or* a baccalaureate degree from an accredited college or university with a major in recreation and 1 year of professional work experience in therapeutic recreation.

Therapeutic recreation specialist. This requires a master's degree from an accredited college or university with a major in therapeutic recreation or a major in recreation with an option or emphasis in therapeutic recreation, *or* a Master's degree from an accredited college or university with a major in recreation and 1 year of professional work experience in therapeutic recreation, *or* a baccalaureate degree from an accredited college or university with a major in therapeutic recreation or a major in recreation with an option or emphasis in therapeutic recreation and 3 years of professional work experience in therapeutic recreation, *or* a baccalaureate degree from an accredited college or university with a major in recreation and 4 years of professional work experience in therapeutic recreation.

Master therapeutic recreation specialist. This requires a master's degree from an accredited college or university with a major in therapeutic recreation or a major in recreation with an option or emphasis in therapeutic recreation plus 2 years of professional work experience in therapeutic recreation, *or* a Master's degree from an accredited college or university with a major in recreation and 3 years of professional

work experience in therapeutic recreation, *or* a Baccalaureate degree from an accredited college or university with a major in therapeutic recreation or a major in recreation with an option or emphasis in therapeutic recreation and 6 graduate credits in therapeutic recreation, *or* a baccalaureate degree from an accredited college or university with a major in recreation and 12 graduate credits in therapeutic recreation plus 6 years of professional work experience in therapeutic recreation.

Additional titles, not part of this formal NTRS structure, might include director of recreation (in a therapeutic setting), supervisor of patient activities, recreation therapist, activities director, and director of sports and athletics.

RECREATION—THERAPY

The rearrangement or words can make familiar expressions take on new meanings. The words recreation and therapy are no exceptions. Based on books by Avedon,[2] Kraus,[10] and the NRPA[13] and several articles in *Parks and Recreation* the following distinctions are offered.

Recreation therapy

This is more medically oriented, dependent almost entirely on a prescription by the doctor, or specific direction by the nurse. There is no freedom of choice here for the patient. The patient is examined, conditions are diagnosed, and a precise schedule is established that is not to be varied or postponed without explicit permission from the attending physician. It is recreation therapy when the physician's order to recreation service reads as follows:

Mr. Brown in recovering well from stroke. Provide patient with _____ twice daily, not exceeding _____. Gradually increase activity tolerance during 1 week. Do not physically tire the patient during first few weeks.

Confine to bedside first week. Record progress notes on chart. Dr. Smith

Obviously, the patient here has no more choice than in selecting his medication or the location of his surgical incision.

Therapeutic recreation

Here the base is the word "recreation," and "therapeutic," the modifier. The broad definition of the word recreation requires: (1) freedom of choice, both of subject area, and schedule, (2) variety available for choice, and (3) pleasure or satisfaction derived is prime reason for the recreation. Presumably, all are present here. The physician's approach to therapeutic recreation service might be shown through his request to the institution's Recreation Service office.

Mrs. Gannon, age 87, advanced cataract condition, eyesight very poor, ambulatory, hearing good. Diagnosis shows patient in good health otherwise, alert, no medical risk at this time. Resident here for 4 years. Request Recreation Service interest her in mixing with other patients, talking, socializing. Also, wish she would try skills with hands—sculpture, pottery, crocheting, stone collecting, etc. Cautions: she is loud, can be irritating to other residents. Don't get her too excited. Keep me posted. Dr. White

Here we see much discretion left to the recreator and also allowance made for personal tastes and potential interests of the patient. By implication, Mrs. Gannon will be persuaded to try different recreations, but, ultimately, she will make a choice of her own and will continue in it because she wants to, not because she is directed to. Admittedly, this is not quite as open or permissive a situation as would be found in a typically democratic community recreation program. However, it is far more permissive than the recreation therapy prescription for Mr. Brown.

Occupational therapy

In some institutions, the term "recreation" is never used in the prescribed and monitored activities of the patients. Occupational therapy (O.T.) includes all day-oriented, specifically planned and assigned skills, movements, and learning experiences of the patients. It includes centers and rooms generously equipped with wall and portable exercisers, bicycle exercisers, hand weights and grips, jump ropes, metal boots for lifting, inclined ramps, stairs, parallel bars, and body-correctional wall bars. Also, there are weaving looms, paints, musical instruments, pinball machines, jigsaw puzzles, rubber balls for squeezing, keys and keyholes, and Jacuzzi heated whirlpools for physical therapy. To say that these pieces of equipment and their appropriate exercises are totally different from recreational therapy is inexact. These activities, aimed at encouraging and strengthening motor activity, are all carefully prescribed by physicians, supervised by nurses, and administered by professional therapists. Some rehabilitative institutions appear convinced that the term "occupational therapy" is more professional and prestigious than "recreational therapy." In such institutions, the word "recreation" is used only to describe the activities enjoyed out-of-doors by patients almost fully recovered and waiting to go home and also the off-duty fun indulged in by medical and administrative staff.

Physical therapy

This is closely related to occupational therapy, except that it is much older in time. Physical therapy (P.T.) is confined almost entirely to large muscle challenges and responses. If anything, it is even more precisely prescribed and monitored than O.T. and is treated as important hard medicine, to be carried out assiduously, with close and determined monitoring by staff. Not much fun here, no choice at all, and not even the color or distraction of games, puzzles, or crafts. Medicine balls, weights, arm, leg, finger, and neck exercisers, treadmills, steps, ramps, canes, and parallel bars —these are the "hardware" of physical therapy, and extremely important to patient recovery.

RELATIONSHIPS

The therapeutic recreator operates in a personnel setting different from most other recreation sectors. In therapeutic recreation, the professional functions in close quarters with and under the scrutiny and control of medical administrators, doctors, nurses, medical interns, and scrutiny personnel. Unlike community or industrial recreators, who perceive a clearly identified superior or "boss" and an equally clear constituency of participants, the structure and chain of command within an institution is more obscure.

In a large private hospital, the therapeutic recreator may be directly under the Administrator, Special Services, Patient Services, or some other category. The recreator may be serving one specific ward or may be available on a hospital-wide basis. As such, recreators move about the hospital and are subject to a variety of disciplines and direction. Conscientiously doing their job in Ward C of a large hospital, the therapeutic recreators plan a Halloween party in the day room directly off the ward. Music, apple-ducking, paper costumes, funny makeup, balloons, candy, ice cream, and singing are on the program. The hospital administrator, in a sudden concern for budget sharply reduces the available funds; the head nurse on duty Halloween evening is a temporary replacement and declares there will be no party without the written approval of the medical director; two ward nurses who were going to assist with the program have been called to assist in an emergency operation; a visiting physician forbids his patient, a serious diabetic, from even taking part in the affair when he finds candy, cake, and ice cream are involved; a nurse from an adjoining ward orders the music turned off because it is disturbing her patients next door; hospital visiting hours prevent the entry of professional clowns who were an important part of the program.

An exaggerated picture, no doubt. However, it illustrates how the lines of authority and chains of command in a large institution are complex and sometimes counterproductive. The therapeutic recreation professional must be extremely patient with the bureaucratic frustrations of the larger institution. Program planning is far more complex and demanding than it is in the outside world. It calls for careful scheduling and arranging to take care of contingencies that may arise from the many-tracked authority structure in which it operates.

RECREATION FOR AGING PERSONS

This segment of the profession is so large and growing that it may well be considered almost a subprofession in itself. This is because, in working with the aging persons, the recreator may encompass a wide range of personality and physical settings. For example:

1. Recreation in an average community, where persons of all ages live at home and recreate communally.
2. Recreation centers for elderly persons in the community.
3. Retirement colonies or residences, for well and fully able elderly persons.
4. Convalescent centers for elderly persons in postoperative conditions.
5. Urban apartment house residences for elderly persons, totally nonmedical.

6. Nursing homes for ill or immobilized elderly persons.
7. Hospital settings for severely ill or preoperative elderly persons.

Each of these settings is different and calls for different planning and programming. Many recreators function in settings that represent a combination of several of these illustrations.

With an aging population nationally and an increased awareness of the potential for enjoying the later years, recreation for advanced age adults promises to be one of the largest and most rewarding sectors of the recreation profession for dedicated workers.

RECREATION IN CORRECTIONAL INSTITUTIONS

An increased national concern about mental disorders, illness, and antisocial behavior must lead inevitably to a study of our prisons and correctional institutions. Until recently, the recreational and therapeutic aspects of confinements were almost totally ignored. Isolated exceptions only underscore this ignorance.[1,3,5]

During the late 1970s, a lively interest in the quality, quantity, and efficacy of prison recreation programs developed. Part of this interest may be explained by the rash of violent prison riots of the mid 1970s in every corner of the country and symbolized most dramatically by the 1971 prison upheavals and deaths at Attica, N. Y. Scholarly discussions of therapeutic recreation may overlook entirely the area of corrections. Yet the inmate experiences the handicaps of being locked in, of being socially ostracized, and of being psychologically traumatized, even if he or she is physically whole and mentally intact.

A typical program of inmate recreation would include indoor and outdoor basketball, jogging, softball, and simple group games such as relay races and tug-of-war.

Inside, crafts and photography are very popular, as is a good, well-stocked library, Painting and music are appealing, but one of the biggest excitements in any such institution is the vaudeville-musical comedy show in which inmate performers blend with visiting performers for an hilarious show. Primitive as this is, it seems to lift the prisoners' morale substantially and make them feel that those on the outside really care. However, further study and development are needed. Fogel,[7] Executive Director, Illinois Law Enforcement Commission, has stated:

As professionals in correctional recreation and the therapeutic use of leisure time, we have a special responsibility to interpret forcefully the necessity of modernization of our fortress prison programs. What worth will our efforts have if we simply continue to be clinical appendages organizing volleyball leagues when the products of our programs are more dangerous on the streets than when we received them as prisoners?

Daniel Walker, governor of Illinois, has stated that "A prison without a comprehensive recreation program is an internal powder keg. A man coming out of such an environment after several years is an invisible walking volcano in our midst."

David C. Park, Executive Secretary of the NTRS, observes that recreation has long had a low priority status in correctional institutions. He believes this is partly because most citizens still regard recreation as "fun and games," and thus regard it as a privilege or luxury afforded prison inmates only when they are good or deserving. He sees a real need for interpreting to the public the deep significance and long-term effects of a well-planned and well-executed therapeutic recreation program in a correctional institution.

A strong program of leisure services can accomplish the following for inmates:

1. Inmates' morale improves.

2. Improved inmates' morale means raised staff morale.
3. Such programs enable the inmates to relate to similar activities after they leave prison (the prisoner who plays the trumpet studies trumpeters and bands on the outside; the stamp collector on the inside reads about and discusses stamp exhibits on the outside, etc.).
4. Recreation activities compel the forming of decision-making habits by otherwise confused prisoners. He or she must make choices, schedule time, collect supplies, store equipment, and gradually progress through a process. For many, this never occurred before.

Unfortunately, prison recreation programs are often poorly financed or supported by management. This puts an extra burden on the zealous recreation professional who sincerely wants the program to succeed. Cast-off equipment and supplies, borrowed musical instruments, garage-style play areas, heavy reliance on volunteers— these are some of the obstacles the recreator must often overcome.

A notable exception to this was the recreation plant and program instituted by Sheriff John Buckley in the new Middlesex County House of Correction, Cambridge, Massachusetts, in 1976. From a crude beginning of a basketball and some boxing gloves, Sheriff Buckley established a four-room complex on the top floors of a new prison facility, complete with showers, locker rooms, whirlpool, boxing and weight-lifting room, meeting rooms, and a small theater. The sheriff's wife opened a new library and this was later taken over by the municipal library system. Sheriff Buckley is a novelty among law enforcement officers since he appreciates the deep significance of recreation to men and women incarcerated for long periods.

Experts see a greatly increased need for leisure services in our correctional institutions. Recreation will be seen as one of the most important and most effective of the rehabilitative tools.

LEISURE COUNSELING

One of the most effective ways that recreation can serve as a preventive measure against individual incapacitation is in the area of counseling. The therapeutic recreator as a counselor, functioning much as a social worker, can do a very great service for patients and retarded and handicapped persons by helping them to live a better and more satisfying life. This is accomplished by guiding them in effectively balancing their daily lives with suitable recreational pursuits during their leisure.

Leisure counseling aims at filling the gaps that result from insecure earlier lives. This insecurity has left the patient or inmate with mute desires, unfulfilled hopes and dreams, and a pervading ignorance as to the joys and satisfactions of leisure. Such counseling for inmates of a hospital or institution should include weekly individual and group leisure education and counseling sessions; day-long trips to discharge locations that include a variety of experiences pertinent to community leisure living; cooperative efforts with other staff members in the education, vocational rehabilitation, social work and nursing services. The overall purpose of a therapeutic recreation and leisure counseling program is to provide the necessary intervention in the existing life style of patients that will enable them to become involved in adequate and appropriate activities of community leisure living.

FEDERAL LEADERSHIP

The U.S. government has provided leadership and guidance to the therapeutic recreation movement. Scattered at first, this guidance has coalesced under the leadership of Senator Edward Kennedy who, in 1967, was responsible for major legislation. This legislation, the 1967 Mental Retardation Amendments, became known as Title V of PL 90-170. It was assigned to the newly formed Bureau of Education for the Handicapped (BEH). The aim of this legislation was to train personnel and promote research in physical education and recreation for the handicapped.

Other agencies that pioneered these efforts included the National Institute of Public Health, the Division of Mental Retardation of the U.S. Public Health Service (now the Division of Developmental Disabilities), and the Office of Human Development. The President's Committee on Employment of the Handicapped, Recreation Division, has been most effective in apprising the general public on the variety and magnitude of obstacles and barriers that prevent handicapped persons from entering the mainstream of life.

Generally speaking, however, the recreation program support for handicapped children generated by the Bureau of Education for the Handicapped, U.S. Office of Education, has had a more significant impact on therapeutic recreation service than any other government agency. In terms of money alone, it has supported more programs of recreation for handicapped persons than all other federal agencies combined.

DEINSTITUTIONALIZATION

Deinstitutionalization is the process by which the hospitalized patients and mentally ill, retarded, and other handicapped persons are moved from larger, formal, sequestered institutions such as mental hospitals and sanitaria and relocated within their home communities. The aim is to make available to these partly ill, partly handicapped people the patterns and conditions of everyday life that are as close to normal as possible. It implies a normal daily routine, including the normal leisure time diversions. It is sometimes called decentralization, normalization, or mainstreaming.

The decentralization of patients from state institutions to community living has great implications for both therapeutic and community recreators. A recent study of programs for handicapped persons shows that only 35% of local recreation and park agencies offer recreation programs for ill, handicapped, and retarded persons. Interest, however, is growing, especially among the 50 individual state park and recreation societies. Typical of many others, the Oregon Parks and Recreation Society in 1973 passed a resolution urging that the state increase its funding of recreation/leisure for special populations.

Community support has not always been automatic. Many local groups fight the coming in of released patients, calling them "intruders, vagrants, criminals, and nuts." The establishment of sheltered workshops, halfway houses, special residences, and hostels has been greeted by more resistance than support. This is especially so when residents or clients are to be drawn from the ranks of the retarded, mentally ill, or those serving time for criminal convictions. But the picture is improving as good examples are set and better public relations programs are developed.

An outstanding example of a fine development is the Recreation Center for the Handicapped in San Francisco, begun in 1952. Year-round recreation and camping programs are provided to 8000 handicapped and retarded children and adults. Mrs. Janet Pomeroy is the founder, director, and major force behind this excellent program and facility. The center is visited by touring recreators and educators from all over the country and the world.

BARRIERS

For a long time, the thought of making *all* recreational activities available to *all* people was unrealistic. Registration qualifications, insurance prohibitions, stairways, narrow doors, lack of exits, restrooms impossible to enter, and doorknobs, switches, telephones, lights, fire extingishers, all too high to reach, were just a few of the barriers that stood between handicapped Americans and the recreational activities for which they so hungered.

On May 4, 1977, the final rules and regulations of Section 504, the Rehabilitation Act of 1973 were implemented by the Secretary of Health, Education and Welfare. These establish a clear mandate to end discrimination against handicapped persons participating in any program or activity that receives federal financial assistance. No qualified or handicapped person shall, because a recipient's facilities are inaccessible to, or unusable by handicapped persons, be denied the benefits of, be excluded from participation in, or otherwise be subjected to discrimination under any program or activity. Further, new facilities are to be constructed so that they are readily accessible to handicapped individuals.[12] This is revolutionary in the opening of full recreation facilities and programs to mentally and physically handicapped people. Thus, minimum standards and specifications have been set for walks, ramps, stairs, doorways, water fountains, telephones, parking areas, rest rooms, and hazard warnings. Full details may be obtained from publications such as the *Design Journal for Therapy and Rehabilitation* and from organizations such as the National Easter Seal Society and the American Red Cross.

Psychological barriers are every bit as real as physical or architectural barriers. The same barriers of previous years that prohibited handicapped boys and girls from entering school and recreation sports and games persist today. Recently, a federal judge granted permission for two football players, each missing an eye, to play varsity football at Missouri Western State College. The stipulation was, however, dependent on a written agreement relieving the college from any responsibility in the event of eye injury to either of the young men.[4] Thus, permission is given under such restrictive conditions that it is tantamount to no permission. The role in this struggle to remove barriers rests heavily on therapeutic recreators. They are the trained, experienced people who can bridge the gap between a sympathetic but relatively ignorant general public and a handicapped population so anxious and so much in need of this vigorous participation that objective planning is beyond their grasp.

CURRICULA

Curricula include both 4-year and 2-year sequences conferring the bachelor or associate degree of therapeutic recreation, respectively. A typical undergraduate curriculum might include:

Courses in major	Units
Sports and games	2
Outdoor recreation	2
Social recreation	2
Dance in recreation	2
Recreation leisure services	3
Techniques of recreation leadership	2
History and philosophy of recreation services	3
Program development in recreation services	3
Organizational patterns for recreation services	3
Administration and supervision in recreation services	3
Directed field work in recreation (comparable to student teaching)	6
Standards and measurement, recreation services	3

Management and organization	4
(business)	4
Foundations of public administration	
Behavior patterns in organization and	4
management	
Recreation for handicapped persons	3
Institutional recreation	3
Sociology or psychology	3
Business writing	2
Research methodology	2
Communications	2

Electives

Special populations (Black, Chicano,	
Indian, Oriental, etc.)	2
Music in recreation	2
Arts and crafts in recreation	2
Drama in recreation	2
Medical anthropology	4
Physical defects	3
Anatomy	3
Social occupations	4

CAMPUSES AND PERSONALITIES

Many excellent colleges and universities offer undergraduate and graduate training in therapeutic recreation in the U.S. and Canada. Some of the finest include Springfield College in Massachusetts, University of Oregon at Eugene, San Jose State, University of Southern California at Los Angeles, University of Connecticut at Storrs, University of Illinois at Champaign, Indiana University at Bloomington, Iowa University at Iowa City, University of Kentucky at Lexington, University of Maryland at College Park, Northeastern University in Boston, and Michigan State University at East Lansing.

Other outstanding curricula include those at the University of Minnesota (one of the most innovative); Lehman College in Bronx, N.Y.; New York University; State University of New York at Brockport; State University of New York at Cortland; Teachers College of Columbia University; University of North Carolina at Chapel Hill; Pennsylvania State University, Uni-

versity Park; Temple University in Philadelphia; University of Utah at Salt Lake City; University of Wisconsin at Madison.

In Canada, outstanding campuses include the University of Alberta at Edmonton; University of British Columbia at Vancouver; University of Ottawa; and the University of Waterloo, Ontario.

Professionals and personalities who have advanced the cause of therapeutic recreation include Dr. Edith Ball, New York University, a pioneer and outstanding educator; Dr. John A. Nesbitt, University of Iowa; Dr. Larry L. Neal, University of Oregon; Dr. Richard G. Kraus, Temple University; Janet Pomeroy, designer and operator of the San Francisco Recreation Center for Handicapped; Dr. Fred Humphrey, skilled chairperson at the University of Maryland; Dr. Gerald S. O'Morrow, University of Georgia; Dr. Fred W. Martin, California State University, Sacramento; William A. Hillman, Jr., Bureau of Education for the Handicapped, U.S. Office of Education.

SOURCES OF PROFESSIONAL INFORMATION

As in all professions, it is vital that the therapeutic recreator maintain contact with writing, research, and thinking in the field. Following are some of the primary sources for literature and information on therapeutic recreation.

American Association for Health for the Handicapped
Physical Education & Recreation Programs
1201 16th Street, N.W.
Washington, DC 20006

American Association of Retired Persons
1225 Connecticut Ave., N.W.
Washington, DC 20036

American Foundation for the Blind, Inc.
15 W. 16th Street
New York, NY 10011

American National Red Cross
17th and D Streets, N.W.
Washington, DC 20006

American Wheelchair Bowling Association
2635 Northeast 19th St.
Pompano Beach, FL 33062

Boy Scouts of America
Scouting for Handicapped Division
New Brunswick, NJ 08902

Girls Scouts of the U.S.A.
Scouting for Handicapped Girl Program
830 Third Avenue
New York, NY 10022

Joseph P. Kennedy, Jr. Foundation
1701 K Street, N.W.
Washington, DC 20006

Muscular Dystrophy Association of America, Inc.
810 Seventh Avenue
New York, NY 10019

National Association of the Physically Handicapped, Inc.
6473 Grandville Avenue
Detroit, MI 48228

National Association for Retarded Citizens
2709 Avenue E, East
P.O. Box 6109
Arlington, TX 76011

National Consortium on Physical Education & Recreation for the Handicapped
Liaison Office
729 Delaware Ave., S.W.
Washington, DC 20024

National Easter Seal Society for Crippled Children & Adults, Inc.
2023 West Ogden Ave.
Chicago, IL 60612

National Paraplegia Foundation
333 North Michigan Ave.
Chicago, IL. 60601

National Therapeutic Recreation Society
1001 North Kent Street
Arlington, VA 22209

National Wheelchair Athletic Association
40-24 62nd Street
Woodside, NY 11377

Paralyzed Veterans of America
7315 Wisconsin Ave., Suite 301-W
Washington, DC 20014

The President's Committee on Employment of the Handicapped
Washington, DC 20210

President's Committee on Mental Retardation
7th and D Streets, S.W.
Washington, DC 20201

Rehabilitation International, Secretariat
219 East 44th Street, S.W.
New York, NY 10017

United Cerebral Palsy Association, Inc.
66 East 34th Street
New York, NY 10016

The major journals in the field include *Threapeutic Recreation Journal, Therapeutic Recreation Annual, Journal of Health, Physical Education and Recreation, Parks and Recreation, Journal of Rehabilitation, American Journal of Nursing, Amicus (National Center for Law and the Handicapped),* and *Rehabilitation World (Rehabilitation International USA).* For specific addresses and other information about the many resources available, contact the National Recreation and Park Association, 1601 North Kent Street, Arlington, VA 22209.

DISCUSSION QUESTIONS

1. On arriving at a new institutional post, the therapeutic recreator will want to get a good feel of the local community recreational philosophy, programs, facilities, and equipment. What is a good step-by-step routine by which this can be accomplished?
2. Several patients in a large convalescent home for the aged have repeatedly asked for broader, more enriched recreation programs. The Medical Director of the home has resisted these suggestions as "too stimulating," or "not worth the trouble." What procedures would you follow, as institutional Director of Recreation, in solving this stalemate?

3. A medium-security state prison for men lies within the jurisdictional limits of a city of 50,000 people. The prison has no organized recreation program and has asked you, the city's Recreation Director, to help them start a program. What steps would you take to comply with their request?

4. You are the Therapeutic Recreation Specialist at a large Veterans Administration Hospital adjacent to a very large city. You wish to involve some of the younger patients as helpers and staff workers in the city's summer recreation program. Describe how you would make this happen, and tell how you would assure the city that unpleasant incidents would be kept to a minimum?

5. The operator of five medium-sized (approximately 50 beds each) private convalescent homes for the aged employs you as Therapeutic Recreation Supervisor for all five. All are located in the same city within 15 minutes drive of each other. You are provided with a small van-type bus. Describe in outline form, with time schedules, how you would set up a recreation program at all five locations, using the bus for transportation.

BIBLIOGRAPHY

American Foundation for the Blind: Utilization and training of recreation assistants, New Orleans, March 1973, The Foundation.

Carlson, B. W., and Gingelun, D. R.: Recreation for retarded teenagers and young adults, New York, 1968, Abingdon Press.

Epperson, A.: SPRE curriculum catalogue, Society of Professional Recreation Educators, Washington, D.C., 1977, National Recreation and Park Association.

Goldstein, J. E.: Enhancing leisure service delivery to handicapped children and youth, Washington, D.C., May 1977, National Recreation and Park Association.

Haun, P. In Avedon, E. M., and Aye, F. B. eds.: Recreation—a medical viewpoint, New York, 1965, Teachers College Press.

Jury, M.: Playtime—Americans and leisure. New York, 1977, Harcourt Brace Jovanovich.

Kaplan, M.: Leisure in America, New York, 1960, John Wiley & Sons, Inc.

Lucas, C.: Recreation in gerontology, Springfield, Ill., 1964, Charles C Thomas, Publisher.

Lucas, C.: Recreational activity development for the aging in homes, hospitals, and nursing homes, Springfield, Ill., Charles C Thomas, Publisher.

New York City Resource Book: A playground for all children, New York, May 1978.

Shiver, J. S., and Fait, H. F.: Therapeutic and adapted recreational services, Philadelphia, 1975, Lea & Febiger.

U.S. Department of the Interior, Bureau of Outdoor Recreation: Recreation for special people, Washington, D.C., Fall 1977.

Wilson, G. T.: Community recreation programming for handicapped children, National Recreation and Park Association Management Aid No. 96, 1974.

REFERENCES

1. Anderson: Recreation in male state reformatories, University of Pittsburgh 1937, Ther. Rec. J. NTRS **6**(3), 1972.

2. Avedon, E. M.: Therapeutic recreation service, Englewood Cliffs, N.J., 1974, Prentice-Hall Inc.

3. Bestman: An evaluation of the recreation program at the federal correctional institution, Tallahassee, Florida, Ther. Rec. J. NTRS **6**(3), 1972.

4. Cramer: First aider **47**(5), January 1978.

5. Dabney: A survey of recreational activities of the penal institutions of the Middle West (with a suggested program for Missouri State Penitentiary, Jefferson City, Mo.), Ther. Rec. J. NTRS **6**(3), 1972.

6. Fain, G. S., and Hitzhusen, G. L. In National Recreation and Park Association Therapeutic recreation—state of the art. Washington, D.C., 1977, The Association.

7. Fogel, D.: Recreation in corrections, special issue, Parks Rec., p. 17, September 1974.

8. Hayes, G. A.: Working with the mentally retarded in therapeutic recreation. In National Recreation and Park Association: Therapeutic recreation—state of the art, Washington, D.C., The Association.

9. Kraus, R. G.: Recreation and leisure in modern society, New York, 1971, Appleton-Century-Crofts.

10. Kraus, R. G.: Therapeutic recreation—principle and practice, Philadelphia, 1973, W. B. Saunders Co.

11. Miller, M. B.: Iatrogenic and nurisgenic effects of prolonged immobilization of the ill aged, Paper presented to the American Geriatrics Society, Nov. 1, 1974.

12. The National Archives: The Federal Register, **42**(86):22681, May 4, 1977.

13. National Recreation and Park Association: Therapeutic recreation—state of the art, Washington, D.C., 1977, The Association.

14. U.S. Public Health Services: Health Resources Statistics 1968, Washington, D.C.

5
INDUSTRIAL RECREATION

Courtesy Champaign Park District, Champaign, Ill.

Industrial recreation is generally considered as those activities, programs, and events arranged and operated for the leisure satisfaction and diversion of workers, managers, and executives in factories and large business complexes. Such places of employment may include remote installations such as scientific bases near global poles where 500 to 1000 scientists and technicians live and work closely together for months at a time. They may also include the luxurious suburban headquarters of major corporate firms where employees drive private automobiles onto campus-like grounds and return home directly after work. Most often, however industrial recreation denotes a program of sports, recreation, and cultural activities for large factory forces whose daily work tends to be routine and repetitive. Since most large factories are located at the edge or outside of cities, such locations usually possess ample open land for outdoor recreation and sports facilities.

Programs generally include highly structured and competitive leagues in softball, basketball, flag or touch football, volleyball, soccer, golf, tennis, handball, and water polo. Instructional classes may offer music, arts, crafts, automotive mechanics, drama, writing, gardening, and similar hobbies and skills. For those less inclined to take instruction, square dancing, hiking, bicycling, travel, and theatre parties may be provided. Major holidays are usually celebrated with huge parties on corporate grounds or in nearby restaurants or clubs.

The basic tenet of industrial recreation from the company point of view is that wholesome recreation fills out the otherwise colorless life of the workers, making them brighter, more enthusiastic, and more productive members of the labor team.

To those who have never worked in a factory or on an assembly line, the monotony and repetition are hard to visualize. A packer in the Gillette Razor Blade factory in Boston reaches up, grasps 10 prepared blades, and inserts them in a tiny box moving in front of him on an endless belt, folding the cover in the process. Again, he reaches up, grasps 10 blades (not 8 or 11), inserts, and folds. Again and again and again for 7 or 8 hours each day. In Detroit, a Chevrolet assembler presses her powered wrench against a specific nut on the automobile frame and spins it tight. Three more nuts and spins and the frame moves past her on an overhead trolley. The next frame arrives and she steps up with her powered wrench to do exactly the same task again. Industrial engineers are keenly aware of the deadening effect such work causes and are constantly searching for new ideas and remedies to relieve such tedium. Industrial recreation is one of those remedies.

Man is not a machine, and his nature is not adapted to long hours of repetitive tasks . . . . Psychologists have repeatedly claimed that for people whose energies are used mechanically and uncreatively, recreation becomes a matter of absolute necessity. Man carries over into other phases of life the regimentation and standardization . . . . Recreation, with its spirit of freedom and action, affords an effective antidote for this unwholesome tendency.[2]

In 1953, the Wall Street Journal estimated that total expenditures by business and industry for employee recreation amounted to $800 million annually. By 1963, the Philadelphia District Federal Reserve Bank assessed company contributions to employee recreation exceeded $1 billion per year and in 1965, $1.5 billion per year.

The National Industrial Recreation Association (NIRA), based in Chicago, Ill., is the prime membership and professional organization that speaks for this subfield of recreation. The NIRA lists more than

1000 major companies that today provide extensive recreation programs for their employees. The Association is nonprofit and aims to provide professional guidance and assistance to its member units and to coordinate an overall movement in the areas of personnel standards, finance, public relations, and legislation. Some 1500 professional directors and managers head up these industrial recreation programs, and their facilities include 150 company-owned golf courses, 400 company-owned parks and camps, and 100 company-owned recreation centers.

HISTORY

The rudiments of industrial recreation may have been scattered throughout history, but they are rare and hard to find. Because most labor, until the nineteenth century, was isolated and small-scale, there was no gathering or clustering of interests. Many production people worked at home, in a room behind the house, in a barn, in an open yard off the main building, in a loft, or in a primitive workshop a few steps from home. Most massive labor forces were slavelike in nature, such as throngs of workers on the Egyptian pyramids, the countless slaves and servants of the Roman conquerors, or the imprisoned crews aboard gallies of warring nations. Slaves they were, and as slaves they were treated; their masters wasted no time, effort, or money on their need for diversion or social refreshment. The same attitude certainly obtained to the majority of Black African slaves transported to the great farms and plantations of colonial America in the seventeenth and eighteenth centuries.

No large laboring or wage-earning class developed in the United States before the Civil War. Although the growing manufacturing and transportation services, trade, and other economic activities employed increasing thousands of people, a substantial majority of the population was occupied in agriculture. As late as 1860, about 60% of gainfully employed persons were farmers.[3]

This began to change rapidly. The census of 1860 showed 1.3 million wage earners engaged in manufacturing, but by 1914 this number had grown to 7 million. When managers, proprietors, clerks, and others were added, there were about 8.2 million people engaged in the manufacturing industries. These figures underscore the remarkably fast growth of industry, transportation, and trade, which provided millions of additional nonfarm jobs.

The workers of this period were generally the young and vigorous from those available. In 1910, three-fourths of adult workers were between 16 and 44 years of age. The number of women engaged in gainful occupations increased steadily after 1870, when only 13% of workers were females. By 1910, that number had increased to over 20%. Large numbers of women were employed in various aspects of the textile industry, in canning and preserving, in confectionery, and in the manufacture of tobacco products.

By the early twentieth century, most of the nation's wage earners were employed by corporations. In 1909, corporations composed about 26% of the industrial establishments, but they employed 75% of the wage earners and turned out 79% of the total value of manufactured products. In 1914, 35% of the nation's wage earners were employed by only 1.4% of the industrial establishments, each of which had an annual product of $1 million or more. The industries that hired the most workers were lumber and timber products, foundries and machine shops, printing and publishing, cotton goods, iron and steel, men's and women's clothing, boots, and shoes. There were only 648 industrial establishments that employed over 1000 wage earners in 1914, but these large businesses had a total of 1,225, 259 workers.

WORKING CONDITIONS

The early wage earners worked long hours for low wages. In 1909, most industrial employees worked between 50 and 60 hours per week, and in a few industries it ran even higher. The cement industry, for instance, pushed its people beyond 65 hours per week, while iron and steel workers put in close to 72 hours each week. Generally speaking, hours were longer for southern industrial workers than for those in the north.

And what of working conditions? Most factories were either chilly and damp from inadequate heating systems or ovenlike from the furnaces, steam engines, and lack of ventilation. Production was the only criterion; all else was unimportant. Small, foul toilets, dim lighting, chemical odors and vapors—the workers and their comforts seemingly were the last to be considered.

Yet something was happening in the 1920s and 1930s. Its specific cause is not certain. It may have been because more and more workers were being assembled in larger and larger concentrations. Perhaps it was a basic democratic independence, indigenous to the American worker. There is the possibility that top management learned early that happy, healthy workers are more productive workers. There may even have been an altruistic tycoon or two who actually wanted the employees to enjoy themselves. Whatever the cause, recreation began to appear, although modest at first—a horseshoe pitching court behind the factory; a fishing club that would meet on Sundays; a few picnic benches for an outside summer lunch; a Christmas party for workers and their families. It began and,

with the burgeoning labor union movement of the time, it grew. Management saw no reason to feed this recreation movement too fast, however. In 1940, the S. H. Kress Company's headquarters included 1200 employees on 13 floors. Recreation consisted on two table tennis tables at the end of the employees' lunchroom, and these were to be used by workers only during their lunch hour. Giant installations such as Macy's Herald Square store in New York City with 3000 full-time and part-time employees, the Merchandise Mart in Chicago, the Bank of the Manhattan Company in New York City, and others that employed from 2000 to 6000 workers regularly all appeared to consider a moderate-sized lunchroom, small reading room, soft-drink dispenser, a radio, and some magazines quite adequate. Some of the more enlightened companies provided a small exercise room with hand weights and a room with 3 or 4 folding cots for workers to nap on their lunch break.

Labor gains during this period included the 8-hour day and a rising wage scale. Unions also fought vigorously for improved working conditions for wage earners, and this had its delayed action effect on recreation accommodations of the time. Certain paid holidays and a modest vacation period were among the early victories of the unions. Soon a baseball field and picnic grove on the plant grounds became commonplace, at least at industrial sites outside cities where space was cheap. A handful of firms, even before World War II, led the way with unusually large programs of employee sports and recreation. The Hershey Chocolate Company established a broad network of games, teams, community center, and evening activities—one that was to become a model for companies to follow later. The Phillips Petroleum Company and the Metropolitan Life Insurance Company of New York were equally forward thinking and espoused the cause of the employee in need of wholesome recreation.

Today, nearly 99% of the total useful work energy of the country comes from machines . . . . The worker at some repetitive tasks may still be fatigued in body at the end of the day's work, but frequently he is merely bored without the satisfaction which once came from creating an object. . . . The current advances in automation indicate that the need to offset this tendency through recreation may be still greater in the years ahead.[2]

WAR INDUSTRY

From 1939 to about 1949, mobilization and war industry aided the expansion and improvement of industrial recreation. Overnight, railroad depots, truck and tank arsenals, aircraft and shipbuilding centers, and a number of huge new administrative complexes sprang up, first to aid our Allies and, later, to service our own war machine. Enormous concentrations of personnel were clustered around these industrial and business centers, and the need for recreational diversion was greater than ever. The reasons for greater program need were:

1. Personnel were siphoned into industrial sites from all over the country, and many had no ties to the community in which they worked.

2. Populations were not the normal age mixture that one finds in society. Because of the heavy drain made on healthy manpower by the military, male workers were either under 20 years of age or over 40 years of age, with few exceptions. Women workers, on the other hand, not only outnumbered males 4 to 1, but they were mainly between 18 and 30 years of age. Even with some military personnel nearby, this arrangement made for great restlessness and great searching for social activity.

3. Management, normally interested in high productivity, now felt the demands of the military to create weapons overnight. Production quotas and tempos rose constantly, and most manufacturing facilities worked on three round-the-clock shifts. Worker morale was extremely important if such frantic production was to be kept up.

4. A pervasive tension, or "war nerves," was evident throughout the country. Everyone had someone, a husband, sweetheart, son, nephew, uncle, close friend, or neighbor in combat or in some dangerous service. Newspapers and radio gave daily reports of dead and injured, and associates regularly reported to one another the loss of this person or the injury to that. There was a fatalistic feeling in many that could easily cause otherwise normal people to act perversely.

Management, both civilian and military, turned heavily to industrial recreation for help. Hundreds of baseball and softball fields were constructed at scores of large industrial sites such as the Electric Boat Company, Groton, Connecticut, producer of scores of fighting submarines; the Boeing Modification Center, McClellan Field, Sacramento, California, where several thousand women did technical changes and modifications on new B-17 and B-24 bombers before they were flown overseas; and at the sprawling Grumman Aircraft Company's plants on Long Island where most of the U.S. Navy's fighter planes were designed and a large portion of them built. Handball walls, weight-training centers, steam rooms, par 3 golf courses, tennis courts, picnic groves, auto repair shops, amateur music units, dramatic groups, woodworking shops, and vegetable gardens were among the most popular activities and facilities.

With the end of the war in 1945, many of these large plants did not cease operating.

Most cut back in production, but their sheer size and complexity prevented any immediate turnoff of their operation. The demands of handling the return home of millions of service personnel, as well as the simultaneous arming of military occupations in defeated nations at opposite ends of the earth, ensured a continued, if modified, demand for war materials. Further, there was a segment of the country's more powerful leaders, influenced by the still very large military establishment, that believed that the world had not yet really settled down to a permanent peace. These people urged the retention of substantial Army, Navy, and Air Force personnel as insurance that Soviet Russia and Red China would not feel free to commit renewed aggressions. Just as these militant voices began to fade, the U.S. was confronted with Soviet belligerence and roadblocks at the entrance to divided Berlin, and a movement toward military readiness was again triggered. Thereafter, a series of international incidents and outbreaks—Korea, Cuba, Viet Nam—forced the U.S. to maintain varying degrees of high production in military hardware. This meant continued large concentrations of personnel, sometimes at very isolated parts of the country, as our arms and their manufacture became increasingly sophisticated.

At first, the design of these sports and recreation facilities and the operation of the recreation programs were left to amateurs. Conscientious volunteers, drawn from the ranks of workers and their families, gave up personal time to organize and guide athletic teams and cultural groups. Gradually, however, the quality and scope of industrial recreation resulted in the employment of professional recreation directors, or at least management personnel whose prime responsibility was the administering of these programs and facilities. But the need for such programs and leadership increased.

OUTSTANDING PROGRAMS

The following corporations and locations have been outstanding leaders in the development of recreation programs and facilities:

1. The Teletype Company, Skokie, Ill., was begun in 1937 with 778 members and today includes 5800. Twenty clubs cater to a wide range of interests for men and women. Basketball, bowling, softball, horseshoes, golf, tennis, and various hobby clubs are included, along with many tournaments and special events. Huge holiday picnics and Christmas parties bring as many as 4000 persons together at one time.

2. General Foods Corporation, White Plains, N.Y., operates a broad activity program for its employees. Recently, a new $1,000,000 recreation and physical fitness center was built on headquarters grounds. A full professional staff operates these facilities.

3. Pepsi-Cola Company, Purchase, N.Y., includes a new physical fitness and recreation center in its corporate headquarters. Outdoors, it maintains a magnificent fishing lake with towering fountain, flocks of ducks and swans, an impressive sculpture garden, and a circuitous jogging track that meanders around the spacious grounds, all for employees and executives.

4. Xerox Corporation, Rochester, N.Y. has probably assembled one of the finest physical plants anywhere for its workers, although it was not one of the first companies with a recreation program. A huge park adjoining headquarters includes lakes, bicycle paths, sports fields, archery ranges, children's play areas, and a host of additional facilities. Main buildings include sophisticated stress testing and exercise equipment, and the entire complex is operated by a first class team of professional recreators. What makes Xerox a standout, however, is the very positive attitude of its top management toward this employee ac-

tivity. Men and women are urged to become active on a wide range of subjects simply because management feels happy workers are more productive workers.

Kraus[4] offers three major reasons for such a substantial effort by industry to provide wholesome diversion for workers:

1. Improvement of employer-employee relations: The aim is to dispel the earlier abrasive relationship between boss and worker, which in early American industry was generally not good. Workers are no longer treated as chattel or regarded as dispensable, and worker morale is considered important for stable operation.

2. Promotion of employee efficiency: Studies have shown that where workers participate regularly in programs of wholesome recreation and sports, absenteeism is reduced. Similarly, recreation combats worker fatigue and boredom, and thus reduces accidents.

3. Recruitment appeal: In today's competitive world, even job sites must outdraw one another. Workers choosing a place of employment will assess the sports and recreation program and facilities with almost as much care as they evaluate salaries. This is especially true when the industry is located far from main population centers.

A fourth, perhaps idealistic reason may well be set forth for some industries. Today's top managers are often youthful, well-educated, and well-traveled and appreciate the fullness and opportunity of life. Also they are probably recreation enthusiasts themselves in one or more areas. Many of these leaders genuinely believe that some part of their leadership ability and the company's resources should be used to improve and enrich the social and cultural lives of the employees. Such a person will often add environmental and cultural activities and facilities to the already established employee program of sports and special events.

FUNDING

Most industrial recreation programs are funded and directed by one of the following methods:

1. Total direct management by the company, with company-employed staff to lead and operate. Small contributions are made by employees in the way of fees and charges.

2. Total employee control through an intricate system of division chairpersons and delegates, with all funds coming from membership dues, fees, and charges. Here, any trained staff is hired by the "employee recreation association," with the company simply providing area and facilities.

3. Some combination of the above, also utilizing the profits from canteens and plant vending machines.

UNIONS

Not suprisingly, many labor unions have taken an increasing interest in industrial recreation and its impact on the worker. Their concern arises from the following:

1. Constantly shortening work weeks and lengthening vacation periods and off-time have presented workers with large blocks of leisure or discretionary time. It is essential that these people "learn" to use this time positively, or it will become a negative drain. In desperation, some workers seek second jobs to fill the disturbing new gap in their schedules presented by the extra leisure time.

2. Unions promote leisure time enrichment by promoting opportunities for workers to raise their intellectual and living standards through travel, study, cultural activities, and hobbies. This has been one of the building blocks of unionism for over a century.

3. Most union officials genuinely feel a responsibility for promoting positive programs of social welfare under enlightened

government. Wholesome recreation, subsidized by local, state, and federal government, represents this kind of government contribution to workers' welfare.

4. Unions appreciate the strong sense of camaraderie that accompanies a sound program of sports and recreation. Union membership is always a problem, and union officials do not overlook recreation as a very strong stimulant for holding old members and bringing in new ones.

The United Auto Workers, one of the largest labor groups in the country, recently changed the name of its recreation unit to the Department of Recreation and Leisure-Time Activities. In addition, a special UAW unit in Detroit was designated Deprived Areas Recreation Team (DART) to develop a network of vest pocket parks by providing financial assistance and working with neighborhood organizations in inner-city areas. DART has also worked closely with the Detroit Parks and Recreation Commission to promote a city-wide federation of neighborhood groups concerned with recreation and conservation.

Perhaps the most solicitous for its members and the best known labor organization in America is the International Ladies Garment Workers Union (ILGWU). The union operates a $10 million vacation retreat in Pennsylvania—Camp Unity—for its members. The camp includes 78 buildings, including a million dollar theatre, large administration center, health club, tennis courts, a swimming beach on a 1-mile lake, and a dining complex that seats 1100 guests. The program ranges from quiet games through all vigorous sports, and from painting to high-level philosophic discussions.

Long active in social concerns for its members, the ILGWU in 1968 announced that it would donate $350,000 to the new Urban Coalition to help improve recreation facilities in urban slums. President of the

ILGWU, Jacob Potofsky, stated at the time:

> In the past, one cause of the aggravated tensions in the cities during the summer months has been a terrible lack of recreation facilities . . . . We must provide the children and young unemployed adults with facilities for recreation, education and entertainment. . . .[5]

Consider the similarity between that statement by the President of the ILGWU and the following one by management on the same subject:

> Nothing is more important to the physical and emotional health of the men and women of industry than proper recreation activities . . . few modern companies would consider locating a new plant of facilities in a community without first surveying its recreation possibilities. Management knows that . . . its ability to attract and hold the men and women it wants often is decided by the Little Theatre, the park system, or the Little League.[1]

CAREER OPPORTUNITIES

The subfield of industrial recreation offers interesting opportunities, but opportunities with realistic numbers attached. Some 1000 major industries presently employ one or more full-time recreational staff persons, so this represents approximately 1500 jobs. At the present rate of expansion and with all the potential economic ups and downs considered, that could mean a total of 2500 jobs by 1980. Generally speaking, industrial recreation jobs are not fast-turnover in nature. People are often selected from worker and lower management ranks and groomed upward. Further, the paternalistic philosophy of many large firms and the concommittant bonuses, travel plans, employee discount stores, and periodic sabbaticals, can make work at this level of management so attractive that people stay for long periods. Metropolitan Life Insurance, Prudential Insurance,

Grumman Aircraft, various telephone companies, Massachusetts Mutual Life Insurance, and Raytheon Corp. are all examples of business firms that have strong holding qualities for their management personnel.

Recreation salaries are modest compared with other divisions within companies. This probably reflects top management's view of the employee recreation program—important, yes; helpful, yes; but not nearly as significant to the financial health of the company as efficiency on the production/assembly line or the sales performance of the merchandising and marketing staff. This is one of the facts of life that the industrial recreator must learn and understand. In the business/industry world, the most important element of all to top management is the triad of production-sales-finance; the rest is secondary. This distinguishes the subbranch of industrial recreation from all other sectors of recreational service. Success here is measured less in quality and quantity of services to people and more in terms of the ''bottom line.'' How did it affect our Profit and Loss statement?—that is the important question.

Salaries for industrial recreation administrators in large firms range from $8500.00 to $14,000.00 and from $15,000 to $26,000 for long-term veterans in super industries. Fringe benefits range from very good to excellent, usually much more comprehensive than in community recreation. They include variations of substantial vacations for beginners, special vacation rates at company camps (International Business Machine [IBM] operates a superb employee camp and club resort near its plant in Poughkeepsie, N.Y.), complete medical and dental coverage for worker and family, eye glasses, discount purchasing plan at many large stores, generous life insurance plan, sick time, employee vacation travel plans and tours at considerable discounts, whole or partial tuition to colleges and training schools, periodic sabbaticals, and a host of additional recreational and cultural features. These enable the workers to stretch their base salaries much further than first seems possible. It is this kind of feature that makes industrial work so attractive and appreciably reduces the turnover.

A potential development area for new positions is in the large number of small business and industrial plants in the U.S. and Canada that employ 100 workers or less. At least 25,000 of these plants exist, but it is quite unlikely that they will ever employ full-time recreation persons to work with their 35, 55, or 75 employees. Instead, they are beginning to realize the advantage of pooling their recreation and physical fitness needs in clusters of four or five companies. Not infrequently, Company A will have three or four employees who would like to establish a drama group. In a firm of 45 workers, it is next to impossible to assemble a full cast, stage crew, etc. Next door, however, at Company B., six employees have expressed interest in dramatics, and in Company C across the street, four would-be thespians have been attempting to launch their own dramatic effort, unsuccessfully. Through a joint effort, these thirteen employees of Companies A, B, and C are brought together, and a budding drama club is underway. This same technique is applicable to sports leagues, bowling, dances, hobby groups, arts and crafts, and countless others.

These loose confederations of small businesses can do many things together in industrial recreation, but their potential is greatly enhanced by employing a trained recreation person to coordinate and develop new programs. This might be accomplished either by formally arranged joint operation in which central budget, policies, and hiring practices are ratified by all the companies involved or by a loose alignment in which interested individuals from the several companies are contacted and invited to gather at some common location (e.g., the cafeteria or lounge of one of the industrial plants) for purposes of organizing their own drama group.

I recently advised a young unemployed recreation person in the Chicago area to create her own job by utilizing one or the other of the methods in the previous paragraph. She did so and 6 months later described her success as follows:

I visited 15 industrial plants, all near each other in a large industrial park, and all employing from 50 to 250 people each. None had any recreation personnel, and very few had more than a semblance of a recreation program. After a month's effort, I convinced six firms to contract with me for $2,000.00 each for one year. I promised them, not a full-time program, but approximately a ⅓ time program, plus training of their own volunteers. I utilized my $12,000 budget as follows: Salary for me, $8,000.00; second-hand small van, $800.00; movie projector, sound system and player, other hardware, $1000. The balance, $2200, I am using for part-time leadership to help me, plus stationery, printing, postage, etc. It isn't much salary, but I am learning a lot and making fabulous contacts. Two months after I started, I had several additional inquiries. If I

wanted, I could be doing 10 plants right now instead of six, but I'm only in it a few months and I want to smooth things out some before I grow.

This technique of pooling three or more small plants and putting the cluster in the hands of a trained professional could produce 3000 to 4000 new positions in industrial recreation by 1980.

BIBLIOGRAPHY

Bagwell, P. S., and Mingay, G. E.: Britain and America—a study of economic change 1850-1939, New York, 1970, Praeger Publishers.
Doty, C. S.: The industrial revolution, Hinsdale, Ill., 1969, The Dryden Press.
Kando, T. M.: Leisure and popular culture in transition, St. Louis, 1975, The C. V. Mosby Co.
Reeve, R. M.: The industrial revolution 1750-1850, London, 1971, The University of London Press.

REFERENCES

1. Bannow, R.F.: What is expected of recreation by management, Recreation p. 15, January, 1960.
2. Butler, G. D.: Introduction to community recreation, New York, 1959, McGraw-Hill Book Co.
3. Fite, G. C., and Reese, J. E.: An economic history of the United States, Boston, 1973, Houghton Mifflin Co.
4. Kraus, R.: Recreation and leisure in modern society, New York, 1971, Appleton-Century-Crofts.
5. Potofsky, J.: Clothing workers to donate $350,000.00 for slum recreation, New York Times p. 24, May 26, 1968.

6
COMMERCIAL RECREATION

© Walt Disney Productions

"There's a sucker born every minute" allegedly declared Phineas Taylor Barnum, the bombastic and most renowned circus showman of all time. And even if this riposte never became an official slogan, it typifies the brash arrogance of that uniquely American phenomenon, commercial recreation. A spicy mix of show business, park planning, entertainment, and glittery escape, commercial recreation is broad in scope and kaleidoscopic in its variety. It might easily include the amusement park, the luxury ocean liner, professional sports, movies, the sale of cameras, stereos, dune buggies, and hula hoops, the lust for gambling and leg shows, and antique car collecting. However, for purposes of identification and focus, the category will be limited to those aspects of commercial recreation that involve structured planning and leadership personnel and programming and those that relate to or resemble the style and scale of community recreation.

Commercial recreation is a relatively new term, having come into use widely only since World War II. It describes that industry, business, or service established to provide public recreation and entertainment for a price and to produce a financial profit for the entrepreneur. It may range from a small bowling alley to a gigantic theme park, from a tiny rowboat concession to a complete skiing complex. Relatively simple and moderately scaled in the nineteenth century and early twentieth century, commercial recreation's growth has been phenomenal in the 1950s and 1960s. Family recreation has influenced that growth substantially. For a century or more, the American family has attached great importance to its weekly, monthly, or seasonal trip to the amusement park, to the seashore, or to the distant historical battlefield, sports park or theatrical district in the big city. The family automobile has played a key role in this fantastic growth of commercial recreation. Because commercial recreation facilities of the past had to be built close to the living centers of their non–auto-owning customers, those facilities were forced to remain small and modest in capacity. When the automobile released the public from that short distance bond, they were able to travel 20 to 35 miles in comfort to reach their amusements, and the facilities moved further away and became bigger. This trend continues today.

Commercial recreation is a multibillion dollar industry and employs millions of people in a broad array of jobs and titles. The simplicity of the 1920s has been replaced by university training, specialized academic degrees, and the use of computer planning and operating. Some in the recreation profession view commercial recreation as the area of greatest growth potential. There is the possibility that this sector may one day absorb all other sectors, as entrepreneurs reach out for greater profit and as governments struggle to keep expenditures subordinate to revenues.

PROFIT

Profit motivation and a balance sheet with "bottom line" strength are basic to commercial recreation. Without them, the color and texture of the operation would change and the effort would be primarily to serve people, to accomplish some social good. Despite the high idealism of some commercial operators and their ethical principles, clean operations, and demonstrated honesty, they are still in the business for a financial profit. In fact, most could not survive without a substantial and consistent return on investment. As will be seen later, this pressure for profit sometimes influences a private entrepreneur to enter shabby areas of activity and to use methods that lack taste or discretion.

Nevertheless, this is all part of the phenomenon labeled commercial recreation and the attraction it exercises over people of all ages in every corner of the globe.

HISTORY

The Circus Maximus of Imperial Rome came into existence under the Emperor Pompey. A showman at heart, Pompey was certain that a large, well-built arena filled with spectacular performances was an unbeatable combination for public appeal, and he was right. Almost 2000 feet long, 625 feet wide, this enormous racetrack-shaped structure comfortably accommodated 250,000 spectators at one time. Elephant acts, horse races, chariot chases, and all manner of simulated battles and pageants were held there to the delight of Rome's common man. Later, the Circus Maximus was phased out by the new Colosseum, smaller, elliptical in shape, but far more attractive and comfortable to its 50,000 seat capacity. Every seat offered a flawless view of the central dirt-floored arena. Nevertheless, the word "circus" had become identified with a central, circular action arena.

In 1770, an animal show in England called "Activity on Horseback by Mr. Astley, Sgt. Major of His Majesty's Light Dragoons," was held in a low, circular enclosure, 42 feet wide, and the modern circus ring was born. This standard size is still in wide use. Circuses and animal acts moved widely through Europe in the eighteenth and nineteenth centuries, some of them even sporting genuine American Indians imported from the New World, who were displayed in the blazing finery of their buckskins, beads, feathers, and headdresses.

If one were to identify the tap roots of commercial recreation in America, there would be many, but three would stand out—1) the Circus–Wild West Shows, 2) the family amusement parks, and 3) the motion picture industry. A fourth, and latter influence, is television, which packages and delivers to the living room a powerfully synthesized combination of the first three. Additional impact came from carnivals, medicine shows, radio, vaudeville, the automobile, and the night club. This potpourri was lubricated by bootleg liquor and bathtub gin in the 1920s and early 1930s. Together, they create a kind of euphoric whole that people now conjure up under such phrases as "The Gaslight Era," "The Good Old Days," "The Roaring Twenties," and "When Mother was a Girl." It was a most colorful period.

THE CIRCUS IN AMERICA

The origins of the American circus are in Philadelphia and New York. The main thoroughfares, before the railroads came to this territory, were the old Boston Post Road and its sideroads. Cattlemen drove their herds into New York by these same roads and often bought various animals from ship captains—parrots, monkeys, and later, larger animals. The idea of exhibiting animals, singly or in groups, originated in this locality.

The year 1792 was very important in American circus history for in that year, John B. Ricketts, a famous equestrian, came to Philadelphia from Scotland and brought his royal circus. . . . On April 3, 1793, the Ricketts Company gave the first complete performance in America. . . . General George Washington attended the Ricketts Circus on April 22, 1793. . . .[2]

Originally confined to the Atlantic seaboard, the circus in America slowly extended its wagon routes in 1802 northward to Boston and southward to Savannah. By 1825 water travel along canals and rivers had been added, and the circuses were appearing farther north, west and south. By midcentury, the circus that travelled by railroad took advantage of the 42,229 miles of railroad tracks in the United States. At its peak, there were more than 1,000 circuses, menageries, Wild West shows and large carnivals crossing and recrossing the nation from March until late fall each year. Collectively, they employed a quarter of a million people in every imaginable show business and maintenance title. Famous names included Sells Brothers Circus, Clyde Beatty–Cole Brothers, Ringling Brothers Circus, Barnum and Bailey Shows, Pan-American Circus, Robbins Bros. Circus, Ricketts' Shows, and Spellman's American Combined Motorized Circus. Some of the better known Wild West Shows were Stone's Great Western Circus and Indian Show, Col. Tim McCoy's Wild West, Langley's Equestrian Circus, and Indian Bill's Wild West. By far, the most famous of these was Buffalo Bill Cody's Wild West with Annie Oakley, markswoman extraordinaire.

Three generations of children grew up dreaming and fantasizing over the sounds, smells, tastes, and dazzling sights of the Circus–Wild West show. The brightly painted wagons, glittering costumes, ragtag clowns, fast music—small wonder that children anticipated by months the announcement, ''The circus is coming, the circus is coming!'' The circus parade through the town, led by a platoon of waddling elephants, chortling calliope, men on horses, women on camels, people in uniforms, flags, banners, colored smoke, amid roars, shrieks, shouts, songs, and the smash of cymbals and boom of drums— surely this had to be commercial recreation at its very best, and America loved it! That kind of entertainment and diversion became a part of America's bloodstream and remains so today. Elements of the circus, the rodeo, and the Wild West show were carried into the next century. The shows are fewer and larger and they travel by high-speed truck, trailer, and diesel train, but the crowds are still there and the lure of the circus may be greater than ever.

EUROPEAN AMUSEMENT PARKS

Like the circus, the family amusement park is a transplanted European concept, developed in the eighteenth century in England and France. Pleasure gardens in and around London included such historic names as Vauxhall Gardens, Ranelagh Gardens, Marylebone Gardens, and others that catered to an amusement-hungry populace. Bowling, flower beds, hot food, wrestling, gambling, fireworks, and music were the bill of fare, with an occasional balloon ascent to provide the spectacular. They were immensely popular.

Unlike the English gardens, which featured old homesteads, taverns, and inns, the French amusement parks were originally designed as such and displayed clever planning and showmanship. The best known group in France was the Ruggieri family, which opened various parks throughout the country. Ruggieri Gardens was a delightful funspot, including an original concept called ''Saut du Niagara.'' It was a sliding boat, loaded with passengers, and released down a steep incline into a pool of water. A half century later, the device began to appear in amusement parks in the United States and is still popular today as the Shoot-the-Chutes. The Ruggieris opened and closed again and again, always expanding and improving. Tivoli, the Parc Monceau, Jardin Beaujon, and the Jardin Marbeauf, another Ruggieri enterprise located at the end of the Champs Elysees near the Chaillot Gate in Paris, were among the most spectacular in Europe.

In Vienna in 1873, a great world's fair

was held, and many of the buildings, including the Great Rotunda, were left standing, These became the Prater, the best known amusement center in all Europe. Every imaginable stunt, vaudeville act, noise, or illuminator, performer, construction, game, device, or entertainment effort found its way to the Prater. The "Riesenrand," or original giant pleasure wheel (we call it Ferris Wheel), was installed in 1904 and became world famous, to be copied a thousand times over.

AMERICAN AMUSEMENT PARKS

One of the earliest American amusement parks was Jones' Wood, along the East River between Seventieth and Seventy-fifth Streets in New York City. Walks and tents, banners and flags surrounded gymnastic equipment and large wooden animals and rides. Bowling alleys and billiard parlors, shooting galleries and side shows added to the jolly bedlam. Beer reigned supreme.

Parker's Grove, located in the Ohio River Valley near Cincinnati, became known as the Coney Island of the West. St. Louis had its Forest Park Highlands, a park created in cooperation with the owners of the Home Brewing Company. Other famous names of the period were Glen Echo Amusement Park, Maryland, near Washington, D.C.; Lake Compounce Park near Bristol, in Connecticut; Riverview Park in Chicago; Schuetzen Park in Union Hill, New Jersey; Kennywood Park near Pittsburgh; Lemon Hill Park in Philadelphia, which later became present-day Fairmount Park, site of the great Centennial Exposition of 1876; Elitch's Gardens in Denver, where Mrs. Elitch Long became one of the outstanding American women in the amusement business; and Playland in Rye, New York. Playland is unusual in that it is fully functioning today after having been carefully assembled and designed in 1925. In addition to its rides, food, and special events, Playland is graced by luxuriant trees, shrubs, and colorful flower beds along walks and between buildings. It continues to be a model for fine family amusement.

Coney Island

The most widely known amusement resort in the United States is Coney Island, located on the ocean beach in Brooklyn, New York at a point where the Florentine navigator Verrazano first set foot on the continent in 1524. The area flourished in the latter part of the nineteenth century, and a cluster of lavish hotels marked the spot. Two large ocean piers were constructed, and two buildings were moved to the site from the Philadelphia Exposition of 1876 and reassembled. All manner of rides and shows followed, and the historic Steeplechase and Luna Park fun centers were created. Despite several devastating fires, the entertainment center flourished and became a model for similar complexes in San Francisco and Atlantic City. George C. Tilyou, a combination of P. T. Barnum and Walt Disney, was the guiding genius behind Coney Island's growth. At the opening of Tilyou's Luna Park in 1903, for instance, 250,000 electric lights were turned on, this in a nation where many people still read by candle or gaslight. Some idea of the popularity of the area may be drawn from a single day's attendance at Coney Island in 1952—1,600,000 visitors.

The explosion

During the first half of the twentieth century, there was no remarkable growth or spread of commercial recreation. Isolated fun spots were busily drawing crowds, as indicated, and periodic splendors such as World's Fairs or International Expositions such as Chicago's Century of Progress in 1933 were held. However, the relative scarcity of quality building materials, the still primitive transportation system, and the absence of visionary designers-builders for this area of the economy, kept new construction and expansion of old to a minimum. Robert Moses, master builder, was one of the few people of that time who saw the potential of commercial recreation. Despite his preoccupation with building playgrounds, beaches, and highways, not to mention helping to cope with a world war, Moses managed to construct not one, but two massive World's Fairs, one in 1939-1940 and one in 1964-1965.

The fun explosion began in the 1950s. Walt Disney, already a creative genius in the field of animated cartooning and motion pictures, began designing and constructing a new amusement park in Anaheim, California in 1950 that was to send a pleasant shock wave around the world. It was to be called Disneyland and was built on 200 acres of wasteland near Los Angeles at a cost of $200 million. Consisting of five main sections, Fantasyland, Tomorrowland, Frontierland, Adventureland, and Main Street, U.S.A., it opened in 1955 and reflected the fastidious detail and painstaking research that characterized all of Disney's work. It was a children's story and picture book come alive, with Bo-Peep, the Big Bad Wolf, Old King Cole, and every other beloved character children had always read about. The children loved Disneyland and its total make-believe fun, but, somewhat surprisingly, the grownups adored it too! Once inside the colorful gates, all guests became as one age and grandparents giggled and pranced about with the same abandon as their grandchildren. Oriental potentates, chiefs of state from abroad, business executives, college presidents—anyone traveling anywhere west simply *had* to visit Disneyland.

Within a few short years of Disneyland's tremendous opening success, 30 large theme parks of various design and magnitude opened in every corner of the country: Busch Gardens and Lion Safari Country in Florida, King's Dominion in Virginia, Six Flags over Texas, Knott's Berry Farm in Los Angeles, Norfolk Gardens in Virginia, Great Adventure in New Jersey, and The Underground in Atlanta. They did not always succeed, however. Freedomland, hailed as New York's answer to Disneyland, opened in 1964 with a theme park depicting every major region of the country on a 72-acre tract of land along the Hutchinson River Parkway in the Bronx. It closed, a dismal failure, in 1966, pulling down thousands of small investors with it.

During the 1950s and 1960s, hundreds of new shopping centers, malls, and covered business plazas were built and many of these incorporated space and facilities for commercial recreation in the form of theatres, amphitheatres, food service, dancing, craft classes, art showcases, and small museums. Expansion of professional sports brought an accompanying rash of giant new stadiums such as the Astrodome in Houston, the Omni in Atlanta, and the Spectrum in Philadelphia. Scores of medium-sized cities and counties decided that to be progressive and attractive to industries seeking relocation sites, it was essential that they have their own arena or sports center and that it have associated with it a substantial exhibition or convention hall. And so the growth continued at a breathtaking rate. Part of this picture was the $50 billion federal highway building program of the late 1950s, which effectively gave the family car the equivalent of 7-league boots. Over 100,000 miles of new superhighway were built, and Howard Johnsons, Ramadas, Hiltons, Days Inns, Marriotts, and Holiday Inns sprouted along these new roads like so many richly colored giant mushrooms. Here again, the element of recreation was added to the ancient craft

Courtesy Knott's Berry Farm

of hostelry. Swimming pools, bars, discotheques, attractive gift shops, teen centers, children's playgrounds, and health spas were made part of many of these 5000 new hotel and motel complexes.

Disney World

Disney World opened in Orlando, Florida, October 25, 1971, on 27,000 acres at a cost of $400 million. This commercial recreation enterprise staggers the mind.

The pattern and highlights are similar to those of Disneyland but the scale is vast, 27,000 acres compared with 200 acres. Consider these facts from Florida and New York newspapers, from *The Story of Walt Disney World* (commemorative edition 1972), and from *Amusement Business* October, 1973:

1. Land involved—43 square miles; purchase cost—$5 million.
2. Annual visitors—10.7 million persons.
3. The inner, active Magic Kingdom area is encircled by a vast resort area, only partially developed.
4. America's largest private construction project ever.
5. Planted 60,000 trees and shrubs.
6. One day's attendance, average—100,000 visitors.
7. Staff of 9,000 employees.

The impact of this project on surrounding areas is, of course, considerable. Before Disney World, Orlando's hotel–motel room total was 5400. Today, the figure is over 15,000, with another 10,000 on the way. At a press conference in 1965, Walt Disney said:

I've always said there would never be another Disneyland. This concept here will have to be something that is unique . . . . so there is a distinction between Disneyland in California, and whatever Disney does in Florida.

If there is a distinction between the two, it has not bothered American or international tourists. They have flocked to California and Florida in increasing numbers, and the Bicentennial of 1976 brought attendance crushes that strained even the vaunted Disney staff equilibrium. Following is one of the greatest compliments paid the Disney approach to design:

. . . the greatest piece of urban design in the United States today is Disneyland. If you think about Disneyland and think of its performance in relation to its purpose, its meaning to people—more than that, its meaning to the process of development—you will find it the outstanding piece of urban design in the United States.[4]

It takes more than hardware and trees to bring out Disney's record-breaking crowds, however, and the following is a sample of the shrewd recreation planning that brings larger and larger turnouts. It is selected from *Disneyland Line* the employee newsletter:

Running on a POO-litical platform that includes 5¢ ice cream cones for everybody, no more afternoon naps, and two visits to Disneyland every year, Winnie the Pooh will be officially nominated as President of the "Little People's Party" at a giant convention planned for Walt Disney World on September 30 and October 1.

Truly, all major amusement park developments in the U.S. may well be identified as pre-Disney or post-Disney. No other adequate bench mark exists.

MEADOWLANDS

In 1975, the Meadowlands Sports and Exposition Complex opened on the Hackensack meadows in New Jersey, 20 minutes driving time from Manhattan and the New York City area. Cost exceeded $400 million, and it includes an 80,000 seat baseball-football stadium, horse and trotter track, administration and convention facilities, with a 20,000 seat ice hockey and basketball arena now under construction. New York professional sports teams are being coaxed to move to the Meadowlands, and New York sports fans are using it increasingly, to the dismay of operators at Yonkers Raceway, Yankee Stadium, Shea Stadium, Madison Square Garden, and the Nassau County Memorial Coliseum in Mineola, all New York State locations.

LAS VEGAS

No discussion of commercial recreation is complete without a brief profile of Las Vegas, Nevada. This adult playspot in the center of mountain-rimmed western desert is the latest and biggest tribute to the adage that opened this chapter, "There's a sucker born every minute." Overlit, overbuilt, overdecorated and overpriced, the Las Vegas complex of hotels, gambling casinos, and nightclubs has no equal in the world. Most construction is new and is either heavily art deco or is built around some designer's romantic theme or motif. Thus, there is the MGM–Grand Hotel, 26 stories high, rising starkly against the china-blue sky, decorated with the memorabilia of hundreds of Metro-Goldwyn-Mayer movies of the past 40 years. Nearby, the Aladdin Hotel sports an Arabian theme, the Circus-Circus is decorated as one would expect—like a huge circus tent, and Caesar's Palace is Greco-Roman. Entrance signs are eight to ten stories high, proclaiming their show business stars and luxury accommodations in blindingly colorful megawatts. Consider these facts and figures about the once-shabby mining town of 500 people that has become the greatest world pleasure city since Babylon:

1. Annually, 10 million persons visit Las Vegas.
2. Gambling proceeds from Las Vegas, Reno, and Lake Tahoe gross $1.2 billion annually, with Las Vegas accounting for $2/3$ of the total.
3. The hotel-nightclub-gambling complex in Las Vegas employs 40,000 persons.
4. Annually, 48,000 people marry in Las Vegas, while 6000 obtain divorces there. On the main street, Las Vegas Boulevard, there are 26 tiny, cute marriage chapels, mini-churches where the entire ceremony can be completed in minutes, including paperwork, ring, flowers, announcements, organ music, and rice.
5. Hotel rooms in Las Vegas now total 40,000 and should reach 55,000 by 1981.

This, indeed, is the commercial recreation supersite of all time and, like Disney World, is still growing.

ATLANTIC CITY

In May 1978, a new star burst upon the commercial recreation horizon. Authorized by a statewide referendum in 1976, Atlantic City, New Jersey, saw her first casino gambling center open in May, 1978. Modeled upon the glittering pleasure palaces of Las Vegas, the first location was the Resorts International Casino Hotel. Opening to record-breaking crowds, Resorts International daily handled over $700,000 in bets and other expenditures. At least six more casinos are ready to open or are in preparation for the next two years, including Great Bay, Hi Ho Industries, Bally (manufacturer of most of the world's supply of slot machines), Caesar's World, Penthouse, and Golden Nugget, all well-known names in the gambling world. Billed as the future "Las Vegas East," Atlantic City's casinos, hotels, restaurants, resorts, and peripheral entertainments and services could one day employ 50,000 persons with a daily "handle" of over $4,000,000. Even a foreign group, the Coral Leisure Group based in London, is planning an Atlantic City gambling casino, according to the *New York Times*.

ATTENDANCE

When the financial and visitor statistics of these giant pleasure installations are added to the growing national sales reports on sport boats, four-wheel drive vehicles, sport planes, hunting and fishing gear, ski equipment, resort homes, and tennis togs, some measure of commercial recreation's growth and potential may be perceived. Consider the following attendance and participation data for 1976[5]:

Museums	78.0 million
Live theatre	62.0 million
Horse racing	51.2 million (25% increase in 10 years)
Camping	58.1 million
Boating	35.2 million
Tennis	29.2 million
Ice skating	25.8 million
Golf	16.6 million
Water skiing	14.7 million
Skiing	11.0 million
Sailing	7.3 million

With the expansion of professional sports franchises, there are now 28 National Football League teams, 22 National Basketball Association teams, 18 National Hockey League teams, 16 National and American League baseball teams, and rapidly growing numbers in golf, tennis, soccer, softball, and bowling. The public's response to these increased offerings may be read in the attendance figures for professional sports as shown at the bottom of the page.

Lest this activity growth be misinterpreted as simply another testimony to youthful exuberance, it should be noted that these attendance figures include substantial numbers of older Americans. Older adults are now the fastest growing segment of the American population. These older adults have many recreational interests, and they include 13 million active partici-

pants in adult education programs in high schools. To quote Sandra Timmermann, Association Dean of the Institute of Lifetime Learning sponsored by the American Association of Retired Persons: "Adult education has advanced far beyond the traditional bridge and checkers activities for the elderly . . . they realize how diverse their experience is, and how much they can learn from each other." This means investments in autos, clothing, cameras, projectors, travel, insurance, painting and sketching materials, and books. Americans spent $11.6 billion in 1976 on books, magazines, and newspapers. The senior citizen leisure dollar is a substantial one and is sought with vigor by the commercial recreator.

MOVIES

The motion picture theatre, like gas stations and nuclear power plants, is the creation of the twentieth century. The premiere of the first real "movie" was held April 23, 1896 in New York City. By the early 1900s, movies were being shown in converted stores with nickel admission charges, hence the name nickelodeons.

The 1920s were called the "Golden Age" of movies because of the fabulous blossoming of thousands of new movie houses and the flood of films from Hollywood. In 1929, there were 30,000 movie theatres in operation. These numbers have been reduced considerably during the 1960s and 1970s, but many have survived through the technique of dividing the old movie "palaces"

Sport	*1966*	*1976*	*Percent increase*
Baseball	25.2 million	32.6 million	29
Football	7.7 million	15.0 million	95
Ice hockey	3.1 million	14.4 million	365
Basketball	2.3 million	8.5 million	270
Soccer	Negligible	2.8 million	—
Tennis	Negligible	2.2 million	—

into twins, trios, and quads by partitioning off sections of the old buildings and showing different films in each one. *U.S. News and World Report* of May 23, 1977 tells us that motion picture attendance in America for 1976 totaled 1.045 billion.

Since the early 1930s, the movie has become increasingly skilled in bringing fact and fancy into the life of every American. African safaris, undersea adventures, blazing Hawaiian sunsets, views from Mt. Everest, a wild horseback ride at midnight, life among the rich—all were made as close and as real as the huge movie screen. All were accompanied by the most clever sound effects and subtle stimuli and were carried on the strains of dozens of the finest violins playing the world's most powerful and sensuous music. America's appetite for commercial recreation in the 1960s and 1970s was being whetted by the movies of the 1940s and 1950s.

Television, so massive a subject that space here does not permit coverage, came along in the 1950s and propelled the same appetite-whetting technique into the American living room. Unlike the movies, however, television was total, ubiquitous, "free," and available daily. Americans devoured it, 25-30 hours per week, spending almost as much time before the television as they did in school, at work, or in any other single pastime except sleep.

FINANCIAL ASSESSMENT

Leisure and recreation, though not exactly new, had been observed by the financial world rather casually or obliquely until the 1960s. An occasional Sunday supplement or a special issue of that unique magazine, *Life,* would be devoted to "Leisure America," or "The Good Life." The emphasis, however, has always been on the vitality, the towering figures, the near hysteria connected with that uniquely American preoccupation, "working hard, playing hard." Little attention was focused on the deep financial investment and personnel expansion of this fast-growing industry.

In 1965, the firm of Merrill Lynch, Pierce, Fenner and Smith began studying the leisure field and turned for advice to manufacturers, teachers, psychologists, business people, and practitioners in the recreation, sports, cultural, and leisure fields. In 1967 they published a pamphlet, *Investment Opportunities in the Leisure Market,* and estimated that the gross value of leisure-related industries annually was $150 billion. The company explored this subject further and stated:

Increasing leisure for Americans is a well-documented trend that we expect to continue. According to the Department of Labor, workers gained an average of about 50 hours a year in free time during the 1960's . . . we believe that the length of the average work week will continue to shrink gradually.[3]

Further, the company predicts that leisure will come in more usable amounts, such as 3-day weekends, excellent for recreation pursuits. Americans will have more money, they say, and will invest heavily in sports gear, photography equipment, hand tools, overseas travel, and home-sewing products. The company predicted that spending on leisure would exceed the rate of disposable income in the 1960s, and they were correct. The number of white-collar workers will grow enormously during the 1970s, said the investment firm, basing their predictions on U.S. Department of Commerce projections. The company booklet included a great deal more on trends and directions for the leisure and fitness movement, and most of it was startlingly accurate. In 1976, the company's estimate of the gross leisure industry's annual expenditures was placed at $250 billion, an increase of

$100 billion in 10 years, *U.S. News and World Report* (May 23, 1977) estimated that gross leisure expenditures will reach $300 billion annually by 1980.

PROFESSIONAL SIGNIFICANCE

The message in all this appears to be that commercial recreation is so massive and growing that conventional studies have missed its true magnitude. Further, these findings would seem to depict a kind of "tail wagging the dog" phenomenon. Some 50,000 professionally registered and active members of the National Recreation and Park Association, the National Industrial Recreation Association, and the American Association for Health, Physical Education and Recreation account for expenditures of from $5 to $10 billion annually and, generally, speak for the profession of "recreation." Meanwhile, a relatively voiceless giant of millions of commercial recreation workers and managers control the expenditures of $200 billion that Americans annually invest in their sports, recreation, cultural activities, and leisure fun through business and commercial channels. Jobwise, this holds major significance for young professionals and those planning to enter the recreation profession, whatever branch or subdivision they choose.

JOBS AND EARNINGS

The following data measure the job potential in the leisure services industry. Based on figures from a study conducted by the Contract Research Corporation,[1] commercial recreation (or hospitality and recreation) represents a current employment in excess of 2,605,000 persons.

This field is large and diverse, including more than 60 types of employers and 200 types of occupations, according to industry sources. These occupations vary in setting, complexity, responsibility, and training requirements . . . .

Careers in this field allow an individual to combine avocation with vocation, involve considerable interaction with people, and offer the satisfaction of contributing to another person's enjoyment.

Hospitality and recreation occupations are those providing services to people away from their homes that enable them to more fully enjoy their nonworking time. The definition stresses the motivation of the consumer to enjoy an activity or event, away from home, during nonworking or leisure time. Hospitality and recreation occupations have been subdivided into six classifications: (1) lodging services, (2) recreation, (3) entertainment services, (4) cultural services, (5) sports, and (6) travel services.

Lodging services

This category includes management and operation of lodging facilities. People are employed at hotels, motels, resorts, convention centers, and steamship companies. Occupations include desk clerk, reservations clerk, bell captain, maid, manager, sales promotion manager, service superintendent, recreation director, fitness trainer, doorman, security chief, etc. There are over 67,000 hotels and motels in America, providing 2.4 million guest rooms. Total annual receipts are $7.2 billion. In 1973, employees numbered 800,000, earning a gross of $4.8 billion annually.

Recreation

This section refers to all employment except the public sector (local municipalities, cities, counties, states, federal employees). Included are occupations with private firms, private agencies, voluntary organizations, industrial and commercial units. Titles include director of recreation, director of special activities, manager, ski instructor, skating instructor, attendant, ticket seller, hunting guide, landscape architect, recreation therapist, recreation aide, golf pro, caddymaster, publicity director, lift attendant, interpretive naturalist, park superintendent, director of maintenance, campground manager, program director, director of conservation, and others. Exclusive of public, community, or municipal recreation, some 420,000 persons are employed in this sector, most on a full-time, or, at least a substantial seasonal basis.

Entertainment services

This category includes the industries and businesses of circuses, amusement parks, theatres (legitimate), movie theatres, booking agencies, carnivals, racetracks, nightclubs, rodeos, and others. Job titles within this sector include producer, publicity agent, ticket broker, ride operator, program coordinator, manager, guide, wardrobe mistress, acrobat, booking agent, motion picture projectionist, rodeo rider, cashier, clown, usher, advance person, makeup person, stage manager, and script clerk. Presently, over 15,000 movie theatres (many doubled, trebled, and quadrupled by subdividing) operate in America, employing some 600,000 persons. (There are 16,000 unionized motion picture projectionists alone.) Additional hundreds of circuses, amusement parks, carnivals, rodeos, nightclubs, and theme parks employ another 300,000 persons, for a total of 900,000 jobs.

Cultural services

This category refers to occupations within museums, zoos, aquariums, music halls, opera houses, ballet halls, art centers, and historical sites. In addition to performers, this subdivision includes curator, director, visual aid specialist, editor, conservator, librarian, dance teacher, music teacher, tour guide, historian, photographer, animal handler, veterinarian, artist, composer, maintenance supervisor, la-

borer, instrument repair person, and others. Approximately 250,000 persons are employed here, most on a full-time or substantial seasonal basis.

Sports

These positions are associated with professional sports teams, their management offices, and the stadiums and arenas in which they play. Occupations are club president, general manager, coach, scout, player, practice pitcher, trainee, trainer, therapist, player personnel coordinator, equipment manager, publicity agent, travel coordinator, finance director, physician, and legal counsel. Professional major and minor league sports teams in all categories total approximately 500 in the United States and each team averages 20 active players, for a total of 10,000 wage-earning or purse-winning pros. This includes baseball, basketball, ice hockey, football, soccer, lacrosse, softball, tennis, wrestling, bowling, and roller derby. An additional 100,000 persons fill the service positions that augment those of the players or performers, for a total of 110,000 persons.

Travel services

This category includes conventional travel agencies, car rentals, bus, train, and plane accommodations, hotel arrangements, steamship lines, airport and terminal services, safaris, world cruises, island trips, and windjammer cruises. Travel agencies in the United States grossed $11 billion in 1974, up from $5 billion in 1970. There were 10,260 travel agencies in America in 1974, employing some 25,000 personnel, with another 100,000 in ancillary travel services.

Commercial recreation represents the real dimensions of this profession and some measure of potential growth for the future. Although all positions are not specifically identified as recreation, today's educational latitude brings many of the categories into close and attainable proximity. Most major universities and colleges in America feature curricula in parks and recreation administration, hotel and restaurant management, travel services, sports administration, and the management of commercial recreation enterprises. Many business schools have broad programs of commercial enterprise management quite adaptable to all phases of community recreation. This is a prime area for careful study by the recreation professional.

DISCUSSION QUESTIONS

1. The entire American professional sports area has remained in private ownership and control with relatively little government intervention. Give three major advantages that result from this freedom from direct government control and three disadvantages. Explain each.

2. Some professionals have suggested that the operation of a city's parks might be accomplished more cheaply and effectively by a profit-making corporation than by a municipal government. Do you agree with this position? Justify your answer.

3. Money and money management increasingly becomes a part of the daily operations of a recreation agency. If you were preparing the undergraduate recreation curriculum at a university, what courses in money and financial management would you include?

4. In certain communities, strong programs in therapeutic recreation exist side by side with quality programs of recreation under a municipality. If several large industrial firms are also present in the same community, suggest three major projects or programs that might be launched for the general public, utilizing the strength of each of these different sectors. On each project, designate whom you think should be the coordinator.

5. Select two organizations that actually exist, one, a municipal recreation department, the other, a successful commercial recreation company. Obtain a budget from each. Compare the elements and layout. Which budget is more readable, and which one provides the most significant information?

BIBLIOGRAPHY

American Association for Health, Physical Education and Recreation, 1201 16th St., N.W., Washington, D.C.

American Association of Museums, 2233 Wisconsin Ave., Washington, D.C.

American Association of Zoological Parks and Aquariums, Oglebay Park, Wheeling, West Virginia.

American Hotel and Motel Association, 888 7th Ave., New York, N.Y.

The Athletic Institute, 805 Merchandise Mart, Chicago, Ill.

Chindahl, G. L.: A history of the circus in America, Caldwell, Idaho, 1959, The Caston Printers Ltd.

Clement, H.: The circus—bigger and better than ever?, Cranburg, N.J., 1974, A. S. Barnes & Co.

Cournoyer, N. G.: Introduction to hotel and restaurant law, Amherst, Mass, 1971, Econo Press.

Fenner, M. S., and Fenner, W.: The circus—lure and legend, Englewood Cliffs, N.J., 1970, Prentice-Hall, Inc.

Freedman, J.: Circus days, Don Mills, Ont., 1975, General Publishing Co. Ltd.

Geduld, H. M.: The birth of the talkies, Bloomington, Ind., 1975, Indiana University Press.

Goldhammer, K., and Taylor, R.: Career education: Perspective and promise, Columbus, Ohio, 1972, Charles E. Merrill Publishing Co.

Hjelte, G., and Shivers, J.: Public administration of recreational services, Philadelphia, 1972, Lea & Febiger.

Institute for study of Sports and Society, Hales Gymnasium, Oberlin, Ohio.

International Association of Amusement Parks and Attractions, 1125 Lake Street Building, Oak Park, Ill. (various publications).

Kalt, N.: Introduction to the hospitality industry, New York, 1971, ITT Educational Services.

Kando, T. M.: Leisure and popular culture in transition, St. Louis, 1975, The C. V. Mosby Co.

Lutzin, S., and Storey, T.: Managing municipal leisure services, Chicago, 1973, The International City Managers Association.

Managing the leisure facility (magazine for the owners and managers of leisure businesses), Billboard Publications, Inc., 1717 West End Ave., Nashville, Tenn.

Mangels, W. F.: The outdoor amusement industry, New York, 1952, Vantage Press, Inc.

McDonnell, V. B.: Careers in hotel management, New York, 1971, Julian Messner Co.

National Academy of Sports, 220 E. 63 St., New York, N.Y.

National Association of Theatre Owners, 1501 Broadway, New York, N.Y.

National Recreation and Park Association, 1601 North Kent St., Arlington, Va.

National Trust for Historic Preservation, 740 Jackson St., N. W., Washington, D.C.

Schickel, R.: The Disney version, New York, 1968, Simon & Schuster.

Since the 1880's, a long and varied run for theaters, Westchester-Rockland Newspapers, pp. G-11 and G-12, Nov. 6, 1977.

Toll, R. C.: On with the show!, New York, 1976, Oxford University Press.

REFERENCES

1. Contract Research Corporation: Occupational preparation in hospitality and recreation, study for U.S. Office of Education, Department of Health, Education and Welfare Belmont, Mass., 1976.
2. O'Brien, E. F.: Circus—cinders to sawdust, San Antonio, Tex, 1959, The Naylor Co.
3. Merrill Lynch, Pierce, Fenner and Smith: Investment opportunities—changing leisure markets, 1972.
4. Rouse, J. W.: Keynote address to the Urban Design Conference at Harvard University, Boston, 1963.
5. U.S. News and World Report, May 23, 1977.

7

PHYSICAL FITNESS IN RECREATION

Courtesy Barry Iverson

Few concerns have occupied the American public during the past 20 years as greatly as that of personal physical fitness and health. At dawn and at twilight, joggers run along tree-lined streets and roads and in parks and playgrounds. Others grunt through pushups on the bedroom floor, pedal bicycles, suffer the shock of medicine balls smacking into fleshy abdomens, and flail their arms in a desperate effort to redeem years of physical neglect. For some, the zeal may even overshadow the desired good. Dr. J. E. Nixon says, "They come into my office, restless for the necessary repairs that will return them to the fray, like so many racing car drivers bringing their battered machines in for a pit stop."

DEFINITIONS

No single definition of physical fitness is precise or comprehensive enough to satisfy everyone. Only by combining several views will a true picture appear. According to the President's Council on Physical Fitness and Sports, physical fitness "is the ability to carry out daily tasks with vigor and alertness, without undue fatigue and with ample energy to enjoy leisure time pursuits and to meet unforeseen emergencies. Thus, physical fitness is the ability to last, to bear up, to withstand stress, and to persevere under difficult circumstances where an unfit person would quit."

Physical fitness, as viewed by physicians and psychologists, is attaining the optimum state of physical tone, readiness, and efficient operation for the *specific* body involved. Morehouse[6] emphasizes this *specificity,* a term drawn from the study of exercise physiology:

Each different type of physical load has its specific conditioning effect. Sprint runs do not build endurance for distance runs. Swimming does not develop muscualr strength. Weight lifting does not improve cardiovascular condition.

Although exercise in any form is beneficial, no one exercise develops general fitness. Several types of exercise are necessary for all-around development . . . . Organic fitness is basic to all activities.

John F. Kennedy called physical fitness "the basis for all other forms of excellence." The first physician of history, Hippocrates, fourth century B.C., stated in regard to the body, "That which is used develops, and that which is not wastes away."

Some obscuring of a clear-cut picture of physical fitness results from our traditional approach to the subject, a situation aggravated by decades of press, radio, and television advertising. Physical fitness has too long been identified with athletic, fully developed males in clinging T-shirts or highly tailored suits. Beach demonstrations of muscular bulges, football prowess, championship boxing, weight-lifting, and similar macho machinations are deeply ingrained in the public mind. On the female side, advertisements utilize sleek, leotarded models whose lines and curves provoke admiring male glances or who are draped in haute couture creations that emphasize the model's height and classic dimensions. Even books and pamphlets prepared to offer day-to-day diet and exercise routines for everyone are illustrated with male and female figures and costumes that seem totally unattainable by the overweight bank teller or the flabby, middle-aged housewife. Physical fitness is a very personal matter and should be thought of as a customized concept that is shaped, tailored, molded, and modified *specifically* for the person involved, along lines, schedules, and objectives appropriate to him or her. The glamor image that attached itself to physical fitness has provoked untold millions of dollars in pointless spending by small wage earners who can least afford the extravagance. Countless numbers of pills, candies, belts, corsets, girdles, rollers, and elixirs have been purchased, along with dubious devices and exercisers that either fail to achieve improved fitness or are of such shoddy design as to be quickly broken or inoperative. Vivacious models, male and female, reaching out from gaudy advertising pages can sell light beer, low-tar cigarettes, electric exercise machines, thyroid pills, "weight-melting" elixirs, and scores of other panaceas and placebos. In the process, the identification of physical fitness and glamorous good looks becomes even more indelibly impressed on the mind of the average citizen. A tragedy.

THE REAL FITNESS

A state of fitness is attainable by every man and woman alive. If by consensus of self, exercise physiologist, medical doctor, and physical fitness technician, this body condition represents the optimum or close to optimum fitness level attainable by this person with his or her age, body conformation, state of organic health, etc., then this person is truly "physically fit." She may be an 82-year-old woman confined to a hospital for care following a stroke, or he may be a paraplegic confined to a wheelchair; she may have chronic diabetes, or he may be recovering from an operation for cataracts. The key to real physical fitness is the sum of the efforts by the individual and the degree of success enjoyed in reaching the optimum operating state for *that* individual possessing *those* specific organic strengths and weaknesses. Thus, physical fitness is truly relative. The 82-year-old woman in the hospital, following sound advice and performing regularly, may be more "physically fit" than a typical 21-year-old male, cavorting on the beach, big, broad-shouldered, and bronzed. It's what you do with what you've got that counts!

THE ROLE OF RECREATION

Recreation is important in the concept of physical fitness for several reasons:

1. Many recreation activities require large muscle utilization and can contribute substantially to the fitness of the person recreating. Examples include jogging, swimming, cross-country skiing, bicycling, and skating.
2. For many people, recreation activities represent the only time they perform vigorously.
3. Recreation offers an attractive vehicle through which lethargic and nonactive people can be stimulated to more activity.
4. Recreation activities, when deeply enjoyed by people, provide the lifelong incentive needed to keep aging people active long after the social structure has lost its hold on them. This would apply to a professional baseball player who might swim or play tennis long after he retired from baseball.
5. The recreation approach, used in hospitals and institutions, offers a low-key and pleasant technique for medical and paramedical personnel to bring otherwise indisposed and reluctant patients and clients back to an improved state of physical fitness.

Thus, it is important that recreation administrators and leaders be thoroughly familiar with the physical fitness movement and its recreational implications.

HISTORY

The history of most ancient cultures and civilizations contains frequent references to health, physical culture, body building, and exercise. Chinese, Aztec, and Mayan records contain much that is physically cultural, and the "sound mind in a sound body" concept of the Greco-Roman golden era is well known. In all of these, it should be noted that only where a lesiure or privileged class was developed, did the matter of body care, health, and fitness become a major preoccupation.

During the Middle Ages in Europe the exchange of information on all matters suffered, and this included research and demonstration in physical fitness. Life was relatively primitive, and the leisure classes were too small and isolated to effect any significant new trends. In colonial America, people were struggling to survive, totally involved in traveling, woods clearing, farming, building, and, frequently, fighting to maintain their small beachhead in the New World. Even at the cusp of the nineteenth and twentieth centuries, hard work and long hours precluded much attention being focused on blood pressure, pulse rates, or obesity. A ripple of concern at the poor physical condition of military recruits in World War I was later magnified in World War II when medical authorities found themselves rejecting 25% of young Americans because of physical defects and other inadequacies. Here was a nation that boasted the most, the best, the greatest of everything material suddenly aware that the flower of its youth was not blooming too impressively. Research and writing began in earnest, and school physical education programs were intensified.

THE PRESIDENT'S COUNCIL ON PHYSICAL FITNESS

All past concern, however, was nothing compared with the explosion of interest that characterized the 1960s and 1970s. President Dwight D. Eisenhower established the President's Council on Physical Fitness, July 16, 1956. Today it is known as the President's Council on Physical Fitness and Sports. Its primary goals were to alert the American public to the alarming state of its collective physical fitness and to provide information and motivation for improving the state of fitness. Much has been accomplished in 23 years; much remains to be done.

In its 23 years of existence, the Council, on a miniscule budget, has motivated hundreds of business firms, thousands of school systems and colleges, and millions of Americans to study themselves, consult their doctors, and begin a fitness regimen. The Council has utilized well-known athletes, dramatic presentations, movies, slide shows, training film strips, books, pamphlets, radio, and television in its campaign, and most effectively. It has worked in close cooperation with the Lifetime Sports Foundation, a nonprofit agency dedicated to stimulating interest on the part of Americans in activities that they can play and enjoy throughout their lives. These include bowling, golf, tennis, badminton, and archery.

To a great extent, the success of the Council's efforts is attributable to the dynamic leadership of its first Executive Director, C. Carson Conrad. Former military man, teacher, and coach, Conrad practices what he preaches by daily running, swimming, and exercising. Through lectures, demonstrations, conferences, and published materials, he and the Council have caused hundreds of campuses and business firms to put new emphasis on methods and techniques for physical fitness. His deep sincerity and high credibility have been major factors in this fitness revolution: "I don't know of a person who is highly regarded in medicine today who doesn't advocate exercise as an essential part of the lifestyle for healthful living." He warns of the danger of spectatoritis, that growing reliance on staged sports events and massive spectaculars: "Every form of entertainment that draws big crowds is passive—at the Super Bowl you'll find 75,000 fans in the stands watching 22 guys getting some exercise on the field!" More than any one sports star, movie or television celebrity, or government official, C. Carson Conrad has made the 1960s and 1970s turnabout time in national physical fitness.

In close cooperation with the President's Council on Physical Fitness and Sports, fifty individual Governor's Council's on Physical Fitness and Sports function in each state. Their activity depth and emphasis vary from state to state. Among the most active are those in Texas, Connecticut, Alabama (among other things, sponsors Alabama Special Olympics), Maryland (where fitness programs for senior citizens' homes have been promoted), and Wisconsin. For further information on any state program, write the President's Council on Physical Fitness and Sports, Washington, D.C. 20202.

MEDICAL PICTURE

Dr. Paul Dudley White of Boston was probably the best known cardiologist in history until he died in 1973. Called in to attend President Eisenhower during his coronary attack in 1956, he brought about Eisenhower's recovery so that he enjoyed several more productive years. A life-long supporter of walking, bicycling, and general fitness, he constantly urged that the American people eat less and exercise more:

Physical exercise is just as essential to good health as rest and sleep, work and recreation, food and peace of mind. Soft, unused muscles do not do as good a job and make clotting in the veins more likely. Thrombosis in leg veins can have serious consequences. Physical exercise tones the muscles, improves circulation of blood in the veins; it is good for the diaphragm and thus makes it easier to bring oxygen into the body and pump carbon dioxide out.

Dr. White observed that middle-aged fitness was the area that deserved attention now. He warned that we must not let the new pressures of education of the mind blind us to the urgent needs of the body. He called this "uneconomical," and a "grave mistake." As Commissioner of Parks and Recreation for Boston, I accompanied Dr. White on several recreational and social occasions. At the dedication of a new city bicycle route in Boston, Dr. White said: "The legs are really a second heart to the body. When they are used vigorously, they help pump the blood back to the heart."

As a nation, we have not heeded Dr. White's advice sufficiently. An estimated 50% of our population is overweight, and 55% of all deaths in the United States result from diseases of the heart and blood vessels—often associated with physical inactivity and obesity. Annually, backaches are responsible for more lost work time than the common cold.

Dr. Roy J. Shepard, professor of Physiological Hygiene at the University of Toronto states that "Loss of production due to premature death in the United States has been set at $19.4 billion per year with further losses due to illness about $3 billion."

Dr. Frederick J. Stare, eminent nutritionist at Harvard University, says: "The talk used to be all 'diet and exercise.' Today it is 'exercise and diet.' Recent studies of obesity at Harvard's School of Public Health quite clearly indicate that most people who are overweight are not that way simply because they consume too many calories, but rather because of lethargy and the lack of exercise."

Forty-five percent of all adult Americans (roughly, 49 million of the 109 million adult men and women) do not engage in physical activity for the purpose of exercise. These sedentary Americans tend to be older, less well educated, and less affluent than those who do exercise.

Only 55% of American adults do any exercise at all, but 57% of American adults say they believe they get enough exercise. Paradoxically, those who do not exercise are more inclined to believe they get enough exercise than are those who do exercise. Sixty-three percent of the non-exercisers say they get enough exercise, while only 53% of the exercisers believe they are as physically active as they should be.[9]

Paffenbarger and Hale[8] conducted an investigation of coronary death rates among longshoremen. They concluded that repeated bursts of high energy output established a plateau of protection against coronary mortality. The study included 6351 men, 35 to 74 years of age, whose work and medical histories were carefully kept for up to 22 years. Their work was computed according to its physical requirements (heavy, medium, light), and adjustments were made to allow for the effect of job transfers from one category to another. The results showed the coronary death rate for the high activity category was 26.9 per 10,000 work years. For those in the medium and light categories, the rates were 46.3 and 49, respectively. The death rate from what is known as "sudden" heart attack was 5.6 per 10,000 work years in the heavy labor workers, as compared with 15.7 in the light and 19.9 in the medium. Put another way, men in the least active jobs have $2^1/_2$ to $3^1/_2$ times greater risk of dying from sudden coronary heart attack than men in the heaviest labor requirement group. They also reported that, men who stayed in the heavy work bracket fared better than their fellow workers who transferred to lighter work jobs.

In 1956, Dr. Jeremy N. Morris, a London physician, and his associates examined 31,000 bus drivers and conductors who worked on the double-deck buses and trolleys in that city. They found that heart attacks caused 30% fewer deaths among the conductors who ran up and down the bus and trolley staircases to collect fares than among the drivers who sat at the steering wheel all day. The doctors later confirmed

this data in a similar study on 110,000 sedentary postal clerks and walking mail carriers. In their most recent study of 17,000 civil servants, reported in 1973, the British scientists showed that vigorous leisure time work promoted heart health. The work included digging in the garden, shoveling snow, sawing wood, cycling, and taking brisk walks of at least 30 minutes on hilly terrain.

Studies have shown that muscle fibers become larger and redder with exercise and contain more myoglobin, a protein that stores oxygen for future use. The liver more readily releases glucose, which provides energy to the body, and better metabolizes the unwanted acids produced during exercise, while the kidneys excrete the metabolic acids more rapidly. Over a long period of regular exercise, the blood volume is increased as are the amounts of hemoglobin and the number of red blood cells, which means that the oxygen-carrying capacity of the blood increases.

Despite this, a major portion of our society still looks askance at regular, vigorous activity.

More than 80 million TV football fans watch 22 athletes play in the Superbowl. Spectator sports continue to outrace sports participation in the U.S.—over a dozen new large-capacity domed stadiums will be built in cities by 1980.

Bowling ranks as America's Number One participatory sport, but few bowl as often as once per week. Doing nothing is the most popular pastime of 49 million U.S. adults, and only 1 in 24 children taking the President's Council National Fitness Test ever wins an award.

Diet fads gross over $100 million each year. Some $500 million is spent by the public annually on cure-all gadgets. Yet an estimated 40 million people are overweight. Deaths related to heart and blood vessel conditions, often related to obesity, account for 55% of the fatality toll.[2]

The research evidence mounts, in California, in New York, in industry, in the armed services, and at the most famous clinics in America—the Lahey in Boston, the Mayo in Rochester, Minnesota, and at Dr. Kenneth H. Cooper's renowned Cooper Clinic in Dallas. Dr. Cooper and his associates administer an average of 75 treadmill stress tests weekly to executives and workers from all sectors of the business and industrial world. He is an ardent supporter of the regular medical checkup and regular, prescribed programs of steady, vigorous exercise. Again and again, the picture comes through clearly and tends to confirm the words of Hippocrates: ''That which is used develops, and that which is not wastes away.''

Despite the apathy of many, however, a substantial portion of the public is awakening and acting on behalf of their health and physiques:

1. More than 60 million adults are exercising, and 30 million say they do it for better health. Tennis players alone spend $100 million on equipment each year.
2. Bicycling is the fitness activity chosen by 20 million adults. Walking is first as favorite, with 44 million Americans rediscovering their legs. Fourteen million swimmers, 14 million calisthenics buffs, and 7 million joggers give further testimony to fitness's growing popularity.
3. Employee fitness and recreation programs and facilities cost 50,000 U.S. companies some $2 billion annually. Over 300 firms have full-time recreation directors.
4. Over 3 million people in America are paying some $300 each, annually, to be made fit by commercial health and fitness clubs, such as Vic Tanney, Elaine Powers, and International Health Spas.
5. The phenomenal growth of formerly low participant sports such as plat-

form tennis, paddleball, volleyball, weight-training, wrestling, and soccer demonstrates the increasing variety of activities being sought by health and exercise aficionados.
6. The sale of books and pamphlets on food, diets, calories, food preparation, and home exercise has quadrupled in 5 years, according to a committee of text book publishers. Never in history have so many worried so much about how few or how many calories are contained in their meals.

BUSINESS AND INDUSTRY

Business and industry have adopted a health and fitness posture in the past 10 years that is very much like business's approach to marketing, manufacturing, and rising productivity curves. It is the business person's approach

Dr. Richard H. Morrison pioneered an executive physical fitness program for the space division of North American Rockwell Corporation and says, ''If our program saves the health of just a few executives, and I believe the score is much higher than that, the cost will have been more than repaid. A healthier executive is a more effective employee. He contributes more when he is on the job, and because he's healthier, he spends less time off the job.'' This is plain business talk, the ''bottom line,'' nothing less.

Two firms that have been national leaders in physical fitness for executives and staff are the Pepsico Corporation and the Xerox Corporation. Pepsico, parent body of the Pepsi-Cola soft drink, sporting goods, snack foods, and truck leasing conglomerate, maintains a modern recreation fitness center at its corporate headquarters in Purchase, New York. Gunnar Ohberg, chief of Pepsico's health and fitness center, supervises an outdoor jogging track plus gymnasium, Gladiator 70 universal stress machine, wall weights and exercisers, hot sauna and needle showers. Strong support by Pepsico Board Chairman, Donald M. Kendall, ensures the future of this valuable program.

Xerox Corporation of Rochester, New York provides a multipurpose recreation building including an exercise area with physical fitness equipment, table tennis, lockers and showers, clothing basket room, executive fitness laboratory, and associated equipment. An outdoor area includes six baseball diamonds, a putting green, a jogging and cycling path, lighted basketball and tennis courts, bleachers, an archery range, and a skating rink. Jogging paths are located at several other Xerox locations, as are softball diamonds and fully equipped exercise rooms.

Other companies have set up similar programs and are expressing very positive opinions.

R. H. Dobbs, Jr. president of Life Insurance Company of Georgia, says, "It's good business to keep our key personnel healthy—is means less time lost. I'm also convinced that if we can add a few years to our employees' lives, it will mean a tremendous financial saving. Our people feel better, stay in better humor and can handle customers better because of participation in our fitness program."

W. W. Keeler, chairman of the board of Phillips Petroleum Co. says, "Physical fitness is good business."

Jim Daniell, vice-president, Marketing Services, North American Rockwell says: "The health and well-being of our employees is our most valuable resource."

The Flick-Reedy Corporation, Bensonville, Ohio, has just built a $90,000 heated indoor swimming pool for its 750 employees.

Ling-Temco-Vought Inc., Dallas, Texas, has invested some $1 million in fitness and recreation facilities for its 23,000 employees.

Timken Roller Bearing Company, Canton, Ohio, stresses running and training under supervision of professional athletes for its workers.

Goodyear Tire and Rubber Co., Akron, Ohio, aims its fitness program at middle and upper management and includes rope skipping, bag punching, chinning, bicycling, weight lifting, shooting baskets, boxing, and jogging. Workouts are followed by steam baths and showers.

Gates Rubber Company of Denver, Colorado began its executive physical fitness program in 1963 "for the purpose of maintaining and improving the physical condition of its executives, thus contributing to their increased stamina, efficiency and longevity." Equipment used is the most modern available, "especially designed to increase breathing, strengthen heart action, and give an improved appearance through weight management."

General Foods Corporation, White Plains, New York, has just completed a new $1 million fitness building and center directly on the grounds of its corporate headquarters. A full professional staff is maintained, and the program caters to all ages and professional levels of the 4000 employees.

The ingenuity of many companies is best illustrated by President Edward Lowe, Lowe's, Inc., Cassapolis, Michigan. In an effort to bring down the weights of his top 14 executives, he invented the *ICATLYC*, the "I Can't Afford To Lose You Club." The company doctor weighed each man and assigned him his optimum weight. Each executive was allowed 1 week per pound overweight to reach his ideal weight. If he succeeded, he was paid $1^1/2\%$ of his annual salary. Thus, a man earning $20,000 per year could collect an additional $300.00 if he brought his weight down. Every year he maintained his ideal weight, the bonus would be renewed. Mr. Lowe is very happy with the results.

MYTHS ABOUT FITNESS

Myths, misunderstandings, and mistakes cloud the concept of physical fitness for the average person and deter many from beginning what could be the most healthful and productive period of their lives. Following are some of these myths:

Middle age begins at age 40. It doesn't. It begins about age 26. Physical performance begins to fall after this age.

Hardening of the arteries is a natural part of getting older. It isn't. It can occur at any age. It is often the result of an inactive way of life. The heart is a muscle that improves with use, and its ability to pump blood depends on what chance you give it to work. The best way to keep the blood vessels fit is through regular, rhythmic exercise.

As you grow older, you should exercise less. Just the reverse is true. A soft, flabby heart will tire more easily than a strong one; it is less efficient and more susceptible to disease, just an an unfit person is likely to be. A conditioning program, in which you exercise just beyond the first onset of fatigue, is best.

Rest or sleep is always the best remedy for fatigue. It isn't. Your physical condition affects emotions too. If you exercise properly, your endocrine glands are affected by the stimulated blood circulation and the glands in turn affect your emotions.

Diet alone is the best way to lose weight. It isn't. You lose weight by dieting, but you also lose fitness. To keep your energy and your sense of well-being, you will do best with a regular exercise program plus a moderate restriction of fattening food.

Alcohol in moderate quantity is a good food. It isn't. It has a high caloric or fattening content, but it has none of such vital nutritive elements as vitamins, amino acids, minerals, or traces of the elements of various substances of value.

It's best to take it very easy when you have a cold. It usually isn't. Moderate exercise will improve your circulation and that is one of the important keys to general fitness and the elimination of colds.

Youngsters aren't equipped for sustained endurance. Yes, they are. Their hearts don't have to pump through as many miles of pipes as does the adult heart. Their hearts are like powerful motors in small cars. When they keep fit, their physical endurance is tremendous.

I know a short cut to fitness. No you don't. There is no short cut for anyone. The secret lies in faithfulness to a continuing program of exercise and activity, sound nutritional habits, a proper combination of rest, sleep, and relaxation, and adequate health care.

Morehouse,[6] offers a few more myths:

Sugar taken before exercise raises the energy level. False. Sugar ingested before a workout or contest can do more harm than good. Sweets can trigger an insulin reaction. The effect is to drive the sugar into the storage organs. The time for sugar ingestion is after an hour and a half of steady exercise, to replace the amount depleted. Extra sugar never gives extra energy.

Put on a warm sweater immediately after vigorous exercise. Don't. There is no point prolonging body heat by encasing it in a garment, and you are not courting a cold. Leave your garment off until the body cools down, then cover it so you don't become chilly.

Avoid sex before athletics. False. The popular notion that abstinence somehow stores strength has no scientific foundation. Athletes are subject to all kinds of constraints. The more constraints you remove from them, the better they perform. Athletes seem to do better after sexual intercourse, even when they have intercourse the morning of competition. Enlightened coaches encourage players to bring their mates along with them on road trips.

Women who train lose femininity. Totally false. They usually become more feminine and more sexy and increase their animal vitality. They are more lithe, they move with greater strength, and they develop the athlete's sense of relaxation—an air of languor under which lies a supply of power waiting to be used.

Bonnie Prudden, outstanding advocate of physical fitness since the 1950s, was one person who encouraged President Eisenhower to establish the first President's Council on Physical Fitness in 1958. Miss Prudden has the lithe, curved figure of the dancer, but is better muscled and in finer condition than most professional football players. She has said of femininity, "Under every curve lies a muscle."

Jane W. Frederick, one of the top female pentathletes in the world and among the finest female track and field athletes in America, is superbly muscled and in the peak of condition. Yet, Mac Wilkins, 1976 male Olympic gold medalist and world record holder in the discus, says of Jane, "I think her body's beautiful. Most American women are marshmallows—physically, mentally, emotionally." This should reassure those young women who always yearned to develop trim athletic figures but feared they would turn into ugly Amazons.

FOOD, DIETS, NOURISHMENT

Exercise and diet are co-partners in attaining optimum health and fitness for any man or woman, regardless of his or her physical configuration. The diet concept has been badly mangled and warped in recent years by a plethora of fad diets, commercial sales pitches, and a series of well-intended by badly engineered nourishment plans. The all-water diet, banana diet for potassium, liquid protein, vitamin C saturation, vegetables only, no-breakfast diet, one-meal-per-day diets, and other such gastronomical freaks have been pounded into the heads of the American public. Many of these diets have some value, but are highly specialized and should be followed only to meet a specific condition under the watchful eye of a physician. Plucking diets and nutrition fads from books, magazines, radio, television, and newspapers is comparable to writing and filling one's own pharmaceutical prescriptions at home with a child's chemistry set. It is unsound, it can make one ill, and it is downright dangerous.

Don't be fooled by fads. Ordinarily, a diet with a variety of foods is a good way to get the vitamins, minerals, protein and other essential nutrients required by our bodies. Vitamin and mineral pills or formulas can be expensive and usually are not needed. . . . Consult your doctor first, before taking any vitamin or mineral pills or formulas.

Special pills, liquids or powders are often sold with promises that they will cure aches, pains and diseases. Be careful! We all like to be safe, but avoid taking products containing many times more than the U.S. Recommended Daily Allowances. Cases have been reported of large intakes of minerals or vitamins, such as A and D, causing adverse side effects when taken routinely without doctor's supervision.

Be cautious about claims that:

Promise a special or "secret" formula, product or pill that cures disease.

Guarantee a quick cure or sensational weight loss.

Use case histories and testimonials in their advertising.

Imply that medical doctors fear competition from the product.[3]

Most food advisors and professional nutritionists recommend a mixed diet, as compared with one stressing vegetables and no meat, or fiber to the exclusion of dairy products. The following is a handy outline, usable by physical fitness enthusiasts and casual recreation consumers alike.

BASIC FOUR FOOD GROUPS

I. Milk group (2 or more servings daily)

One serving equals:
 1 cup milk
 2-inch cube Cheddar-type cheese
 1¹/₂ cups cottage cheese
 1 cup plain yogurt
Includes milk products used in cooking as part of the total servings.
For variety: Skim milk, nonfat dry milk, buttermilk, cheeses, fruit or plain yogurt, ice cream, milk custard.

II. Bread and cereal group (4 or more servings daily)

One serving equals:
 1 slice bread
 ¹/₂ to ³/₄ cup cooked cereal, noodles, or rice
 1 ounce ready-to-eat cereal
 1 small biscuit or muffin
Includes whole grain or enriched breads and rolls, enriched noodles, macaroni, rice, or fortified cereals.
For variety: ready-to-eat cereals, cooked cereals, cornmeal, hamburger or frankfurter buns, pancakes, wheat germ

III. Vegetable and fruit group (4 or more servings daily)

One serving equals:
 1 cup raw vegetables
 ¹/₂ cup fruitjuice or cooked 1 medium or 2 small fruit
Includes citrus fruit or vegetable important for vitamin C daily, dark green or deep yellow vegetable for vitamin A at least every other day
For variety: peas, green beans, Brussels sprouts, cabbage, squash, tomatoes, sweet or white potatoes, apricots, dried fruit, oranges, watermelon

IV. Meat or meat alternate group (2 or more servings daily)

One serving equals:
 2 to 3 ounces meat, fish, or poultry
 2 ounces cheese*
 2 eggs
 4 tablespoons peanut butter
 1 cup cooked dried beans, lentils, or peas
Includes lean meats, well-trimmed, or meat alternatives such as dairy products, dried beans, dried peas, nuts, or nut butters that supply animal or plant protein
For variety: Beef, lamb, pork, liver, veal, turkey, shellfish, tuna, textured vegetable protein, cottage cheese, yogurt*

EXTRA FOODS

Sugars and sweets provide additional calories, but few nutrients. Sweets include candies, syrups, jellies, honey, cakes, pies, and cookies.

Fats provide essential fatty acids and contain some vitamins but are also the most concentrated source of calories in foods. Fats include vegetable oil, shortening, lard, animal fat, margarine, and butter.

Alcohol provides almost as many calories per ounce as fat and has little or no nutritional value.

FLUIDS AND FIBER

Don't just take water and fiber for granted. Both are useful for proper body functioning. Water is present in many foods, but additional water or other beverage is usually needed.

Water and other fluids (4 to 8 cups daily)

Functions: replaces water normally lost by the body in sweat and urinary excretion; aids elimination and normal function of body
Good sources: beverages such as water, milk, juice, soft drinks, coffee, or tea and foods such as soup, fruit, vegetables, or meats

Fiber (undigestable portion of foods)

Function: aids in elimination
Good sources: bran, whole-grain cereal products, fruits, and vegetables

---

*If used for meat group, additional dairy products should be consumed to meet milk group servings.

The *Health Letter*[4] has this advice for fitness-minded people concerned about diets:

Obviously, the goal in dieting is to eliminate excess fat stores safely while maintaing good health. Beyond that, it is just as important to *keep the fat off. You do that by learning about nutrition.* You can prepare good food with a well balanced diet that helps you avoid excess calorie intake . . . *This is accomplished in the kitchen in food preparation.* In short, *what we need is not a "diet revolution," but a "kitchen revolution."*

YMCA

Long before many recreation and health agencies had awakened to the importance of regular physical fitness programs, the YMCA was the leader in this significant field. The YMCA was born in London, England, in 1844 and, from the beginning, was concerned about the healthy body as a vessel for the healthy spirit. A prime goal was "the improvement of the spiritual and mental condition of commercial young men." In 1851, it was brought from England to Boston, Massachusetts, and by 1860 there were 205 Y's with 25,000 members in the United States. Throughout the latter part of the nineteenth century, Y's spread, and one of the basic tenets was bodily fitness and health. The first major gym appeared in 1869 as part of the "physical department" of the new McBurney YMCA at 23rd Street in Manhattan, and the first "swimming bath" or pool was installed at a Brooklyn YMCA in 1885. It was 45 feet long.

In 1887, a Department of Physical Training was established at Springfield (Mass.) College by Luther H. Gulick, one of the most renowned leaders in the physical education field. This institution became the training center for YMCA leaders and the place of origin of two new games. In 1891 James Naismith, a young staff member, formulated the game of basketball. Four years later, William C. Morgan, YMCA training leader, developed the game of volleyball.

YMCAs, YWCAs, YM-WHAs today continue to be the most vigorous centers for physical fitness activities, with over ten million men and women participating in some phase of their programs. New York City YMCA spokespersons state that fitness interest in this decade has "really taken off." The YWCAs have opened "fitness studios" at several of their municipal branches. Gladys L. Brown, YWCA health and environment consultant says, "Women like to do more interesting things, like Yoga and Tai-chi-chuan, an ancient Chinese system of exercise. One of the most popular classes at the YWCA now is Mediterranean dancing—belly dancing—which is considered an excellent method of strengthening the abdominal muscles."

Outstanding "Run for your Life" programs, a systematized schedule that includes medical examination, prescribed jogging-running routines pitted against time statistics, and careful post-activity monitoring, have flourished at YMCA's in Cambridge and Boston, Massachusetts; in Niles, Illinois; in New York City; in White Plains and New Rochelle, New York; in Los Angeles; and in Washington, D. C. Edward F. Fendt, 70 years old and an insurance executive of Des Plaines, Ill., is a devoted YMCA runner and sums it up thusly:

"A physically fit person is a happy person, and a happy person is a disciplined person. Physical fitness changes your lifestyle; it becomes part of your daily routine. You feel a lot better, without stress or strain."

AMERICAN RED CROSS

The American Red Cross has been the major source of public enlightenment regarding cardiovascular vulnerability and the urgent need to improve one's state of fitness. Cardiovascular pulmonary resuscitation (CPR) is now part of the program at every ARC branch, and millions of citizens are being trained to take the all-important lifesaving steps in the first few minutes of a heart attack. In addition, the ARC continues its widespread program of basic swimming instruction, lifesaving, and "Swim and Stay Fit," with over 50,000 persons registered in the latter.

THE COMMERCIAL SIDE

The commercial or profit-making aspect of physical fitness consists chiefly of three sectors:

1. *Professional consultants and advisory firms catering to individual needs or those of organizations.* These usually consist of exercise physiologist, medical doctor (most often cardiologist or internist), and auxiliary personnel for administration and management. Firm names include Olympic Fitness Inc., City Island, Bronx, New York; Aerobics and Dance, Inc., Executive Fitness Corp; Physical Fitness Laboratory, Ltd., Westport, Conn., and All-American Physical Fitness and Health, Inc. For a fee, such consultant firms will test selected employees and prepare a detailed exercise, nutrition, and life style program for them. For an additional fee, the consultant will actually operate the program and serve as monitor on results.

2. *Health, body-building, and fitness clubs, organizations, and spas.* These are usually situated in or near business concentrations or shopping centers and cater to the individual health and fitness seeker. On a short- or long-term contractual basis, such spas will provide luxurious surroundings, personable staff, swimming pool, lockers, lounges, and a full array of modern exercise equipment. If clients wish detailed activity plans, they are also provided.

Otherwise, clients are left to develop and progress at their own speed and taste. Among the best-known names are Bonnie Prudden, Inc., Vic Tanney Gymnasiums, Elaine Powers' Studios, International Health Spas, Susan Marlowe Figure Salons, and European Health Spas. The European chain is the largest in the nation, with 145 clubs and adding 12,000 new members every month. Despite the fact that commercial health spas have a slightly tarnished reputation and are often identified with pornography and massage parlors, those that are soundly established and well operated make a major contribution to public fitness. Some 350,000 persons exercise three times a week at European, with over 70% under 35 years of age. The firm is increasing its sales promotion to older people, however, and expansion here is expected. European urges all new applicants to have a medically supervised stress test before beginning an exercise program.

3. *Manufacturing firms in the business of producing health and fitness equipment.* Largest among these is American Machine and Foundry Corp., Fitness Equipment Division, White Plains, N.Y. Others include Benlee, Everlast, Universal Gym, Medart, and Medalist. Two of the most enterprising of these manufacturing firms are the Jayfro Corporation of Waterford, Conn. and the North American Recreation Convertible Co. of Bridgeport, Conn. Both of these companies, while producing and distributing conventional recreation and sports equipment, have researched and developed a wide range of special adaptive gear. Jayfro's emphasis has been on portability and street mobility and has come up with a full line of folding, wheeled, attachable, and packaged volleyball, baseball, basketball, tennis, and water polo units that lend themselves to easy transportation and quick assembly on rugged street surfaces, vacant

lots, shopping centers, parking lots, and playgrounds. North American, on the other hand, has spent years studying the special problems of handicapped children, men, and women who want to be more active and more physically fit. They have assembled a full line of adjustable pool tables, Ping-Pong tables, benches, chairs, weight-lifting racks, and training devices, all adjustable and all usable by both severely handicapped people and fully able people.

RECREATION RELEVANCE

Certain activities, for reasons of convenience, low cost, and ease of learning, lend themselves better than others to recreation and everyday use by the public.

Walking

This is certainly the most convenient exercise and the one involving the least vigorous effort. It is a great endurance and fitness builder, but does little to test those

Courtesy World Leisure & Recreation Association Photo Library

already in good condition. It must be done briskly to achieve a training effect. Nevertheless, walking for fun, for health, for a generally good feeling, is still undisputed king where overall body tone and state of mind are concerned. Men and women are more at home, more comfortable, while walking leisurely than they are while standing or sitting still. A mild stimulant to circulation, an exercise in balance and coordination, a stimulant to breathing and heart action—walking is all of these and more. There is no cheaper, easier, nor relaxing exercise known, and it is one in which very few people lack the necessary skills. Few people must invest in teachers to be taught to walk. Small children demonstrate clearly the natural inclination of humans to walk when they struggle on their spindly legs to take those first halting steps. It is almost impossible to convince infants that they should lie down or sit when the drive in them is to walk.

Physical educators, recreation professionals, doctors, and people in all lines of work are urging their fellow Americans to walk, and to walk frequently. The old-fashioned stroll down the main street, window shopping, conversing with chance acquaintances, the walk to the movies, to the store, to a neighbor's house two or three blocks away—these were commonplace practices 25 to 30 years ago. Deep inroads on our walking habits have been made by the automobile and its instant availability. Men, women, and children need a postive attitude toward walking, or the habit will simply not reassert itself.

Jogging

The "in" exercise, jogging is enjoying great popularity in America after having been popular for years in Europe and Asia. *Datsun Action* calls this "one of the best for heart, lungs and circulation," and it is one of the most efficient and inexpensive ways to get in shape. The unfit should start slowly, however. Results do not come quickly. The President's Council finds that positive effects include (1) cardiovascular improvement, (2) reduction in likelihood of coronary attacks, (3) effective modality in postcoronary care, (4) strengthening of bone and muscle systems, (5) aid in fat reduction and increase in lean body tissue, (6) protection in decline in work capacity with age, and (7) enhancement of self-image and social poise.

Some jogging tips from the President's Council include:

1. Run upright, avoid leaning. Keep the back straight, don't watch the feet (unless the terrain is rough, of course).
2. Hold arms slightly away from body, elbows bent, forearms roughly parallel to ground. Occasionally shake and relax the arms and shoulders.
3. Occasionally, take several deep breaths and blow them out explosively.
4. Land on the heel and rock forward so that you drive off the ball for the next step.
5. Keep steps short.
6. Dress comfortably and as lightly as weather will permit.

Millions are jogging today in parks, on beaches and tracks, around gyms and arenas, on boardwalks, and along downtown streets. No single health "fad" has ever gripped America as has jogging. It is hoped that it will become a permanent part of the public life style and not fade as have other fads of the past. A steady jogger burns up 450 calories per hour.

Bicycling

This is a good weight reducer and overall fitness inducer if done vigorously. It is suitable for all age groups and brings a special element of fun and sight-seeing when done over extended distances. To be effective, bicycling must be done so that maximum leg extension occurs. Dr. Paul Dudley White was one of its greatest advocates, and, in 1957, in the Boston-Cambridge area, created the Committee for Safe Bicycling, Inc. Research shows that a vigorous bicycler burns off 270 calories per hour. Bicycling has been growing rapidly and should continue into the 1980s. Although the 3-speed or 10-speed bicycle represents a substantial startup cost, there are few costs thereafter so long as reasonable care is given the bike. The rider should dress comfortably with no loose pant legs or sleeves to become snared or hooked, and a lightweight bicycling helmet is recommended. All other cautions one would observe for running or jogging should be observed in bicycling.

Swimming

Swimming is one of the best all-around body conditioners and is hampered only by the difficulty of finding a swimming pool in the colder climates for year-round workouts. Swimming is excellent for building endurance but should be balanced with jogging or calisthenics. A vigorous swimmer burns off about 300 calories per hour.

Tennis

This can be a great fitness maintainer, if played regularly and vigorously. It stimulates endurance, flexibility, and balance. A choice must be made in it however. Intense interest in skill, style, power, grip, and strategy of the game will appreciably reduce its value as a body conditioner. Ironically, the "dubs" who play tennis as a casual volleying game with a steady back and forth return of the ball probably derive greater body value than the highly skilled stars who aim their shots and strive to shorten the game for purposes of winning. To play vigorous singles tennis, a high level

of fitness is required. The tennis enthusiast in action is burning off 425 calories per hour.

Others

Other calorie burners are:

Activity	Calories per hour
Ice skating	360
Skiing, cross country	594
Rowing	300
Golf (walking)	300
Walking (briskly)	216
Volleyball	210

Other excellent activities that can have a pronounced effect on one's fitness, if done regularly and systematically, are rope skipping; roller skating; arm, shoulder, leg, and abdominal calisthenics; rope climbing; boxing; and wrestling. Of course, each of these implies vigorous and continuous action.

THE PARCOURSE

An interesting new development in the physical fitness inventory during the past 10 years is the Parcourse or Fitness Trail. This circuit or sequence of exercises, generally outdoors, was developed several years ago in Zurich, Switzerland by the Vita Life Insurance Company for its employees. It consists of some 18 individual stations or exercises laid out around a 1-mile jogging course. Each station is marked with a small permanent sign demonstrating the particular exercise and describing the level of performance expected of the beginner, intermediate, and advanced. Exercises include bends, stretches, push-ups, chin-ups, lifting of small logs, etc. The first few stations call for easy, warm-up routines such as toe-touching, torso stretching, and arm circling. Progressively, the routines become more demanding, with the course ending in a series of relaxation exercises. Participants who encounter problems with any one of the stations may bypass that one and continue on. Completing the Parcourse (named from the French "par cours," for running, that is, a track for running) corresponds roughly to a 1-hour gym class.

The concept was brought to America in the 1970s, and now there are many such circuits laid out at industrial plants and military bases. Some firms are marketing the concept commercially under the names "Fitness Trail," "Vita Parcours," "Parcourse," and others. The first municipal Parcourse in eastern America was installed in New Rochelle, New York in 1977 by the Department of Parks and Recreation. Cost of the packaged unit was paid by the Manufacturers Hanover Bank, and the entire installation was handled as a training project by the New Rochelle unit of the U.S. Marine Corps Reserve. The Parcourse, located in Huguenot Park and circling a city lake, has become one of the most popular recreation and fitness installations in the city and has since been copied by several neighboring communities.

FITNESS FOR AGING PERSONS

If any one myth is headed for its end, it is the old bromide that exercise and physical fitness are only for the young; old people are beyond all that. Daily, we see new demonstrations of the fallacy in this thinking. It is admitted that some modest concessions must be made to age—reactions, vision, tendon resiliency, all are less at 60 than they are at 20. This is only a small part of the picture, however, and does not justify the fatalistic mood of so many 50-year-old persons who explain their deteriorated condition with, "Well, what do you expect at my age, Tarzan?"

Extensive testing and research by the President's Council on Physical Fitness and Sports, as well as that pursued on several university campuses, has established that soundly planned and executed programs of regular physical exercise are good for men and women of middle and advanced years. Dr. Theodore Klumpp, a member of the American Medical Association committee studying problems of aging, has a prescription for separating fatigue from aging. Except in advanced organic disease, one should engage in a regular routine of physical exercise such as golf, hiking, swimming, gardening, bicycling, badminton, even tennis, according to Dr. Klumpp. Find one that is fun, he recommends, and then he presents a fascinating comment to all of us who might view with alarm exercising at an advanced age. He says, "It is interesting to note that only 2% of all heart attacks occur during exercise, most of them occur during rest and 50% occur during sleep!" He goes on to add that any power plant, engine, or human body functions best when it is used regularly and vigorously; when it is permitted to idle too long, it responds sluggishly and may even cough and die.

Activity is the key to a human's health and youthfullness. Muscles and glands require exercise to stay young. Recreation can be of enormous help here. The variety of activities available, the convenience and low cost for participation, the social advantage of exercising with another person, all work to make physical exercise more comfortable, more familiar, more fun. The growth of senior citizens centers and programs have made this matter of regular exercise much easier and much more attractive.

C. Carson Conrad, Executive Director of the President's Council lists four attitudes that militate against elderly people participating in vigorous exercise:

1. They believe their need for exercise diminishes and eventually disappears as they grow older.

2. They vastly exaggerate the risks involved in vigorous exercise after middle age.
3. They overrate the benefits of light, sporadic exercise (a game of golf, a frolic in the surf).
4. They underrate their own abilities and capacities.

Most studies presented show clearly that older people are trainable in respect to physical fitness components even though they may have been sedentary for many years. Exercise and recreation cannot stop a person from getting older, but when properly applied, they can retard the aging process and add vigor to living throughout life.

FITNESS FOR HANDICAPPED PERSONS

As with most atypical groups within society, physically and mentally handicapped persons have, until recently, been regarded as beyond the reach of conventional vigorous, fitness-producing activities. Because of birth defects, children were allowed to grow fat and lethargic, waited on hand and foot, and pampered. Comic books, movies, candy, ice cream, and saturation television has constituted the daily diet of many of these young people. Sports, recreation, and vigorous calisthenics were considered totally inappropriate. Happily, this has changed.

Several studies have explored the value of physical activity programs—including games and sports—for the mentally retarded. One study carried out in England by J. N. Oliver brought about marked improvement in athletic achievement, physical fitness, and strength (mentally retarded children are often poorly coordinated and obese) and also was responsible for an average increase of 25% in I.Q's of its subjects. Similar efforts with educable mentally retarded boys demonstrated improved scores on the Wechsler Intelligence Scale for children after only 20 days' duration.[5]

Case[1] notes that eurhythmics, including social, folk, and square dancing, are particularly attractive to sightless persons. Blind persons of all ages can be highly motivated to take an interest in their bodies, but it may never take the same form as that of fully sighted persons. Although they are, theoretically, capable of all types of weight-lifting, gymnastics, wrestling, and isometric exercises, they may respond more dynamically to socially oriented programs and events.

A number of special running tracks for non-sighted people have been created with wire cables strung alongside each lane. The blind runners, by placing their hands on the cable, can guide themselves in dashes or multilap long distance runs. Two cities that have been leaders in recreation and fitness activities for the blind are Detroit, and Long Beach, California.

The development of the Special Olympics, with substantial encouragement by the Joseph P. Kennedy, Jr. Foundation is another indication of the refreshingly new attitude concerning fitness and people with handicaps. Persons with paraplegia, paralysis, partial sight, cerebral palsy, muscular dystrophy, diabetes, and cardiac problems along with dozens of other optimistic people have been entering track and water races, archery, basketball games, weight lifting, and a variety of similar events. Their spirit, their strength, and their adaptability are a delight to behold, and many of these people were brought into the active fitness area through recreation activities and dedicated leadership.

RECREATION OPPORTUNITIES

Numerous recreation activities and special events lend themselves to the improvement of physical fitness, whether it be a hospital, correctional institution, campus, or community. A few illustrations follow.

Track and field meets

Instead of the conventional events—distances and standard to be met—these programs can be scaled down. High jumps can be lowered, broad jumps shortened, and distances reduced to meet the average levels of the participants. In addition, fun events such as tug-of-war, the carrying of heavy dummies in races, the balancing of objects on the head, etc., all emphasize the delight and excitement of participation rather than that exclusively of winning. This way, many of the normally nonparticipatory people will be involved, and a percentage of them will be encouraged to continue their fitness activities after the meet.

Walkathons and bikeathons

These marathon-like events lend themselves very well to institutions and communities, and most are staged as fundraisers for charities and other worthwhile causes. Each participant arranges his or her sponsor in advance and assures the promoter that the sponsor will donate to charity a unit sum (e.g., $1.00) for every mile or lap completed. This technique can be used for walking, jogging, swimming (pool laps), bicycling, tennis (number of games played or games won), rowing, bowling (number of games bowled or won), badminton, volleyball, football kicking, push-ups, sit-ups, and many others. In the process, charity is served, but it also stimulates large numbers of youth and adults to test themselves and to expand their interest in fitness. This is particularly appropriate for community recreation departments.

Competitions

Recreation agencies are using competitions in many sports and body challenge activities. These serve as attention-getters and also provide a stage on which athletes who are improving themselves can demonstrate their new prowess. Illustrations include weight-lifting contests, track meets, survival tests in the wilderness, mountain-climbing, speed skating, cross-country skiing, rope and tree climbing, swimming and lifesaving competitions, and foot and bicycle marathons. New York City's Annual Marathon, only a few years old, has already drawn fields of 11,000 entries who challenged the five-borough, 26-mile course. Almost every major city in America now hosts one or more annual marathons while just a decade ago the only marathon the average citizen heard of was the 50-year-old Boston Marathon, 26 miles from Hopkinton, Massachusetts, to the downtown Prudential Center in Boston.

Throughout, the recreation leader has an almost unequaled opportunity to bring the concept of physical fitness into closer and more understandable form for the average citizen. Most citizens know and trust their local department, and in institutions, the recreation leader is a known and liked person. Rather than finding fault with fat people, heavy smokers, gluttons, lazy bodies, and other people who have lost their zest for trimness, tone, and high self-image, the recreator has special access and opportunity for reaching and motivating. The party setting, outing, picnic, hospital softball game, beach party, boat ride, fishing trip, or mountain junket all offer unique opportunities to show a skill, to comment on an accomplishment, and to advise sympathetically on further steps available for improving one's capacities. These opportunities represent one of the greatest reasons why recreation professionals must know about physical fitness, understand its deep significance in the lives of their constituents, and be skilled at bringing about a steadily improving state of fitness, regardless of the age, physical configuration, or mental skill of the people served.

SOME ADDITIONAL TRICKS FOR FITNESS

The trim body and that general feeling of fitness need not involve enormous muscles or the body of a gymnast. Naturally, many white-collar workers cannot find the time or dedication to work at building enormous biceps or washboard stomachs. There are ways, however, that average Americans can keep themselves trimmer and firmer than they ever believed possible.

1. Draw in your stomach. Do this frequently through the day. Sure it sounds like something out of Annapolis or West Point but it can have a marked effect on the tone of the stomach muscles. Do it quietly and inconspicuously and your friends will never detect you are doing it. They will admire the trim, firm tummy that this can produce. Creating a tucked-in tension and holding it for 10 seconds is all that is necessary. If this is done often enough it will become an unconscious habit, tending to keep these muscles in a trimmer tighter position, producing finer muscle tone and appearance.

2. Walk "tall." Imagine that your are a puppet with a string running from approximately your stomach straight up through your body and coming out the top of your head. Imagine that this string is pulling upward and your body will follow. An inclination to walk straighter and to put more muscles to work should follow. Whatever your height, the additional half inch this gives will benefit your overall carriage and will certainly make your walk more graceful.

3. Climb stairs occasionally. This does not mean racing up at a heart-breaking pace nor does it mean climbing eight to ten flights at a time. It does mean that for climbs three floors or less you might walk up half the trips and ride the elevator the other half, all going up of course. Done at a moderate pace, stair-climbing is a simple form of leg exercise and mild heart stimulant.

4. Pick up objects of bulk, such as a hassock, small chair, heavy piece of wood, or objects weighing 8 to 15 pounds. Grasp them firmly, raise them to various positions about your body and head, extending and retracting your arms and moving them in a slow and graceful manner. Such weights should not strain you, and at the same time you will develop increased arm and chest muscle tone.

5. "Push" on resistant surfaces such as door jambs, mantle pieces, stairways, etc. Privacy here is important or strange questions will be asked by observers. Avoid strain or injury but press in such a way that arm, back, chest, and stomach muscles as well as thigh muscles are put to work. This is a form of the old Charles Atlas "dynamic tension."

6. Rotate at the waist as frequently as possible. Nothing focused more attention on the American waistline than the twist dance and the hula hoop. Though they may be gone, the bulging waistline is still with us. Deliberately turn right and left at the waistline as far as possible several times a day. Stretch while turning and reaching for objects in inconvenient locations, which forces twisting at the waist, a simple technique for toning up the back and the sides of the torso.

None of these steps requires purchase of equipment, payment of any fees, or registration in any expensive fitness program. All around us are simple ways by which we can keep our bodies in better tone and our figures looking trimmer. Clutching a rubber ball, reaching for the ceiling, touching our toes, bending at the waist, walking—these are the simple things so often classified as calisthenics and discarded as regimented and unpopular. Though there is no short cut or easy way to general fitness, there are certainly many ways in which we can, inexpensively and conveniently, keep the body moving, supple, and in the kind of tone that makes our leisure time recreation more fun than ever.

CAREERS

There is great potential for job expansion in recreation physical fitness during the years ahead. Some have said that physical fitness and self-help health care represent the third largest growth industry of the 1980s. There is a fast-spreading belief that medical costs will never come down until Americans learn to take better care of their own bodies. Job titles in this area would include recreation director, recreation leader, recreational therapist, activity leader, physical fitness director, and exercise specialist.

For further information on such careers, write to:

National Recreation and Park Association
1601 North Kent St.
Arlington, VA 22209

National Industrial Recreation Association
203 N. Wabash Ave.
Chicago, IL 60606

President's Council on Physical Fitness and Sports
Washington, DC 20201

DISCUSSION QUESTIONS

1. As recreation director for a group of paraplegic veterans, you are requested to arrange a field day of events for 100 patients, utilizing the hospital's large wood-floored gymnasium. Assemble a list of games and events for the day and point out at least seven potential problems or hazards that must be accommodated in the planning.
2. The mayor of your city (50, 000 population) has become suddenly enthusiastic about citizen physical fitness and demands that, as recreation director, you institute a city-wide program immediately. What are at least five basic steps that should be taken before launching the program?
3. In a city of 250,000, surrounded by several dozen large industrial plants and business headquarters, the Director of Parks and Recreation undertakes to open a new physical fitness program through recreation. What are some of the assets and facilities that the director may find in this concentration of business firms? How can some of these assets be put to work for community fitness?
4. Knowledge of the cardiovascular system is valuable information for the recreation director who wishes to put participants into physical fitness programs. Using reliable medical texts and resources, prepare a simple sketch of the human heart, lungs, and major blood vessels. On the sketch, mark and describe various points where common cardiovascular diseases and weaknesses frequently appear. Relate these to the cautions that must be exercised by fitness leaders before they put clients into vigorous body-building programs.
5. As a professional recreator, you are faced with an aging staff and an elderly clientele in a nursing home. It would appear that a modest program of physical activities would be helpful to the residents, but strong resistance prevails. Outline a program of action to motivate both the staff and residents in the direction of a more active program.

BIBLIOGRAPHY

Business Week, January 5, 1974.
Butler, G. D.: Introduction to community recreation, New York, 1972, McGraw-Hill Book Co.
Editorial: How to live it up and live longer! *Prevention*, Emmaus, Pa., 1974, Rodale Press.
Emmerton, B.: Running for your life, New York, 1970, World Publishing Co.
Kraus, R. G.: Recreation and leisure in modern society, New York, 1971, Appleton-Century-Crofts.
Kusinitz, I., Freedman, M., and Fine, M.: The challenge of physical fitness, Westport, Conn., 1969, Physical Fitness Laboratory, Ltd.
Lutzin, S. G., and Storey, E. H.: Managing municipal leisure services, Chicago, 1973, The International City Managers Association.
Miller, D. B.: The extended care facility, New York, 1969, McGraw-Hill Book Co.
Myers, C. R.: The official YMCA physical fitness handbook, New York, 1975, Popular Library.
O'Neil, J. F.: A feasibility study of the need for corporate physical fitness programs, Master's project, Northeastern University, Boston, 1976.
President's Council on Physical Fitness and sports:

Physical fitness in business and industry, Washington, D. C., 1973.

President's Council on Physical fitness and Sports: Research digest, Series 2, No. 3, Washington, D.C., 1972.

US. News and World Report, January 14, 1974.

The World Almanac and Book of Facts, New York, 1975, Doubleday.

REFERENCES

1. Case, M.: Recreation for blind adults, Springfield, Ill., 1966, Charles C Thomas, Publisher.
2. Datsun Action, 1976.
3. General Mills Corp.: Meal planning for the golden years (free pamphlet on nutrition), Minneapolis, 1976.
4. Health Letter, Communications, Inc., 1900.
5. The mentally retarded need recreation, Parks Rec. p. 575, July 1966.
6. Morehouse, L. E.: Total fitness in thirty minutes a week, New York, 1975, Simon and Schuster.
7. Nixon, J. E.: The fitness craze. In World Book Yearbook, Chicago, 1974, Field Enterprises Educational Corp.
8. Paffenbarger, R. S., and Hale, W. E.: Work activity and coronary heart mortality, New Engl. J. Med. **292:**545, 1975.
9. President's Council on Physical Fitness and Sports: Newsletter, Special edition, Washington, D. C., May 1973.

8
LEADERSHIP IN RECREATION

Courtesy Boston Parks and Recreation Dept.

115

Leadership is that quality or characteristic by which certain people are able to influence others, the followers, and cause them to do what the leaders wish or desire. Sometimes the leader dominates or intimidates the followers, as when a tough football coach roars and commands in an intensive drill or practice; sometimes leadership is exercised in a gentle, persuasive manner, as seen in the group motivation tactics of a psychological counselor serving a home for aged medical patients. Always, leadership is a major responsibility. Cruel or unscrupulous leaders have the power to misguide and even destroy their innocent or less knowledgeable followers. The sincere, sympathetic leader can raise humble, pessimistic people to new heights of hope, optimism, and success.

Leadership is an inexact substance/characteristic without which little occurs in human affairs. It surfaces in myriad forms and at unexpected moments. It has no sex or size, this being more true in the 1980s than ever before. Unbound by past prejudices, double standards, and anachronistic legislation, leadership will explode in shapes, forms, and personalities totally unexpected in the past. In business, religion, politics, industry, leisure services, the armed forces, and medicine, physically small people of both sexes are assuming leadership roles and opportunities formerly reserved only for physically attractive males. This is truly the age of genuine leadership cultivation, a period when new leaders are emerging, unfettered, in every walk of life and level of society. This has great significance for the field of recreation and leisure.

DEFINITIONS

The *American Collegiate Dictionary* defines the leader as: "a guiding or directing head, a conductor or director"—a woefully understated definition! To be fully appreciated, the concept of leadership calls for adjectives such as courageous, ruthless, dynamic, subtle, inspired, gifted, sensitive, harsh, blind, or distracted. Anything less simply suggests the milder labels of influence, persuader, guide, helper, direction marker, or aide. To appreciate leadership, one must consider the power and impact of some of the great leaders of all time. For simple analysis, such leaders may be grouped into three categories: superleaders, great leaders, and agential leaders.

Superleaders are those few persons in history whose individual characteristics and resources are such that they accomplish great deeds without the need for formal structures or the backing of large governmental units to fuel their power. Their impact on people, time, and life, nevertheless, is enormous. Such "self-starters" might include Jesus Christ, Napoleon Bonaparte, Moses, Christopher Columbus, Martin Luther, Adolf Hitler, Martin Luther King, and Elvis Presley.

Great leaders are those men and women who receive the means, the structure, and the power from some formal promotion, election, assignment, or appointment by others. They are then placed in official positions of strength and leadership, and they succeed. But because of inner fires, ideals, and energy, the great leader then moves beyond the original position and framework and leads or influences others toward heights of service and accomplishment through his or her newly found synergic resources and strengths. Some great leaders eventually attain the next level of superleader. Examples of great leaders are John F. Kennedy, Pope John XXIII, George Washington, Queen Victoria, General Douglas MacArthur, and Czar Alexander.

Agential leaders are those persons of substantial intelligence and skill whose leadership success, however, depends almost entirely on the formal governmental or societal framework into which they are ceremoniously placed. There is likelihood that, without this structure, the agential leader might pass through life leaving no visible mark or impact on people or history. In brief, the job makes the person. This group would include President Gerald Ford, President Diem of South Viet Nam, Emperor Hirohito, Prime Minister Neville Chamberlain, J. Edgar Hoover, Governor Nelson A. Rockefeller, and Queen Elizabeth.

Klapp[2] puts this concept in slightly different terminology:

A symbolic leader is one who functions primarily through his meaning or image (for example, Gandhi meant much as a person to the masses of India—indeed, of the earth—regardless of his official status). Thus I make a distinction between a symbolic leader and an organizational leader; the latter works within a certain social structure or organized group and may not mean much to people otherwise.

Verba[10] presents a similar interesting point of view on leadership differentiation:

Leadership vs. Headship—Leadership exists when the consent of the followers is given spontaneously because of a recognition of the leader's contribution to the group goal; headship exists when followers obey because of the organizational position of the headman or for any other reason but the spontaneous recognition of the leader for the particular task on hand.

These definitions have particular significance for recreation leaders. There is little chance for leadership success in this field unless the leader relies heavily on subjective resources and momentum rather than on mere structural support or organizational status.

LEADERS IN RECREATION

Meyer and Brightbill[4] believe that "The success or organized recreation depends more upon its leaders than on any other factor. Quality leaders, trained and experienced, form the very foundation of a recreation program."

Inevitably, the old questions are asked by lay persons and must be answered anew. "Why do you need leaders in recreation and leisure? Are not recreation activities supposed to be spontaneous, unfettered, unstructured, with beginnings and endings only where the participant feels they ought to be?" Of course the lay person is not wrong when recreation is viewed idealistically or theoretically. Is not the school a setting for delightful learning, for hungry young minds to feast on the flow of educational nourishment passing before them every day? Is not the church or synagogue an idyllic retreat solely for quiet, individual thought and prayer, unbothered by bells, schedules, collection plates, public address systems, hymnals, organs, and heating bills? Of course recreation in the abstract is a simple, self-led movement into and out of things and experiences, a free spirit tapping the immense wealth of fun, thrills, joys, and new information surrounding us. But life is not quite so simple. Viewing the surf, counting herons in the sky, picking buttercups, and jogging along lonely roads require little or no leadership, but, will this meet and satisfy the many tastes, needs, wishes, hopes, and curiosities of millions of different people? The answer is that it will not, and to seek out and meet these needs, talented leadership is required.

THE RECREATION LEADER

Much has been written on the qualifications for recreation leadership. From it one might infer that a paragon is needed. Yet when one compares these demands with employment opportunities, compensation, and recognition, the rewards are entirely too meager for the quality of leadership demanded. This has always been true in the professional fields of education, religion, welfare, and recreation. It is only in recent years that social responsibilities have received increased recognition and wage conditions have improved. There is still much room for improvement, as well as a shortage of desirable personnel in all four fields resulting from inadequate financial compensation.

In all positions that involve dealing with human personalities, there are general qualities expected in every leader: (1) a broad interest in society, a genuine enthusiasm for one's work, ideals, good judgment, integrity, responsibility, initiative, and resourcefulness; (2) patience, dependability, devotion, a sense of humor, and courtesy; (3) the related qualities of efficiency, thoroughness, accuracy, promptness, and industry; and, (4) a feeling that the leader has a good amount of common sense and with it a scientific attitude and approach to the job.

Almost every profession desires its leaders to possess these qualities. They are needed in teaching, social work, the ministry, medicine, and law, as well as in recreation. Practical methods of ascertaining the extent to which a potential employee possesses these qualities are difficult to find, and every effort should be made to ensure a practical and liberal approach to any measurements and tests that are made. Letters of recommendation, interviews, words from friends, teachers, and others can all bear fruit. At the same time it must be understood that different people interpret these qualities in different ways and visualize them according to personal experiences and relationships.

Leaders should also broaden their information base and should have a knowledge of the following:

1. History: Philosophy and theory of recreation; development of recreation; stages, transitions, and trends; concepts of recreation; background knowledge and study of recreation in the cultures of peoples.

2. Basic concepts in understanding individuals: General biological and physiological functions, general psychology, psychology of personality, social psychology, child and adolescent psychology.

3. Principles and methods of leadership: Objectives and techniques of leadership; interests, needs, abilities, and limitations of leadership; leadership and the group process; leadership in program planning and activities and techniques of administration, supervision, and direction; understanding volunteers.

4. Recreation needs and resources to meet these needs: Sponsorship and purpose; areas, facilities, and equipment; clientele served; program building and emphasis; legislative factors; financial policies and practices; personnel; public relations. Special knowledge of the problems, frustrations, and opportunities presented by ward or institutional life is of special importance to therapeutic recreation leaders.

5. Knowledge of skills: Mastery of one or more skills, practice of numerous skills and recognition of the place of other skills in the total, balanced program of athletics, sports, and games; dramatics, music, and dancing; arts and crafts; reading and storytelling; nature and outing activities; social events; place, use, and direction of recreation program skills.

6. Methods of social research: Research projects, studies and surveys, analysis and interpretation, evaluation techniques, clinical experiments, and reports and records.

7. Field work in recreation: Practical experience—procedure and methods; schedule and time elements; supervision and guidance; standards.

PERSONALITY TRAITS

Personality and skill are inextricably combined in effective leadership. Successful leaders have a blended combination of these precious qualities. A positive personality is a must. Lacking this, potential leaders are doomed to mediocrity and near-success. With it, seemingly average people can reach the heights of leadership.

Other attributes necessary for success in this field are (1) a sense of humor, (2) a desire to work with *people* instead of with *things* to help others learn to help themselves and to live their lives more abundantly, (3) a knowledge of what makes people of all ages act as they do, (4) an understanding of recreation, its importance, and how to use the fun approach instead of the perfectionist approach in building a well-balanced program for all ages, (5) good health and a zest for life, (6) common sense, (7) knowledge of how to use democratic methods, how to lead rather than drive others, and how to work with people without using them, and (8) resourcefulness.

Areas of study in the professional preparation of the recreation leader should include social sciences, english, education, cultural arts, sociology, government, physical education, and recreation.

Professional field work, supervised leadership assignments, visits to as many different kinds of recreation areas as possible (including hospitals, mental institutions, schools for retarded or handicapped children), personal interviews with local leaders in the field, actual experience in conducting recreation surveys and in community organizations should all be a basic part of leadership preparation. Summer employment at a camp, playground swimming pool, country club, or sporting goods store is a very important source for leadership experience. "There is no substitute for qualified leadership, and any compromise in this matter is false economy. The best leadership possible is none too good to guide and serve the leisure-time interest of the American people."[5]

The concept of leadership has undergone considerable change and sophistication during the 1960s and 1970s. In the early days of the movement the primary consideration was to provide interesting activities for small groups of young children. Recreation leadership today takes many forms, involves widely different functions, and has varied objectives. Leaders in different positions deal with children, young people, and adults; they help organize and conduct programs comprising a wide variety of activities; they administer many types of indoor and outdoor facilities; and they have relationships with recreation boards and committees, public authorities, community organizations, and the general public.

PLAYGROUND LEADERSHIP

Leadership on the playground means more than the maintenance of discipline and order. Guards can look after the equipment, and policemen, who represent organized force and authority to the child, can enforce good behavior; but this discipline has only negative value. It lacks the vital, positive influence on the growing child that a competent leader brings to the playground. Unlike policemen or guards who act only when some disciplinary problem arises, leaders are in constant association with the children and youth. They keep the children happily engaged in activities that interest them, and conduct the activities in such a way that occasions for dispute are minimized. When disagreements do occur, leaders help the children settle their difficulties and reach a solution through understanding. They seek to enlist the children's active cooperation in curbing an undesirable activity for an understandable and worthy end. In this way, children learn self-control and restraint in their social relationships; they learn the value of discipline by experiencing the good it brings them, not by resisting its restraints.

LEADERSHIP IN INSTITUTIONAL RECREATION

The recreation leader in a sanatorium, prison, or convalescent hospital faces a different set of circumstances from those of a community recreation leader. The clientele is confined and compressed for various reasons. Most activities take place indoors and within confined spaces. Patients, residents, or inmates have a problem, or several problems, or they would not be there, and this problem can seriously interfere with their response to even the finest leader's overtures. Moreover, the leader is surrounded by other professionals and staff, all doing their thing to bring about the patient's or inmate's rehabilitation or return to health. This is a complex and, in a sense, an unnatural situation when compared with a typical community recreation setting.

The therapeutic recreation leader should possess several of the following characteristics:

1. Gentle, dignified approach—the fragile balance of a ward or prison setting can easily be upset by a too strong or too strident voice or approach. A steady, low-key personality is desirable.

2. Careful planner—small details, ignored or forgotten, may cause failure in an otherwise fastidiously prepared event or program. One gift too few, the name of a key participant left out of a program, a time conflict that places two groups in competition—these are but a few of the tiny details that can destroy a program. Attention to details is essential.

3. Optimism—the mood of the location or setting may become very depressed. Therapeutic recreation leaders must have the capacity for rising above it and gently buoying up those around them.

4. Capacity to forgive—ill, handicapped, or incarcerated people can sometimes be unintentionally cruel. A word, a shrug, a collective joke, a cold reaction to a program attempt—these are often the reward of conscientious therapeutic recreation leaders after they have worked hard to start a program or launch an activity. The leaders must realize the root causes of this discourtesy or truculence and compensate through their own optimism and buoyance. A quick "forgive and forget" is in order.

MANAGEMENT

There are those who would separate management from leadership. In their book, leaders are tall, charismatic personalities, radiating confidence and promise. Managers are small, wizened personalities, short on social electricity but long on charts, graphs, statistics, and systems. This sharp distinction is fallacious. The two labels intertwine and are mutually contributory. Rice[7] puts it this way:

I find difficulty in differentiating between management and leadership. At the manifest level of behavior, a leader has to be able to carry his followers with him, inspire them, make decisions on their behalf, with or without their collaboration . . . A manager has to get the best results out of the resources he has available—money, time, materials and people. Both leaders and managers have to deal with numbers of followers and subordinates, extending all the way from the small intimate face-to-face group of immediate colleagues to extended commands and even crowds.

CREATIVE LEADERSHIP

We have discussed the basic elements of leadership. Creative leadership is a step beyond. Creative leadership calls for greater awareness, for a sense of timeliness, the ability to weave together seemingly unimportant details so that a task of particularly imposing size is brought down to scale and accomplished. The creative leader might be expected to use one of those familiar bromides: "The difficult we do immediately, the impossible takes a little longer." Consider this excerpt from Bellows:[1]

Creative leadership is needed if our present civilization is to survive. The thought has been voiced that physical science has made it possible for all men to die together; our growing knowledge of creative leadership must make it possible for men to live together.

Creative leadership is something more than management. It possesses an element of taking the available and producing that which was before unavailable. It involves the arranging and rearranging of situations so that predetermined goals and objectives are attained on schedule. It is the rearranging, the realigning, the compensating, the substituting, the adjusting, and the searching for and finding of missing parts that characterizes this particular form of leadership as "creative." Bellows decries the notion that certain people are "born leaders." He maintains that they can be trained, developed, and brought to high levels of productivity through sound educational processes. He bases this on extensive experience with such talent-hungry agencies as the U.S. Army, Navy, and Air Force, Burroughs Corp., National Bank of Detroit, E. R. Squibb & Sons of Olin-Mathieson, Western Electric Co., and the American Management Association.

Examples

The Director of Recreation of a large municipal hospital has been informed that she should expand her program of services to patients. Simultaneously, the budget director notifies her that her new budget will be reduced 5% because of financial constrictions. If she flatly refuses to improve the program, she is a questionable leader. If she cheerfully assumes her administrative responsibilities and promises to expand the program, but makes it clear the budget director must give her additional money, she is of leader caliber. However, if she assumes her responsibility and manages to (1) launch some new fund-raising events, (2) exhort her staff to new ingenuity heights, and (3) motivate business and industry in her city to assist by underwriting certain programs and activities—then she is a creative leader.

A recreation leader working for a municipal department of recreation, arrives at his evening community center, only to find his small equipment locker rifled and bare. No basketballs, bats, softballs, jump ropes or craft equipment remains, and he faces 35 adolescent boys and girls eager for vigorous activity. Left behind by the thief are a 30-foot length of heavy rope and a basketball official's whistle. If he complains of the situation to the young people and suggests they go home, he is no leader. If he draws the youngsters together and lectures them on the evils of theft and its consequences, he has demonstrated a degree of responsible leadership. If, on the other hand, he improvises several tug-of-war matches and other original activities using the long rope and the whistle so that the young people go away singing his praises, he is a true creative recreation leader.

CREATIVE DEVELOPMENT

The developing of creative vision, the capacity to design, to improvise, to relate seemingly unrelated objects or concepts, is within the grasp of every thinking man and woman. Following are some steps that can enhance people's capacity for creative thinking:

1. *Read.* Read rapidly, hungrily, frequently. Read a rich variety of periodicals, not only those on recreation, but also professional, tabloid, scientific, political, photographic, travel, labor, and trade journals.

2. *File.* File mentally, and physically, the vast array of significant and provocative material your reading unearths.

3. *See.* Use your eyes to "see" life and living about you. Look at what others overlook. Look under, behind, above, and below the obvious. Look again later and see differently. *Move* about physically so that a constant supply of *the new* is provided for your visual appetite.

4. *Listen.* In a manner similar to *see.*

5. *Meet people, talk, tolerate, and cultivate newness in others.*

6. *Juggle many ideas simultaneously! Creativity* here must not be confused with *creation.* Creative leadership, or creative ideas, does not mean "something out of nothing." It means the assembling of new ideas, concepts, and things out of relationships among old, familiar, unrelated ideas, concepts, and things.

Stereotypes

Too often, "creativity" is linked only with long hair, eccentricity, and artists such as Leonard Bernstein and Walt Disney. However, it is also a very real part of the work of batting champions, golfers, home builders, politicians, doctors, clergymen, racketeers, generals, policemen, and lovers.

The cultivation and development of a "creative idea" can be one of the loftiest functions of human minds. The creative idea, in the hands of the creative leader, can be of enormous impact. Ancient civilizations and their languages acknowledged the value and impact of the *revolutionary new idea.* Today, a prime ingredient in the dynamic, problem-solving executive is his *creative idea power.* Many executives lack this power. A far *greater* number *have* the potential but do not exercise it fully. In a highly structured society, such creative ability is essential for dynamic leadership.

Synectics

Synectics is the technique or skill by which things are made to relate or brought into relationship. It is a procedure or process by which the human mind lays parts or units together in varying patterns, and from these patterns extracts a new, fresh relationship that earlier was totally unseen. A process I originated is labeled as follows:

Synectic Perspection produces *Ideational Hybrids*
SP leads to IHs

In this, the word "perspection" denotes vantage point, vista, point of view, scale, ability to see comprehensively. "Ideational" signifies that connected with ideas, concepts, abstracts, mental images, visionary subjects. "Hybrids" indicates that these ideational units or offspring are crossbred, mixed, unusual, unique, and distinctly the result of interface and interrelationships of other, less interesting ideas. They resemble their parents, but are new entities in themselves.

New and creative ideas are typically the *combination* of 2 or or more previously *unrelated* ideas. A creative idea is both *original* and somehow *potentially useful.* A creative *technique* brings familiar objects, function of objects, ideas, abstracts, etc. into proximity, so that they will rub, scratch, ignite, affect one another. The result is a new entity or idea!

Visual

In this case, A and B represent familiar but previously unrelated ideas, concepts, or things.

Mathematically:	A + B = A + B
Creatively:	A + B = A + B + C
Eventually:	A + B = C (maybe)

Creative idea power is *not* mathematical, and it is very *subjective*.

Practice

This kind of creative exercise must be practiced if it is to grow and become part of the creative recreation leader's arsenal of tools. At home, at play, at the office, in church, on the beach—almost every daily living situation presents opportunities for putting synectic perspective to work. Consider some of these creative ideas, in which a problem plus some available familiar things, produced an exciting new idea.

1. *Piggyback trains:* the result of costly highway trips by loaded trucks and trailers, crossed with sagging sales reports on long distance freight trains. From these two unrelated problems, came the great new idea of loading trailers on flatbed rail cars for long-distance hauling.

2. *Hula Hoop:* an overloaded inventory of colored plastic tubing, plus a search for new and exciting children's toys gave us the Hula Hoop, a sales sensation in the 1960s and a still quite popular toy.

Others include glamorous support hose, pizza-flavored mustard, plastic milk bottles, the one-man police car, Ticketron reservations, printed electrical circuitry, and many of the new diet-exercise regimens.

Deterrents

The major deterrent to creative leadership is *mediocrity*. It is omnipresent. It is cozy and painless, and it is easy to be mediocre. There are many excuses that thwart imaginative creativity. Just a few are: "It's not in the budget," "Too big for us," "Don't you have enough to do now?" "We've tried that before," "We're not ready for it," "It's too hard to administer," "We don't have sufficient staff," "People here are different—they'll never go for it," "You're moving too fast," "Why hasn't anyone else tried it?" or "Come down to earth—be realistic." Everyone has heard these and more. These are to be avoided at all cost. Do not use them and do not be abused by them. Too many people use this tired defense to turn off the creative talents of their neighbors.

Creative people

Creative people are not necessarily bearded, wild-eyed, bohemian, or Austrian. Nor do they all come from Oxford or M.I.T. Creative people are *usually* collectors of information, especially observant, bright but not brilliant, often having average or below-average scholastic records; visionary, seeing pictures, relationships, and patterns in everyday things; capable of holding many ideas "juggling" about at the same time; generally vigorous, interested in life, "joie de vivre" types; livers of more complex lives than average; very often self-conscious and quite self-critical; and more primitive and more cultured, more destructive and more constructive, crazier and saner, than the average person. Some say that creative people love more passionately and hate more bitterly. Readers must decide for themselves.

ADDITIONAL SKILLS

The finest recreation leader potential may go unused if the person's skills and talents are not developed. Recreation leadership calls for visibility, communications, and field generalship if it is to be effective. Some of the complimentary skills to be developed include the following.

Public speaking

This means the ability to be heard and understood. It does not mean a deafening voice. Plain, clear speech is the most desirable, accompanied by articulate wording and sufficient modulation so that people want to listen to the leader and can understand him or her. Many fine recreation leaders have limited impact because they never learned to address a group or audience in a strong, clear, convincing manner. Since crowds and audiences are not always completely friendly, the dynamic recreation leader must learn ways and means for capturing attention in noisy rooms and for influencing crowds persuasively rather than attempting to do battle with them.

Methods of improving one's public speaking ability include reading a selected text or two from the wealth of fine books available on the subject; attending an adult education class or seminar on public speaking, or enrolling in a professional poise and speech organization such as the Dale Carnegie School or the Berlitz School of Languages.

Constant practice is the best way for recreation leaders to improve their speaking skills. One way to practice is by doing a few minutes deep breathing daily, and forcefully shouting the alphabet, forwards and backwards. Short, choppy words that induce inhaling and exhaling of air are helpful in developing a stronger, more resonant tone. A second way to practice is by accepting frequent public speaking assignments before PTAs, youth clubs, social clubs, and neighborhood organizations. Each of these assignments should be regarded as very important, with appropriate attention given to subject research, speech outlining, practice, and a substantial, dignified presentation. Greater skill and ease follow almost inevitably.

Appearance and presence

One of the strengths of today's society is the freedom to dress and appear in a wide variety of styles and patterns. Nevertheless, the general public is still quite conservative when it looks at men and women who serve as visible leaders and spokespersons for government and human service agencies. For this reason, it behooves recreation leaders to learn and practice the rules of good taste and attractive dress style appropriate to the activity and setting. This does not mean expensive or flamboyant clothing, but rather a comfortable mix of working and dress clothes that enhance one's appearance.

Body hygiene is another major factor in the leader's makeup. It is one characteristic quickly discerned by followers in a leader, especially if those followers are typically bright, observant children. Thus, beards and mustaches should be trimmed and neat, and hair should be clean, combed, and groomed. In every way, recreation leaders should use their appearance to support and strengthen their leadership role and effectiveness.

If the leader functions in a prescribed uniform, be it T-shirt or more formal attire, that uniform should be clean and attractive at all times, with no exceptions. The public may tolerate grease stains and the smell of sweat on the work clothes of a maintenance work or sanitation laborer, but it finds a similar condition repugnant in a recreation leader.

For ideas and suggestions on how civilian dress and uniforms can be controlled and beautified through sound planning, a few of the finest such operations include the Rockettes of the old Radio City Music Hall, Los Angeles and New York City lifeguards, beach attendants at Jones Beach, New York, and the staff of Disneyland.

Communication skills

Speaking publicly is important, but no more important than communicating effectively within a department, staff, or official family. This means staff meetings that are scheduled and worth the time, and memoranda and directives that are long enough to carry the message but short enough to stimulate reading and response. It behooves recreation leaders–administrators to learn and use every technique and device for reaching and informing their staffs. Everyone has had some experience with leaders who are brilliant, attractive, and fully knowledgeable in their fields, but who fail badly when it comes to communicating their brilliant and attractive ideas and programs to those staff people who must carry them out. A leader is expected to lead others, not to function solo simply because he or she can't make himself or herself clear to the staff.

Recreation leaders should make use of the many attractive guide books and pamphlets on office communications distributed by the American Management Association, the National League of Cities, the International City Managers Association, the National Recreation and Park Association, and the National Public Relations Association. If one or more major corporate headquarters of industrial centers are located nearby, their personnel and internal communications staff people can be most helpful in this area. Industrial companies such as Exxon, Xerox, Standard Oil, IBM, Minneapolis-Honeywell, and Litton Industries have been particularly effective in this area.

Personality

It is helpful for leaders in recreation, as in related areas, to have a viable personality, an individuality, of their own. Part of that personality should include one or more skill areas and the recreation leader should be highly skilled or thoroughly knowledgeable in at least one of those subject areas. This subject area need not be directly in the line of the recreation leader's work, but if it is, its professional value is even greater. I have known several outstanding recreation leaders, each of whose personality was enriched by an unusual skill, hobby, former profession, or just pastime. One such leader could speak for hours on the finest details of surf-fishing—poles, reels, bait, favorite beaches, and the seasons of the year. Another leader, an accomplished amateur actress, was at home in every aspect of drama and stagecraft, and her associates were keenly aware of it. A third leader owns and pilots his twin-engine aircraft, a never-ending source of stories and unique experiences connected with his work. Further, recreation leaders should develop quickly the necessary curiosity, enthusiasm, and research capability for browsing through and enthusing over new pursuits and leisure activities, not solely for themselves, but for their staff and constituents.

Put another way, it is difficult to imagine a strong leader-follower response by a recreation staff to a leader who is so bland, so imperturable, and so lacking in individuality that he or she excites or stimulates no one, under any conditions. Rather, a recreation leader who is a good singer or dancer and occasionally displays these talents at a show or party develops more rapport with staff and constituents. "Let's have a

Courtesy Pepsi-Cola Co.

song!," "Did you bring your guitar?," or "We hope you'll come to our square dance and call a few dances for us," are the kind of overtures received by a recreation leader who possesses a few personal skills. In addition to actual skills, leaders should improve their knowledge and familiarity with things such as drama and dance, sports, arts and crafts, special hobbies such as collecting, travel, card playing, chess, gardening, jewelry making, and puppetry. Obviously, recreation leaders cannot be omniscient but, as pointed out earlier in this chapter, one key to expanding a leader's capacity for creative thinking is reading, reading, and more reading. Similarly, the personality and dynamism of recreation leaders are directly enhanced by the volume and quality of their reading. There is no substitute for it.

The recreation leader is in a field that in-volves emotion, posture, high levels of interaction, and movement. A vibrant personality, built on a broad range of life experiences and skills, has to be a major asset. The recreation leader whose career decision was made at an early age has the distinct advantage of being able to build up one or more high skill areas and personality characteristics during the developmental years, a task not so easy as one enters middle age. Young professional leaders, therefore, are urged to experience deeply the great variety of sports and cultural, historic, mechanical, and artistic skills and hobbies that are available at modest cost in this country.

THE EXECUTIVE LEADER

The executive leader—it sounds stuffy, but isn't. It simply means that, unlike the face-to-face activity leader in recreation programs and activities, the executive leader is the group motivator, the staff organizer and stimulator, the administrator who heads the leadership organization chart.

Executive leaders are every bit as important to the sound delivery of recreation services as are the direct interface leaders. Executive leaders carry titles such as Director of Recreation or Director of Recreational Services in a large hospital or prison; Superintendent of Parks and Recreation or Commissioner of Recreation in a medium-sized or large city. Staffs beneath them may number from 10 to 3000 persons and may include stenographers, artists, musicians, horticulturists, nurses, tree surgeons, carpenters, electricians, administrative assistants, recreation leaders, and deputy commissioners. Budgets under their supervision may range from $250,000 to $25 million annually. Leadership here is vitally important.

Kraus and Curtis[3] state that the "successful recreation and park administrator must have certain key qualities, such as intelligence, motivation, drive, willingness to work hard and communicate effectively with others, and planning and organizing ability." Further, they recommend a package of skills and aptitudes that are invaluable to the executive leader:

1. Specific knowledge of the recreation and parks field.
2. Awareness of the chief role and subroles played by the effective administrator (e.g., actor, catalyzer, disciplinarian, friend, etc.).
3. Human relations skills and sensitivities.
4. Capacity for intelligent decision-making.
5. Skill for communicating effectively.
6. Competence and respect for the mechanics of practical politics. This is

true whether the setting be a military base, nursing home, industrial plant, hospital, or city hall.

Failures

Many tests and research projects have sought to determine why and how certain executive leaders fail, while other succeed. The following are the eight most frequently quoted reasons for the failure of top management executives: (1) inability to delegate responsibility, (2) inability to analyze and evaluate, (3) inability to judge people, (4) inability to cooperate with others, (5) decision inability, (6) lack of drive, (7) lack of responsibility, and (8) lack of perserverance.[11]

Stodgill[8] conducted an examination survey of 124 studies on leadership. He concluded that a classification of personal factors associated with leadership would be:

Capacity (intelligence, alertness, verbal facility, originality, judgment)
Achievement (scholarship, knowledge, athletic accomplishments)
Responsibility (activity, sociability, cooperation, adaptability, humor)
Status (socio-economic position, popularity)
Situation (mental level, status, skills, needs and interests of followers, objectives to be achieved, etc.)

If the situation is very important, and Stodgill and other research people believe it is, this is "devastating evidence against memorable traits." Traits that work in one situation do not work in another if leadership depends on the situation. Stodgill concludes: "The findings suggest that leadership is not a matter of passive status, or of the mere possession of some combination of traits. It appears rather to be a working relationship among members of a group . . . ."

Thus, all current research notwithstanding, the pivot of whether an executive leader succeeds or fails seems to be: Does he or she lead when leadership is required? Or, does the pseudo-leader simply posture, gesture, and make articulate but useless words and sounds? Fine clothes, the leadership stance, articulate speech, knowledge of the field, and a host of subfactors do not the leader make, if the leader does not lead. *Psychology today: an introduction*[6] lists several basic requirements for the dynamic executive leader, which include moderately powerful personal resources, high verbal output, intelligence, and likability, and then says:

> But even the combination of dominance and likability is not normally enough for leadership. Group members typically take one further factor into account: the ability of the leader to bring about the success of the group in their main instrumental tasks. Task success to some degree is a must if rewards are to be obtained from the external environment, and many groups are heavily dependent upon task success.

Executive leaders in recreation should demonstrate the kind of vitality and self-starting capacity that enables them to brighten up and galvanize into action a hospital or prison recreation system that has fallen into dull, repetitive program ruts. It is the leadership vitality that helps a new recreation superintendent to enter a city noted for its shabby facilities, sulky staff, and lack-luster programs and, in short order, motivate staff and community to sweep out the cobwebs and move to new heights of enthusiasm. This is executive leadership at work in the field of recreation.

THINGS TO AVOID

The price of dynamism, of being a self-starting leader, is sometimes the loss of contact and empathy with those who would follow. This is no less true in recreation than in any other field of endeavor. Follow-

ing are some pitfalls that should be avoided by the recreation leader.

Do not move too fast for your group or your community. They will become confused and resentful. Psychologists point out that group reactions are generally slower and more primitive than those of an individual. Recreation leaders must set a mental "least common denominator" for their group and gear their directions, speeches, warnings, and other communication at this specific level. The faster levels or strata will simply have to be patient even though they listen and learn faster. To do otherwise is to invite chaos. This is particularly true in a hospital or correctional institution.

Never talk down to or otherwise alienate the group or community you would lead. This is a common error among recreation leaders. Groups of constituents, segments of public, or an audience can sometimes be careless, rude, even cruel. The recreation leader must never succumb to the temptation to fight back, to tell them off, to shut them up. The leader's role is not that of boss, commander, or common conscience. The leader is a sympathetic member of the group, elevated to the post of leadership because of a number of professional and social credentials, none of which makes the leader better, stronger, or more virtuous than the followers. The leader must never commit the deadly error of taking on the group as an antagonist—the leader can never win such a joust.

Meanness, discrimination, partiality, and grudges toward constituents are unforgiveable in a recreation leader. Basic to sound leadership is a confidence on the part of followers that the leader, despite any harshness or remoteness, is always fair and impartial. This is absolutely uniform through successful leadership. Thrasher[9] points out clearly that grudge-free, firm but impartial leadership is an absolute must among the street gangs of Chicago. Gang members, tough and unschooled, can tolerate many abuses by police, the public, and other gang members, but they are seriously wounded and sometimes destroyed by a gang leader who displays partiality, grudges, or favoritism or who fails to fill the father-leader role.

Always keep in mind the need for humility and objectivity on the part of the leader. The leader exists only because of the needs and frailties of the followers. Arrogance or a sense of superiority in leaders is totally out of order.

DISCUSSION QUESTIONS

1. A large private resort facility is opening in Florida. It will feature adult recreation of the highest quality. A professional recreation leader is needed to take over responsibility for the program as well as the supervision of a staff of 10 persons. Describe the type of professional recreation person best suited to such a situation. Include three characteristics that would be most unwelcome.
2. The newly elected mayor of a city of 100,000 persons declares that the first department he will reorganize is the Recreation and Parks Department. As head of that department, what steps would you take to prepare for the mayor's questioning and departmental examination?
3. At a large, terminal cancer hospital for elderly patients you are a new member of the small recreation staff. Your director states that the program is weak and ineffective. She tells you to examine the staff and make recommendations for changes and replacements. What type of leaders would you retain and what type would you recommend for transfer to other institutions?
4. As a guest speaker, you are addressing the junior and senior classes in a medium-sized high school, some 1000 boys and girls. Your purpose is to tell them of career opportunities in recreation. Mention and describe the types of personalities and qualifications that identify those who should investigate career possibilities in recreation.
5. "Leaders are born, not made" is a familiar saying. If you agree with it, explain how it applies to the recreation profession. If you disagree with it, tell why.

BIBLIOGRAPHY

Butler, G. D.: Introduction to community recreation, New York, 1959, McGraw-Hill Book Co.

Dible, D. M.: Up your own organization, Santa Clara, Calif., 1973, Entrepreneur Press.

Drucker, P. F.: Landmarks of tomorrow, New York, 1965, Harper & Row, Publishers.

Drucker, P. F.: Managing for results, New York, 1964, Harper & Row, Publishers.

Ghiselin, B.: The creative process, New York, 1960, Mentor Books.

Gouldner, A. W.: Studies in leadership, New York, 1965, Russell & Russell, Inc.

The International City Managers Association: Municipal recreation administration, ed. 4, Chicago, 1960, The Association.

Lutzin, S. G., and Storey, E. H.: Managing municipal leisure services, Chicago, 1973, The International City Managers Association.

Mason, J. G.: How to build your management skills, New York, 1965, McGraw-Hill Book Co.

McClelland, D. C.: Power—the inner experience, New York, 1975, Irvington Publishers, Inc.

Meyer, H. D., and Brightbill, C. K.: Community recreation, Englewood Cliffs, N.J., 1964, Prentice-Hall, Inc.

Rodney, L. S.: Administration of public recreation, New York, 1964, The Ronald Press.

Taylor, C. W.: Creativity—progress and potential, New York, 1964, McGraw-Hill Book Co.

Trecker, H. B., and Trecker, A. R.: How to work with groups, New York, 1965, Association Press.

Vannier, M.: Methods and materials in recreation leadership, Philadelphia, 1956, W. B. Saunders & Co.

Wilson, W., and Vail, T. H.: Leaders of men, Princeton, N. J., 1952, Princeton University Press.

REFERENCES

1. Bellows, R.: Creative leadership, Englewood Cliffs, N.J., 1959, Princeton-Hall, Inc.
2. Klapp, O. E.: Symbolic leaders, Chicago, 1964, Aldine Publishing Co.
3. Kraus, R. G., and Curtis, J. E.: Creative administration in recreation and parks, ed. 2, St. Louis, 1977, The C. V. Mosby Co.
4. Meyer, H. D., and Brightbill, C. K.: Recreation administration, Englewood Cliffs, N.J., 1956, Prentice-Hall, Inc.
5. Prendergast, J.: Personnel standards in community recreation leadership, New York, 1957, The National Recreation Association.

6. Psychology today, an introduction (an anthology), Del Mar, Calif., 1970, CRM Books.
7. Rice, A. K.: Learning for leadership, London, 1965, Tavistock Publications.
8. Stodgill, R. M.: Personal factors associated with leadership: a survey of the literature, J. Psychol. **25**:35-71, 1948.
9. Thrasher, F. M.: The gang, Chicago, 1963, University of Chicago Press.
10. Verba, S.: Small groups and political behavior—a study of leadership, Princeton, N.J., 1961, Princeton University Press.
11. Why executives fail, Pers. Psychol. **10**:16, 1957.

9
PERSONNEL

Courtesy Huron-Clinton Metropolitan Authority, Detroit, Mich.

In Chapter 8, emphasis was placed on the importance of dynamic leadership in recreation. In this chapter, however, the means and methods of obtaining, training, supervising, and evaluating that leadership personnel will be explored. It is not an easy job, but it is an extremely important subject.

Of all the tasks confronting a recreation administrator, none provides more benefits to the organization than that of selecting a competent and effective leadership staff. Such personnel determine the tone of operations and the quality of the program. Indeed, the ability of staff enhances the success and efficiency of the recreation service.[7]

Despite this, some agencies, managers, and elected officials are still skeptical as to the importance of recruiting and hiring qualified recreation leaders and administrators. "Anyone can do that work, if they like children," is a familiar comment made by unenlightened hiring authorities. "I've got a good generalist available," says a political official paying off a promise or campaign debt. "Let's put him in the Recreation Department; they'll teach him what to do," is another invitation to administrative disaster. Throughout an expanding and improving profession and in the face of conferences, books, pamphlets, and lectures extolling the virtues of high professional standards and careful selection of staff, the same old mistake is frequently repeated.

A large recreation department is turned over to a superintendent or director whose background is in insurance, auto sales, or a term in the state legislature. A thriving recreation center is assigned to a young woman trained in nutrition, political science, or office management. The development of a hospital-wide program of recreation activities is placed in the hands of a physical education major with little or no experience in management, staffing, public relations, or the art of drawing participants into the planning process. In almost all such cases, program planning and staff administration suffer markedly, and associates ask again and again, "How did *he* ever get here?" "Who put *her* in charge of this mess?" This has been exacerbated by increased municipal dependence upon the federal Comprehensive Employment Training Act of 1975 (CETA), which funds the employment of unemployed persons in the community. The solution is an unequivocal commitment by the managing agency to seek, select, hire, train, supervise, and evaluate the finest professional talent they can afford and obtain.

Personnel in recreation belong roughly in two general categories, similar to that of the military. They are direct contact personnel and service or support personnel. *Direct contact personnel* include the recreation leader in a small hospital ward, the recreation director at a neighborhood recreation or community center, the interpretive nature instructor in a large state park, and the arts and crafts instructor in an evening community center. These people are face-to-face with the public, the clients, or the patients, sometimes on a one-to-one basis. They specifically lead, guide, touch, and assist recreation participants in their play or instructional programs. People actually "recreate" under such leaders' direction; they *do* the things this textbook is all about, and if the leadership personnel is effective, these participants are better, happier, healthier people for it.

Service or support personnel, on the other hand, are those who design, plan, assemble, and supervise the recreation operation but rarely do the actual leading or recreating. These people, every bit as important as the direct contact personnel, must provide the planning, designing, programming, and administrative skills that enable the recreation activity program to exist. Job titles would include the director of recreational services in a large hospital, the superintendent of parks and recreation in a medium-sized city, the coordinator of activities for handicapped persons, and the supervisor of public affairs for a large private recreation agency.

BACKGROUND

In the early days of the recreation movement,[1] recreation staff personnel were considered primarily for their skill in working with children. They were thought of as somewhere between nursery school teachers and day-care attendants. Warmth, sensitivity, and a knowledge of children's games, songs, and crafts were regarded as the only basic tools of the professional recreation leader.

The role has changed radically in recent years. The recreation staff person of today finds work in varied settings, involving diverse functions, needs, and skills. In a variety of positions, leaders deal with children, but they also work with young people, adults, elderly persons and entire families. They help organize and conduct programs ranging over a broad spectrum; they administer many types of indoor and outdoor facilities; and they have complex relationships with recreation boards and committees, institutional staffs, public authorities, community organizations, and the general public. What was once a mere slice of the public service profession has become a recognized profession in itself, professional recreation leadership personnel.

RECRUITMENT

No matter how small the institution, agency, or department, a well-planned recruitment program is essential if fresh and dedicated professional personnel are to continue entering the field and filling key positions. In fact, this matter of constant recruitment is of concern to the entire profession of recreation. Chapter 17 describes relationships between recreation practitioners and the high school guidance staff so that likely candidates may be identified early and assisted toward their choice of career. The diligent efforts of the various national organizations such as the National Recreation and Park Association, the National Industrial Recreation Association, and the American Association for Health, Physical Education and Recreation give a nationwide thrust and continuity to this recruitment movement. Additional information and support is derived from the fifty state recreation societies and associations, as well as from such specialized subunits as the American Park and Recreation Society, the National Therapeutic Recreation Society, the Society of Professional Recreation Educators, and the Armed Forces Recreation Society. Local and regional recreation organizations provide still further contact and motivation to potential candidates. Interestingly enough, however, despite all this structured and staffed recruitment work, the most effective device still seems to be the direct contact by an enthusiastic practitioner. The young man or woman fortunate enough to meet or work with a dedicated and articulate recreation professional person will hear and see the job in action without false buildup and without any loss of the psychic income that is part of the work. One has only to poll a sampling of enthusiastic young leaders in recreation work across the country. In four out of five cases, the young professional will likely answer, "Oh it was my local recreation superintendent who got me into this work. He loved it, and told me I would enjoy it too," or "I saw her working in a hospital and she seemed so happy, so satisfied with her work. Then she told me how I could go to college and learn to do the same thing." These often turn out to be the most dedicated of the new leaders, and so the recruitment process continues as enthusiastic leaders communicate that enthusiasm to potential leaders.

Realistically, of course, a flood of new talent cannot always be absorbed in paying positions. Depending on the current economy, demographic trends, size of agency or institution, and other factors, there will be times when jobs are scarce and only a trickle of new candidates can be absorbed. Nevertheless, a constant recruiting movement is necessary to maintain a viable personnel supply over 10- and 25-year periods. Unlike tap water, personnel talent supplies cannot be turned on and off abruptly, and a steady supply of trained, dedicated recreation leaders and administrators is vital to the health of the movement.

ACADEMIC PREPARATION

With the advent of more sophisticated recreation planning and delivery has come the need for professional training and study. Beginning with the National Recreation School, a 1-year graduate level course of instruction established in 1926, the educational aspect of the recreation movement has burgeoned. Today, there are almost 400 individual curricula and campus programs, involving 1000 faculty members and some 100,000 students at junior colleges, 4-year colleges, and universities. Evening programs, continuing education programs, 2-year curricula leading to associate degrees, 4-year curricula leading to bachelor degrees, and graduate programs leading to master's and doctor's degrees are involved.

Formerly, the great majority of these curricula were centered in the college or university's Department of Physical Educa-

tion, but this has changed with the branching out of the profession. Now, recreation may be found, not only in conjunction with physical education departments, but in some arrangement with health, dance, therapy, planning, landscape architecture, forestry, environmental science, and even restaurant and hotel management. On some campuses, recreation has been included under a new diversified title, Leisure Services. This is a good development, since recreation had been handicapped for years by appearing to be a stepchild or poor relation to physical education. This is not meant as a criticism or in any way a belittling of that noble profession that has played such an important role in American education—sports and physical fitness. Unfortunately, however, recreation had for too long been exclusively identified with gyms, locker rooms, and bats and balls, and people thought there was little else to the field. This obscured the fact that art, music, drama, dance, hobbies, travel, aquatics, camping, teen centers, playground design, and therapeutic recreation were all distinct and basic part of the recreation whole.

Although many practitioners in community and therapeutic recreation were busily involved in these varied programs, it took the perception and courage of the educators, members of the Society of Professional Recreation Educators (SPRE) of the NRPA to establish these new identifying titles, a few of which follow: Southern Connecticut State College, New Haven, Conn.: *Recreation and Leisure Education Department;* San Diego State University, San Diego, Calif.: *Department of Recreation;* Arkansas Polytechnic College, Russelville, Ark.: *Department of Recreation and Park Administration;* Michigan State University, East Lansing, Mich.: *Recreation and Youth Leadership Curriculum;*

Missouri Western State College, St. Joseph, Mo.: *Leisure Management Curriculum;* Springfield College, Springfield, Mass.: *Community and Outdoor Recreation Department;* and the University of Massachusetts at Amherst: *Program in Leisure Studies and Resources.* (which is part of the Department of Landscape Architecture and Regional Planning, College of Food and Natural Resources). The variety continues on dozens of other campuses.

Undergraduate education

There is much agreement that the preparation of professional recreation personnel should include a firm foundation in liberal cultural education. The student should take a variety of courses in the humanities, social sciences, natural sciences, and communication arts. Some 50% of the content of the undergraduate program should be devoted to broad cultural education, 25% to specialized professional education, and 25% to related areas of competency.

The first group includes such subjects as sociology, psychology, mental hygiene, history philosophy, the cultural arts, physiology, anthropology, and government—courses that will help the student gain an understanding of people as individuals and as social beings. The second group, professional specialization, includes leadership techniques, methods of dealing with people, and familiarity with recreation materials.

Presented another way, the student's preparation should include:

1. Understanding of recreation, its nature, development, and significance to our civilization, as well as the nature and scope of the recreation movement.
2. Familiarity with the various program areas, with advanced personal skills in at least two of them; the ability to organize and lead arts and crafts, games and sports, social recreation, dramatics, music, dance, outdoor recreation, hobbies, and other special events.
3. Understanding of methods and procedures needed to organize and administer a recreation program. This would include procedures and topics such as:
   a. Operation of indoor and outdoor recreation centers
   b. Planning, organization, supervision, and evaluation of recreation programs
   c. Recruitment, selection, and training of personnel
   d. Design, selection, installation, and maintenance of playground equipment
   e. Budget preparation and control
   f. Reports and record keeping
   g. Public relations and publicity
   h. Departmental structure, organization, functions
   i. Legal aspects of recreation
   j. Relationships with other agencies engaged in recreation and leisure services
4. Intern experience or professionally supervised field work. This is described in more detail in Chapter 17.

In addition to this rather specialized preparation, it is important that professional personnel have a good background in political action and its implications and in the area of business management and finance. An absence of these constitutes a chronic Achilles heel in many present recreation executives, and this weakness should not be perpetuated in new recreation personnel. The following is a typical undergraduate 4-year curriculum in recreation. It is a composite drawn from several campuses.

DEPARTMENT OF RECREATION EDUCATION
Recreation options

I. Public recreation and park administration option (12 elective hours)

This option is for students interested in supervisory and executive levels of leadership in public park and recreation services departments of cities, towns, villages, and counties.

Suggested courses	*Credits*
Audio-visual education	3
State and local government	3
Principles of public administration	3
Public personnel administration	3
Public financial administration	3
Urban sociology	3
Collective behavior	3
Social control	3
Rural-urban relations	3
The city	3
Government and mass communications	3
Business enterprise	3
Introductory physical geology	3
Introduction to the art of landscaping	3
Elements of forestry	3
Basic landscape composition and	3
conservation of natural resources	3-3
Urban geography	3
Supervision	3
Measurement and evaluation	3

II. Outdoor recreation option (6 required, 6 elective)

Required courses	*Credits*
Recreational use of natural areas	3
Concepts and issues in outdoor recreation	3

Suggested courses	*Credits*
Principles of conservation	3
Field botany and taxonomy	2
Plant ecology	3
Soil and water conservation	3
Introduction to astronomy	3
Introduction to anthropology, archeology, and physical anthropology	3
Introductory entomology	3
Introductory physical geology	3
Descriptive and synoptic meteorology	3
and Cartography and graphics practicum	3-3

Outdoor education workshop	6
and Conservation of natural resources	3-3
The biology of marine and estuarine invertebrates (Prerequisite—1 year of Zoology)	4
Elements of forestry	3

III. Therapeutic recreation option (12 elective hours)

The therapeutic recreation option is designed for those recreation majors gearing their preparation for work with any of the various disability groups.

Suggested courses	*Credits*
Introduction to therapeutic recreation	3
Field laboratory and workshop	1-6
Recreation programming for the aged	3
Problems in therapeutic recreation	3
Avocational choice—theory and information	3
Personality and adjustment	3
Social psychology	3
Introduction to special education	3
Characteristics of exceptional children—mentally retarded	3
Characteristics of exceptional children—gifted	3
Adult health and developmental programs for the aged	3
Children's physical developmental clinic	1-4
Adapted physical education	2
Social problems	3
Criminology	3
Juvenile delinquency	3

IV. Program option

This option is designed for the student who plans a career in programming or who wishes to have a program specialization, i.e., crafts, music, dance, aquatics, drama, physical recreation. These opportunities are developed on an individual basis with the student and the advisor (12 hours— limited to no more than two of above mentioned skill areas).

V. Unspecified

Students who find that their career goals cannot be met through the administration, therapeutic, outdoor, or program options are invited to petition the undergraduate curriculum committee stating their interest in the creation of additional option alternatives, e.g., industrial, armed forces, tourism.

Graduate education

There has been a steady increase in men and women seeking training and studies beyond the 4-year undergraduate level. In 1950, some 18 colleges and universities were providing graduate level study in recreation. By 1977, this number had risen to 84. There are many reasons for this, but according to Hutchinson[3] the prime purposes of graduate education are: (1) to conduct research, (2) to apply research, (3) to develop scholarly leaders, (4) to develop the ability to communicate, and (5) to specialize in a particular area. Doubtless, many students experience the additional pressure for higher level leadership skills and knowledge and for help in coping with the constantly more complex nature of the work. Some additional incentive may be in the form of improved job salary opportunities that follow receipt of graduate degrees. This is, however, far more prevalent in the teaching profession than it is in recreation.

The following is a typical program on the graduate level, leading to a master's degree in recreation and park administration. It is a composite of several of the finest campuses in the country.

MASTER OF SCIENCE DEGREE IN RECREATION AND PARK ADMINISTRATION
Admission requirements

1. Graduation from an accredited college or university with a minimum cumulative grade point average of 2.5.
2. Undergraduate preparation should include
   a. Course work in each of the following: philosophy and history of recreation,

Program planning and delivery systems, Leadership, Facility design and maintenance, Basic supervision and administration, and Introduction to field of therapeutic recreation (valuable to all students, regardless of their specialization)
   b. Supportive course of work in fields directly related to the area of specialization.
   c. At least one basic course in psychology, sociology, political science, or government
   d. Some practical experience in the field
3. Master's degree requirements (36 credits)

Course	Credits
Contemporary issues and Philosophy of recreation and leisure services	3
Programming and delivery systems	3
Facility design and maintenance	3
Legal aspects of recreation	3
Management, finance, and advanced administration	3
Research and evaluative procedures	3
Concentration area—field of specialization	3
Master's thesis	3
Electives to be selected with advice and counsel of department staff, may be selected from any department or curriculum on campus as long as they are relevant to students major and are approved by advisor	12

JOB TITLES

A glossary of job titles in the recreation and recreation-related fields would be long and confusing. Instead, I have grouped or clustered jobs so that the personnel picture may be perceived more clearly. In addition, comments are made on the availability of certain positions and trends regarding that type of position. Salary parameters are also indicated, though this is sometimes a sensitive area.

Many professional writers believe that the inclusion of any salary figures immediately dates a book or study, since salaries seem always to be moving up. Unfortunately, this ostrich-head-in-sand attitude prevents readers from knowing general salary figures and eliminates one of the most critical informational factors in the job and career decision-making process. A further criticism of using salary estimates is sometimes that insufficient study was made or that complete regional and national data is not available. The answer to that criticism must rest in the knowledge, experience, and resources of the writer. Besides having over 200 annual reports from departments, hospitals, and institutions throughout the United States and Canada, I also have recreation salary studies completed by departments in ten states during the past 15 years. Service in recreation agencies and departments in three different states, active participation on national committees and panels on professional salaries, and a large inventory of articles, monographs, and budgets, are some of the additional resources. In 1965, I co-authored a book[5] that includes analysis of current and future salary trends. Thus, there is a substantial base of experience and data when job comments and salary estimates are made. Finally, it is clearly acknowledged that salary figures are provided as reference points only.

Executive level

These are the people who supervise major offices, recreation departments, or recreation divisions in hospitals, military bases, large resorts, prisons, cities, counties, and states. These people receive the glory of success, the brickbats of failure, and the daily wear and tear of being the prime source of direction, motivation, and originality for the department. They personify the "self-starter–leader" phenomenon. Various titles include commissioner of recreation, director of recreation, superintendent of parks and recreation, administrator of leisure services. Titles may also

include deputies, associates, or assistants to the above.

Duties

1. Working with all groups and organizations within the community or the institution.
2. Planning the budget and financial structure of the operation and enforcing same.
3. Recruiting, selecting, supervising, and evaluating the department staff.
4. Design, construction, operation, and maintenance of facilities. (In some instances, the facility aspect of the park and recreation operation is delegated to another agency.)
5. Communication of schedules, ideas, and general public relations program to the public.
6. Representing the department in a wide range of public meetings, appearances, speeches, and community activities.
7. Service as executive secretary or liaison with the citizen board, commission, or other lay body that guides the policy of the department or agency.

Qualifications. Such an executive level person should possess a college degree, preferably with a major in recreation and/or parks administration, physical education, or some substantial combination of social sciences. Also, graduate work of at least 1 year in an accredited university in above or related fields is most helpful. Three to 5 years full-time experience as a management or supervisory person in recreation work should be a minimal requirement. The chief executive should display those dynamic leadership qualities described in Chapter 8 and demonstrate the several capacities needed to serve as prime mover and motivator for the department or agency.

Salary. Executive level personnel of this type generally receive annual salaries as follows:

Large agencies and cities of 500,000 population or more—$35,000 to $55,000

Smaller agencies and municipalities with populations of from 100,000 to 500,000 —$25,000 to $45,000

Smallest units, but professionally based —$20,000 to $35,000

Such positions sometimes include what politicians and executives call "perks," or perquisites. These are the amenities, status symbols, accommodations, or small luxuries that sometimes go with the position, ostensibly as recognition of the pressures and responsibilities borne by the executive. A city car, an automobile provided by the agency, an attractive private office, reasonable allowance for books, professional training and conferences, freedom in the choice of vacation periods and occasional time away from the office, direct access to the board president, the mayor, or the town council—these are among the extra features that make executive level recreation work attractive.

A decade or two ago, many of these executive level positions were filled by untrained, poorly equipped friends of politicians and agency policy makers. These jobs were regarded as rewards for people on the basis of favors owed. Today, although not uniformly so, most agencies and government departments recognize the need for and value of careful recruitment and selection on the basis of qualifications, training, and experience.

Young professionals who aspire to be recreation chief executives should note that most people work hard in these posts, perhaps harder than any member of their staffs. They are driven by the need for accomplishment and a taste for excellence, by

their own creative fires within, and by their simple enjoyment of the work. The executive's role can sometimes be a lonely one, since it is often impossible to convey full details of a problem, condition, or challenge to anyone else, even to a trusted assistant. President Truman memorialized the saying, "The buck stops here," in reference to the isolation and responsibility of the presidential decision-making process. On a smaller scale, but weighty nonetheless, "the buck stops here" for the man or woman who supervises a major recreation operation and daily faces the opportunities and pressures of making important final decisions.

Managerial-supervisory level

These are the professionals who function under the overall direction of the executive. Their role is to interpret orders, accept delegated authority and re-delegate it where necessary, and apply their skills and expertise to getting the major tasks accomplished. Depending on the degree of authority and responsibility, these people sometimes exercise substantial control over staff and programs below them. In this category are titles such as supervisor of music, community center director, director of recreation for a single ward or wing of a hospital, program coordinator, supervisor of cultural activities, ice rink manager, golf course manager, and supervisor of athletics.

Duties

1. Operation of one or more specific facilities such as ice skating rink, swimming pool complex, community center, etc.
2. Direct assignment and supervision of recreation leadership and maintenance personnel.
3. Distribution and processing of administrative forms such as vacation

lists, time sheets, accident reports, inventories, sick reports, program reports, etc.

4. Coordination of one specific program activity or speciality, such as drama, music, or crafts.
5. Administration of programs and activities in one geographic area of a city, town, or county.
6. Supervision, training, and evaluation of subordinate personnel.
7. Representing the department or agency in one specific geographic area.

Qualifications. Recreation supervisors/managers should have a good knowledge of recreation theory, history, and practice; community organization; and supervisory techniques. These people must have the capacity for coordinating large numbers of subordinates so that morale and productivity both remain high. A bachelor's degree from a recognized college or university with a major in recreation, physical education, or a substantial combination of social sciences is most important. Experience of at least 2 years in a strong leadership or supervisory role is basic to the development of an effective recreation supervisor or manager.

Salary. Salaries for middle management and supervisory persons range from $18,000 to $30,000 annually, depending on the size of the municipality or agency. If a military analogy were used and executive level recreation positions represent field grade and general officers (majors, colonels, and generals), the managerial-supervisory recreation positions may be likened to company-grade commissioned officers (lieutenants and captains). Higher ranks of noncommissioned officers (sergeants) would represent long-term, veteran members of the recreation profession, people who may have few academic credentials but much service, experience, and dedication. Such people develop strong rapport with lower-ranking staff members and with the public. They are the sturdiest cushion against the frequent commissioner or director changes at the top. Often, this middle management core of dedicated supervisors, center directors, area coordinators, and assistant directors are the primary links that bind past, present, and future in a department searching for continuity of philosophy and program. This has been particularly true in older, big city departments such as Philadelphia, New York, Detroit, Baltimore, Boston, Los Angeles, and Washington, D.C. *The New York Times* once called these people the "Depression Virtuosi," since many of them entered the field at the bottom personnel steps during the lean years of the 1930s and the early 1940s. The same article deplored the passing of this group of hard-working, long-term civil servants, many of them retiring with 30 to 40 years of municipal service. Because of changing cultures and a modern casual attitude toward job-hopping, this group may never be replaced.

Leader positions

Recreation leaders are the front-line positions of the profession, the people who meet the public in direct contact. They show how to paint, set the key for singing, hold the hand of the beginning ice skater, call the directions in a square dance, signal the turns on a bicycle convoy, and supervise the banking of fires at a wilderness campsite. The leader is what the entire personnel structure is all about. There is a beautiful simplicity about the role of leaders—they reach out, touch the participants, and gently guide them in the direction of action, experience, learning, and satisfaction. Formally, the leader has responsibility for planning, organizing, and directing a specific event, program, sport, or a piece of a large structure such as a community center or an institutional plant.

Duties

1. Planning, organizing, promoting, and conducting specific recreation activities and events.
2. Assigning and supervising subordinate personnel on occasion.
3. Maintaining records of attendance, petty cash, accidents, etc.
4. Aiding in the preparation of basic publicity and communications.
5. Serving as sports officials when required.
6. Encouraging groups and individuals to participate in recreation activities.

Qualifications. Leaders need an elementary knowledge of recreation theory and practice; community organization; people motivation and leadership; first aid, sports, games, and recreation skills and details for teaching these; and a broad and warm sensitivity for people and their needs. A 4-year undergraduate program and bachelor's degree in recreation, physical education, or a closely related field are most desirable, but not always possible. More realistically, requirements should be an associate degree (2 years) in recreation plus at least 1 year's paid experience in the field. Because of the tremendous breadth of skills, interests, and special characteristics sought in recreation leaders, broad recruiting latitude should be given here so that talented and dedicated people are not lost as a result of the application of too stringent, too exclusive standards.

Many departments and agencies divide this category into Senior Recreation Leader and Junior Recreation Leader or, in larger departments, Leader I, Leader II, Leader III, Leader IV, etc. This is simply an internal classifying of the general title to provide entrance level positions and a promotional progression of higher ranks with higher salaries and greater responsibilities.

Salary. Salaries for recreation leaders range from a beginning of $8000 to $16,000 for veterans of 20 years or longer. Salaries in this title are generally higher in municipal recreation than in private agency or institutional recreation.

Activity specialist

This is the professional or technical expert whose skills and experience are extremely high in one specific area or category. Distinguished from general recreation leaders who usually have a broad leadership skill coupled with two or more areas in which they are reasonably familiar, the specialist is typically knowledgeable in one activity. Often the skill area is comparatively rare. Because of this, it exposes some remarkable personalities coming from unusual sources. Thus, we have the bank vice-president who loves to teach advanced water skiing or the clergyman who is an expert instructor in all forms of pottery-making and draws great satisfaction from his classes. The specialist position involves the teaching or conduct of an activity with considerable latitude as to method, site, and materials. The position may require the actual conduct of the activity, or it may consist of organization and initiation of activity groups and the instruction of their recreation leaders.

Duties

1. Planning and conducting programs in arts and crafts, music, drama, dance, aquatics, nature, social recreation, sports, and games.
2. Arranging and directing sports clinics.
3. Teaching musical instruments, folk and square dancing, producing complete plays, operettas, pageants, etc.

Qualifications. Degrees and special schooling are irrelevant here except as they pertain to the specific program or skill area. A deep, thorough knowledge of every aspect of the activity or skill area is essential. Locating books and supplies, a wealth of history and related lore, a group of talented aides to assist the operation, appropriate public relations, and other fine points of the special activity are what make a specialist so valuable and so effective in a recreation program.

Salary. Full-time activity specialists receive modest annual salaries in the range of $15,000 to $30,000 when they remain with an agency or recreation department for some 10 years or longer. Actually, however, more can be accomplished by the agency through the strategic use of several top quality part-time activity specialists. The per-hour or per-session salaries of these part-time people range widely because of the informal nature of recruitment. Nevertheless, most specialists identified with any one very popular activity or skill will earn hourly rates of from $7.00 to $25.00. Obviously, the more numerous the working hours, the lower the hourly rate. However, it is not unusual for a sought-after operetta coach or an outstanding square dance caller to receive $100.00 for a 3-hour evening session. In addition, the specialist may ask that at least one additional 3-hour work session be added to the weekly time sheet to accommodate time spent at home or in the library reading and preparing for the scheduled assignment. In view of the high skill demonstrated by such people and the fact that their work hours in this area bring no fringe benefits or permanent employment status, it is not surprising that their hourly rates are high.

Trainee positions

Trainee level positions include interns (see Chapter 17) and a variety of field work arrangements with high schools and colleges. These are usually broken schedules, that is, certain hours 1 or 2 days per week, certain evenings and weekends, or 8- to 12-week long sessions of 40 hours per week. Salary arrangements vary with the department or agency, the hours involved, and the acedemic level of the trainee. Productive work is often the result of such arrangements, but it is unfair to the trainee or intern to place productivity and work performance in the highest priority. The intern's or trainee's orientation, experience, and growth should be the prime concern, with the work as a low second priority.

Part-time leader positions

The leader position described earlier applied to full-time, professionally oriented persons, people who regard their recreation position as their first and major job and source of income. For budgetary reasons, departments and agencies are limited in the number of such full-time leaders they can afford. Moreover, in today's highly unionized labor structure, such full-time workers are usually limited to 35- to 40-hour work weeks and, except in emergencies, have a right to refuse extra duty, even at high overtime pay rates.

To augment expanding programs at a reasonable cost, there is the resource called the part-time or seasonal leader. These people, whose qualifications and credentials may vary widely, are selected for their great interest in certain specific skill areas, their practical experience, personality, and, above-all, their demonstrated ability as on-the-spot leaders. This leadership pool includes such diverse people as housewives, unemployed plumbers or electricians, military personnel on leave, clergymen, college students, school teachers, and off-duty police officers. These part-time recreation leaders, working at hourly rates ranging from $3.00 to $15.00, serve as bowling instructors, roller skate attendants, teen center leaders, lifeguards, archery instructors, basketball officials, parking attendants, and disc jockeys.

It is important to note that some of the positions and lines of work may suggest a routine not including actual leadership, e.g., lifeguard and parking attendant. But experience has taught that a recreation operation benefits greatly when all those contacting the public are "leadership oriented." Many instances occur when the seemingly unimportant job of parking attendant becomes pivotal in solving a problem or a threatening situation. For example, a busload of teenagers arrives at the site of a major recreational event. Only the parking attendant is present to find the visiting person in charge, park the bus conveniently, send for local contact people, and direct or lead the group to the right location. As another illustration, a lifeguard, trained for safety and lifesaving techniques, is suddenly confronted with a fist fight among a group of teenagers on the crowded beach. The lifeguard's alertness and appropriate action can do much to defuse this potentially explosive situation. My experience confirms that good training and careful selection of part-time leaders is a wise investment in safety, better programming, and effective public relations.

Auxiliary personnel

In addition to executive, middle management, supervisory, and leadership personnel, a recreation operation requires certain staff people whose jobs at first do not identify directly with recreation and leisure services. These are the office receptionists, typists, stenographers, file clerks, and telephone operators. At the warehouse or large centers, they may include shipping and receiving clerks, gardeners, janitors, painters, carpenters, truck drivers, bus opera-

tors, motor mechanics, and gasoline dispensers.

On the professional level, larger departments and agencies may also include staff attorneys, planners, medical doctors, horticultural experts, public relations consultants, and chiefs of security. These people, for the most part, have achieved their titles and professional status in jurisdictions or spheres outside recreation and have later joined the staff of the recreation organization. They are extremely important as staff advisors and in-house consultants to the recreational chief executive in matters of advertising, personnel, union negotiations, budget preparation, facility design, land acquisition, lawsuits, and the occasional socio-political confrontation.

Apprentice personnel

This term refers to persons in junior and senior high school who serve as nonsalaried aides and assistants. In this era of emphasis on the importance of "earning a living" and the anticipated high cost of college, this type of help is difficult to obtain. People do not seek out recreation department offices, hospitals, prisons, YMCAs, or mental institutions so that they may serve without pay. Even conventional advertisements in newspapers and on the radio underscoring the "development qualities, satisfaction, and psychic rewards" of the work may bring only a mere trickle of inquiries.

Nevertheless, such people do exist and in substantial numbers, and proper methods can bring them forth. One of the most effective techniques is for the recreation executive to address junior and senior high school assemblies and clubs. Since such audiences are often large and restless, it is important that such presentations be kept crisp, lively, interesting, and brief. The use of films, slides and other demonstration items is most helpful, but the most effective device is including two or three young people of the same age as the audience in the presentation. If the assistants come from within the specific school population, all the better. In the few minutes that their attention is captive, a positive and exciting message should be put forward in the student's language:

1. The deep social significance of wholesome recreation in today's culture.
2. The need for young persons as leaders, and why they are, in some ways, more effective than older persons.
3. The honest facts about the lack of paying jobs for people under 18 years of age.
4. The fun, excitement, challenge, and warm satisfaction that come from recreation service.
5. The distinct possibility that apprentices of today *may* be paid staff members 3 years from now. Emphasis must be placed on the conditional *may*.

Volunteer personnel

Volunteers are extremely valuable to the recreation movement, yet some professionals characteristically underestimate them or ignore them completely. During research, I scanned a full dozen of the finest texts on professional recreation administration, and only three paid more than passing attention to volunteers.

Butler[1] says:

Volunteer service has played an important role in the development of community recreation . . . . many present-day public recreation departments grew out of the work of the voluntary playground or recreation association which sprang up in the 1890's or later . . . . During World War II the volunteer really came into his own. It was demonstrated that volunteers will work long and hard when they feel they are needed and when they are given interesting work along with training that increases their confidence in their own abilities.

Meyer and Brightbill[6] say:

The organized recreation movement began with volunteer leadership. Most public recreation systems are the results of volunteer organizations and efforts. Private interests have prospered in proportion to volunteer contributions and services. Today, and for a long time to come, the volunteer will have a significant place in the recreation pattern of the United States in both public and private programs.

Kraus and Curtis[4] say :

The real potential of volunteer leadership in recreation work has yet to be explored. Many recreation and park executives take the position, "Volunteers are okay, but they take too much of my time, and they're not reliable." In truth, few executives give sufficient attention to the screening, training, and supervision of volunteer workers, and thus their success or failure is left largely to chance.

Volunteers bring to a program a dedication, a sincerity, a singleness of purpose beyond that of the finest professional. The professional is, after all, doing a salaried job, however well, while the volunteer is there primarily because he or she wishes to give, to serve, to help. Actually, the two functions, paid and volunteer, are different and defy direct comparison. They are both at their best when they work cooperatively with each other.

The vastness and complexity of recreation operations is such that scores of productive openings and jobs exist for the volunteers. Fitzgerald[2] points out a few major areas for volunteers:

1. Agency and board members
2. Special activity leaders
3. Club leaders
4. Campaign solicitors
5. Agency committee members

6. Community and neighborhood advisory committee members
7. Study and survey team members
8. Athletic coaches and managers
9. Sports officials
10. In-service training staff members
11. Clerical staff members
12. Consultants on technical matters

Based on experience with volunteers in many settings, the following could be added: contest judges, track meet personnel, cooks and bakers, costume makers, parade participants, teen center chaperones, ice skating instructors, sign painters, dramatic coaches, music leaders, special event organizers, home-party hosts/hostesses, and dozens of others. The list is endless, and it is a tragedy that otherwise talented professionals do not make more use of the skills and generosity of these fine people.

As in everything human, use of volunteers is not without some psychological and administrative problems. By its nature, the system is fluid and changeable, and the professional supervisor or administrator must be prepared. A few of the problems are:

1. Volunteers have their own lives, and many have paid jobs. This may sometimes interfere with their volunteer duties.
2. Some volunteers enter service with great enthusiasm but after awhile, this enthusiasm may turn to boredom.
3. Training is needed, but training is difficult when people are volunteers and work on varied schedules.
4. Once in the program, a militant or antagonistic volunteer leader is difficult to remove.
5. Sometimes a clash arises between a volunteer and a professional leader working in the same program. Both may be intolerant of the other's position.

All these problems can be solved, however, with care, sensitivity, and intelligence. Despite these disadvantages, the proper use of volunteer personnel is one mark of a bright and effective recreation administrator. To accomplish the most in working with volunteers, trained recreation leaders should do the following:

1. Announce clearly and broadly exactly the type of volunteers and talents that are invited and what their definite duties and working conditions will be.
2. Screen them carefully and sensitively, directing likely candidates into the proper sectors and courteously turning away those who present obvious personality or leadership problems.
3. Provide as much informal, realistic training as possible.
4. Repeat specific assignments and desired goals when volunteers are actually put to work.
5. Supervise and assist them adequately and helpfully.
6. Evaluate their service and reward them appropriately. Recognition for services rendered is one of the surest ways of thanking volunteers and a fairly good guarantee they will return for future service.

In a department that can afford it, a sound investment is to assign one capable staff person to work regularly and fully on the recruitment, training, and supervision of volunteer personnel. It is one of the least developed assets in most recreation departments and agencies.

PERSONNEL POLICIES

The establishment of sound personnel policies is vital to accomplishing important goals in the delivery of park and recreation services. A personnel policy is a broad but clearly written statement, enunciating to all who read or hear it the agency's, hospital's, or department's position on some major issue or administrative process relating to personnel and recreation. A few examples would be:

Policy: All professional staff shall be employed solely on the basis of training, experience, and academic qualifications.

Policy: Professional and paraprofessional personnel shall be required to reside within the limits of this city.

Policy: The Director of Recreation is the chief executive of the Recreation Department, and all administrative direction and decisions shall emanate from his/her office.

Naturally, the administrative structure of the agency or department involved governs to a great extent the manner in which personnel policies and procedures are developed. In some instances, the recreation departments perform personnel functions independently of the local city council or central personnel agency and in so doing have wider latitude in establishing and filling recreation positions, fixing salaries and conditions of employment, and performing other personnel activities. Some private agencies (large camps, prisons, hospitals) may have split or multiheaded organizational structures that result in two, three, or even more personnel policy tracks. Needless to say, this multitracking makes personnel policy difficult, and frequent contradictions or misunderstandings may arise.

RECRUITMENT AND PROMOTION

The National Recreation and Park Association, the National Therapeutic Recreation Society, the National Industrial Recreation Association, and others offer excellent channels for announcing openings and recruiting professional personnel. In addition, the services of the local, municipal, county, and state civil service agencies should be used so that the finest type of pro-

fessional talent available will be drawn into the procedure. Announcements for such positions should include: (1) title of position and department or agency, (2) specific and general duties, (3) educational and experience qualifications, (4) salary, (5) fringe benefits, (6) residence requirements, if any, (7) locations where applications are available and where they should be filed, and (8) final date for filing.

Promotion policies must be based on merit and a series of examinations or self-preparation steps, or the morale and loyalty of the department or agency will suffer. Despite the fact that an occasional worker will sometimes get ahead or obtain a choice post through friendship, nepotism, or an illicit exchange of gifts, these negative exceptions are very few compared with the great majority of workers who fully expect to be promoted on the basis of merit and performance. The wise recreation administrator will establish a firm and reliable reputation for honest and consistent personnel practices, including work evaluation, testing, and promotion based on performance. Once such a reputation is sullied by a preferential or prejudicial promotion or favor, it is almost impossible to have it fully restored again in the eyes of the staff.

OPERATING MANUAL

The soundest administrative device for communicating to all staff the basic policies, procedures, rules, and regulations of the department is the administrative manual, or manual of rules and regulations. This should be carefully researched and prepared by top personnel within the agency or department or by highly qualified experts brought in from the outside. The manual should include: (1) policies and objectives of the departments, (2) working schedules and in-out procedures, lateness, etc., (3) vacation arrangements, (4) illness procedures, medical follow-through, (5) emergency procedures in office, out of office, during trip to work, etc., (6) procedures on fringe benefits such as pension, Social Security, insurance, medical protection, etc., and (7) accident compensation forms and procedures.

The manual should, of course, contain a great deal of additional information on various services and functions of the department such as operation of activity programs, attendance sheets, supply room rules, use of motor vehicles, etc. However, experience has proved that new recreation employees are much more at ease and enthusiastic in their new position when the employer appears *most* concerned about their early personal needs. This is one of the best ways to convince new workers that they have joined a department, city, or agency that cares about them and one of the most reliable methods for early establishment of professional loyalty.

UNIONS

Unionism in the public service has been growing rapidly. Public and agency recreation personnel long ago became heavily unionized. There are two main reasons for this. First, government on its own has enacted legislation authorizing its workers to unionize. President Kennedy gave unionism in the federal service a boost in 1963 when he issued Executive Order No. 10988, which recognized the right of employees to organize, to be formally recognized for the purpose of collective bargaining, and to have a dues checkoff system from government pay checks. State legislation is still very spotty and inconsistent. However, the trend toward greater recognition of unions in the public service is clear.

Secondly, employees themselves, seeing the gains attributed to unionism in private industry, have demanded the right to organize and bargain. Frequently, a union may develop because of unfair labor practices, practices that the administrator may be unable to correct because of political meddling, unsympathetic ears, or tax burdens. Whenever government wages and working conditions fall far behind those found in private industry, the situation is ready for organizing. When one recalls the 50- to 55-hour weeks of recreation workers in the 1930s and 1940s, 2-week vacations after 10 years' service, and no compensation when injured on duty, it is not difficult to see why unionism has advanced.

The professional worker in recreation joins a union for the same reasons as does a blue-collar worker or dock laborer—for better pay and improved working conditions. The trend toward unionization has brought advantages and disadvantages to the recreation movement. The recreation administrator who has not yet become involved with unions, grievances, delegates, stewards, negotiated agreements, and job actions is an administrator who has some sharp training and rough conditioning ahead. However, if such administrators have developed clear and fair personnel policies, if they are aware of personal safety factors affecting their staffs, and if they have established channels for the resolution of grievances, their future union problems may not be insurmountable. Still, they can be almost certain that those union problems and negotiations will be time-consuming and will require substantial effort.

PERSONNEL MOTIVATION

Many recreation administrators become deeply absorbed in their jobs and fail to recognize that, to most staff personnel, their jobs are not the most important thing in their lives. True, fringe benefits do help improve employee performance, morale, and add to the spirit of a hospital team or department. Their importance, however, is outweighed by other less tangible factors that appear more important in making employees happy and content. Studies prove that management's interest in the worker is still the most important single item in the worker's attitude toward the job.

Workers like to achieve. They want challenges and they enjoy their work when they overcome obstacles. Employees want to be recognized for the work they do. A fine summer playground program, a reduction in vandalism, a commendation by parents— these are real accomplishments in the eye of the workers. They want to be recognized for it by management, by the director of recreation.

Recreation workers like to participate with management in meeting management's problems. They gain satisfaction from being able to share their ideas as to how a job should be done or how a process could be improved to provide more efficient services. This participation process becomes especially important as a motivating factor as agencies grow larger and more impersonal.

Finally, motivation is possible as recreation workers believe they have opportunities for personal growth within the department or agency. These growth opportunities are more effective if they provide advancement with additional responsibility and if they require intellectual ability along with the knowledge. Economic growth alone falls short of carrying this impact.

If recreation administrators give ample opportunities for achievement, recognition, participation, and growth, they will lead staff personnel who can be motivated to the high performance necessary for successful operation. Personnel in recreation, as in all other professions, respond warmly and positively to enlightened and sensitive leadership from superiors; they balk and grumble when they are treated as lackeys or automatons. The golden rule, "Treat others as you would have them treat you," is marvelously appropriate.

DISCUSSION QUESTIONS

1. As the Director of Recreation at a private leisure residence for retired, elderly persons, you are asked to expand your recreation program on a broad scale. At the same time, your budget for the coming year will be increased only $15,000. Explain how you would invest that amount of money in additional personnel and the sources to which you would turn for people.
2. Many recreation agencies find difficulty in convincing middle management staff personnel that they should return to school to improve their skills and knowledge. Specify five advantages accruing to recreation professionals by their returning to school to attain a graduate degree.
3. In larger recreation and park departments, the administrative structure may contain people who carry professional and technical titles that appear to have little or no relationship to recreation. For example, lawyers and librarians. Specify five additional such titles and point out what item or service is provided by each as part of the overall operation.
4. Currently, many men and women who have no formal training in recreation are seeking and getting jobs as recreation leaders and administrators. Give five arguments that justify the employment of recreation-prepared personnel as the most productive policy. Give five arguments favoring open employment with no concern for academic qualifications.
5. Some college campuses are better equipped than others in preparing students for professional work in recreation. What are five attributes that mark an effective recreation education department as compared with a mediocre one?

BIBLIOGRAPHY

Bellows, R.: Creative leadership, Englewood Cliffs, N.J., 1959, Prentice-Hall, Inc.

Doell, C. E.: Elements of park and recreation administration, Minneapolis, 1963, Burgess Publishing Co.

The International City Managers Association: Municipal recreation administration, Chicago, 1960, The Association.

Kraus, R. G.: Recreation and leisure in modern society, New York, 1971, Appleton-Century-Crofts.

Lutzin, S. G., and Storey, E. H.: Managing municipal leisure services, Chicago, 1973, The Association.

McChesney, J. C.: Personnel policies in parks and recreation, National Recreation and Park Association, Management Aid Bulletin No. 63, 1966.

Meyer, H. D., and Brightbill, C. K.: Community recreation, Englewood Cliffs, N.J., 1964, Prentice-Hall, Inc.

National Recreation and Park Association: SPRE—recreation and park education curriculum catalogue, 1976-1977 Biennial directory.

New York State Recreation and Park Society: Personnel standards, rev. ed., New York, 1968, The Society.

Sternloff, R. E., and Warren, R.: Park and recreation maintenance management, Boston, 1977, Holbrook Press Inc.

REFERENCES

1. Butler, G. D.: Introduction to community recreation, New York, 1959, McGraw-Hill Book Co.
2. Fitzgerald, G. B.: Leadership in recreation, New York, 1950, A. S. Barnes & Co.
3. Hutchinson, J.: Recreation **22:**134, March 1956.
4. Kraus, R. G., and Curtis, J. E.: Creative administration in recreation and parks, ed. 2, St. Louis, 1977, The C. V. Mosby Co.
5. Lederer, W. W., and Curtis, J. E.: Personnel standards in community recreation leadership, rev. ed., New York, 1965, National Recreation Association.
6. Meyer, H. D., and Brightbill, C. K.: Recreation administration, Englewood Cliffs, N.J., 1956, Prentice-Hall, Inc.
7. Rodney, L. S.: Administration of public recreation, New York, 1964, The Ronald Press.
8. Stein, T. A.: SPRE—Report on the state of park and recreation education in Canada and the U.S., National Recreation and Park Association, 1977.

10
CHILDREN AND RECREATION

Courtesy White Plains Recreation and Parks Dept., White Plains, N.Y.

Many adults think of recreation only in terms of children's playthings. Often, a well-intended adult committee will instruct the architect to "be sure to design it so the young people will want to use it." All this, despite the fact that the country's population has been aging appreciably during the past 10 years, the birth rate is down, and larger numbers of mature adults are taking advantage of the many recreation facilities and programs now available to them.

Nevertheless, there is a bond between recreation and children that is unique and that should be studied carefully by both professionals and students. The intriguing possibilities for the growth and development of children offered by recreation represent a primary reason for its rapid growth and for the interest shown in recreation by professionals from other fields. Medical doctors, psychiatrists, psychologists, clinicians, exercise physiologists, teachers, and guidance counselors are some of the experts who have studied recreation and the ways children enter and perform within it.

No other setting presents a child so clearly and so completely at ease as does recreation. A delight for the clinician, the child aroused, the child energized, the child reaching out hungrily for experience and sensation—these are triggered in recreational settings. The following sample situations should help to illustrate that valuable link between children and recreation.

Situation A

It is a warm, sultry, summer evening. In the run-down playground of an inner-city school a group of boys is playing basketball. The court is littered with broken glass and garbage. Not far off, another group of boys watches. They have no ball and they call out to the other boys for a turn to play, but they are ignored. Listlessly, they begin to taunt the boys who have the ball, throwing cans and insults at them. Soon a fist fight has broken out.

Situation B

At two o'clock each Wednesday afternoon a certain public elementary school's fifth graders have physical education class. Referred to as "gym," the class is 30 minutes long and replaces recess for that afternoon. The school employs only one certified physical education teacher who must supervise three classes at the same time. As a result, the class is led by a person unskilled in physical education techniques who tosses the children a ball and suggests they play kickball. When teams are finally selected, only 20 minutes remain in the class period.

Situation C

The grandstands are filled to overflowing. It is the bottom of the ninth inning, and the Midget Yankees and the Midget Dodgers are tied 5 to 5. Both teams have been previously undefeated, and the winning team today will be the Midget World Series champs. Parents and coaches are shouting. The players on the Yankee bench sit tense, eyes riveted on the play. One small boy stands up, knees shaky, and walks to home plate. He knows the Yanks have two outs and a failure to bring home the man on third will give the Dodgers an opportunity to win. His face is sweaty and his stomach so nervous he feels sick.

Situation D

A group of high school students stands on the street corner in front of their favorite deli. School has just let out and they don't want to go straight home. They are bored. Some drink Cokes and some smoke cigarettes, while others just drape themselves across the store fronts wondering what to do for excitement. Someone suggests going to the movies, but without a car that is impossible. Finally, for lack of a better plan, they return to the school yard for more hanging around, looking for an outlet.

The above four situations are real. Each was taken from a particular observation by me, but all, unfortunately, are commonplace. The first occurred in a disadvantaged neighborhood in Cambridge, Massachusetts. It might have occurred in any underprivileged neighborhood lacking recreational facilities and leadership. The second situation describes a public school in an affluent city in suburban Westchester, New York. The school is typical in that its physical education programs are sharply limited and understaffed, a common administrative problem today. The third situation is characteristic of virtually every community where Little League programs have become popular. It occurs when the real goal of sports for children is replaced by the vicarious and aggressive competitiveness of adults. Winning becomes everything and losing becomes a humiliation. This can leave deep emotional scars on sensitive children. The final situation is perhaps the most harmful to all. Boredom can lead teenagers to do many potentially dangerous things and make them a threat to society and to themselves.

The common thread connecting these situations is the frequently deplorable state of children's recreation programs. The important changes needed here are both attitudinal and administrative. By focusing on the emotional, physical, and social needs of children, we may formulate comprehensive programs that help develop their physical and emotional muscles. At the same time we will be benefitting society by adding to its population of healthy, active people and diminishing the stresses that lead to drug abuse, teenage alcoholism, gang violence, vandalism, unwanted pregnancies, and suicides. One has but to scan the problems of today's youth to appreciate the staggering need for healthful recreation as a major aid in reducing juvenile deterioration.

The boxed material briefly outlines the developmental stages for the child, 4 to 13 years of age. The more complex needs of the special child are discussed later. Some of the more important points should be noted. First, psychological changes are given equal importance with physical developments. This was a fact often over-looked by physical education and recreation institutions in the past who mistakenly thought that it was possible to fully develop the body while ignoring the mind. However, in recent years, with such mentally disciplined fitness experts as the Eastern martial artists, transcendental meditation proponents, yoga practitioners, and others influencing our somewhat one-sided Western view of physical conditioning, this is changing.

Today, millions of Americans meditate, experiment with yoga and mind control, and do psychic healing and a host of activities to put themselves in harmony or touch with their bodies. Rather than merely exercising the body, experts now say you must know and understand it too. "Learn to listen to your body," they say. "Know when it's tired, what muscles need exercise, what it's hungry for, when to stop eating. Be conscious of everything from your posture to your blood pressure, and you cannot help but improve your health."

This is a marvelous change in attitude. It is especially significant regarding the curriculum of children's physical education and recreation programs. Along with activities to teach skills and coordination, children require instruction in basic physiology and anatomy. They must learn what their bodies need and how to maximize the benefits of good nutrition and healthy exercise.

In summary physical education and recreation must be a broad experience. It must encompass thorough understanding of both mind and body. Further, it must incorporate respect and pride in that wondrous and beautiful machine, the human body.

COMPETITION

Social psychologists describe two basic ways in which group members define their relationship to a situation from which they

Text continued on p. 157.

Summary of growth and development characteristics and implications for physical activity

Preschool, grades 1 and 2

Characteristics	Needs	Types of experience
Spurt of growth of muscle mass	Vigorous exercise requiring use of large muscles	Running, chasing, fleeing type games; hanging, climbing, supportive type exercises
Gross movement skills becoming more refined	Exploration and variations of gross motor skills; opportunities to refine skills	Self-testing activities of all types; dance activities and movement tasks
Manipulative skills still unrefined, but improving; will catch ball with body and arms more so than with hands	Opportunities to manipulate large or medium-sized objects; throw small balls	Ball-handling activities; work with beanbags, wands, hoops, progressing from large to smaller objects
Imaginative, imitative, curious	Opportunity for expression of ideas and use of body	Creative dance, story plays, creative stunt and floor work; exploration with all basic skills and small equipment
Very active, great deal of energy	Ample opportunities for vigorous play, particularly at the onset of the physical education period, recess needed in other half of day	Running games, stunts, large apparatus; more locomotor work than nonlocomotor activities
Short attention span	Activities that take short explanation and to which some finish can be reached quickly; frequent change in activities or tasks	Simple games, simple class organization so activities can be changed quickly; conversations in movement
Individualistic or ego-centric	Needs experiences to learn to share or become interested in others; engage in parallel play alongside of other children rather than with them	Much small group work, self-testing activities, exploration of movement factors

Continued.

Summary of growth and development characteristics and implications for physical activity—cont'd

Grades 3 and 4

Gross motor patterns more refined and graceful	Use of skill for specific purposes	Introduction to specific sport skills; in expressive style skill utilized in dance; traditional dance steps
Hand-eye coordination improved; growth in manipulative skills	Opportunities to handle smaller objects; more importance placed on accuracy; throw at moving targets	Ball-handling activities; use of bats, paddles, target games
Sees need to practice skills for improvement of skill and to gain social status	Guided practice sessions, self-testing problem situations	Drills, skill drill games, self-testing practice situations; task setting
Balance more highly developed; better body control	Opportunities to work on higher beams, bars; more activities requiring static balance	Large apparatus work, tumbling, stunts
Increased attention span	Activities with continuity, more complex rules, and understandings	Lead-up games to sports, low-organized games with more complex rules and strategy
More socially mature, interested in welfare of group	Make a contribution to a large or small group, remain with one group for a longer period, help make and accept decisions with a group	Team activities, dance compositions with small groups
Greater sex differences in skills; some antagonism toward opposite sex (grade 4)	Ability grouping	Combative-type stunts; folk dance; afterschool activities for grade 4
Great interest in proficiency and competitive spirit (particularly boys) may drive to fatigue	Recognition of symptoms of fatigue and place of rest, relaxation, and moderation in competition	Self-testing activities; relaxation techniques; interval training with developmental exercises
Spirit of adventure high	Activities requiring courage; adventure, initiative; recognition of safety factors	Self-testing activities of all types; use of large apparatus; low-organized games demanding courage; creative dance compositions

Summary of growth and development characteristics and implications for physical activity—con'd

Tendency toward poor posture	Understanding of body mechanics; development of endurance and strength	Developmental exercises, vigorous running games, large apparatus, and fitness activities; individually planned program for those below average in posture and fitness
Intellectually curious	Learn mechanical principles of movement, similarities of movement patterns, and physiological principles	Self-testing activities of all types; problem-solving method used in analyzing own skill patterns; creative dance; developmental exercise programs; set own goals

Grades 5 and 6

Coordination highly developed, keen interest in proficiency in skills	Need to learn more difficult skills; more coaching on refinement of skills; use of skills in games, routines, and compositions	Lead-up games to sports in season; instruction and practice in sport skills; more advanced dance step patterns and folk dances; track and field; apparatus routines; intramurals
Greater sex differences in skills, interests; most prefer to play and compete with own sex; boys play more vigorously and rougher than girls	Separation of sexes in classes or within classes for some activities	Coeducational dance; swimming, gymnastics, recreational games; sexes separate in team sports and fitness activities; intramurals for each sex
Good skills and physique important to social acceptance, particularly for boys	Instruction and practice sessions in skills, understanding of fitness elements, understanding of changes in growth and abilities resulting from puberty	Fitness tests; developmental exercises; work with apparatus; classroom discussions and movies about puberty (may be done in cooperation with nurse or parents)

Continued.

Summary of growth and development characteristics and implications for physical activity—cont'd

Grades 5 and 6—cont'd

Group or gang spirit is high; allegiance to group is strong	Need to belong to a group with some stability; make rules, decisions, and abide by group decision; longer term of membership on a squad or team	Team games, tournaments, group dance compositions, gymnastic squads with student leaders, gymnastic meets, track and field meets
Social consciousness of need for rules and abiding by rules; can assume greater responsibility	Participate in setting rules; opportunities for squad captains or leaders	Student officials; plan and conduct tournaments in class and after school; students plan own strategy, line-ups, etc.
Flexibility decreasing	To maintain flexibility within structural limitations	Stunts, tumbling, apparatus, developmental exercises
Muscle growth of boys increasing; most girls in puberty	Interest in maintaining good posture, fitness level; build good attitudes toward activity and proficiency for girls; knowledge of methods of increasing strength and endurance for boys	Apparatus, developmental activities, track and field, more individual and dual activities, intramurals

Grades 7 and 8

Coordination very highly developed; skill level increasing more rapidly for boys than girls; skill level for girls reaches a plateau	Learning more advanced sport skills; opportunities for refinement and use of skills in sports, routines, compositions	Modified team and individual sports, more demanding dance skills and composition work, intramurals for both sexes and individuals
Sexes differ in skills and interests; boys' muscle strength much more than girls'	Separation of sexes in classes sometimes undesirable; male and female teachers for both sexes; sexes brought together for some activities	Team sports for both; recreation in individual sports, volleyball, gymnastics, social, folk, and square dances
Most girls in puberty and some in grade 8 reaching full stature; some boys starting puberty; less sex antagonism; boys' interest in opposite sex increases	Understanding of changes caused by puberty, better understanding of body mechanism	Fitness activities, body mechanics

---

**Summary of growth and development characteristics and implications
for physical activity—cont'd**

Prestige associated with good skills for boys; lack of interest in activity for many girls as a result of cultural influences	Many opportunities for individual coaching and practice of skills; girls need to be encouraged to maintain fitness and an interest in activity	Much game play and individual coaching in class and in intramurals; interest clubs
Intellectually very capable and knowledgable; ability to deal with the abstract	Opportunities for logical reasoning and creative thinking	More emphasis placed on strategy in game play; creative dance composition work; more involved routines in gymnastics; setting own goals; selective programming
Feeling of insecurity, unsure of self in group (particularly grade 7); great desire to be a part of group	Need to have feeling of acceptance by teacher and other members of class; great understanding and patience needed by the teacher (especially in grade 7); children need recognition	Involved in selecting teammates; work in small groups; expected to produce in group work projects; involved planning special events and after-school tournaments and play days; social service projects related to movements; peer teaching

---

get their rewards: cooperation and competition.

If members feel that what one gets, the others must lose, they define the situation as one of competition. However, if they believe that no one will get rewards unless they all work together, the define the situation as one of cooperation. Very often, in a work group, an external authority sets up the way in which pay, recognition, grades, or other forms of reward are distributed among the members. In this case, the members are under strong pressure to define the situation in the way the authority defines it, and cooperation or competition will prevail in the group as determined by the conditions set by authority.[2]

This is the crucial role of recreation leaders. They will set the tone for competitive or cooperative group activity.

In recent years, a new breed of recreation scientist has sprung up. Usually well-acquainted with both physiological and psychological aspects of fitness, these writers and philosophers have expressed the view that preoccupation with winning and defeating our opponents is best left to the Super Bowl, not to children's recreation programs. Foremost among these thinkers is Dr. George Leonard, author of *The Ultimate Athlete* and contributor to *The New Games Book*. Both books take a fresh view of the goals in athletic games. The *The New*

Games Book holds that one must become totally involved with activity, "play hard, and play fair, nobody hurt," but only to reach one's *own* highest potential, not to better one's opponent. Enthusiasts of this idea would like to see an end to most elimination games that relegate the majority of players to idly spectating from the sidelines. The book outlines "new" games, designed to maximize the fun, healthful exercise, release of tension, and growth of communication between participants in creative play.

While this change in recreation attitude is beneficial to all ages, it is especially significant to children. In the past, programs singled out a few "superstars" and either ignored the majority of children or subjected them to great pressure and anxiety for "success." This new philosophy of physical education and recreation will encourage leaders and teachers to concentrate on each individual's complete development and personal fulfillment.

The time has come to move on, to create new games with new rules more in tune with the times, games in which there are no spectators and no second-string players, games for a whole family and a whole day, games in which aggression fades into laughter—new games.[1]

RECREATION PROGRAMMING: BEYOND THE BICEPS

There was a time when community recreation programs for children consisted almost entirely of Little League baseball teams for boys. The only developmental challenge was the mastering of a specific physical skill or learning to play on a team. Girls were virtually ignored in the process.

Today, recreation programming is limited only by the administrator's imagination. Modern programs include the arts, music, drama, and dance. Children benefit greatly from exposure to these art forms as well as from instruction in crafts, quiet games (backgammon and chess), etc. Modern camps include many introductory lessons in these art forms. The fundamentals of dance, basic steps and warmup exercises, graceful movement, and an appreciation of music can be introduced as early as the first grade. As for the dramatic arts, children can be instructed in voice projection and elocution. Shyness can be overcome by a gradual introduction to speaking, singing, and dancing or simply dressing up in funny costumes for a small peer group. Finally, and perhaps most important, is that a love of the fine arts can be cultivated through the child's exposure to them. Recreation programs may include trips to the theater, the opera, and the ballet.

Our most joyous and receptive participants in the field of recreation are our children. The young are imaginative, energetic, and daring. They have the courage to attempt virtually anything and have the potential to participate in countless skills, sports, arts and crafts, and recreational activities. The key word here is *potential*. The child has boundless opportunities for recreational development, but without proper guidance this potential is wasted. The child is like a rough, unmolded slab of clay. In the hands of a professional recreation leader, this clay can be molded into any one of a million beautiful shapes. Through careful instruction, patience, and creative stimulation, the leader can help children reach their recreational potential. Children, 4 to 13 years of age, have particular strengths, problems, and needs peculiar to the recreation setting.

FITNESS FOR CHILDREN

A popular misconception by many adults is that the ability to play is instinctive with all children. While children will usually run and be physically active without too much encouragement, this does not constitute creative play. It does not always maximize the benefits of recreational activity for the child. When guided by a recreation professional or physical education teacher, however, the child's play becomes a developmental experience. The professional leader can develop programs of athletic activities geared specifically to each age group and sex. Once properly taught a happy and satisfying activity, children will practice it ceaselessly in their unsupervised play time. Having mastered a skill, they find play much more rewarding and interesting.

Schurr[3] wrote a book devoted solely to the development of better recreational and physical education programs for young children. She uses scientific and humanistic studies of their physical and mental needs as her basis.

The central purpose of education is to help each child toward becoming a fully functioning self-actualized person. The primary purpose of Physical Education is to contribute to this broader purpose, by helping each child realize his movement potential.

Therefore, it can be reasoned that recreation and physical education must contribute to the skills and awareness necessary to reach one's highest movement potential. Schurr[3] outlines them in her supportive purposes of recreation and physical education:

1. Understand the structure of movement.
2. Move completely and confidently.
3. Communicate feelings through and about movement.
4. Meet and solve new movement demands.
5. Interact with his fellow beings in and through movement.
6. Find personal meaning and significance in movement.

While these goals are of obvious value to all, they are especially significant in children's play. For, as any psychologist or psychiatrist from Sigmund Freud to Benjamin Spock will agree, it is the childhood experiences that have the greatest single effect on adults. A child whose curiosity and imagination have been fed and encouraged will be an eager inquisitive adult. By the same token, children brought up on healthful, vigorous movement will most likely continue these well-established exercise habits throughout their adult life.

The following observations from Schurr's research give a broad picture of the child's physical development. While these developmental factors may vary from child to child, they give an accurate overview of children's growth and their corresponding physical needs. A thorough understanding of these needs is essential to ensure the development of comprehensive and complete recreation and physical education programs.

In addition to the arts, the complete recreation program also includes social events. Children need places to congregate, to visit with friends, and to get to know the opposite sex. From the sixth grade on, it is especially important to have recreation centers for teens and adolescents to meet, talk, laugh, dance, and learn how to "interact" with each other.

Some activities that bring children together are ice skating, skiing, and trips to museums, zoos, and major athletic competitions such as tennis tournaments and basketball and baseball games. These trips are particularly convenient in large urban city areas, many such major events happening almost every day of the year. Most sports organizations offer discounted group rates on tickets, and appreciate the publicity of a large group attending. Transportation is as simple as renting a bus or starting a car pool.

The important things to remember are to:

(1) select an activity geared to the age group attending, (2) provide adequate chaperones for the group, (3) make certain each child has parental permission to attend the activity, and (4) remember that the opportunity for the children to socialize is as important as the activity itself. Give them time to talk to each other, perhaps by meeting somewhere after the scheduled activity is over.

Besides trips, a complete recreation program for teenagers and adolescents should include dances, games, and other activities held in the same central meeting place, be it a school, church, YMCA building, or synagogue. These buildings are good for recreation centers and teen centers because of their size and easy accessibility. In summer, a city's parks and outdoor facilities can be the site of concerts, dances, and other outdoor teen activities with the needs of children in mind.

The key to successful social programming for children is to know the community well. Know what is needed (facilities, activities, supervision, and instruction). Know what is available (the community may have many resources not widely known). Know what the community's youth wants. This knowledge will enable the programming of exciting, diverse activities, including "something for everyone." Finally, one should not be discouraged if an activity is at first not popular. Sometimes, it is impossible to anticipate children's likes and dislikes. One can only learn from mistakes and modify the program accordingly.

Teaching goals in these social and artistic programs are much the same as in physical education and recreation programs. Development of the individual is of the utmost importance, as is the gaining of self-confidence and physical and mental competence. For the adolescent and teenager, peer group recreation activities should aid in easing interaction between the sexes and in gaining a sense of belonging to a group. Finally, recreation activities keep children constructively active and can help prevent drug use, crime, and other forms of juvenile delinquency.

SPECIAL SITUATIONS: RECREATION FOR THE EXCEPTIONAL CHILD

So far we have discussed the physically and mentally able, the emotionally secure and stable child. We have not mentioned the problems of leadership, teaching, and recreation programming for the exceptional child. The remainder of this chapter will deal specifically with this area of development. According to Schurr, major objectives of recreation and physical education are the same for all children, but she also indicates that children must learn to be "self-directive" in regulating the extent of their participation in activities. Finally, they must acquire knowledge of, and skill in, a variety of games and activities.

In adapting recreation activities to the special child, Schurr uses the following basic criteria:

1. Adaptive does *not* mean giving the child some nonphysical task such as keeping score. It means adapting for participation. In activities calling for a great deal of individual work or self-testing, this is not at all difficult.
   Summary: Emphasize activity.
2. Adaptation has its limits. It cannot be so great that it will interfere with other children's normal progress.
   Summary: Be realistic
3. Sometimes mastering a recreation skill will require extra time at home or with a teacher.
   Summary: Allow for extra time.
4. All other children must understand the child's handicap to a certain degree. This will make them more eager to accept him or her and help out. The child will learn that best effort is rewarded by group support.

Summary: Encourage understanding and support of these children.

In the past, it was believed that special education classes should be separate from the schools and camps for normal children. This thinking no longer prevails. Today, most schools and recreations camps integrate special and normal classes and groups whenever possible. Certain guidelines must be set, but according to Schurr,[3] "Fitness levels and skills will probably be lower for the handicapped than for the so-called normal." She goes on to say that handicapped children, with time, patience, and guidance, can improve their motor skills almost on a par with nonhandicapped children. The problem seems to be in the decision-making mechanism. Because handicapped children do not make their decisions as quickly as other children, they become easily confused in games that require application of rules or quick changes in direction of play. Careful attention should be given to placing these youngsters in settings that do not demand too many decisions until they are more comfortable in and confident of the conduct and direction of the game itself.

The following special situations deal with: (1) the physically handicapped child, (2) the mentally retarded child, (3) the developmentally disabled child, and (4) the emotionally disturbed child.

The physically handicapped child

This category covers all problems from impaired vision or hearing to limited motor control. Schurr makes some useful suggestions for successful recreation fitness programs with special children. First, obtain a full physician's report on the child and his or her limitations. Find out what motor skills the physician recommends that the child work on. Meet with the child's parents to get a picture of their situation and to reassure them of the safety of the recreation program.

When goals have been clearly established, the following is a good basic outline to follow:

1. If locomotion is the problem, emphasize recreation skills requiring little movement.
   Example: The child can bat a softball, but have someone else run the bases.
   Example: The distance of a relay race can be altered; the child need run only half of the conventional distance.
2. If vision is the problem, targets can be made larger, balls thrown more slowly, etc. If a child cannot perform an activity alone, such as throwing the ball, perhaps a partner can help.
3. When hearing is the problem, a partner is also helpful to demonstrate instructions, signal moments of action, etc.

In nonathletic activity, the same basic rules apply. The physically handicapped child may find great delight in arts and crafts, drama, music, working with audiovisual equipment, quiet games such as chess and backgammon, and other nonphysical activities.

A sensitive teacher must be aware of such children's early and frequent fatigue and frustration with active games and provide a balanced diet of quiet recreational occupation. Teaching tips include (1) discouraging individual athletic competition *between* teammates and (2) encouraging team unity.

The mentally retarded child

There are a variety of definitions of mental retardation. Numerical measures vary, ranging from a lower than "average" intelligence quotient ("average" being about 100) to the more profoundly retarded victims of Down's syndrome.

Suggested recreational activities for mentally retarded children include (1) swimming, (2) hiking, (3) nature study, (4) bicycling, (5) fishing, and (6) simple crafts. Here, as with the physically handicapped child, the child's doctor, parents, and other teachers should be consulted.

Aside from physical activities, many other skills including crafts, music, painting, story-telling, and drama can be enjoyed by retarded children and young adults. With patience and individual attention, there is no limit to the progress that can be made in these areas.

Some teaching tips for recreators include (1) use simple instructions, restated often and slowly, (2) allow extra time for mastering each skill, (3) spend as much time as possible with each individual, without penalizing the group, and (4) apply self-evaluation constantly.

The emotionally disturbed child

The problems of the emotionally disturbed child are usually not of a physical nature. They can stem from any traumatic experience and often result in crippling shyness, depression, aggression, or other compulsive behaviors. Primarily, the emotionally disturbed child needs acceptance and encouragement. He or she has lost confidence, self-esteem, and a sense of security. Emotionally disturbed children may demonstrate these emotional problems in several ways.

One demonstration is through extremely aggressive behavior. Much more of a problem with boys than with girls, aggression is believed to be a learned response. Berkowitz believes that aggressiveness is a habit learned through the rewards and punishments life metes out. In studying the child rearing and family relationships of aggressive boys and their more acceptably socialized counterparts, some definite patterns emerge. The hostile boys respect their mothers, but feel rejected by both parents

and are resentful and critical of their fathers. They express aggression in a direct, uninhibited fashion, have fewer positive feelings toward their peers than other boys, and are distrustful and fearful of situations that might force them to become emotionally dependent on others.

Psychiatrists tend to think of aggression as a learned reaction brought on by parental and/or societal rewards and punishments. If children learn to see personal frustration in every nook and cranny of life, then each new frustration will reaffirm their expectation that, for them, things will *always* go wrong. Thus, the following points should be stressed in working with aggressive children in recreation: (1) de-emphasize competition, (2) emphasize personal achievement, and (3) strive for a cooperative mood—show that all people are not against them.

In programming for the aggressive child, the use of *The New Games Book* is highly recommended as a guide in tension relieving. Team games emphasizing unity and cooperation, such as ''Rock-Paper-Scissors,'' ''Knots,'' and ''Siamese Soccer'' are also appropriate. Another tension-easing game is ''Snake-in-the Grass.'' For fast-paced individual competition, there is ''Hug Tag.''

Nonactive, individual activities are extremely important to the calming and reassuring of the very aggressive child. Painting, sculpting, building simple toys, and listening to classical music do not generally trigger disappointments, arguments, and frustrations. Keeping a well-stocked area of quiet playthings will allow the children to browse, select something that interests them and occupy themselves, privately and peacefully.

Another way in which the emotionally disturbed child exhibits emotional disturbance is through depression. Depression is the result of the individual's feelings of failure. Rather than compete and conflict, the individual withdraws from life. Unlike the aggressive child who may seek notice of any kind, the depressed child may wish to disappear completely. The goal of the physical education instructor or recreation leader must be to stimulate new interest in self-activity. It should be remembered that the depressed child easily loses interest in any activity. Therefore, activities with brief explanations and clearly defined goals are best.

Teaching tips include (1) simple explanations and (2) lively, fast-paced recreation activities, with changing situations. The secret to reaching the depressed child is to capture his or her interest. Once taken "out of themselves," depressed children quickly progress to greater involvement in the outside world. A recreation leader is permitted greater emphasis on direct involvement in the activities and games because the child will be very reluctant to begin on his or her own. Starting the child on a group project where he can do his own work with others, such as painting a large mural with other children, building a group campsite, or singing a group song with his mates should work well.

The developmentally disabled child

Developmentally disabled children were once thought to be mentally retarded. As knowledge of learning disabilities increased, it revealed that a "slower child" is often the victim of a disability (such as dyslexia), that conceals his or her otherwise normal I.Q. Such sensorimotor disorders can affect any one of the child's main areas of development: motor, symbolic, social, and numerical.

Since such disorders can seriously hamper the child's potential for both academic and physical progress and will probably not be evident until the child is compared with others of the same age, recreation leaders must be constantly alert for any signs of developmental disabilities. Schurr[3] cites the following problems.

Problems in balance

Activities. Walk on a line painted on the floor. Walk forward, backward, and sideward on a low balance beam. Stand on one foot for 10 seconds. Balance on a rocker board.

Suspicious behavior. Failure to maintain balance. Consistent use of only one arm or one side to regulate body weight or inconsistent use of arms in symmetrical fashion. Need to run or walk very fast to maintain balance. Hesitance or need to look backward to maintain balance. Hesitance and trouble in shifting direction. Hesitance in sideward walking. Child attempts to cross over with trailing foot when going to the right or left foot when going to the left. Behavior such as this indicates a general lack of postural control and flexibility, lack of sense of laterality, and poor spatial orientation.

Problems in laterality and rhythm

Activities. Jump on one foot, then on alternating feet. Do same, in hopping position. Skip. Hop in pattern of right-right-left, left-left-right, left-left-right-right.

Suspicious behavior. Inability to shift weight to maintain balance when jumping or hopping on one foot; difficulty in using feet alternately; difficulty in maintaining rhythm or flow of pattern in hopping. Behavior such as this indicates a general lack of body control and coordination, poor sense of laterality, inability to alternate movements across the midline, or poor control of rhythm or flow of movement.

Problems of body image

Activities. Play "Simon Says," a game in which the leader directs the group to touch different parts of their bodies or use different parts of their bodies to do something. Play "Mirror Game," in which leader moves various limbs in various combinations but gives no verbal command. Followers must imitate the movements of the leader.

Suspicious behavior. Errors or slowness in response to touching and using the correct body parts; hesitance in movements; confusion in matching leader's movements; use of wrong limbs or matching behavior of opposite limbs; reverses patterns of leader. Behavior such as this indicates a lack of awareness of location of body parts, a lack of coordination and control of body parts, a poor sense of laterality, and a poor idea of body image.

Problems in eye control, hand-eye, foot-eye coordination

Activities. Using a tether ball attached to the end of a rope suspended from the ceiling, child should follow the ball with his or her eyes as it swings across in front, backward and forward, and in a circle. The child should reach out and touch the ball; hit the ball with a hand; hit the ball with a large paddle; catch objects of various sizes from varying distances; kick a stationary ball, a moving ball. Set up a pattern of squares painted on the floor or newspapers arranged on the floor in an irregular pattern so that the child must use varying lengths of steps and alternate feet to step on squares as he or she progresses around the room.

Suspicious behavior. Difficulty in keeping eyes on ball as it crosses midline of body; moves head instead of eyes. Inability to touch or hit the ball as it moves; difficulty in catching ball; reaching out for ball and moving head back; closing eyes as ball reaches child; hesitance in deciding which foot to use to step on square; always trying to use the same foot; trouble adjusting length of step to varying distances between squares. Behavior such as this may indicate

a malfunction of the muscular system of the eye or a lack of coordination with the perception and motor action. The former must be treated by a physician. If the latter is the case, a lack of sense of laterality, directionality, and spatial orientation is indicated.

Problems in spatial orientation

Activities. Set up a low hurdle or use a low table (or another person on hands and knees). Have child go over and under the obstacle; pass between two objects placed close together. Tell the child to throw to and at a large stationary object; throw to and at a moving object; run and throw a ball up in the air and catch it.

Suspicious behavior. Inability or difficulty in estimating height of obstacle and size of step needed to clear it; difficulty in judging amount of space and necessary body adaptations needed to go under the obstacle or through a narrow space; difficulty in judging distance target is from self; difficulty in judging how far ahead of person ball must be thrown so ball and person will meet (this is a difficult task for a young child); difficulty in judging where ball is in space while one is moving. Behavior such as this indicates that a child has problems of awareness as to body parts in space and of body in relation to other objects in space.

Since these problems are often newly detected by the physical education teacher or recreation instructor, the first step after detection should be referral to a medical specialist. Often disabilities are correctible with expert therapy, but the depth of the problem and steps to help the child must first be ascertained. After the specialist's diagnosis and with his or her permission, Schurr[3] recommends a thorough study of the area of weakness, complete with steps to help the child "catch up" to the normal level. "Activities similar to those used in screening provide good practice devices."

Besides the physical therapies, most coordination, control, and orientation problems can be aided by quiet activities that require manual dexterity and depth perception. These might be drawing, finger painting, sculpting, weaving, and other simple handcrafts.

A most important factor to keep in mind when recreation programming for the exceptional child is the instructor's attitude. This handicapped child offers both teacher and fellow pupils a wonderful opportunity to be creative. When a positive attitude is demonstrated in programs for both special and normal children, the response can be enormous. A review of the main goals of recreation for the exceptional child follows:

1. Emphasize activity. The child must not be simply a spectator.
2. Be realistic. Set reasonable goals that the special child can reach without hindering the programs of others.
3. Allow for extra time for the exceptional child.
4. Encourage the understanding and support of other children in the group.

SUMMARY

The central goal of children's recreation should be the attaining of their highest athletic, creative, and social potentials. The benefits of recreation are not limited to the classroom, the field house, or the gymnasium. Truly complete programs extend their influence into the total life style of children. Not only must their education be strengthened, but also their free, unsupervised group play, their meditative, quiet times, and every other aspect of their lives. Staff must not dwarf or warp their futures by resorting to television as their sole entertainment. Rather, every bit of modern programming knowledge, facilities, and creativity must be utilized to ensure a total recreation experience for these developing human beings.

Recreation is not, as so many still believe, solely the domain of children. But, because of the long lives that lie ahead of them, children should be assisted to learn early and savor deeply, the thrills, delights, and profound satisfactions that healthful recreation can bring them through all their years.

BIBLIOGRAPHY

Avedon, E. M.: Therapeutic recreation service, Englewood Cliffs, N.J., 1974, Prentice-Hall, Inc.

Donnelly, R. J., Helms, R. G., and Mitchell, E. D.: Active games and contests, New York, 1958, The Ronald Press.

Leonard, G.: The ultimate athlete, New York, 1975, The Viking Press.

REFERENCES

1. Leonard, G.: In Fluegelman, A. (ed.): The new games book, New York, 1976, Doubleday & Co.
2. Psychology today, an introduction (an anthology), Del Mar, Calif., 1970, CRM Books.
3. Schurr, E. L.: Movement experiences for children, Englewood Cliffs, N.J., 1975, Prentice-Hall, Inc.

11
PROGRAMMING AND SPECIAL EVENTS

Courtesy Dade County (Fla.) Parks and Recreation Dept.

The program is what recreation is all about. All else—personnel, supplies, budget, public relations—are solely to see that the program occurs and that people enjoy the program. It is true that some phases of recreation, so-called passive activities, would seem to deny the need for structured, formalized programming. These activities include strolling, fishing, bird watching, or just sitting in the park. Despite this, however, most people think of recreation as "doing" something and frequently seek out a program structure in which to "do" their thing. Golfers seek tournaments, basic instruction, and classes; sculptors enjoy demonstrations and technique classes; bicycle enthusiasts are forever joining clubs, learning about their bikes at training sessions, and entering carefully arranged bicycle competitions. The general public, enlightened though it may be, is a fickle and sometimes lethargic entity. Without programs and programming, far fewer youths and adults would ever tear themselves away from the television set, or they would perpetually slip into the spectator seat at a tennis match or sailing event. Human nature, particularly in our rather soft, affluent environment, tends to lack the self-starting mechanism that transforms a watcher—admirer into a doer-enjoyer. Program makes the difference.

The community recreation program is the term applied to the total experiences of individuals and groups resulting from community action in providing areas, facilities, leadership and funds. These experiences represent a wide range of activities, planned and spontaneous, organized and informal, supervised and undirected.[2]

OBJECTIVES

The objective of program planning is to provide those experiences that will bring to the participant the most satisfying values, and that in addition will have desirable social effects. It should be kept in mind that in many cases the planning process itself has recreation values.[1]

The objectives of the ideal recreation program include the following.

It should provide substantial opportunity for all segments of the population to be served—the neighborhood, the hospital, the city. To say it should provide "equal" opportunity to all is grossly unrealistic in view of the endless list of variables that are part of every community. "Substantial" opportunity is a very great accomplishment.

All ages and both sexes should be accommodated in the program plan. Here again, the assumption is that we are talking about a broad spectrum of games, activities, and special events. Individual activities may be aimed at one age group or ethnic group rather than all groups.

The special needs of the family in recreation must be recognized and accommodated. Today's family is already beset by myriad divisive forces. Recreation programs have a bringing together influence.

A wide and varied range of activities and pursuits should be made available. One of recreation's greatest strengths is freedom of choice, which distinguishes it from military training, schools, formal physical education, or other tightly structured spheres of activity. Variety and depth are needed to accommodate this search for free choice.

Basic activities in a recreation program should have carry-over value into later life. These activities include things such as swimming, sewing, hiking, and photography. Less likely to be carried over are high diving, team football, boxing, skydiving, and competitive swimming.

Recreation programs should be an exercise in democratic planning and leadership with substantial input by participants.

It should provide a year-round, flexible schedule of activities covering all kinds of work and leisure schedules so that all have substantial opportunity to participate.

Activities should be designed to stimulate spontaneous activity and to create new programs and activities on the part of participants.

The recreation program should be aimed at motivating and accomodating the atypical people—the ill, handicapped, embittered, imprisoned, hospitalized, poor, disenfranchised and those who are physically prevented from participating with ease. For the program to serve only the able is to deny its greatest value—that of serving those who need it most.

Recreation should be a platform for teaching citizenship, courtesy, honesty, and brotherhood through programs and activities. Through fun, thrills, and competition, children and adults can learn great truths of social behavior and can become better men and women.

A recreation program can serve as life in miniature, with all the preparations, challenges, unpredictables, trade-offs, and final evaluations. People can learn the lessons of life under circumstances where a loss does not mean a permanent wipeout.

These objectives may be reviewed and restated as follows. The sound and vigorous recreation program aims at developing (1) emotional and physical health, (2) character, personality of substance, (3) everwidening interests. (4) citizenship, community spirit, and pride, (5) skills of all kinds—simple and advanced, (6) sense of social communication and rapport, and (7) community strength, vitality, and economic vigor.

ELEMENTS OF PROGRAM PREPARATION

The stable, attractive, and effective recreation program reflects a careful consideration of several key factors that are vital to the program's success. Sadly, too few recreation administrators really consider these factors carefully. Rather, there is a tendency to jump into the program planning as if it were one's own private party, selecting those events and stunts the planner likes best and with which he or she is most familiar. Ignored are a host of items that should dictate the length, breadth, and depth of the program.

Age of participants

The tastes and responses of people change radically as they grow older. This may seem obvious when one compares the childish, primitive chase games of the 5 year old with the subtle, highly skillful competitions that appeal to a 30 year old. However, many in-between changes also occur as adolescents pass into early adulthood and into later stages. Frequently, these transitions are not fully considered by the program planner.

Sex

This is a very important element, even as the traditional walls between the sexes continue to fall. The physical, temperamental, and taste differences between the sexes are still substantial for the majority of people. To ignore them is to invite program failure.

Physical plant or location

Settings for a teen center and a ski competition differ widely. The physical accommodations are a major consideration, whether it be a swimming pool, ball field, curling rink, discotheque, kitchen, gameroom, or airport. A silk purse out of a sow's ear is often impossible in promoting a new recreation program.

Skill or knowledge of the participants

This can be a major explanation of early failure of some programs when compared with the successes of others. People do not enjoy being embarrassed, nor do they like to feel they have no chance at winning or excelling. Effort must be extended to bring people together at appropriate skill levels and then to move forward together as they advance in skill development. Whether we are discussing skiers, swimmers, painters, or bridge players, people seek a level of participation or competition that is reasonably close to their personal level.

Group size and makeup

The administrator must consider whether the program will serve a small group of highly motivated participants or will be offered as a mass demonstration before thousands. A women's club from a single profession, all the bathers on a single beach at noon on a summer day, the occupants of a small mountain hotel, and twenty young, married couples—each of these is a different group and size to be considered, and the program must be adapted to meet their specific needs and interests.

Nature of community

Makeup of the potential participants in terms of their environment is important to the recreation planner. Blue-collar or white-collar, youthful adults or retired persons, welfare recipients or corporate officers—these are the community characteristics that determine the program. Further elements include ethnic and national makeup, religion, cultural heritage or absence of same, occupations, and attitudes toward governmental leadership.

Program structure being considered

The nature of the program itself must be considered. Shall it be free choice, highly structured, a single event, or a long sequence of sessions or periods? Each of these characteristics influences the type of program that can be accommodated and the format most suitable. A New Year's Eve party is, by definition, a once-a-year event, with much planning and an explosive climax. On the other hand, the development of an amateur guitarist involves a long sequence of relatively short, repetitive, training sessions.

Budget and staff

The program planner must face the fiscal realities of the activity and make appropriate adaptations. Appropriated sums, possible fees and charges, and outside gifts are all weighed against leadership, supplies, and rental and advertising costs. The structure of the new program will reflect the fiscal parameters.

PROGRAMS AND HUMAN SERVICES

Human Services, Human Resources, and Community Services are relatively new departments in many cities. Basic to the concept of these new departments is the conviction that cities and urban centers must improve their delivery of simple but critically important services and amenities if cities are to survive and if people are to remain within them. An integral part of such thinking is the premise that a sound and broadly based recreation program can have major social significance for the community. Rather than viewing recreation as simply "fun" or a "time-killer," supporters of Human Services see the recreation program as one of the most underrated elements on the urban scene.

Recreation department programs and activities have experienced tremendous changes over recent years, many of which are the result of Human Services concerns. Traditionally, the recreation program for any community has been almost exclusively involved in the operation of athletic programs. These programs were designed to serve the youth of the community who were not involved in school athletic programs, as well as young adults who wished some form of athletic activity.

The recreation department typically organized leagues for competitive sports in baseball, softball, soccer, football, swimming, etc. . . . During the 1950's this situation began to change. The department's role changed from merely organizing athletic programs to developing a wide variety of programs to satisfy a broad cross section of community interests . . . . thus, the Human Services aspect of recreation took on new significance.[3]

SAMPLE PROGRAMS

The following is a series of lists suggesting the potential richness of program planning in recreation. Many activities are of such a varied nature that they might be classified under two or more headings. Some of these activities are primarily for children; others are ideal for youth and young adults; many are suitable for all ages. Some are essentially for men and boys because of their traditional play habits and their biologically bigger and stronger bodies; others are favorites of girls and women. Note well, however, that today's culture is altering many of these stereotypes. Certain games and activities require large spaces and elaborate equipment; others may be carried on at home or in a tiny college dormitory room. Solitude is essential for the fullest enjoyment of certain games and pastimes; others yield their greatest enjoyment when engaged in among laughing, jesting throngs. Universal appeal characterizes some; others are participated in only by rare aficionados. Some are informal; others are structured and disciplined. Some are dirt cheap; others are extravagantly expensive. The richness and diversity facing the recreation program

planner is one of the most delightful aspects of this profession.

Active games and sports

Low organized games

Bull in the ring	Hill dill
Cat and mouse	Prisoner's base
Club snatch	Relays
Fox and geese	Snow games
Hare and hounds	Tag games
Hide and seek	Three deep

Individual and dual games and activities

Athletic tests	Hopscotch
Badminton	Horseshoes
Baseball fundamentals	Indoor bowling
Billiards	Jacks
Boccie	Marbles
Bowling-on-the-green	Paddle tennis
Box hockey	Quoits
Clock golf	Ring tennis
Croquet	Roque
Curling	Smash
Dart baseball	Squash
Golf	Table tennis
Golf croquet	Tennis
Hand tennis	Tether ball
Handball	Top spinning

Gymnastics and stunts

Apparatus work	Pyramid building
Bag punching	Rope jumping
Baton twirling	Trampoline
Calisthenics	Tumbling
Lariat throwing	

Group or team games

Baseball	Goal-hi
Basketball	Ice hockey
Bicycle polo	Kickball
Cage ball	Lacrosse
Captain ball	Longball
Cricket	Newcomb
Dodge ball	Polo
Field ball	Roller-skate hockey
Field hockey	Shinny
Football	Soccer

Soccer baseball
Softball
Speedball
Touch football

Sports

Aquaplaning
Archery
Aviation
Bicycle riding
Boating
Bobsledding
Boxing
Canoeing
Coasting
Crew racing
Cross-country running
Diving
Fencing
Field events—jump-
  ing, pole vaulting,
  etc.
Figure skating
Fly casting
Horseback riding
Horsemanship
Hotrod racing
Ice sailing
Ice skating
Ice boating
Junior Olympics

Tug-of-war
Volleyball
Water polo

Kite flying
Lifesaving
Model airplane flying
Model boat sailing
Motor boating
Parachute jumping
Pistol shooting
Rifle shooting
Roller skating
Sailing
Ski-hiking
Skiing
Skijoring
Skijumping
Skin and scuba diving
Soaring
Swimming
Synchronized
  swimming
Tobogganing
Track events
Trap shooting
Water skiing
Wrestling

Old home weeks
Parties—
  barn warming,
  birthday, block,
  college, costume,
  hard times,
  holiday—Christ-
  mas, Halloween,
  New Year's, St.
  Patrick's, Twelfth
  night, Valentine's
  day, Washington's
  birthday
Pencil-and-paper
  games
Picnics
Quilting parties
Sailing parties
Scavenger hunts
Social dancing

Social games—Buzz
  Crambo, Going to
  Jerusalem, I have a
  face, Murder, etc.
Socials
Splash parties
Square dancing
Straw rides
Table games—
  anagrams, back-
  gammon, carrom,
  checkers, chess,
  Chinese checkers,
  crokinole, domi-
  noes, parcheesi,
  Scrabble
Treasure hunts
Visiting
Wiener roasts

Music activities
Vocal

A capella choir
Action songs
Choruses
Christmas caroling
Community singing
Glee clubs

Informal singing
  groups
Opera groups
Quartets
Singing games
Verse-speaking choirs
Whistling groups

Social activities

Banquets
Barbecues
Barn dances
Basket suppers
Beach parties
Card games—bridge,
  canasta, hearts,
  pinochle, pit, etc.
Clambakes
Community social
  evenings
Conversation
Dating
Entertaining

Family or club
  reunions
Father-and-son
  dinners
Fun nights
Get-acquainted stunts
Lodge and club
  meetings
Masquerades—pro-
  gressive contests,
  progressive games,
  tacky
Mother-and-daughter
  dinners

Performances

Band concerts
Cantatas
Glee club concerts
Incidental music at
  pageants, festivals,
  etc.
Music competitions
Music festivals

Old fiddler's contests
Operas
Operettas
Oratorios
Orchestral concerts
Original song contests
Radio or television
  concerts
Record concerts

Instrumental

Accordion
Bands
Bugle corps

Chamber music groups
Cigar box fiddlers
Fife and drum corps

Continued.

Harmonica bands
Instrumental choruses
Kazoo bands
Mandolin and guitar
  groups

Orchestras
Rhythm bands
Saxophone ensembles
Symphony orchestras
Ukulele orchestras

Miscellaneous

Composing music
Listening groups
Making musical instru-
  ments

Music appreciation
  courses
Music study clubs
Music weeks

Arts and crafts

Basketry
Bead craft
Block printing
Book binding
Cabinet making
Cardboard construc-
  tion
Carving—soap, wood,
  bone, etc.
Cement craft
Ceramics
Cookery
Costume design
Drawing
Dyeing and coloring
Embossing
Embroidery
Etching
Fabric decoration
Finger painting
Furniture refinishing
Home decoration
Jewelry making
Knitting
Leather craft
Making scrapbooks
Making sports equip-
  ment
Map making
Mechanics

Metal craft
Millinery
Model aircraft
Model making
Modeling
Mosaic crafts
Needlework
Painting
Paper craft
Photography
Plastic crafts
Poster making
Pottery
Printing
Quilting
Radio
Reed and raffia
Rug making
Sand craft
Sculpture
Sewing
Ship model building
Sketching
Snow sculpture
Stagecraft
Tin craft
Toy making
Visiting museums
Weaving
Woodworking

Drama activities

Carnivals
Charades
Children's matinees

Dramatic stunts
Fairs
Fashion shows

Feast of lanterns
Festivals
Follies
Impersonations
Informal dramatiza-
  tions
Making scenery
Marionettes
Mask making
Masquerades
Mime exercises
Minstrel shows
Mock trials
Movie making
Movie shows
Musical dramas and
  comedies
One-act plays
Pageants
Pantomimes
Parades
Peep shows

Play-exchange circuit
Play reading
Play tournaments
Play writing
Play-writing contests
Punch and Judy shows
Puppetry
Radio dramas
Shadowgraphs
Song impersonations
Stagecraft
Stage lighting
Story dramatization
Story plays
Story telling
Television produc-
  tions
Three-act plays
Traveling theatre
Vaudeville acts
Water pageants
Workshop

Dancing

Acrobatic
Ballet
Classic
Clog
Eurhythmics
Folk

Gymnastic
Interpretive
Modern
Social
Square
Tap

Nature and outing activities

Astronomy
Auto riding for plea-
  sure
Bee culture
Bird walks
Camping—auto, day,
  family, group, over-
  night
Caring for home
  grounds
Caring for pets
Dog obedience classes
Excursions or trips to
  art galleries, indus-
  trial plants,
  museums, parks,

places of historic or
  scenic interest,
  public buildings
Exploration
Fishing
Flower arrangement
Fruit raising
Gardening—flower,
  miniature, vegetable
Hiking
Hunting
Log rolling
Making nature trails
Microscope study
Mountain climbing
Nature games

Nature hikes
Nature museum projects
Nature study collection and identification—animals, birds, flowers, fossils, insects, marine life, minerals, mosses, reptiles, trees
Nature tours
Nature treasure hunts

Orienteering
Pet shows
Picnicking
Pigeon clubs
Plant exchange days
Playground zoo or aquarium
Raising poultry
Sand play
Snow tracking
Travel
Visiting zoos
Wading

Mental and linguistic

Book clubs
Charm school
Conservation
Creative writing
Debates
Discussion clubs
Foreign language study groups
Fortune-telling
Forums
Guessing games
Lectures
Listening to radio
Magic
Mathematics
Mental games

Poetry groups
Public speaking
Puzzles—crossword, jigsaw, etc.
Radio programs
Reading—silently and aloud
Reciting
Spelling bees
Study groups
Storytelling
Television programs
Tricks
Verse-speaking choirs
Writing letters

Collecting

Antiques
Autographs
Bookplates
Books
Bottles
Buttons
China
Clocks
Coins
Dime novels
Dolls
Etchings
Firearms
Furniture

Glassware
Indian arrowheads
Lamps
Match covers
Medals
Miniatures
Natural objects—butterflies, fossils, sea shells, etc.
Paintings
Pictures
Postcards
Pottery
Ship models

Silver
Stamps
Tapestries

Toys
Weapons
Woodcuts

Service activities

Group leadership in settlement house, boys' club, or playground
Membership on park, school, or recreation board or city council
Service as scoutmaster or troop committeeperson
Service as assistant at playground or recreation center
Directing glee club, orchestra, dramatic group
Helping conduct a hobby, craft, or nature project
Assisting in organizing a holiday celebration, a city beautiful week, or a campaign for a civic improvement
Assisting with publicity, money raising, or public relations program of a recreation or other agency
Teaching a Sunday school class
Helping with Red Cross projects and with activities in veterans, hospitals, homes for the aged, or other institutions
Transporting aged or handicapped persons to recreation centers

PREPARATIONS

From beginning to end, the systematic creation, planning, preparation, execution, and evaluation of recreation program or activity is what separates order from chaos. The fact that a great many programs meet early failure or mediocre success is often directly attributable to the inadequate planning and preparations by professional staff. It is hard to believe that so many intelligent leaders who have adequate training begin activities and programs based on the flimsiest of preparations. A few of the errors or violations that invite failure include:

1. Inadequate announcements of date, time, place, and any unusual circumstances

2. Faulty public address equipment, or none
3. Insufficient staff present, or poorly briefed
4. Failure to obtain street permit or permission to use the facility involved
5. No medical or first aid service available
6. No plans for rain or other inclement weather.
7. Insufficient food, prizes, or athletic equipment
8. No press coverage
9. Police department not notified in advance of major outdoor event
10. No arrangements for trash or garbage removal

These are a few of what could be a long list. Even if all these items were properly handled, there is also the need to plan the program itself so that it has maximum chance of succeeding. Following are some general steps that will lay the proper groundwork for new recreation programs and activities. Programs may be classified either as a *scheduled sequence* or as a *special event*.

A *scheduled sequence* consists of a beginning date for registration and start, a series of specifically scheduled dates of activity, usually the same time and place, and a definite termination date. Sequences may be: every Wednesday night for 10 weeks, from 7:00 P.M. to 9:00 P.M.; every Saturday and Sunday morning for 6 weeks from 9:00 A.M. to noon; or every evening, Monday through Friday from 6:30 P.M. to 10:00 P.M. The program may include activities such as bridge instruction, basketball practice, free swimming, or guitar lessons.

A *special event* is the planned, one-time occurrence. All planning and arrangements are aimed at making this well-publicized and carefully staged incident a major success. Events may include the Kite Flying Rodeo, Saturday from 10:00 A.M. to 5:00 P.M.; the Boxing Tournament, 9 bouts, Friday night from 7:15 P.M. to 11:00 P.M.; or the Mini-Marathon of 5 miles, Sunday morning at 10:00 AM. Championship sports events, track meets, the play festival, the walkathon, the Fourth of July fireworks, the Thanksgiving Day Parade—these are more examples of a special event that demands careful planning and execution for success.

The planner must ascertain that there is a *general receptivity* for the program or event before starting preparations. Questioning local people of different types will help, as will questionnaires aimed at determining local recreation interest and needs. Although good recreation program planners do insert some of their own professional tastes and ideas, it is futile to force an event or program if there is no community receptivity for it. Sports atmosphere, ethnic interests, past history, local culture and mores, and the general life style of the community play a major role in deciding whether a certain activity or program will be warmly or coldly received. Neighborhoods with large concentrations of old, foreign-born people are not generally receptive to rock music or performing arts activities that border on the obscene. They do respond well to old-fashioned dance music, small children's events, and outdoor handcraft displays. Neighborhoods that contain large numbers of young adults, college students, singles, and young, childless couples are far more receptive to avant-garde art displays, ballet, flea markets, wine-tasting events, sophisticated rock music, and sports car exhibits.

CHECKLISTS

To be sure that planning is complete, a simple checklist or punchlist is recommended. For the *scheduled sequence,* observe the following suggestions.

1. Announce the program, with specifics, sufficiently in advance so that all interested persons will have a chance to inquire and register. This varies with the activity. For summer camp, at least 2 months' advance notice should be given; for a 10-week bridge class, at least 2 weeks' notice is recommended. Handbills, posters, and the local newspaper and radio station are desirable media for announcements.

2. Provide a phone and/or office so that inquiries may be made for further details on the program. Be specific about days and time that the phone will be staffed.

3. Obtain the finest recreation leader or instructor for the program early enough so that he or she can help in announcing the activity and in answering the preliminary questions. Put the leader's name and background on all announcements.

4. Secure a clean, attractive location for the activity. Visit the site and check it out for convenience, safety, rest rooms, light, and good work space. Beware of vague promises by custodians such as, "Don't worry, we'll find you a place," or "I know it looks messy now, but we'll have it all ready for you when your people come." Insist that all rooms, equipment, preparations be ready in advance.

5. Prepare a list of required supplies and equipment. Go over this list in advance with the leader/instructor. Make certain no item is left to chance.

6. Arrange a tight, secure, and convenient procedure for handling registration fees. Make certain each participant receives a cash receipt. Complete this cycle all the way from first payment through banking until a bookkeeping credit is entered.

7. Arrive early (or your designated representative) at the first session and check

everything out with the leader/instructor. Allow enough time for "panic-runs" to pick up missing items.

8. Ideally, the administrator should greet the group at the opening session, introduce the leader/instructor, and observe the first part of the program. This makes the group feel received and raises the spirit of all involved.

9. If the scheduled sequence involves progressive skill training or education, certificates or diplomas are sometimes awarded to those completing the program course. These are usually prepared by the department and presented to the participants by the administrator and the leader/instructor.

A helpful additional step in such programming is to distribute a simple critique or evaluation sheet to all participants just before the conclusion of the last session. Request that they fill it out and turn it in before they leave. Their signature is optional. Questions should include: Did you find the program pleasant and productive? What was missing, if anything? What would you like added, when program is repeated? Please add any additional comments you wish on leader/instructor, fee, time schedule, physical accomodations.

The checklist for the *special event* is more basic and resembles the approach to a space vehicle launching or a theatre opening night.

1. Check out the site the day before the event. Weather, traffic, accident, or bureaucratic bungling may have changed the site radically since earlier designation. For example, an outdoor art show has been scheduled for Saturday along a chain link fence edging a sidewalk. Visiting the site on Friday, you discover that an automobile has crashed into the fence recently, destroying half the fence. Last minute switches or accomodations are a must if the

art show is to come off on schedule. Similarly, in advance of the planned Friday night teen center dance, the recreation planner visits the room on Thursday and finds the floor has just been freshly varnished. A quick switch of location, with announcements, is a must.

2. Prepare a list of required supplies and equipment, whether this be chairs and tables, gymnastic equipment, music stands, scenery, or an ancient touring car. Check a day in advance and again early on the day of the event. Things have a way of moving off or being damaged.

3. More programs of all kinds are destroyed by faulty or missing public address equipment than by any other hardware problem. Make certain of the number of microphones required, the physical layout, turntable and records if desired, source of power, and someone to operate the set. Then insist that a completely separate back-up public address unit be available in case the first one fails. Arrive at the event site at least 1 hour before scheduled time and carefully check out the entire system as well as the backup unit. Take no one's word— listen to it work for yourself.

4. Small supplies include bats, balls, bases, marbles, kites, food, bicycles, prizes, and a host of associated items depending on the event. Each item should be on the checklist and each item carefully checked out. Only such handling will avoid the disaster of starters' pistols without cartridges, kites without string, roller skates without keys, balls without bats, and the whole system suffering because of lack of scissors, twine, or masking tape. Casual assurances such as, "They're bound to have it," or "Don't worry, someone will supply those things," are invitations to disaster in recreation programming.

5. The presence and preparation of paid staff and volunteers is critically important in the success or failure of a recreation event. Days in advance, the key personnel should be designated and notified. Vagueness and ambiguity should be avoided: "You can help me if you'll come" or "Come by and I'll see if we can use you." This invariably results in too many or too few recreation leaders. Assignments should be definite and unmistakable. If the administrator or supervisor expects to be absent, a substitute should be named and directed to take full charge of the event. It is very disconcerting for the public to arrive at the Easter Egg Hunt or Winter Ice Carnival and be met by a group of busy personnel with no one in charge. The leader must be clearly identified and should be present sufficiently early to take complete charge.

6. For events involving even small risks of accident, arrangements should be made to handle emergencies. If the group is small, the activity mild, and youngsters are involved, the presence of a complete and clean basic first aid kit should be sufficient. If the event is large (several hundred people) or if the group is predominantly elderly or physically handicapped, plans should be more extensive. The presence of a registered nurse is recommended, and the presence, at least part of the time, of a doctor is desirable. For special events that add higher risk factors, such as ski tournaments, fireworks displays, channel swims, mountain climbing, speedboat races, and hang-gliding demonstrations, a fully-equipped ambulance should be parked at the scene and staffed by trained paramedics. In addition, the nearest hospital should be alerted one day in advance and advised of the type of event and the nature of the risk factor. This preparation can appreciably reduce the danger of serious casualties.

EVALUATION

Evaluation of the program is the surest guarantee against repeating planning mistakes in the future. Some departments and agencies use a specific form or questionnaire. Whether or not a form is used, the following items are important:

1. Name of the event, date, time, location.
2. Number of participants, spectators, staff.
3. Quality of location.
4. Adequacy of supplies and equipment.
5. Comment on how general preparations could be improved.
6. Safety hazards involved.
7. Public reaction—collect several comments from persons at the event.
8. Cost of the program.
9. Comments on holding the program/event again.
10. Signature of supervisor or leader.

After a special event or program has ended, it is wise for the agency or department to assemble a kit or file of materials fully describing the program. Included should be: (1) copy of each flier, mailing, and instruction sheet distributed on the event, (2) several good photographs of the event, (3) copies of all news releases written and clippings of all printed materials, and (4) evaluation sheet completed by staff person in charge of the event.

This complete file should be assembled in such a way that all events and programs of the year are reachable at any time and in compact form. They may each be mounted on their own clipboard; a wall of some 30 to 40 clipboards represents a quick retrieval program file. Manila folders may be used for each program and filed in conventional fashion, or each program batch of material may be stored in a large mailing envelope. Whatever the pattern, the aim is to present a total storage and retrieval system for all the programs and events of the year. The availability of such a master program file is of great value in the evaluation process and in the process of planning future programs. It is one of the prime weapons in the war on "program-sclerosis," the ailment in which recreation departments become encrusted with old, tired events and repetitious program activities. The ancient programs are repeated, year after year, despite their failing attendance, dreary planning, high unit cost, and general anachronistic quality. Good programming means fresh, informed objectivity, making room for the new by discarding the old.

COSPONSORSHIP

Through cosponsorship, the programming capability of a recreation agency can be greatly expanded. Two or more organizations combine their talents, personnel, and resources to produce an event or program larger and better than either could have done alone. Such combinations might be a public recreation department and a local YMCA, the parks and recreation departments of two neighboring cities, the recreation division of a large hospital and the public high school across the street, or a local shopping center and a nearby boys' club. The combinations are endless and present a creative programming challenge to the recreation administrator.

Advantages of such cosponsored combinations include (1) more trained personnel available, (2) expanded budget, (3) property, sites, equipment, and supplies on a larger scale, (4) more creative thinking, and (5) better contact with communications media. Perhaps more than all the above, however, is the advantage of presenting an image of agencies and industry working together. Like motherhood and honesty, the concept of teamwork-cooperation is a perennial winner for support from all persons. Following are some illustrations of how cosponsorship produced programs or events that might otherwise never have occurred.

1. The Recreation and Parks Department

of White Plains, N.Y. joined with the White Plains Jaycees to produce a giant Easter Egg Hunt and Festival. The department provided the park, the stage and public address system, and a dozen recreation staff personnel. The Jaycees provided 5000 candy eggs, prizes, gift baskets, costumed bunnies, music, and several uniformed volunteers. Over 2000 children and adults participated in the event.

2. A western Pennsylvania city was plagued by constant friction and competition between the local YMCA and the YWCA. Finally, an enterprising aquatics leader decided to bring both agencies together (each owned an indoor swimming pool) in a city-wide "Y-SWIM" Water Festival, emphasizing the need for basic swimming instruction on all age levels. Thereafter, all swimming programs were operated jointly between the two agencies and the public enjoyed greater access to both pools.

3. In Bedford, Mass. the U.S. Veterans Hospital teamed up with the nearby Hanscom Air Force Base to produce a series of sports and recreation competitions between patients at the hospital and airmen and dependents at the base. Over 3000 persons participated, and all costs and logistics were shared.

Some recreation administrators believe they have exhausted the potential of cosponsorship when they do three or four promotions or they persuade a large industry to purchase and donate a piece of new playground equipment. This is shortsighted. The possibilities for coprogramming are enormous and far beyond the conventional few special events. Following are types of agencies, departments, and organizations in any urban center of 50,000 persons or more that can be joined together in projects by a skilled recreation program planner: churches and temples, taverns, large industries, small business offices, polic

officers and firefighters, medical societies, auto dealers, professional sports teams, seminaries, colleges and universities, movie theatres, marinas, unions, veterans' organizations, service clubs, travel agencies, hospitals, nursing homes, gasoline stations, fast food outlets, and many more.

A special form of a cosponsored program is that designed and marketed by a national product or firm in conjunction with a local recreation department or private youth-serving agency. Illustrations of this are Ford Motors' "Punt-Pass-Kick," a football skills competition; Pepsi-Cola's "Mobile Tennis" and "Hot Shot" (basketball) programs; Chevrolet's "Soap Box Derby;" Ken-L-Ration's "Pet Show," and others. Some 25 such major programs are available, with a variety of rules, regulations, territories, schedules, and a huge amount of sophisticated printed literature. In most cases, these programs are well put together and are aimed at genuinely expanding local recreation programs. Usually, the materials and rules are placed in the hands of local recreation people, who are then given a time frame in which to run their local competitions. These are then followed by city, county, state, regional, and national competitions.

Much of the value of these programs rests with the local recreation units. If the competitions are kept vigorous and honest from the beginning, the experience is good for the youths involved. However, since the prime business sponsors are usually heavily preoccupied by the successful running of their businesses, such distractions may receive short shift or careless handling. Overall, these programs are very helpful to local recreation programs when the originating firm or industry is conscientious and consistent and when the local recreation department or agency adheres strictly to the rules and monitors the activity closely.

For information on "Punt-Pass-Kick," contact Ford Motors, Detroit, Michigan; for "Pepsi-Cola Mobile Tennis" and "Pepsi-Cola/NBA Hotshot" contact Pepsi-Cola Co., Anderson Hill Road, Purchase, New York; for all others, contact the National Recreation and Park Association, 1601 North Kent St., Arlington, Va. 22209.

YOUTH PROGRAMS

Over 100 national sports and recreation programs for youth exist in the United States today. The best known of these are Little League Baseball, Pop Warner Football, Babe Ruth Baseball, Pony League Baseball, Biddy Basketball, and Little Kid Basketball. This youth sports movement

Courtesy Pepsi-Cola Co.

began in the late 1940s and saw its greatest growth from 1955 to 1965. Over 8,000,000 boys and girls are registered in these organizations, and an enormous amount of training and competition is generated through them.

Such programs offer additional opportunities for program expansion in the community. With heavy emphasis on volunteer leadership and fund raising, these national organizations assemble working teams and support groups that would cost local recreation departments hundreds of millions of additional budget dollars were it necessary to use the tax dollar to pay these people. A good recreation planner makes certain that this explosion of talent, spirit, fund-raising, and sincere care for youth is properly plugged into the overall community recreation program. It is not always easy to work with hyperactive, totally dedicated volunteers, and it takes a skilled recreation professional to keep the proper mix of familiarity plus objectivity. Nevertheless, these people represent a massive program factor, the vast majority of it for the good, and such organizations and their activities must be woven in as part and parcel of the basic community recreation program.

The headquarters for national Little League Baseball is Williamsport, Pennsylvania. For all other such organizations, it is suggested that contact be made through the National Recreation and Park Association.

DISCUSSION QUESTIONS

1. A vacancy for a program planning person has opened on your hospital recreation staff. Qualifications are flexible. List at least five places you would contact in your search for such an individual.
2. You are superintendent of a department of recreation in a small middle-income, suburban community. Your entire activity program is under public criticism for being too limited in schedule and for failing to serve family needs. Outline a series of steps you would take to correct this situation.
3. Very often, practitioners criticize campus recreation education programs for turning out inadequately prepared recreation leaders. Is this a valid criticism? Why? How would you correct it?
4. In some communities, a major portion of the residents are young singles, living alone without the conventional family structure. How would you reach and program for these people?
5. Many program activities tend to be rooted in the past and out of step with the 1980s. As program director of a large recreation-providing private agency, what steps would you take to keep your program abreast of the times?

BIBLIOGRAPHY

Berne, E.: Games people play, New York, 1964, Grove Press, Inc.

Calkins, E. E.: Care and feeding of hobby horses, New York, 1933, Leisure League of America.

Depew, A. M.: Cokesbury game book, New York, 1952, Abingdon Press.

Eisenberg, H., and Eisenberg, L.: The family fun book, New York, 1957, Stratford Press, Inc.

Eisenberg, H., and Eisenberg, L.: Skits and stunts, New York, 1959, Association Press.

Fleugelman, A. (ed.): The new games book, Garden City, N.Y., 1976, Doubleday & Co.

Goodrich, W.: Science through recreation, New York, 1964, Holt Rinehart & Winston.

Harbin, E. O.: The fun encyclopedia, New York, 1950, Abingdon Press.

The International City Managers Association: Municipal recreation administration, Chicago, 1960, The Association.

Kohl, M., and Young, F.: Games for grownups, New York, 1951, Hill and Wang.

Kraus, R. G.: One thousand family games, New York, 1973, McGraw-Hill Book Co.

Mason, B. S., and Mitchell, E. D.: Active sports and games, New York, 1945, A. S. Barnes & Co., Inc.

Mason, B. S., and Mitchell, E. D.: Social games for recreation, New York, 1949, A. S. Barnes & Co. Inc.

Meyer, H. D., and Brightbill, C. K.: Recreation administration, Englewood Cliffs, N.J., 1956, Prentice-Hall, Inc.

McVicar, W.: Clown act omnibus, New York, 1960, Association Press.

Musselman, V.: Making family get-togethers click, Harrisburg, Pa., 1968, Stackpole Press.

Nash, J. B.: Spectatoritis, New York, 1945, A. S. Barnes & Co., Inc.

National Recreation and Park Association: Games for boys and men, Arlington, Va., 1956, The Association.

Rodney, L. S.: Administration of public recreation, New York, 1964, The Ronald Press.

Strobell, A. P.: Bicentennial games 'n fun handbook, Arlington, Va., 1975, National Recreation and Park Association.

Strobell, A. P.: Creative recreation programming handbook, Arlington, Va., 1977, National Recreation and Park Association.

REFERENCES

1. The Athletic Institute: Recreation for community living, Chicago, 1952, The Institute.
2. Butler, G. D.: Introduction to community recreation, New York, 1959, McGraw-Hill Book Co.
3. The International Managers Association, Managing human services, Washington, D.C., 1977, The Association.

12

LEGAL ASPECTS OF RECREATION

Courtesy University of Oregon News Bureau

Legal aspects of recreation work should be a concern of every recreation leader and administrator. Like money matters, however, law is an area in which most recreation personnel feel they are "over their heads" or in some alien jurisdiction. This attitude is out of step with the times. We live and function in an era of litigation, and the like fire, some legal action will enter the lives of almost every reader of this book. Our efforts, then, shall not be in the direction of "instant lawyers," but rather toward that of familiarizing recreation personnel with basic legal fundamentals that they can use in their work.

Usually when park and recreation writers cover the subject of legal aspects of recreation, the major emphasis is placed on state enabling acts and the so-called legal basis for recreation services. This emphasis may have been appropriate during the early stages of the recreation movement—the 1930s to the 1950s when the majority of new departments were just starting. Now, however, most heavily populated states, counties, cities, towns, and villages have created some type of recreation department, and the private recreation agencies are also well established. Today's legal problems are more complex and involve insurance, liability, risk management, OSHA, human rights, affirmative action, and other sophisticated aspects of the law. Thus, after a brief overview of enabling acts and permissive legislation, the more relevant matters of contemporary law will be discussed.

HISTORY

The concept of municipal responsibility, concerning the park aspect of parks and recreation at least, is not new. From colonial times, the city fathers set aside public squares, plazas, and gardens for ornamental beauty. The Boston Common is probably the most famous of these parks, or "common lands," as they were known in the late seventeenth century. In 1852, New York City made the first actual park acquisition by purchasing, specifically for park purposes, the land that later became Central Park. Cities across the nation acquired and developed great systems of delightfully landscaped urban parks, forests, and preserves. Excellent examples of this include the park systems of Los Angeles, Kansas City, Milwaukee, Minneapolis, St. Louis, Philadelphia, Chicago, Boston, Baltimore, and Washington, D.C.

Recreation, however, did not gain such early acceptance as a municipal function. For the most part, government considered recreation a very personal matter—the concern, the prerogative, and the responsibility of the individual. This attitude prevailed until the end of the nineteenth century, when the rapid growth of cities and their concomitant crowding and interaction brought the recreation movement to the fore. More and more, parks became the site of active games rather than merely passive meditation, and isolated forests suddenly found themselves in the midst of downtown development. A need for more "legal basis" for the municipality's involvement was needed to guide cities, towns, and villages in this new government service.

It is necessary to have legal authority for a public recreation system to acquire, develop and maintain recreation areas, to construct and operate buildings and facilities, and to carry on the duties necessary to develop a program of activities. Therefore, a local recreation system can only function through authority granted to it by state law. In short, recreation agencies must operate within a legal framework specified by state statute.[4]

Most states have passed laws permitting every local governmental unit within those states to conduct a broad recreation program under any form of organization it considers most suitable or effective. In many cases, the legislation was drafted and promoted with the cooperation of the National Recreation Association (now the National Recreation and Park Association). These laws are commonly called enabling acts.

ENABLING ACTS

By constitutional law, all municipalities are the "children" or "off-spring" of their respective states. Thus, the enabling act must be enacted on the state level. The enabling act, simply put, is a state law that emphasizes and confirms home rule for municipalities in that particular state. Home rule is the political-legal term that denotes local government's powers to make its own local laws, usually called ordinances, exercise its own prerogatives, and govern its own destiny. The enabling act gives the option to use or to ignore the law's permissive features. It allows the establishment and operation of recreation and park services by cities, counties, towns, villages, school districts, or by any combination of these political entities.

Features and details of enabling acts vary from state to state, but there is a general similarity. The following are some of the basic characteristics of all state enabling acts:

1. Applicable to all cities, towns, villages, counties, school districts, and other governmental subdivisions within the state.
2. Applicable to any two or more of the above in combination.
3. Authorizes municipalities to acquire and set aside land for recreational use.
4. Legalizes the expenditure of public monies for land acquisition and for the building of recreation facilities.
5. Legalizes issue of bonds to accomplish 4.
6. Permits municipalities to establish and operate playgrounds, teen centers,

parks, recreation centers, and to expend public funds for this purpose.
7. May authorize the establishment of a citizen board, commission, or similar body for the purpose of setting policy and operating the recreation system or facility. This includes employing professional personnel, preparing a budget, and conducting the administrative affairs of the agency.
8. If no board or commission is put in charge, the authority remains with the municipality to accomplish 7.
9. Legalizes the acceptance of public gifts for the good of the general public (land, facilities, money, real estate, easements, equipment, etc.).

The foundation of municipal recreation was laid in the early decades of the twentieth century when the state legislature of New Jersey enacted enabling legislation in 1915. New York, New Hampshire, and Michigan did the same in 1917, as did Connecticut and New Hampshire in 1919. Today, every state has some form of general enabling legislation relating to recreation or a combination of parks, recreation, and conservation.

Frequently, the state enabling act will specifically authorize the local governing body to assign the recreation operating power to a locally assembled or existing unit. The Florida act,* for example, says "The governing body of any such municipality or county may vest the power to provide, maintain and conduct playgrounds, recreation centers and other recreation activities and facilities in the school board, park board or other existing body, or in a playground and recreation board as the governing body may determine." The

---

*From an act empowering cities, towns, and counties to equip and operate playgrounds and recreation centers, State of Florida, passed June, 1925.

Alabama act, on the other hand, specifies that a permanent park and recreation board be established to carry out these duties. In the Kansas enabling act* no mention of counties is included, only cities and/or school districts. Consequently, when a county in Kansas wishes to provide such recreation services, another act is necessary to make it legal. The New York State enabling act† is probably more specific and inclusive than most. It authorizes (1) "the setting apart for use as playgrounds or neighborhood recreation centers any land or building owned by such municipality and not dedicated or devoted to other inconsistent public use," (2) acquisition of "land for such purposes by gift, private purchase or by condemnation," (3) lease of "land or buildings for temporary use for such purposes," and (4) equipping such "playgrounds and recreation centers, and the buildings thereon" and "constructing, maintaining and operating in connection therewith public baths and swimming pools."

The Michigan enabling act, passed in 1917, is a good example of a typical law:

"An Act authorizing cities, villages, counties, townships and school districts to operate systems of public recreation and playgrounds
123.51 Public Recreation System—Section 1. Any city, village, county or township may operate a system of public recreation and playgrounds; acquire, equip and maintain land, buildings or other recreational facilities; employ a superintendent of recreation and assistants; vote and expend funds for the operation of such a system.

---

*General Statutes of the State of Kansas, Chapter 12, Article 19, Public Recreation and Playgrounds.
†From law granting authority to cities and counties to equip and operate playgrounds, New York State, passed 1917, amended 1920, 1922, and 1924.

123.52 Same; power of school district—Section 2. Any school district may operate a system of recreation and playgrounds, may vote a tax to provide funds for operating same; and may exercise all other powers enumerated in Section 1.
123.53 Same; operation—Section 3. Any city, village, county or township may operate such a system independently or they may cooperate in its conduct in any manner in which they may mutually agree; or they may delegate the operation of the system to a recreation board created by any or all of them, and appropriate money, voted for this purpose to such a board.
123.54 Same; location—Section 4. Any municipal corporation or board given charge of the recreation system is authorized to conduct its activities on (1) property under its custody and management; (2) other public property, under custody of other municipal corporations or boards, with the consent of such corporations or boards; (3) private property, with the consent of the owners.

LOCAL LEGISLATION

In a state in which enabling legislation exists, the local municipality may take advantage of this permission by passing an ordinance (local law) or resolution that sets forth in detail the organization, powers, and duties of the proposed recreation system. In many instances, the managing authority for recreation is given to a board or commission. Here again, whether an ordinance provides for an administrative and policy-making authority or one that acts merely in an advisory capacity depends on the powers provided by state law and local charter. California, for example, does not allow general law cities and counties (as distinguished from charter cities and counties) to establish administrative or policy-making boards.

A number of states have passed legislation authorizing the establishment of recreation districts or park and recreation districts. The general purpose of such districts is to provide a managing authority or vehicle when the existing municipalities cannot meet the task. Reasons for this inability may include the following:

1. Partisan politics prevent two or more adjoining municipalities from joining on a project or operation.
2. Physical geography that places obstacles such as mountains, deserts, or rivers in the way of efficient jurisdictional lines.
3. Statutory features in one or another charters preclude the providing of certain recreation services or prohibit the joining of two or more municipalities.
4. Very specialized nature of service to the proposed district.
5. Sheer size of the district.

To meet any or all of these obstacles, a special district is established that lays out a new service and jurisdictional boundary. This boundary may lie totally inside a single village or may run across the boundary lines of two cities, two towns, or five counties. This district then becomes a new, if unusual, quasimunicipality in itself, with its own board or commission, its own governing rules, and its own power to levy taxes and spend monies. Such special districts are numerous in many states and are not set up exclusively to meet recreation and park needs. Most states have their special fire districts and districts for water supply, sewage, highways, environmental conservation, ambulance service, education of handicapped persons, special transportation, and other purposes.

LIABILITY

This is the real problem in today's economically oriented culture. Common expressions such as "You can be sued!" or "You're liable!" can arouse terror in even the most fastidious recreation professional. Such expressions conjure up images of hostile courtrooms, glowering judges, unsympathetic juries, and browbeating prosecutors. These frightening images are reinforced by newspaper stories of huge cash judgments and settlements that make our courts look like television giveaway shows and appear to ignore all efforts for safety of participants by conscientious recreation administrators. Things are not as bad as they seem. A few points should first be established:

1. The stories of colossal cash awards in the courts are often blown up by the press. True, a few unusually large awards do occur from time to time, but the full facts in these cases are often obscured from the public for purposes of news story appeal.

2. The few massive "windfall" money judgements are overshadowed by the tens of thousands of unsuccessful suits and those in which fair, modest awards are made. All such cases mean the investment of time, effort, money, and frustration, and often, after years of litigation, they are dismissed for insubstantiality. Winning a suit is not easy or quick.

3. The majority of judges are sound, understanding, and thoroughly professional jurists who sincerely wish to adjudicate matters before them on merit, not on emotion or notoriety.

4. Alert recreation professionals can prepare themselves for possible court action by a combination of knowledge, in-service training, good administration, safety procedures, and sound legal counsel.

Liability is defined as an obligation of payment. When laypersons speak glibly about being sued or being liable, they really are not making such a shocking observation. Most of us are, at every moment of the day and night, constantly subject to suit. A homeowner may file suit against his neighbor for a marauding dog who menaces his children; the neighbor may sue the homeowner because his children have made his dog ill; a pedestrian may sue the city after tripping on a crack in a sidewalk; a child's family may sue their daughter's teacher because he implanted disturbing thoughts in her mind resulting in nightmares and expensive psychiatry bills—the possibilities are endless. Suing simply means that one party decides he or she has been wronged by another and wants redress or cash payment to compensate for that wrong. The person hires a lawyer and a suit is begun. But there is nothing, absolutely nothing, in this action that says the plaintiff, or person filing the suit, has even a slight chance of recovering any money at all, even after years of litigation. Therein lies the whole message of this liability–suing–judgment thing—what kind of a case is it? Anybody can sue anybody else, anytime, for any amount, but only the substantial, carefully researched, heavily documented, painstakingly prepared case has a chance of winning, and even the winner may only receive costs. The recreation professional definitely has ways and means at hand to cope with this kind of legal onslaught.

Tort liability

An area of major concern to the recreation administrator is that of tort liability. The word *tort,* is from the Latin *torquere,* meaning to twist or wrench aside. It denotes a private or civil wrong or injury done to an individual or a specific group of individuals. In contrast, a crime denotes injury to the public or society as a whole. Liability in tort can be created by either intentional or unintentional conduct—by an act or by an omission.

Tort differs from crime in that, when a crime is committed, the state steps in to prosecute and punish the wrongdoer. When a tort is committed, the state takes no judicial notice of it, but it does provide appropriate remedies to the injured party if he cares to avail himself of them. The tort, then, is legal wrong resulting from failure to do something that one should do or from doing something wrong that results in injury to person or property. Most tort liability suits involve negligence and/or nuisance.

Negligence is the violation of an absolute duty or failure to take into consideration the interests of others and resulting in injury.

A generally accepted definition of negligence is:

Negligence is failure to act as a reasonable and prudent person would have acted under the circumstances. A more precise and legal definition which appears in "Corpus Juris," states that negligence is an unintentional breach of legal duty, causing damage reasonably foreseeable without which breach damage would not have occurred.[5]

Examples of negligence are:
1. Leaving your post without permission as a swimming pool lifeguard, and a drowning occurs.
2. Failing to repair a broken playground swing, on which a child later breaks an arm.
3. Ignoring fire department occupancy regulations at a crowded teen center, resulting in fire casualties.

Nuisance is a violation of civic duty to neighbors, a failure to use the degree of care required. The nuisance may be a thing, a sound, or a condition tolerated or caused by the instigator consciously or unconsciously; it may offend the senses, violate decency, attract dangerous activity, or obstruct the use of property. Examples of nuisance are:
1. Storing a huge pile of sand on a street, unmarked or unprotected, near the play site of young children. Children subsequently dig in the sand and a suf-

focation occurs. This is sometimes referred to as "creating an attractive nuisance."

2. The owner of a powerful stereo unit plays rock music into the window of a neighbor. An elderly resident of the house is prevented from sleeping and becomes ill.

3. A park department employee stores a mound of fresh horse manure on a small parking lot under the windows of a neighbor's apartment. The neighbor becomes nauseated, calls for a doctor, and requires treatment.

In general, under tort law, one is entitled to (1) the safety of his person and freedom from fear of bodily harm; (2) the safety of his property, both real and personal, from trespass or conversion; (3) his good reputation, and that it not be defamed; (4) freedom from interference in his domestic relations.[1]

Only adults can be held responsible for their torts; persons under 21 years of age are not liable for their tortious acts.

Governmental versus proprietary liability

The question of tort liability or non-liability of governmental agencies is centered, for the most part, on a very interesting concept of *governmental immunity* dating back to the early courts of England. This theory or concept of public right and wrong, said, "The King can do no wrong." Unfair as that appears to most democratic tastes, it was, nevertheless, the way peasant, nobleman, and monarch judged events and viewed justice of that era. If a peasant took another peasant's land, the law was swift and exacting, and the perpetrator probably lost his head. If the king took a peasant's land, the matter ended there on the assumption that there must have been good reason, some ameliorating circumstance, etc. because, since he is the king, he is incapable of doing wrong.

This principle, carried into modern legal activity simply places government in the position formerly occupied by the king, on the assumption that governments work *for* the people and, therefore, may err but not through any malice or wrongdoing. Now this principle, whether justified or not, is relatively simple seemingly and should be easy to adjudicate. When a government is doing the things that a government is mandated to do, those activities are declared *governmental,* and the concept of immunity from liability should prevail. If, on the other hand, a government is performing acts that may be desirable, helpful, and important to the public, but are deemed optional rather than required by statute, these actions are declared *proprietary.* These acts resemble the functions of private business rather than those of government, or so goes the theory.

Here the ambiguity arises. What is a *governmental* act and what is a *proprietary* act? Under which heading does recreation belong? In some states, California, Illinois, Massachusetts, Michigan, Minnesota, Washington, and Wisconsin among others, the courts have generally interpreted municipal recreation to be a *governmental* function. In other states, Indiana, Ohio, New York, Pennsylvania, and Texas, the courts have held it to be a *proprietary* function. In many states, no clear-cut distinction can be made, with various decisions falling to both views. Generally speaking, the municipality located in a state that classifies recreation a *governmental* function runs less of a liability risk than the municipality that lies within a state labeling recreation services *proprietary.* Note well the word "generally," since this does not hold true in every case and there are a great number of extenuating circumstances that can influence a court decision.

Thus we have this situation. Anyone or

any group can file suit against a recreation agency at any time for any real or imagined cause. The real challenge is not in *filing* a suit but in *winning* the suit, and this is based on the merits of the case.

Tort liability is the principle by which a person or group is responsible for acts or omissions that cause injury, loss, or both to another. Contributing to the guilt or innocence of the defendent (the person, group, or agency against whom the suit is filed) is the question of whether there is negligence or nuisance present, and to what degree.

In a court case of tort liability against a municipal recreation agency, the likelihood of being found liable for damages is *less* if the recreation agency functions within a state that regards recreation as a governmental act. A judgment against the recreation department is *more* likely to succeed within a state that deems recreation a proprietary function of government.

IMPACT OF FEES AND CHARGES

The act of charging fees or of not charging fees, can have a significant effect on court decisions regarding liability in recreation activities and facilities. Reed[3] puts it this way: "Court decisions relating to liability have rested largely on the question of whether the municipality administering the public recreation facilities was performing a governmental (public) or proprietary (private) function." He goes on to say that a city generally acts in a governmental capacity when it is engaged in the performance of a public service in which it derives no special advantage or privilege, but which it is bound to see performed in pursuance of a duty proposed by law for the general welfare of its inhabitants. The proprietary function, he counters, is one voluntarily undertaken by the city for its particular advantage or *pecuniary* profit.

In cases tested before the courts, the amount and purpose of the fee or charge levied by the recreation agency seemed to have more effect on the courts than the fact of the fee itself. The "profit motive" therefore is a key factor. If the fee or charge were only incidental and not for the purpose of making a profit, courts decided that the fee did not change the nature of the recreation function from governmental to proprietary. Courts, generally, take a very idealistic view of public recreation services and regard them as essentially wholesome, uplifting, highly desirable, and free, especially for people of low incomes. Thus, although there is no specific doctrine or rule, the growing tendency by municipalities to charge fees for park and recreation programs and facilities increases the likelihood of negative judgments in recreation lawsuits. The effects of charging fees vary in different states. It appears generally, however, that in states in which recreation is regarded as a governmental function, incidental changes do not affect the nature of the function. When recreation is regarded as a propriety function or when there are substantial secondary profits accruing to the recreation operation, the function and liability are changed by assessment of fees. Where the intent of fees and charges is clearly and solely to produce profits, the function is definitely affected, whether in a governmental or proprietary state, and the possibility of financial damanges in suits against the agency becomes much greater.

Thus, to determine the liability impact of proposed new fees and charges or any increase of existing fees and charges, a public recreation agency should ascertain:

1. Whether the state in which the agency lies regards recreation services as governmental or proprietary.
2. Whether the purpose of the fee or charge is to bring a direct profit or to

accomplish some other goal such as control of attendance, segregation of clientele by residence, defrayment of some related cost.

3. Whether any profit resulting from the proposed fee or charge schedule could be judged by a court to be large or substantial.

4. The history of related lawsuits within the state.

The thoughtful answers to these questions will give the recreation administrator a good estimate as to the possible tort liability impact if the proposed fees and charges are invoked.

ACCIDENTS AND INSURANCE

The ten leading causes of death in the United States of persons 1 to 44 years of age and their annual incidence are:

1. Accidents (57,427)
2. Cancer (21, 864)
3. Heart disease (16,534)
4. Homicide (15, 455)
5. Suicide (13,897)
6. Cirrhosis of liver (5,516)
7. Cerebrovascular disease (4,601)
8. Pneumonia (3,354)
9. Congenital anomalies (3,269)
10. Diabetes mellitus (1,688)[2]

Accidents and their complications are by far the greatest legal concern to most recreation administrators. Playgrounds, ice rinks, gymnastic equipment, tobaggan runs, swimming pools—all have such tremendous accident potential that many recreation directors have completely avoided one or all of these in their operations. Now, however, since accident insurance has quadrupled in cost during the late 1970s, this fear of accident and devastating lawsuit has been greatly aggravated.

A sound insurance policy is a must for any recreation operation. The municipality may choose to purchase a policy or to "self-insure." The latter is the practice followed when a long history of no suits or successfully defended lawsuits makes it infeasible for the municipality to pay out high insurance premiums. Instead, it sets aside a specific sum annually (approximately $1.00 per resident of the municipality as a minimum) and hopes that in 3 to 5 years it will have accumulated at least a quarter of a million dollars. With good luck and tight administration, such a fund, once accumulated, can save the city the cost of conventional insurance overhead. Needless to say, a sudden catastrophic accident and heavy financial judgment could wipe out such a fund and even put the municipality in debt.

Whether insured by a firm or self-insured, the recreation agency should institute a program of safety control, accident prevention, and risk management if it is to cope with today's expensive accident insurance premiums. This is particularly true in those states in which recreation services are deemed a proprietary function of government. Insurance should be of a comprehensive nature and give coverage to the total recreation program regardless of whether the program is conducted on or off the property of the recreation agency.

Coverage for individual employees, or agents as the law identifies them, in excess of $1,000,000 is no longer unusual, though such amounts are rarely paid in judgment. The insurance policy should cover the entire recreation agency and its employees so that if a suit is filed against one employee or the entire agency the same insurance policy will cover everyone involved. This points up an interesting practice in accidents and suits. Lawyers and their clients usually regard it as advantageous to file the same suit against every individual involved in the accident, various clusters of persons, and the entire agency. For example, a 12-year-old boy is working out on the parallel bars in the local high school gymnasium under the supervision of a part-time, paid recreation leader and a volunteer adult. The apparatus was set up by the regular building custodian. Suddenly, half of the extended parallel bar slips in its post and the boy falls and breaks his arm. The parents sue shortly thereafter for $25,000 charging collective negligence and lack of supervision. Named in the suit are the custodian, the custodian's superior, the paid leader; the volunteer leader; the board of education, individually, each member of the board; the chairman of the recreation commission; the recreation comission; individually, all other members of the commission; the mayor; individually, members of the city council; and the superintendent of recreation. The theory seems to be, "find the softest spot." All persons and areas are probed early, and through hearings and investigations, the plaintiff's attorney finally decides on the softest target and attacks. The case is then focused on one or two individuals.

After insurance protection is obtained, the next most important thing is a strong accident prevention procedure. This should include: (1) staff instruction, (2) accident and emergency procedures, (3) sound facility layout, (4) regular inspection and repairs, and (5) supervision.

Staff instruction

Proper training of staff and rehearsal of procedure is basic to accident prevention. Every member of the recreation agency, including secretaries and file clerks, can contribute something to the prevention of accidents. Further, it may be that when a small disaster occurs in the office, only the secretary is on hand to cope with it. No one, no section, and no department is immune to accidents. No excuses should be tolerated. Needless to say, certain areas and jobs are more vulnerable than others. Lifeguards, truck drivers, gymnastics instructors, and people working with fuel, furnaces, refrigeration, building materials are all among those who deal most frequently with dangerous accidents. Nevertheless, accident prevention is everyone's business.

Accident and emergency procedures

Each basic type of accident, e.g., pool drowning, beach drowning, skating injury at the ice rink, coronary attack, should be carefully analyzed and written out in the accident procedure manual. Every employee should have this manual and be reasonably familiar with its contents. Preparations should include location of first aid supplies and equipment and telephones, availability of ambulance, police, and fire services, and extreme steps to be taken when all conventional services fail to arrive.

First aid instruction should be given to all staff members—advanced instruction to those in accident-prone situations, elementary first aid to all others. The local chapter of the American Red Cross can be invaluable in the teaching of first aid and in periodic check-ups and retraining.

Sound facility input

Many accident potentials can be avoided by sound planning and construction. Glass, steps, windows, pits, pools, coping, doors, moving partitions, deck space, skylights, electrical work, overhead pipes—these are just a few of the features of a recreation facility that can result in many unnecessary and costly accidents. The proper placing of a handrail or the lowering of a step just 1 inch are the small design features that can make a building or facility much safer.

The installation of basketball backboards, indoors and out, and the great variety of new metal and wood playground equipment offer countless opportunities for carelessness or poor workmanship. It is well worth the time and money by management to scrutinize all such new equipment both on arrival and after installation.

As an added precaution and, incidentally, to meet most state building requirements today, recreation designers should adapt their facilities to accomodate handicapped people. The NRPA provides written material on ramps, rails, door widths, toilets, and the like that accommodate the needs of handicapped persons and meet state requirements.

Regular inspection and repairs

Regular inspections, and all repairs to damaged or worn equipment should be tightly scheduled and never left to chance. Loose handrails, crumbling steps, broken glass, and exposed wires are the kinds of conditions that invite trouble. Recreation administrators should establish a comprehensive inventory of potential accident sites and conditions and schedule regular personal inspections or inspections by qualified subordinates. Written records of these inspections should be kept along with records of the carpentry, plumbing, painting, or rewiring that was done to correct the situation. These records could be vitally important in a later court case.

Supervision

Supervision, or the lack of it, is probably the most often mentioned factor in lawsuits in which negligence is charged. No one can ever determine, by formula, exactly what constitutes "good supervision," as distinguished from "poor supervision," at an ice rink, on a rifle range, at the beach, in a gymnasium. Numbers are not the simple answer, as in "one lifeguard on duty for every 10 swimmers" or "one leader stationed in each corner of the gymnasium when a full gym class is in progress." The

matter of supervision and negligence, unfortunately, is more complex than that. Among the questions often asked in court include: Were the lifeguards clustered together? To whom were they talking? Was the sun in their eyes and, if so, why were they not wearing sunglasses? Where was their supervisor? Were all equally well-trained? When had they last been inspected?

As long as one understands that the goal of the plaintiff's lawyer is to prove negligence, or at least inadequate supervision at the recreation site, it is clear why he or she will continue one line of questioning until the witness, defendant, or both look lazy, stupid, careless, or poorly trained.

The best advice to the recreation administrator is to provide the best trained and most adequate leadership and supervision the budget will permit. Careful selection of staff, sound training in accident prevention and first aid, and regular inspections represent the best administrative process. "Reasonable and prudent supervision" is a phrase frequently used by courtroom attorneys in describing the type of supervision they believe should be exercised over recreation activities and facilities.

NRPA SAFETY

For several years, the NRPA has maintained a permanent task force for the purpose of establishing saftey standards for playground equipment. Equipment manufacturers, recreation and park administrators, workers, leaders, safety specialists, medical doctors and college professors are liberally represented on this task force. Work has included analysis of designs, materials, paints, fittings, and other construction features, and several major steps have been completed for improving the quality of equipment and installation. Reputable playground manufacturers such as Gametime, Miracle, Belson, Mexico Forge, Jayfro, American, Burke, Everwear, North American Recreation Convertible, Timberform, Big Toys, and Play Timber are likely to profit through the effectiveness of this safety task force. Safer, sturdier equipment can only result in the sale of more units and the modernization of thousands of playgrounds.

OSHA

With the passage of the Occupational Safety and Health Act (OSHA) of 1970, public recreation managers began to discover what good industrial managers realized decades ago—that good safety is good business. It not only saves lives and limbs, it saves time and money.

Although public employees are initially exempted by the act, Executive Order No. 11612 requires federal agencies, including the National Park Service, to develop effective and comprehensive occupational safety and health programs. Further, the separate states are encouraged to establish and enforce strict safety and accident programs that will cover state, county, city, town, and village employees. A major encouragement is the fact that such state OSHA programs are 50% reimbursable by the federal government.

OSHA inspections for safety are generally feared by businesses and government agencies because of their thoroughness and potential penalties, but they have done much to relieve dangerous working conditions in certain areas. Today, close to 90% of the individual states have established OSHA programs for industrial safety.

CIVIL RIGHTS

In an era of expanding awareness of individual rights and freedoms, it is essential that recreation administrators be alert to their legal implications. In all programs and administive matters, diligent efforts are required to ensure that no individuals or groups are excluded, discriminated against, or in any way abused because of age, sex, race, or other socioethnic factor. In matters of jobs, training, promotions, membership eligibility, use of facilities, admission charges, no discrimination or preferential treatment is to be tolerated, unless one wishes to face substantial civil rights charges and court action. Particularly sensitive spheres are employment interviews, dress and hair regulations, official memorandum language, special holidays and celebrations, work assignments, and selections for advance training. Careful study of basic civil rights legislation and a sound judgment should help the recreation administrator to avoid such legal pitfalls.

COURT APPEARANCES

Precautions notwithstanding, there is every likelihood that the professional reader of this text will someday be summoned to appear at a lawsuit proceeding or other litigation connected with recreation. It is wise to be prepared.

Before the accident or incident:

1. Maintain complete files on maintenance inspections, checkups, and repairs of facilities and equipment.
2. Keep the staff alert to accident procedures and reports.
3. Maintain reasonably detailed files on every reported accident for at least 5 years.

At the time of the accident or incident:

1. Have site or unit of equipment thoroughly photographed. Obtain at least 5 clear, black-and-white, 8 × 10 inch photos, all angles and perspectives.
2. Obtain all witnesses' statements, names, and addresses immediately.

Do not delay and do not overlook anyone. Put all statements in writing and have them signed or initialed.

3. Read accident report carefully: then question all persons involved fully, quietly, and meticulously. Record all statements. Give staff member a copy.

4. Notify the corporation counsel, town attorney, legal counsel to the institution, or the insurance company's lawyer. If none exists, consult a reputable attorney and brief him or her on the facts.

5. Wait for further developments.

A pretrial hearing is frequently arranged to establish facts and strategy. Your attorney, the municipality's attorney, or the insurance company's attorney will contact you. You will be asked to relate facts as you recall them as will other members of the staff who may have been involved in the accident or incident. The conversation is carefully recorded by a stenographer and/or a tape recorder. Be candid and honest with the attorney, giving only the facts. You will later receive a copy of your testimony for your approval. If you believe it to be accurate, sign the statement and return it to the attorney. This will be used as an exhibit in court, and a copy will be made available to the plaintiff's attorney.

In the meantime, do not discuss the case, the facts, or the personalities with the plaintiff, the plaintiff's family, the plaintiff's lawyer, the press, or anyone not connected with your own attorney's office. Never, under any circumstances, discuss the case with anyone on the telephone, regardless of what names, credentials, or other approaches they use.

When summoned to court, observe the following suggestions:

1. Arrive at least one quarter of an hour early to meet your attorney and become oriented.

2. Do not speak to the plaintiff, the plaintiff's family, or the plaintiff's attorney before the trial. An innocent comment can easily be misconstrued.

3. Dress neatly but conservatively so that your appearance does not distract from the proceedings.

4. When called to the witness stand, be prompt and courteous at all times.

5. Answer questions clearly and briefly so that the judge, jury, and others in the room can hear.

6. Do not embroider or embellish answers. If the answer to a question is "Yes", or "No," leave it at that. If possible, avoid vague answers such as "Maybe," "I think so," "Could be." Such responses will weaken your testimony considerably.

7. When in doubt, stop and think. If you do not understand the question, ask that it be repeated. If you become confused, turn to the judge and ask his or her advice, *not* on the answer, but on what is being sought or how you should phrase it. The judge is a friend, not an enemy, and is there to be used.

8. Do not be intimidated or rushed by an aggressive prosecutor. The plaintiff's lawyer has no right to rush you as long as you are trying to be cooperative and are following the directions of the judge. You have every right to pause, to think, and when necessary, to ask for additional time before answering.

9. When excused from the witness stand, leave promptly and make no additional statements.

10. Thereafter, discuss the case with no one except your own attorney until a decision is announced. This could be many months later.

The message in the above ten steps is to prepare yourself well in advance of the trial with the facts, be composed in the courtroom, and discuss the case only with your own lawyer and when called on in court. Do this, and your chances of winning the lawsuit will be considerably improved.

PUBLIC GIFTS

The prospect of receiving public gifts is a pleasant one for the recreation administrator. Public gifts mean such things as a new piano for a YMCA, new playground equipment in a park, a new outdoor swimming pool for the community, and the like. Usually, the gift is in the form of cash or a check made out to the agency and is specifically intended for a favorite project of the donor. Often, the donor will identify the gift as a memorial to a specific person, to a war veteran, or to the city or town in which the donor was born. These public or community gifts are to be encouraged, but the realistic recreation administrator should also be aware of the legal responsibilities and concerns that accompany such gifts. Following are a few tips that should facilitate gift reception without legal problems.

1. At first offer of the gift, request courteously that the gift offer be put in writing with as much detail as possible.
2. Inform your superior and your legal counsel, providing them with copies of the written offer.
3. Analyze the motives of the donor. If any ulterior motive surfaces, be it politics, excess profit, or personal grudge of some kind, decline the offer.
4. If the gift is tangible, such as a piece of property, a building, a vehicle, or some type of sports equipment, examine it. In the past, unscrupulous persons have used this method to unload unsightly property, stolen goods,

or just plain junk on an unsuspecting city hall.
5. Make certain that full title to the gift goes with it, with no liens, restrictions, or hampering provisions that will prevent the full use of the gift in the public's interest.

If everything appears legitimate, request legal counsel to outline steps by which the gift can be accepted by the municipality or agency and become fully the property and responsibility of same. Never, under any conditions, accept such a gift in your own name.

Gifts of park land are quite common and some of the motivations include memorials to members of old families, perpetuation of the wooded or rustic atmosphere of some portion of the community, a tangible "Thank you" to city or community for a happy youth or satisfying life, genuine love for mankind, disposal of rugged or hilly pieces of property useless for other development, and tax deduction under Internal Revenue laws.

A new park may bring reflected benefits on adjoining property resulting in greater beauty and higher real estate values. This has been a motivation in the donation of many parks in the past. The cash value of such gifts is deductible from taxable annual gross income. To distribute the tax benefit, parts of a given parcel are often donated in different years. The inheritance tax operates to encourage liquidation by public donations of properties before the death of estate builders.

One of the country's finest park systems is in Minneapolis, where 22 complete parks and a substantial portion of other parks were gifts. Probably no other city service rendered is supported to this extent by gifts from citizens. Los Angeles, with a total park acreage of 12,820 acres, may be cited as another example. It has 169 parks and playgrounds, not including off-street park-ways and triangles. Of this number, 41 were gifts, totalling 3474 acres. The largest single gift was 3200 acres, Griffith Park, added to by purchases and now totalling 4254 acres. The donation of land was followed by a gift of $1 million trust fund to provide cultural facilities in the park. Other donations have included 2 miles of extraordinarily fine public beach property and a playground of 30 acres next to a school property. According to estimates, one third of the local park and recreation acreage in the United States has been acquired through gifts.

Positive steps must be taken to create an atmosphere for such gifts. News stories, statements by municipal officials, both elected and appointed, working policies, and department literature and speeches before local organizations should make clear to the public that such gifts are welcome. The advantages to the donor, as described previously, should be pointed out. Above all, these methods must generate a real desire to give, to build, to establish something lasting and good. When donors come forward, they must be met by the appreciative but mature reception they logically anticipate.

Similarly, public officials must exercise discretion in accepting gifts that may become public liabilities. A bottomless swamp, a minute piece of real estate, a dangerous piece of equipment, and other items of this type must be avoided even at the declining of the gift. The motives of the donor may be unimpeachable, but the municipality must not be burdened with a public menace or a "money-gobbler" simply because it is offered.

One successful "gift" project, completed and tastefully publicized locally, can trigger a chain of such gifts over the years. Through such gifts, long-range plans for park and recreation improvements can be greatly accelerated, and cost to the individual taxpayer can be kept within reasonable limits.

The warning to recreation administrators is that they must "look the gift horse in the mouth" when public or community gifts are involved. To do less, is to set the stage for a long-term public nuisance or a serious legal problem.

LEGAL COUNSEL

Wise recreation administrators, early in their careers, come to realize the importance of sound legal counsel and advice. In a municipality it is the corporation counsel, county attorney, or city attorney; in institutional recreation, it is the staff counsel. The recreation professional should meet such counsel, exchange ideas, and establish a good working relationship. When new ideas are proposed or problems begin to emerge, recreators should discuss this with the attorneys, getting their ideas *before* deciding on an action. With a background such as this, it is easy to come together and plan strategy when a major incident or lawsuit occurs.

DISCUSSION QUESTIONS

1. The state enabling act is the legal basis for recreation services in a muncipality. Explain what such an enabling act permits and why it is called a permissive piece of legislation.
2. Explain the difference between *governmental* and *proprietary* when applied to the acts and functions of a government agency. Specify five such acts that might easily be interpreted as governmental in one state and proprietary in another.
3. A recreation agency is liable for its torts. Explain what a tort is and describe five everyday situations in a YMCA that, if neglected, might easily produce tort liability situations. Describe how each of these tort liability situations might have have been prevented.
4. A playground accident has occurred. Rumor reaches you, the recreation director, that a lawsuit will be filed. Outline the steps you would take in preparation for the lawsuit.

5. You are the new recreation director of a large maximum security prison of 500 male inmates. What steps would you take to ascertain your legal status and possible liability in the carrying out of recreation programs?

BIBLIOGRAPHY

Butler, G. D.: Introduction to community recreation, New York, 1959, The Ronald Press.

Bulter, G. D.: Recreation areas, their design and equipment, ed. 2, New York, 1958, The Ronald Press.

Doell, C. E.: Elements of park and recreation administration, Minneapolis, Burgess Publishing Co.

Dyer, D. B., and Lichtig, J. G.: Liability in public recreation, Appleton, Wis., 1951, C. C. Nelson Publishing Co.

Legislative manual, state of New York, 1971-1972, Albany.

Lutzin, S. G., and Storey, E. H.: Managing municipal leisure services, Chicago, 1973, The International City Managers Association.

Metropolitan Regional Council: The race for open space, Regional Plan Association Bulletin no. 96, New York, 1960, The Association.

Nash, J. B.: The administration of physical education, New York, 1931, A. S. Barnes & Co.

Nash, J. B.: The organization and administration of playgrounds and recreation, New York, 1927, A. S. Barnes & Co.

Outdoor Recreation Resources Review Commission: Outdoor recreation for America, Report to the President and the Congress, Washington, D.C., 1962. State enabling legislation for local recreation, recreation circular no. 3, Washington, D.C., 1937.

Van der Smissen, B.: Legal liability in cities and schools for injuries in recreation and parks, Cincinnati, 1968, W. H. Anderson Co.

REFERENCES

1. Mounce, E. W., and Dawson, T. L.: Business law, Boston, 1958, D. C. Heath & Co.
2. National Safety Council: Family Safety 36:23, Fall 1977.
3. Reed, C. E.: Recreation, 1932.
4. Rodney, L. S.: Administration of public recreation, New York, 1964, The Ronald Press.
5. Sternloff, R. E., and Warren, R.: Park and recreation maintenance management, Boston, 1977, Holbrook Press, Inc.

13
FACILITIES

Courtesy Huron-Clinton Metropolitan Authority, Detroit, Mich.

Recreation facilities are the real estate, the hardware of the recreation program, whether they are located in parks, on school sites, college campuses, industrial reservations, or private camps. Facilities are the third point of a triangle that also includes leadership and program. This was not always so. In the earlier stages of the recreation movement, facilities were not thought of as critically important. A shed, an open field, or a hill were regarded as adequate to meet the needs of motivated people, and they often did. But highly motivated, knowledgeable people are a small minority. Most people are uncertain, unskilled, or ignorant of the meaning and significance of recreation; they need motivation and the right opportunity. This is where the facility is so important.

The widening impact of public recreation, of physical education, and of a number of health problems has aroused public consciousness to the importance of more and improved provision of health education, physical education and recreation programs and services. It has also directed attention unmistakably to the need for additional areas and facilities to meet the growing demand and enable these programs and services to function fully and effectively.[1]

Among the factors that have accelerated this demand for new and improved recreation facilities are:

1. The nation's population is still increasing, despite a so-called zero birthrate, and will grow appreciably until the year 2000.
2. An increase in leisure brought about through longer school attendance, longer vacations, and more labor-saving equipment.
3. Incomes, after taxes and adjusted for inflation, are still on the rise.
4. Greater mobility is the freedom with which families and individuals pick up and move to distant places, often for new jobs and new careers.
5. Most of the country's large, concentrated metropolitan areas have grown phenomenally from 100% to 800% since World War II, both in population and in developed acreage.
6. This metropolitan growth has reduced appreciably the free, open spaces formerly available to urban and suburban dwellers.
7. The rapid change in assembly line production and the arrival of new business systems and equipment have taken much of the personal input and pride from labor. Workers are left with a great hunger for experience, self-fulfillment, and exercise. Recreation facilities are a major factor in fulfilling this hunger.

Recreation facilities range in size from the tiniest park or plain brick wall for a game of balls and strikes to such giants as the Meadowlands in New Jersey, the New Orleans Super Dome, and Disney World in Orlando, Florida. Some are natural—lakes, forests, hills, and beaches; others represent the design genius and construction skills of man—Lion Safari Country and The Windows, a restaurant atop the World Trade Center in New York City. The number and array, especially in the United States, is unbelievable.

For practical purposes, however, we shall concentrate on those areas and facilities that are most frequently found within the purview of community, recreation, therapeutic, and institutional recreation. These include parks, swimming pools, golf courses, basketball courts, skating rinks, bicycle paths, sports and athletic fields, recreation centers, playgrounds, tennis courts, picnic areas, and beaches, lakes, and ponds. Contained within several of these larger facilities are benches, restrooms, checker tables, fountains, shuffleboard, handball, street hockey, badminton, volleyball, paddle tennis, archery, boccie, horseshoes, table tennis, and others.

This overall group contains 90% of the areas and facilities that make up the "hardware" inventory of most recreation administrators. A list of rarer facilities includes skiing and sledding slopes, water chute-the-chutes, hang gliding and soaring hills, underwater facilities, amateur rocketry pads, skateboard slopes, drag strips, and rifle or skeet ranges.

PLANNING

How does a recreation facility come into existence? Is it the genius of one planner, or do a group of people put it together? Is it spontaneous, or does it take many years? How does a new recreation administrator react when a citizen group says, "We want you to build us a park." Despite the increased sophistication of the recreation profession, sound planning of new facilities is still the exception rather than the rule. In spite of all the meetings, architects, sketches, and so forth, key elements of the process will frequently be left out, unforgiveable errors made, and golden opportunities lost that could have produced near-perfect combinations of need matched with facility. Consider the following two examples.

A shower room floor in a new junior high school was so tilited that shower water flowed downhill under the door of the director's office. Extra curbing had to be built to keep the water out—ugly, inconvenient, and expensive. New light towers on a softball field were accidentally installed *inside* the baselines of the ball field! The day before construction began, some children moved the marker stakes prankishly. Laborers arrived, respected the stake locations exactly as they appeared, and sank the concrete footings for the steel poles inside the baselines. Later, the entire ball field had to be moved to accommodate the mislocated floodlights. Substantial time was lost, and extra expense incurred. I can verify these two errors, since both took place at locations where I was in responsible posts.

Reports of design and construction errors are numerous and, in most cases, unforgiveable. In addition, many facilities that are built soundly from a design and engineering standpoint miss their mark because they do not meet the tastes or needs of future users. They are the right facilities, but in the wrong place or in the wrong time, or they are constructed to meet conditions that never occurred or that occurred too long ago to be relevant.

Regardless of whether the facility is large or small, if it comes under the authority of a recreation department, the following procedure will be most helpful. Before commencing, note these basic principles, commit them to mind, and make certain they are accommodated in the new facility:

1. Recreation opportunities should be available to all, regardless of age, race, color, creed, or ethnic or economic status.
2. The facility should provide as wide a variety of activity as possible. This is economically advantageous.
3. Esthetics of the design should be considered immediately after the use factor. Appearances are important.
4. The facility, small though it may be, should represent a distinct improvement or addition to its neighborhood.
5. The new facility should be conceived as giving maximum activity or use potential, while requiring the least maintenance care and cost.

Study the need

A careful analysis of the immediate area is a must. How many people live within $1/2$ mile of the site? Are similar facilities nearby and unused? These and dozens of questions on neighborhood tastes, habits, ethnic preferences, traffic flow, noise, lights, safety, and local religious practices must be researched and answered. From this comes the true neighborhood or community profile without which the new facility would be a mere shot in the dark. Small meetings of 10 to 15 people at a time, in homes, schools, temples, churches, restaurants, and markets are extremely helpful in arriving at this profile.

The financial plan

Assembling a sound, workable financial plan is the next step. The recreation administrator, whether in a city, town, hospital, retirement resort, or prison ascertains a rough cost estimate for the facility. The city engineer or staff technical expert can provide this as long as the recreation person informs the engineer of general outlines and requirements of the project. Such an outline might read, "An athletic park and playground, build on existing flat land, with two softball fields, six tennis courts, small children's play area, and parking for fifty cars." Another possibility is, "An olympic-sized swimming pool outdoors, a small locker room, ample deck space for an average attendance of 200 people, and the entire area fenced by chain link, 6 feet high." Such descriptions are quite easily converted to rough estimates of cost.

Following this comes a series of studies and decisions as to how and when the project will be financed. Sources include federal revenue sharing funds, sales tax revenues, special recreation levies, state grants for park and recreation facilities, U.S. Land and Water Conservation Funds, gifts from local donors, local reserves, advance family registrations for the facility, or some combination of the above. For example, a new artificial outdoor ice skating rink,

covered by a dome, with overall area 100 feet by 200 feet, is desired, and estimated cost is $1 million. The local city government may choose to finance it as follows:

Special recreation revenue bond	$500,000
Land Water Conservation Funds	250,000
Advanced skating registrations for local families	50,000
Local reserves	200,000
Total	$1,000,000

A great many variations are possible, but a sound financial plan is absolutely necessary before any decision is made to proceed further.

Architectural services

Except for the tiniest and most simple installation or construction, the talents and skills of a licensed architect should be used. In a very large agency or department, an architect or architectural services may be directly available within the organization. Use them. If no such person or services is available because of the small size of the department or because of administrative policy, go outside to get such assistance. Advantages include: (1) knowledge of materials and substances, (2) esthetics and taste, (3) strength and stability in design, (4) knowledge of building codes and laws, (5) skill at bringing together utility, economy, appearance, and the many people and agencies who influence the creation of a new structure, and (6) supervision while the project is under construction.

Architects are normally selected under the heading of "professional services," much as a lawyer, doctor, dentist, or registered nurse is selected. It is recommended that the recreation department or agency establish a few construction criteria on paper, distribute a printed description of what is desired to several reputable architects, and then conduct interviews. The architect selected should be:

1. Familiar with recreation and park services and needs
2. Experienced in designing recreation facilities
3. A capable person, skilled in working with public officials, agency personnel, and all segments of the public sector.
4. A designer of original, fresh concepts, rather than a mere reprinter of stereotypes
5. In a position to marshal any and all personnel needed, full-time or part-time, such as draftsmen, surveyors, licensed engineers, and other technicians

When the architect has been selected on the basis of his or her proposal for doing the job, a formal written contract should be drawn up by legal counsel. Thereafter, the architect is part of the planning team.

Obtaining the site

If a piece of property is already available, no site selection is needed since the property is specified and already owned. If not, a search must be made. To do this, the planning team should look at all sites available within the chosen area under the guidance of municipal real estate staff and/or private real estate brokers. Great caution must be exercised by the planning team while looking at potential sites. Ask questions, take photographs, study the properties in the finest detail, but do not give any indication which properties are favored, for fear the prices on such pieces may escalate. Only when all studies are complete should the owner be approached for negotiation and then in complete privacy. A few important characteristics of good recreational properties include: (1) accessibility to populations requiring the service, (2) good natural drainage, (3) as remote as possible from such hazards as highways, railroad beds, sanitary landfills, canyons, gullies, swamps, or offensive industries, and (4) of such a contour and texture as to permit normal grading and restructuring.

Developing the site plan

This is the step in which the raw property is converted, on paper, into the park, playground, or recreation facility desired. Here the licensed architect's guidance is most important. Photographs taken in various weather conditions and at various times of the day are helpful. From them and from meetings with neighborhood residents come the first preliminary sketches and drawings of the facility. These are studied by the professional staff and by citizen groups, and, inevitably, many comments, suggestions, and changes result. The architect redraws the sketches, accomodating as many of the changes as possible. The process is repeated some three or four times until a good compromise pattern has been determined. This, then, becomes the base plan, and more advanced technical drawings are begun. In the process of discussion and redrawing, some of the elements to be considered are:

Program. Does the site and facility grow out of community program need? Are spaces, doors, closets, etc. especially suited to anticipated programs?

Utility. Have maximum use, convenience, and sensible working layouts been considered in planning toilets, washrooms, storage, etc.?

Safety. Do any activities or building components threaten any others? Do balls fly in the wrong direction? Is the parking area a hazard to participants? Are there any health or sanitation problems?

Flexibility and adaptability. Has the design considered the need for many different programs, with minimal time needed for changeovers? Is the unit flexible enough to include new and unanticipated activities in the future?

Beauty. Has the plan utilized all the existing natural features, and has it brought the complex together in a way that is pleasing to the eye and an asset to the neighborhood? Lack of beauty or ugly utilitarianism has haunted many a noble recreation project long after its completion. Architectural guidance here is extremely important.

Going to contract

When all technical drawings have been completed by licensed architects and engineers, the project is advertised for bids. This advertising is placed prominently in one or more recognized local newspapers and is often sent to several local contracting and construction firms inviting them to submit sealed bid proposals on or before an official deadline (usually, several weeks are given).

On the specified date and time, the bids are opened in a public room, each specification is noted and tallied, and the contract for construction of the facility is awarded. Criteria for this award are usually adherence to specifications, lowest total cost to the recreation agency, agreement to meet the time schedule, and general quality of the proposal. With such a variety of criteria, it is not difficult to determine which bid proposal offers the most to the city or agency for the least cost.

Construction

At an agreed-on time, actual construction begins under the watchful eye of the architect and the recreation administrator. The architect's job here is to see that there is strict adherence to the bid proposal and contract in every way, including time schedules, quality of materials, construc-

tion skills exercised, the use of union personnel is specified, and cooperation with all city, state, and federal regulations on Affirmative Action, building codes, and general safety. At completion of the project, the recreation agency inspects the facility, accepts title for the city or agency, and authorizes final payment to the contractor.

Cautions

Based on many years' experience, many mistakes, and the advice of several other recreation experts, the following cautions are offered regarding contracting work and construction.

Make certain that quality and density standards for concrete are met, that pourings are scheduled, and that no pourings are done when temperatures approach freezing. The handling of concrete is very technical and should be closely supervised by an engineer or technical expert. Free advice on concrete may be obtained from the Atlas Cement Institute.

Similar cautions should be observed with asphalt as with concrete, though temperatures and characteristics are different. The Asphalt Institute offers a free, excellent reference book.

Other construction materials such as lumber, glass, granite, steel, insulation, and electrical materials must all be scrutinized *before* they are installed if serious structural problems are to be avoided.

Delivery and completion dates are probably the most often violated factors by contractors. Delays are usually extremely costly. Care must be taken to ensure that time schedules are realistic, and then they must be enforced.

The innocent recreation agency may be placed in an awkward position by the unscrupulous tactics of certain builders. If the contract calls for union workers, the builder should not bring in nonunion personnel as a speedup or as a cost-cutter. Further, the builder must enforce all OSHA safety regulations on the job, including hard hats, elevators, tools, explosives, gasoline, lights, first-aid, and so forth. Carelessness in this by the builder-contractor can delay the project weeks and months and may end up in lawsuits filed by unions or individual workers.

RECREATION STANDARDS

Following are a series of standards or guides for planning recreation and park facilities. Based on anticipated population use and geography, they are to be thought of only as guides, not absolutes. Most of these were established by the National Recreation Association (now the National Recreation and Park Association) during the 1940s, but they have been updated periodically since then.

Types of facilities

The neighborhood playlot. Frequently called the totlot, kiddy playground, or vest-pocket park, this facility serves a city block or less and includes a few elementary pieces of play equipment. A space of 2000 square feet to 5000 square feet is considered adequate, and the users are primarily preschoolers and children under 7 years of age.

The neighborhood playground. This facility is for children 6 to 14 years of age, chiefly, with some small accommodation for older youths and elderly persons. It usually contains basketball, boxball, and small softball areas along with a battery of five to ten pieces of metal play equipment. Ideally, its size runs from 4 to 8 acres, though many congested urban areas can only provide $1^1/2$ to 2 acres.

The community playfield. This facility should provide some accomodation for every age and for family groups. A central

playfield is used for sports such as baseball, softball, soccer, football, lacrosse, and a variety of special events. Auxiliary features include a shelter building, rest rooms, small picnic area, and parking. A standard of 15 to 20 acres is desirable, though not always attainable in crowded cities. A rule-of-thumb is 1 acre for each 800 people residing in the city or municipality. A playfield should lie within $1/2$ to 1 mile of each home.

The large urban park. Unlike the carefully laid out and rather sharply defined pattern of the playfields and playgrounds, the large urban park is usually irregular in shape and tends to follow some natural or artificial contours or boundaries. It may follow a stream, such as Rock Creek Park in Washington, D.C., or it may occupy a huge center area of property as do the 800 acres that make up Central Park in New York City. Many smaller playfields or playgrounds may lie within the perimeter of a large urban park, along with hills, forest groves, lakes, bridle paths, picnic areas, and uncommitted open space. A minimum of 100 acres is desirable, but 300 or more acreas should be sought. A rule-of-thumb is one such large park for every 50,000 persons residing in the municipality.

The reservation. This is a large tract of land kept in its natural state, some sections being made available for activities such as bicycling, horseback riding, biking, camping, nature study, and riflery. Such facilities require substantial acreage, as in the South Mountain Reservation, Essex County, N. J. and the Blue Mountain Reservation, Westchester County, N.Y., and are most often located at the edge of large cities, or considerably beyond their borders. A minimum of 1000 acres is considered adequate, with many urban and suburban reservations in the Midwest and West running to 5000 acres or more.

Special areas and facilities. These are sites and areas set aside and/or developed for one specific activity, each activity requiring a substantial piece of acreage. These might include a golf course, beach, large swimming pool, athletic field, tennis center, or sports stadium.

A 9-hole golf course requires approximately 50 acres, an 18-hole course requires 110 to 160 acres, and 2 complete 18-hole courses require 250 acres.

Beaches are flexible, but no beach worth its name should have less than 2 to 3 acres of clear, attractive sunbathing area at high tide. From here, beaches can range up into the tens of miles, such as Los Padres National Seashore in Texas or Cape Cod National Seashore in Massachusetts.

A large swimming pool with necessary locker rooms, office, shelter, service buildings, and parking requires from 3 to 10 acres.

An athletic field of modest proportions calls for 6 to 8 acres, but a large sophisticated plant with stadium, parking, and auxiliary services will need from 25 to 50 acres. Shea Stadium in New York City sits on 52 acres, while the Tampa Memorial Stadium in Florida is on 44 acres.

The neighborhood park. This tiny facility has many other names—parklet, greenspot, minipark, vestpocket park, and cameo park, to name a few. It should possess all major park features, but on a smaller scale. Its purpose is quiet, informal recreation, mixed with some amenities for small children and their guardians. Benches, shrubs, small trees, decorative fencing, hedges, drinking fountain, chess-checkerboard tables, sculpture, fountains, and memorial pieces are the type of "furniture" found in the neighborhood park.

Probably the most important park unit on the crowded urban scene, the neighborhood park usually consists of 2 acres of parkland for every 1000 people in a neighborhood of multifamily dwellings. In neighborhoods of one- or two-family dwellings, this requirement is reduced to 1 acre for every 1000 residents. Since neighborhoods vary widely, this requirement may be better understood by this further breakdown of space:

> 2000 residents—2 to 4 acres
> 3000 residents—4 to 5 acres
> 4000 residsnts—5 to 6 acres
> 5000 residents—6 to 8 acres

Acreage

Two factors must be carefully considered when computing acreage needed for a new recreation facility.

Be conservative. Land is expensive and difficult to acquire. If the acreage sought is too large, much time will be consumed seeking it and much frustration experienced until it is found. Further, if the oversized site includes residential "taking" and municipal negotiations on streets, easements, zoning changes, and so forth, the litigation connected with site acquisition may be endless.

Be visionary. Extra acres acquired as part of a large land purchase are not nearly as difficult to obtain as they will be at some later date. A pinched, warped property line resulting from a too conservative land purchase may produce a pinched, warped facility design, starved for a few extra acres. Since many facilities, after successful planning, quickly find themselves physically inadequate for the crowds of users, it is a great asset to have a few extra acres for expansion.

Recommendation: Err slightly on the side of too much acreage rather than too little.

An overall guideline for providing the adequate space to accommodate a city recreation program is: *One acre of publicly owned open play space for every 100 persons.* Despite an endless variety of people, geography, tastes, needs, budgets, and communities, this guideline continues to be very useful.

The space requirements for some popular facilities listed at the bottom of this page refer to the space needed for use by the largest and most vigorous participants, since such facilities can easily accommodate smaller, younger, and less skilled players.

Helpful information on certain facilities

Based on experience and on the observations of several outstanding recreation executives from cities, resorts, schools, industries, and private agencies, the following list has been compiled. These represent the most popular and most frequently encountered recreation facilities. Some helpful information and advice is offered on each.

Ice skating rink, artificial. Although there are a variety of techniques available for natural ice skating such as lake and pond surfaces, and frozen tennis courts, the sophisticated taste of today's ice skater means requests for artificial ice skating surfaces. Space needed for the actual rink is 100 feet by 200 feet, if official ice hockey is to be played. The overall need for rink, shelters, locker rooms, food and skate service, and so forth is approximately 3 acres, with an additional 3 acres for parking.

Today's costs suggest a construction figure of $750,000. This does not include a roof or cover, which, if included, increases the cost to $1,000,000 to $1,125,000. High energy costs have made this an expensive facility to operate, and annual fuel and electricity charges could run from $5000 to $25,000, depending on the amount of sunshine and the length of the season. Staff is important and costly because of the high accident potential.

With careful management and a moderate fee, a publicly owned rink can almost break even financially. This will require careful use of every piece of time and ice, however, for public skating, school skating, special instruction, private parties, pageants, ice shows, and other events. Intensive renting for hockey events, sometimes for 24 hours, will bring in the extra revenue that will make the rink almost solvent. A top quality ice rink manager is essential if the rink is to be a financial and program success. Reliance solely on public skating, even where it is very popular, is not enough since most

Baseball	90 ft. diamond	122,500 sq. ft.
Basketball	60 ft. x 100 ft. average	6,000 sq. ft.
Boccie	20 ft. x 80 ft. average	1,600 sq. ft.
Field hockey	210 ft. x 330 ft. average	69,300 sq. ft.
Football	190 ft. x 420 ft. average	79,800 sq. ft
Handball	32 ft. x 44 ft. average	1,408 sq. ft.
Horseshoes	12 ft. x 52 ft. average	624 sq. ft.
Ice hockey	100 ft. x 220 ft. average	22,000 sq. ft.
Lacrosse	225 ft. x 360 ft. average	81,000 sq. ft.
Paddle tennis	35 ft. x 70 ft. average	2,450 sq. ft.
Shuffleboard	10 ft. x 60 ft. average	600 sq. ft.
Soccer	225 ft. x 359 ft. average	81,000 sq. ft.
Softball	60 ft. diamond, 275 ft. x 275 ft.	75,625 sq. ft.
Tennis	60 x 120 doubles court	7,200 sq. ft.
Touch football	190 x 420 ft. average	79,800 sq. ft.
Volleyball	45 ft. x 80 ft.	3,600 sq. ft.

public skating crowds are concentrated on Saturday, Sunday, and holiday afternoons.

There are several types of skating rinks. One is based on a concrete slab that rests on a bed of crushed gravel that breathes, vibrates, and moves slightly with earth action. A system of wrought iron pipes is installed within the concrete slab, and a freezing solution such as ammonia or brine is pumped through these pipes. This chills the concrete and freezes the surface water. The second type is a similar gridwork of metal pipes containing a refrigerant, permanently laid within a slab of sand or extra fine gravel, not solid concrete. The third type, called "roll-up" or "take-up" rink is like the second in that sand or fine gravel is used as a bed, but the pipes are plastic tubes or hoses and the entire system can be picked up and stored during the off season. Still another, newer arrangement eliminates pipes or solid slab altogether. This arrangement blows jets of highly chilled air across a paved surface bearing a 1-inch surface film of water, thus freezing the surface water in the process.

Recently, a firm named Slick has marketed a plastic material that, when applied in sheet form ³/₄-inch thick to the surface of plywood panels, 2 feet by 3 feet by 1 inch, provides a skating surface that almost equals that of real ice. These panels, when tightly assembled into composite slabs of approximately 500 square feet, serve as good skating practice areas. They eliminate all refrigeration, hardware, energy, and construction. A full-sized rink of this material, laid out on any hard, indoor floor, would cost from $75,000 to $100,000 but would not give the speed or skate response of genuine high quality water ice. Periodic surfacing treatment is necessary as the material does erode and wear at the heaviest contact points.

Any plan, large or small, for artificial skating construction, should include the purchase and operation of a mechanical ice resurfacing machine. These machines have been on the market for about 20 years, and there are over 1000 in operation today all over the world. They have revolutionized the care and quality of artificial ice surfaces. Formerly, between skating sessions or after rain and snow storms, all smoothing and resurfacing was done by skaters with shovels, brooms, hoses, mops, and squeegees. It was a slow and costly process for management, and still left a rough, soggy, and lumpy surface of varying thicknesses.

The mechanical ice resurfacer (commonly called the "Zamboni" after the California firm that first developed and marketed the machine) is a small truck-like machine built on the chassis of a jeep or other 4-wheel drive vehicle, with a 4-cylinder engine and low truck gear ratio. It contains tanks of warm water and a hopper for storage of 2 to 3 cubic yards of snow or slush. Devices on the machine enable it to perform the following functions in one operation:

1. Pick up 1 inch of loose snow and slush.
2. Deposit slush in hopper by means of endless belts and cups.
3. Shave skating surface for rough edges and splinters with a worm gear blade.
4. Gently lay out a film of warm water to fill cracks and holes with a water distributor.
5. Wipe away excess water with a squeegee.

Within 15 minutes, the entire ice surface is dry, smooth, and glistening, providing the kind of quality surface required for an ice show, expert ice skating competition, or professional hockey. *Note:* the ice rink resurfacer is not to be mistaken for a snow plow. It is helpless on snow surfaces more than 1 inch thick and can quickly be damaged when so used. Cost of these vehicles, sold by Zamboni Co., Rinkmaster Inc., and others, ranges from $8000 to $25,000, depending on the size and features of the vehicle.

Large, outdoor swimming pool. Probably the most popular single facility in the recreation inventory and, despite the limited outdoor season in northerly climates, the swimming pool's popularity continues to grow. Most large installations are located in or very close to medium or large parks. To be considered large, the pool should measure at least 150 feet by 50 feet. Many, such as the New York City pool in Astoria, Queens, are much larger and almost resemble artificial lakes.

Space required for a large pool, with its lockers, auxiliary diving and kiddie pools, service areas, and parking is similar to that of the outdoor artificial ice skating rink, from 5 to 10 acres. In fact, some communities have found it advantageous to build a swimming pool to the right and ice skating rink to the left of the same central core of dressing and service facilities, thus getting double use out of the core unit during different seasons of the year.

Costs for large pool complexes run from $1,000,000 to $2,000,000, depending on the extent of luxury features and the condition of the building site.

Vulnerable points, not unlike the ice skating center, include lifeguard staff and a battery of very delicate mechanical equipment. The threat of death is always present. If guards and staff are careless or ill-trained, the piping, chemicals, water purity, power, controls, and so forth make the pool maintenance and operation a very demanding one. An alert, trained staff and a qualified and reliable pool manager are absolutely necessary if disaster is to be avoided.

The recreation center. This is the fully enclosed building especially designed and built for private agency or public recreation use. Despite the availability of thousands of fine school buildings, there is an increased demand for separate modest-sized but well-built recreation centers. Such buildings definitely have advantages over conventional school buildings, and the only deterrent to most communities wishing to build them is the cost. They are better designed for recreation use than schools—they are available during the day and at other times when schools are committed to their own programs, and they offer storage and activity facilities and rooms that are often denied to recreation programs by school administrators.

To be considered a recreation center, a building should have at least 5000 square feet and should contain a large multipurpose room or floor, rest rooms, director's office, simple food service, and one or two small meeting-activity rooms. Since the range of variety is limitless, a cost parameter could range from $1,000,000 to $3,000,000, the latter containing an ice skating rink, cafeteria, library, and amphitheater.

Tennis center. An outdoor tennis center should include four or more tennis courts. Fewer units make it uneconomical to staff or manage. Ideally, the cluster should include from six to ten courts. The center will be even more popular if there are also four to six platform tennis courts. A small utility building should contain locker rooms, rest rooms, tennis supply shop, showers, lounge, and simple food service. A steam room or sauna is a much desired additional feature.

While grass and clay are the more traditional and charismatic tennis court surfaces, the agency or recreation department will do much better surfacing its courts with an asphalt composition. Dozens of brand names and mixes are available, and most are very good. Construction steps are usually:

1. Preparation of ground surface, earth-moving
2. Waiting period, 6 months to 1 year, while soil settles; air pockets are compressed by heavy rolling
3. Coarse crushed stone layer, 2 feet to 4 feet
4. Fine gravel layer, compacted, 1 foot to 2 feet
5. Prime black bituminous asphaltic surface, 4 inches to 8 inches thick
6. Fine colored asphalt veneer $^3/_4$ inch to 1 inch thick (most popular colors being green for the playing court, red for the outside court) applied and smoothed: contains asphaltic bond and finely pelletized rubber and cork
7. White baselines painted
8. Four-week drying period
9. Nets installed for play

The effects of this installation are medium-fast play, no puddles, quick drying, gentle on the calves, and very pleasing to the eye. Costs, very generally, are $25,000 per tennis court (with wide variants dictated by conditions of soil and area) and $25,000 per platform tennis court. This latter figure includes the latest in all-aluminum, no wood construction, plus built-in lights and antisnow heaters. There are more modest installations for $15,000.

The golf course. Comprising some 120 to 150 acres per 18-hole course, the golf course is one of the loveliest and most environmentally attractive of all recreation facilities. The original design and construction of a golf course are what make one "exciting," attractive, and of championship quality, as compared with just another "dog." The course should be designed by a landscape architect, preferably one who specializes in golf courses such as Robert Trent-Jones, the greatest name in the field.

Westchester County, New York, with its 52 public and private golf courses, is called the "golfingest county in the nation." Maintenance costs have skyrocketed, however, and many of these courses are in serious danger of being sold to developers. Estimated cost for acquiring acreage and building a new 18-hole golf course today, regardless of region, ranges from $2 million to $4 million. Annual maintenance, including staff, utilities, water system, and other items, ranges from $75,000 for a modest course to $250,000 for the more luxurious centers.

Par-3 golf courses, sometimes known as "pitch-and-putt" courses because of their short distances to the greens, can be built on areas from 5 to 25 acres. Costs for such facilities, which feature from 9 to 18 holes, are approximately $500,000.

The bathing beach. It is the unusual private agency or recreation department that today possesses a safe, clean, attractive bathing beach close to urban centers. Those that do are priceless additions to city living during the warm summer months. In the deep south, this period can be as long as 8 months of the year.

The beach is basically a gently sloping shoreline gradually leading within $^1/_2$ mile from water that is only inches deep to water that reaches depths of 100 feet or more. Ocean beaches frequently include tumbling surf, which provides one of the most delightful sources of physical pleasure. Inland beaches, beaches on bays, coves, rivers, and lakes are generally calm except for tiny lapping waves at their edge.

Beaches should extend right and left at least $^1/_2$ mile to give the feeling of space, though many fine beaches are a bare 1000 feet long. Primary requirements at a managed beach, after clean water and an attractive sand, grass, or roundstone shore area, are security patrol by trained lifeguards and a program to keep the beach free of ugliness and environmental intrusion. Parked automobiles, too much nearby residential development, over-commercialization, noise, and smoke should be avoided or at least minimized.

New beaches are rarely bought as such today. Either the municipality has owned the beach waterfront for many decades, or a new beach is developed from empty, characterless waterfront. Today's cost of such development can be enormous, as evidenced by New Rochelle's (New York) development of two small beaches surrounding a 14-acre island in the Long Island Sound just off the city's shore. Four million dollars was earmarked for this important new recreation construction; yet the area involved was very small. Even money is not the sole obstacle to new beach development. Environmental impact studies have become so complex and so demanding that any attempt to put sand, soil, or rock beyond the water's edge may call for a series of applications, research, hearings, and decisions that can postpone construction for 2 years or kill it completely. Building a beach today is a tremendous challenge. Those communities fortunate enough now to possess fine beaches protect them and enjoy them fully.

Safety equipment is essential at a bathing beach. Well-situated lifeguard towers, rowboats, life rings, ropes, surfboards, oxygen and a resuscitator, first aid equipment, and blankets are basic to beach safety. These must be handled by the finest lifeguard staff available. There is no room for cost cutting here.

Nonswimmers or beginners can be accommodated by safe areas marked by ropes, buoys, floats, or flags, and this area should be under constant surveillance. At many beaches, a diving float or platform is placed some 50 to 60 yards offshore where deep water is guaranteed at both low and high tides.

The care, maintenance, and cleanliness of a public beach is a major recreation responsibility.

The athletic field. This urban recreation facility is usually 10 to 25 acres in size. Its main purpose is to provide opportunities for both informal play and highly structured varsity or semiprofessional sports activity. Facilities would include combinations of baseball and softball fields with backstops, running track, battery of tennis courts, grandstands, football–soccer field, and general purpose field house. In some cases, the indoor facilities of a nearby school building can substitute for the field house. Storage space for athletic equipment, practice backstops, football blocking dummies, goal posts, and other gear should be provided in safe, dry surroundings.

Viewed as a recreation facility, such a site may also be built around a stadium seating up to 10,000 spectators or, in a very large installation such as a college campus, seating for 20,000 to 30,000 persons. Here, the facilities for crowd control, feeding, parking, policing, and sanitation become very important.

In round figures, the creation of a small athletic field, 15 acres in size, with modest appointments, represents an investment of $700,000 to $800,000. A large, opulent plant may be as high as $3,000,000.

The outdoor theatre or bandshell. Regarded as old-fashioned during the 1950s and early 1960s, the outdoor theatre enjoyed a resurgence in parks and resorts during the late 1960s, and 1970s. The outdoor theatre, site for puppet shows or glittering extravaganzas, may range from a diminutive corner of a neighborhood playground to the vastness of the Marine Theatre at Jones Beach, New York. Wolf Trap Park near Washington, D.C., Robin Hood Dell in

Philadelphia's Fairmont Park, and the outdoor theatre in San Francisco's Golden Gate Park are illustrations of this facility on a grand scale.

Most municipal outdoor theatres are designed in a naturalistic manner to conform to the character of their setting. Slopes, groves of trees, rocks, water, and combinations of these with brilliant sunrises or sunsets characterize the truly dramatic outdoor theatre. Red Rocks, a vast, rocky outdoor roofless theatre on the outskirts of Denver best symbolizes this type of facility.

Fine acoustics are essential if the proper effect of the production is to be appreciated. A lack of fine acoustics can only be corrected by a good public address system. Other necessities include dressing rooms, lighting, orchestra pit, and a variety of security devices to move large numbers of people in and out, sometimes in dusky light or darkness.

Some of the more modern locations have invested great sums in backdrops, buffers, baffles, and other creations resembling the proscenium arch of the traditional indoor theatre. These ensure fine acoustics, lighting, and stage effects for more complex theatrical productions.

The marina. This is an extremely expensive but very popular recreation facility, especially in semitropical regions such as San Diego, Los Angeles, Corpus Christi, Miami, and Ft. Lauderdale. This is essentially a boat garage–motel, including from 100 to 1000 boat berths. It requires at least 25 land and water acres for construction and operation. Shoreside facilities include restaurants, laundry, ship repair and supply shops, motel, discotheque, clothing boutiques, parking, garage, barber shop, and beauty parlor. Boat owners are usually fairly secure financially and will demand and pay for the finest of services and accomodations.

Large marinas cost from $1,000,000 to $4,000,000 to build and from $100,000 to $500,000 per year to operate, including staff, utilities, insurance, and physical upkeep. A well-run marina can cover all its expenses and still return a small but regular profit to its owner or municipality. Two of the largest, best known, and most luxurious commercial marinas in America are the Marina del Rey in Los Angeles and the Bahia Mar in Ft. Lauderdale.

Lighting

Lighting a recreation facility can transform it from one of dependence on daylight to one that can extend its services far into the evening. In congested communities and cities where space is at a premium, the lighting of a sports facility is almost like doubling its use or like building a duplicate of the original at a tenth of the cost. This is because, although the tennis court or softball field is available 24 hours a day, its heaviest use time on weekdays is from 6:00 P.M. to dusk, or about $2^{1}/_{2}$ hours. With lights, the same facility can be used until 11:00 P.M. or later, thereby more than doubling its prime use time.

Facilities that lend themselves best to lighting are softball, baseball, field hockey, soccer, and football fields, ice hockey rinks, and basketball and tennis courts. Excellent assistance in designing the lighting of sports areas can be found in the handbook of the Illuminating Engineering Society.[2] Table 3 lists characteristics of various light sources.

Based on studies of hundreds of lighting installations, the following general suggestions are offered to recreation personnel who are contemplating lights for their facilities.

1. Study the site carefully before doing anything else. View it when it is empty and crowded, in good and bad weather, and dur-

Table 3

Comparative characteristics of light sources for general lighting purposes

Source	Lumen output per lamp	Efficacy	Life expectancy	Color acceptability	Degree of light control	Maintenance of lumen output
Incandescent	Fair	Low	Low	High	High	Good
Tungsten halogen	Fair	Low	Low	High	High	High
Mercury	Good	Fair	High	Low	Good	Good
Phosphor mercury	Good	Fair	High	Fair to good	Fair	Fair
Metal halide	High	Good	Fair	Good to high	Good	Fair
High-pressure sodium	High	High	Fair	Fair	Good	Good
40-watt fluorescent	Low	Good	Good	Good to high	Low	Good
High-output fluorescent	Fair	Good	Good	Good to high	Low	Good
1500-MA fluorescent	Good	Good	Fair	Good to high	Low	Fair

There are four ratings for each characteristic—high, good, fair, and low. (From committee report, Illuminating Engineering Society, New York, 1972.)

ing the day and night. This will make it intimately understood and familiar as the design point is reached.

2. Visit at least three or four nearby lighting installations similar to the one contemplated. Ask the recreation person in charge what improvements would be made if the installation were to be redone. Incorporate these suggestions in your own plans.

3. Retain the finest electrical engineering advice or consultant services available, preferably someone who has done earlier flood-lighting work. Make certain that this design expert knows *exactly* what is desired.

4. Carefully select the type of fixture, the service, and the number, height, and composition of lighting towers. Insist that the consultant-expert discuss every detail with you.

5. Give careful attention to current energy costs and to where estimated costs may be 3 to 5 years from now. This is a dangerously expensive area if carelessly overlooked. Do not accept offhand, round figures from utility executives or casual statements such as "It won't cost much" or "You can keep your costs down by shutting them off early." It never works out that way. Estimate your costs on the *high* side. Lights are an excellent recreation addition, but they are costly. An incorrectly placed light pole can create havoc.

6. Stake out the *exact* locations of all light towers. Have them reviewed and second-guessed for safety and utility by a committee of recreation people, sports people, team players, and coaches who will be among the prime users of the facility. Again, be present at the very moment that the contractor begins excavation. The slightest error on location can cause many problems later.

7. Do not accept the light installation until every aspect of lighting, maintenance, and bulb replacement has been thoroughly demonstrated and explained to your satisfaction. Learn what the high-voltage risks and dangers are.

A few estimates may help the recreation professional considering plans for lighting a recreation facility:

Standard, 6-pole recreation softball installation	$80,000±
Tennis center, 6 courts, side by side	$50,000±
Football field, 8 towers, 4 each side, 80 feet high	$120,000±
Horseshoe pitching area, 10 courts	$15,000±

OPERATIONS

Any discussion of design and construction of recreation facilities without mention of daily operations is short-sighted indeed. Efficient operating procedures and a recognition of the problems of vandalism and misuse are basic to the sound administration of such facilities.

During the 1960s, there was a surge of facility building, stimulated by many federal grants for the construction of "outdoor recreation facilities." In their haste to take advantage of this money boon, many recreation departments and agencies rushed blindly into massive construction programs, apparently with little thought or accommodation for the costs of maintenance and operation. Artificial ice rinks, public swimming pools, recreation centers, lighted ball parks, ski slopes, and band shells blossomed everywhere. In the fiscal crunch of the early 1970s, however, many of these new facilities were understaffed or were closed for long periods. Some were completed but never officially opened.

A recreation rule-of-thumb, based on the substantial experience by many leisure service executives in various parts of the country, dictates that the annual operating costs of a new recreation facility will approximate 10% of the gross initial cost of the construction of that facility. This is a broad estimate, of course, but it could vary between 5% and 15% without losing its value. It still gives a rough idea of how important it is to include funds for maintenance and operation when a construction project is being priced.

The rule works most effectively when applied to such conventional, familiar facilities as the large outdoor swimming pool, the artificial ice skating rink, the recreation center, and the golf course. Construction estimates on the unusual, the rare, the highly customized facility such as the ski slope, the sports flying airport, or the target shooting range are such to make this rule-of-thumb much less reliable.

Thus, a $1 million artificial ice rink should require approximately $100,000 per year to operate. A larger, more elaborate and luxurious ice skating center, costing $2 million to build, will cost from $175,000 to $225,000 per year to operate in a top professional manner. This figure includes administrative staff, skate guards, instructors, first aid personnel, utilities, paint, repairs, insurance, parking, and miscellaneous supplies.

The recreation facility planner, when conceiving and designing the new facility, must accommodate many future cost factors, including:

1. Maintenance union pay scales and the possibility of substantial increases every 2 years
2. The unpredictability of utility costs and fuels
3. Possible damage caused by well-intended, but careless participants at the facility
4. Vandalism
5. Act of God damage—earthquake, flood, snow, lightning
6. Theft or pilferage by staff
7. Unanticipated breakdowns in important, expensive machinery

Next to fuel costs, these unanticipated breakdowns are probably the most exasperating item in the operating budget. Electric motors, generators, transformers, circulating pumps, refrigerators, compressors, Zamboni and Rinkmaster ice resurfacers all represent a staggering repair or replacement cost when breakdowns occur. Murphy's Law—"Whatever can go wrong, will"—is painfully accurate where the operating of a large recreation facility is concerned.

VANDALISM

Willful and pointless destruction, defacement, or defilement of property is known as nagging and expensive nuisance vandalism. The term comes from the word *Vandals,* a barbarian race from northern Europe who sacked Rome in 455 A.D. Some examples of vandalism follow:

In 1971, Boston estimated $1½ million damage and destruction to its parks, subway cars, and school buildings; also in 1971, Los Angeles tallied up $250,000 damage to several of its park facilities; in 1973, New York City Parks and Recreation facilities suffered direct vandalism damage of $1,167,904, and the same city that year spent $2 million cleaning graffiti off its subway cars and stations; in the first 4 months of 1974, Detroit police recorded 5061 cases of malicious property damage, a rise from 4227 for the same period in 1973; repair of vandalized facilities in national forests is estimated at well over $2 million annually and does not include manpower and time lost from other projects nor the extent of damage to the environment.

Kraus' 1972 study of 53 of the largest cities in the United States disclosed that destructive vandalism had become a major problem in more than two thirds of the cities studied. Vandalism has not only resulted in major financial costs to park and recreation departments, but it also poses a strong threat to the continued existence of such departments. Charles Nutter, New Orleans Recreation Director, stated that 30% of all park maintenance is cleaning up or repairing vandalism.

Categories of vandalism

Petty or impromptu vandalism. Petty vandalism includes acts such as conscious street littering; tearing down banners, flags, and ropes from flagpoles; breaking small windows in storage and shelter buildings; tire slashing; and defacing walls, memorials, and billboards. Petty vandalism is relatively unpremeditated, low in unit cost for correction, and much more of a nuisance and eyesore than a severe damage. It does represent an enormous annual task of repetitive cleaning and is, ultimately, quite expensive. Far worse is the esthetic befoulment and the discouraging effect is has on recreation personnel and the general public. The appearance of any city is badly blemished when its public areas and parks display the results of petty vandalism.

Aggravated or minor planned vandalism. This category includes destruction of rest room facilities; the mass breakage of windows in public buildings; theft or damage to park and recreation vehicles; grass fires; and the deliberate crashing of automobiles into baseball backstops, chain link fences, decorative iron fences, and expensive park bench arrangements. This type of vandalism represents a degree of planned premeditation, spurred on by alcohol or drugs perhaps, and an attitude of avenging oneself on the establishment. Such vandalism usually involves three to five males, most likely between 10 and 16 years of age. The individuals involved generally have records of previous similar behavior in school or in connection with recreation programs. Damage is often considerable and frequently is sufficient to incapacitate vehicles, playgrounds, swimming pools, or other public facilities. Patterns of vandalism are discernible because once successful vandalism attacks are committed without arrest they usually are repeated at the same location or nearby.

Grossly destructive or premeditated vandalism. This category includes the severe cases of vandalism that appear to have been carefully planned. Theft is usually not involved, but rather a destructive act is committed that will damage or destroy a location or a facility permanently or for a long time. Such acts include pouring gasoline into a large recreation center and igniting it, resulting in the total destruction of the building, or smashing a vehicle into or setting fire to school buses or recreation/park department vehicles, causing damages of $100,000 or more. A third illustration might be the deliberate reversal of swimming pool machinery or the turning off of safety valves causing the system to destroy itself and thus putting out of operation a swimming pool, an ice rink, or a complete lighting system for weeks or months. These grossly destructive acts are the workings of disturbed minds. Unlike aggravated vandalism, grossly destructive, premeditated vandalism is not particularly patterned and seems to occur when individuals or groups are under severe mental or social stress. Racial unrest or street gang warfare could trigger such acts. It might be caused by consumption of liquor or drugs or by a psychopathic state of mind. The act frequently includes wanton destruction, suggesting that such a person would be physically violent or dangerous if confronted. Damage is major and occasionally is such that the building or facility cannot ever be restored at reasonable cost.

Preventing vandalism

Much research and many interviews with park and recreation officials and operators in all parts of the country has resulted in the following steps that will reduce, though not completely eliminate, vandalism.

Construction. There are many ways that new facilities can be constructed to reduce the possibilities of vandalism. For example, fewer and smaller windows placed higher in the walls, one-piece roofs without shingles or tiles, doors with flush-mounted locks that cannot be forced, high window sills that prevent fluids such as gasoline from being poured in across them, high roofs that cannot be easily scaled, and drinking fountains recessed into walls so that large instruments cannot be brought down to smash them. These and a number of other preventive measures should be included in the designs of all buildings.

Lighting and policing. Every new facility, regardless of its susceptibility to vandalism, should be planned so that it is well lighted throughout the night. Lighting a buidling from all sides constitutes a 50% or better chance of it escaping major vandalism. Police action is equally important and should be instituted from the opening of a new facility. With all facilities, this requires a meeting to stimulate police interest in what was formerly a stereotype vandalism target. The point to be emphasized is that when police become accustomed to a facility or a building being vandalized, they tend to ignore it. Thus, small acts of vandalism can grow and grow until the unit or facility is reduced to a total shambles.

Staff education. Much effort is needed to enlighten the staff, particularly middle-aged and older members. Positive attitudes toward the visiting public and understanding of the causes of vandalism are important. When staff members believe that vandalism can be curbed and that the general public does appreciate good facilities, the administrator has come a long way toward improving the situation.

Community education. A continuous community and city program is required if the public (remember that the public changes with each new generation) is to be

enlisted in an active antivandalism program. Blaming or chastising is not the answer. The public must be reminded constantly that they paid for and own park and
recreation facilities, and that use will be
curtailed if vandalism continues. Further-
more, they must be urged to bring about the
apprehension and conviction of people who
commit acts of vandalism on public
facilities.

Program and leadership. In any facility,
the employment of spirited, dedicated, reliable recreation and maintenance workers is
a major deterrent to crime and vandalism. If
the leadership is active, it will involve
young, middle-aged, and elderly people and
it will help the community to identify with a
happy feeling on the playground. Maintenance personnel who go out of their way to
keep the facility particularly attractive are
an asset since they give the public reason to
be protective and proud of the facility.

Participants and visitors. Without a
doubt, the most important antivandalism
ingredient is the people using the facility.
The crowded beach, the busy picnic area,
the recreation center bustling with traffic,
has a better chance of avoiding vandalism
than the remote, isolated, or little-used facility. Active participants are the best "policemen," and recreation administrators
must see that their facilities are used positively as much as possible to reduce the incidence of vandalism. Acts of vandalism reflect a low ebb in man's behavior; yet there
is no justification for a negative, defeatist
attitude on the part of the staff. However,
our relative affluence and our reliance on
technological devices tends to make us less
sensitive to vandalism and destruction. As
recreation and park managers, we must
constantly work to keep vandalism in
check. This is done through education,
through positive programming, and through
repeated demonstrations that the department is serious about reducing vandalism.

CONSULTANTS

The recreation planner/builder will find
great value in the selective use of professional consultants. Whether the task be
massive rehabilitation of parks, a new safety lighting pattern, the design of a new
park, or an answer to vandalism, the professional consulting firm can be very
helpful.

The consulting firm in recreation and
parks differs slightly from the professional
architectural firm in that the consulting firm
is usually an experienced specialist in
things recreational. Further, the consulting
firm offers itself as a broad, advisory agent,
capable of doing research, day-to-day
analysis, and staff work that lead to policy
decisions as well as any physical construction. On the other hand, the architectural
firm is usually employed to do a specific design task, with only modest amounts of research and field work. Most architectural
firms handle a wide and varied selection of
projects, in and out of recreation. The following illustrations may clarify the difference.

Problem: A recreation agency would like to
build a ski slope and lodge on a hill that it owns.
Solution: Employ an architect.

Problem: A recreation department finds its
beach, pool, and service buildings are out of date
and losing money. Need is for the redesign of the
structure to meet new public demands and a
reorganization and retraining of professional
staff to serve the public better.
Solution: Employ a recreation consultant firm.

Most reputable consultant firms are made
up of three to five professional people including structural engineers, architects,
landscape architects, industrial engineers,
and business/marketing people. No rigid

pattern exists in this, of course, and each firm represents a slightly different combination of people.

Certain of the consulting firms have included on their staffs outstanding parks and recreation administrators, men and women who have demonstrated brilliant leadership in one or more major municipal jobs. Some give part-time advice while still employed full-time in their municipal or agency posts. Other people accept positions with consulting firms after they retire.

It is wise to check references and previous jobs given by any consulting firm seeking your business. An excellent checkpoint for overall quality is the Council of Parks and Recreation Consultants (COPARC), a branch of the National Recreation and Park Association. COPARC was formed in 1974 and consists of representatives from over 100 reputable professional consulting firms. Queries to this organization on any one consultant firm or a request for lists of firm names will be promptly answered.

DISCUSSION QUESTIONS

1. The recreation division of a large hospital has been authorized to build a small multipurpose and roller skating surface in the inner courtyard of the hospital. As recreation administrator, outline the steps you would take in getting this project accomplished.
2. There is a 50-year-old, medium-sized swimming pool in an old park that is too cracked and leaky to hold water. It is otherwise mechanically sound. A modest sum of money ($50,000) is available, and the recreation director is uncertain as to whether the old pool should be repaired or a new pool built. Give several advantages and disadvantages of each of these two choices.
3. A park is being built along an open water shoreline in a temperate climate. List several advantages and disadvantages of this location, viewed from program and maintenance standpoints.
4. Two adjoining villages, each about 10,000 population, seek to build community swimming pools. Both have money but neither can fully afford the pool on its own. Outline steps by which these two

villages might combine resources and construct the pool. Indicate how planning chores might be shared.
5. Many devices and pieces of equipment on the market today are helpful in doing all kinds of tasks quicker, more effectively, and more cheaply. Many of these devices are still not being used widely in recreation operations. Give several illustrations of such devices or machines and tell why they would have special value in recreation and park work.

BIBLIOGRAPHY

Asphalt Institute: The asphalt handbook, University Park, Md., 1947, University of Maryland.

Butler, G. D.: Introduction to community recreation, New York, 1959, McGraw-Hill Book Co.

Butler, G. D.: Recreation areas, their design and equipment, ed. 2, New York, 1958, The Ronald Press.

Dahinden, J.: Urban structures for the future, New York, 1972, Praeger Publishers.

Eckbo, G.: Urban landscape design, New York, 1965, McGraw-Hill Book Co.

Friedberg, M. P.: Handcrafted playgrounds, New York, 1975, Random House.

Friedberg, M. P.: Play and interplay, New York, 1970, The Macmillan Co.

Gabrielson, M. A.: Swimming pools, a guide to the planning, design and operation, Ft. Lauderdale, Fla., 1975, Hoffman Publications, Inc.

Hogan, P.: Playgrounds for free, Cambridge, Mass., 1974, MIT Press.

An instructional playground for the handicapped. Albany, N.Y., 1975, State Education Department.

Lutzin, S. G., and Storey, E. H.: Managing municipal leisure services, Chicago, 1973, The International City Management Association.

Rodney, L. S.: Administration of public recreation, New York, 1964, The Ronald Press.

Rutledge, A. J.: Anatomy of a park, New York, 1971, McGraw-Hill Book Co.

Sternloff, R. E., and Warren, R.: Park and recreation maintenance management, Boston, 1977, Holbrook Press, Inc.

REFERENCES

1. The Athletic Institute: Planning areas and facilities for health, physical education and recreation, Washington, D.C., 1966, American Association for Health, Physical Education and Recreation.
2. Kaufman, J. E., and Christensen, J. F. (eds.): IES lighting handbook, ed. 5, New York, 1972, Illuminating Engineering Society.

14
POLITICS AND MINORITIES

Two of the more turbulent influences in modern life are politics and minority dissatisfaction, separately and together. These two have had and continue to have a substantial effect on the growth, development, and quality of the recreation movement in America.

Politicians like to call politics the "art of compromise"; citizens are less sanguine in their descriptions. "Crooked," "dirty," and "deceptive" are adjectives heard all too often when people talk of politics, and this is not merely the result of Watergate, the Korean bribing of Congressmen, or the current series of legislative exposés. The ancient Greeks and Romans wrote caustically of devious and vicious in-fighting and corruption among their Senators. Shakespeare's tragic play, *Julius Caesar,* revolves around the intrigues and villainous politics of Roman statesmen and soldiers. Other views of politics include the following:

Politics is not an exact science—Otto Von Bismarck, nineteenth century German statesman, in a speech before the Prussian Chamber, December 18, 1863.

Politics are nothing more than a means of rising in the world—Samuel Johnson, eighteenth century English essayist in a letter to Sir Joshua Reynolds, 1775.

Politics is perhaps the only profession for which no preparation is thought necessary—Robert Louis Stevenson, premier storyteller of nineteenth century England, in *Familiar Studies of Men and Books.*

The mules of politics, without pride of ancestry, or hope of posterity—John O'Connor Power, in H. H. Asquith's *Memories and Reflections.*

The politicians in the ordinary American city secure their incomes by plunder and graft, and keep their control by the distribution of patronage—G. K. Turner, The City of Chicago, *McClure's Magazine,* April, 1907.

Governmental promises, followed by governmental compromises, cannot help but lead to long, hot summers—Dick Gregory in *Dick Gregory's Political Primer.*[1]

But these are only negative viewpoints, and they do not give the full picture. All politics are not bad; all politicians are not corrupt. The same percentages of good, decent, conscientious, intelligent, fair, poor, and corrupt apply to politicians as to clergymen, doctors, farmers, and professors. The goldfish bowl life of politicians and the impact of their decision-making processes tends to focus a harsh light and magnifying glass on all of their activities. Thus, any impropriety immediately makes the news.

THREE CATEGORIES

Three categories of politics and political action are discussed in this chapter, including their impact on recreation.

Big Fed—laws and political activity on the national level by President, Congress, the courts, and the federal bureaucracy that affect the policies and lives of the entire country.

Medium State—political action laws and projects in one or more states that influence park and recreation planning, programming, land acquisition, personnel, and the like within that certain state or states.

Little Local—the myriad actions, laws, and ordinances by mayors, city council members, village managers, city administrators, boards of selectmen, corporation counsels, and others that affect the day-to-day operations of recreation on a local level. These may appear insignificant when compared with a piece of federal legislation, but they loom very large and important in the eyes of local professionals and citizens. Departments have risen and fallen, jobs have been created and destroyed, careers have soared and dived through the workings and malfunctions of "Little Local" politics.

Big fed

The political hand of the federal government was first felt heavily on recreation during the Depression and the 1930s. National legislation passed in 1932 by President Franklin D. Roosevelt was called the National Recovery Act (NRA). Under this act, the Works Project Administration (WPA) and the Public Works Administration (PWA) were created. These agencies put thousands of unemployed men and women to work in recreation leadership posts as crafts instructors, dancers, singers, physical education teachers, and a host of similar jobs. In addition, hundreds of parks and playgrounds were built in cities and suburbs throughout the nation, utilizing hundreds of thousands of unemployed artisans and unskilled laborers. Finally, the national forests, parks, watersheds, and endangered environmental resources of the nation were substantially rehabilitated by the Civilian Conservation Corps (CCC). This quasi-military organization assembled tens of thousands of unemployed young men and assigned them to reforesting projects in every corner of the nation. Millions of new trees were planted, roads and dams built, and primitive camping facilities constructed.

In more recent years, political action has created the Bureau of Outdoor Recreation (since renamed Heritage Conservation Recreation Service) and several other federal agencies focusing on the outdoor recreation and leisure habits and needs of national America. Some of these are Outdoor Recreation Resources Review Commission Report, 1962; Bureau of Outdoor Recreation, PL 88-29, May 28, 1963; Land and Water Conservation Fund, PL 88-578, September 1964; Wilderness Act, PL 88-577, September 1964; Wild and Scenic Rivers Act, PL 90-542, October 1968; National Trails System Act, PL 90-543, October 1968; and River and Harbor Act, Title I of PL 87-874, October 1962.

In addition, there are the major regulatory agencies, created by acts of Congress and each having its own direct and indirect influence on matters recreational: Federal Communications Commission, Civil Aeronautics Board, Federal Power Commission, Securities and Exchange Commission, Interstate Commerce Commission, Federal Trade Commission, Atomic Energy Commission, and Federal Energy Commission.

Each of these agencies has had its own political pluses and minuses, its infighting, and its local overtones. "Politics" is a word raised often when federal investigators are deciding how much land to buy, where the access roads will be constructed, and whose property will be taken in condemnation proceedings. Such massive land projects as Lake Mead, Boulder Dam, Los Padres National Seashore, Cape Cod National Seashore, and Everglades National Park (4 million acres) inevitably stir up jealousies, greed, and bitterness along with the basic good purposes and consequences of the project.

In most such federal recreation projects, however, the greater good prevails and, when the noise subsides and the dust settles, the public enjoys the resulting park or recreation area for generations to come. That politicians see the great impact of recreation on their constituencies was clearly evidenced in the presidential campaign of 1976. Two weeks before the election, President Gerald Ford's staff released a headline story, *One and one half billion dollars for parks,* crediting the President as the source of this windfall. Actually, it was only a proposal by Ford for a reallocation of certain monies and a suggestion that these figures be extended over a 10-year period. Thus, the $1.5 billion figure, which looked very impressive, was actually only a $150 million per year increase, and it was not yet a fact of life but only a legislative suggestion for the future by the President. However, it did make a very impressive headline even if it failed to get him re-elected. I believe that this was the first time in history that the phrase, "parks and recreation," was uttered formally as part of a presidential campaign.

Medium state

Political action for recreation in most states has focused on state parks, campsites, parkways, beaches, protected lakes, rivers, streams, and wilderness areas. In addition, individual states have one or more of the following bureaus and agencies that have an impact on recreation and represent the end products of political action: (1) state youth board or bureau, (2) department or office of parks and recreation, (3) recreation certifying bureau (Civil Service), (4) state planning agency, and (5) office or department of education.

Such offices are sources of substantial funding on park and recreation projects at the local level, so it is no surprise that vigorous efforts are made to lobby this money downward from the state level to the respective localities. Lobbying includes personal visits, phone calls, letters, elaborate proposals, brochures, films, project models, slide shows, printed materials, and combinations of all these. Many states (aiming for federal grants) and municipalities employ full-time "grantsmanship" experts, people who are skilled at finding mother lodes of grant money and in completing successful paper offensives to dig out and carry home large chunks of it from the scores of federal departments, agencies, bureaus, and commissions.

A new technique was added to this hunting exercise in the late 1960s. Originally, only state agencies and municipal governments were eligible for these large money grants. Other youth-serving, private agencies could only hope for part of the money by serving as a subcontractor or backup unit for the local governmental unit. Faced with failure by many municipalities to spend their grant funds effectively, the federal government, and later most state governments, began awarding large money grants *directly* to local and regional nonprofit agencies, organizations that had no direct links with any unit of government. These included the Boy Scouts, Boys' Clubs, Girl Scouts, B'nai B'rith, Community Action Agencies (CAP), police boys' clubs, police athletic leagues, YMCA's, YWCA's, United Funds, and similar organizations.

If there was jockeying and politicking before, it was now compounded ten-fold. For example, if a Boys' Club in Boston wanted to obtain a $50,000 special federal grant from the U.S. Department of Health, Education and Welfare to combat a serious youth delinquency problem near one of its centers, it had to show substantial negligence or failure in the job on the part of conventional recreation agencies, including the Boston Parks and Recreation Department. But, since government funding sources prefer to give aid to combinations of agencies or team efforts, it was necessary for the Boys' Club to claim full and close cooperation and coordination with local agencies, including the very same Boston Parks and Recreation Department. Thus, it was necessary for the Boys' Club to ally itself with the very agency that was being chastised for nonfeasance—a curious "through the looking glass" situation. State, local city or village, private youth-serving agency, federal representatives, volunteer spokespeople for local needs are sometimes all involved at the same time, jabbing, withdrawing, offering, snatching, dividing up, placing blame, and protecting themselves. It was also necessary to return frequently to "base camp," to ascertain the current attitude and policy of governor, senator, mayor, city manager, or agency director involved. Somewhere down the line, drug users, low-income families, potential delinquents, developmentally disabled children, elderly persons, or neighborhoods were waiting and hoping for new recreation programs and facilities while this multi-structured fight continued.

Is all of this "politics"? Well, the citizens and professionals involved in this mixture of gamesmanship, grant chasing, and budget stretching certainly do not hesitate to cry, "Politics" when their competition is awarded the money. Oddly enough, when such a recreation-funding effort is successful, and they frequently are, despite the fights, no one remembers to declare "*Good* politics," and this may explain in part why "politics" and "bad" are almost always identified automatically.

Little local

This is the most sensitive area, the region of the personal stab, the intimate crunch, the close-by hatchet job. The fact that dozens of people spend weeks and months and hundreds of thousands of dollars lobbying and beating the drum for the enactment or defeat of a recreation-related federal law may mean little to us. It is far away and impersonal. But let a brother or friend be passed over for appointment to a lifeguard position at the local beach in favor of a city councilman's son, or let someone hear of a deal favoring the location of a new playground on street A instead of street B and then the pain and anguish are intense and real, and the shrieks of "dirty politics" are heard everywhere.

Local political frictions and crises involving recreation seem regularly to derive from a few familiar situations: appointments to top professional positions, funding of special recreation programs and construction projects, distribution of part-time jobs, prestigious board and commission appointments, and publicity and ego trips.

Appointments to top professional positions. The placing of a man or woman in a key salaried post or the removal of someone summarily is a very sensitive situation. In most agencies and municipalities, professional qualifications and job specifications have been established and published for such posts as director of recreation, superintendent or commissioner of parks and recreation, deputy commissioner, and so forth.

In the normal progression of events, an incumbent will be promoted or will announce his or her resignation to accept another position and will give some 30 to 60 days notice. Death or a totally debilitating health condition might also create a vacancy. The local personnel officer, aided by a 3- to 5-member screening committee, then invites application from qualified persons, sifts them through, interviews, and recommends a final 3 or 4 to the appointing authority (town board, chief selectman, mayor or city manager). Appointment follows shortly, and all agree the best qualified candidate has obtained the post.

Often, however, it does not work this way. A new mayor will insist on "cleaning house," and all department heads, regardless of quality or performance, are dimissed from office summarily. Newly elected public officials will sometimes announce they want "familiar, reliable, loyal department heads, people I can trust." This may be a sincere statement, but it does suggest the spoils system. It certainly discourages career recreation professionals when they see the superintendent's office or other responsible job filled by a young lawyer, beer salesman, or school teacher who helped the mayor win the election. Bitterness and lackluster performances usually follow.

I have heard mayors in a dozen American cities make statements such as:

Why search out a recreation professional from some distant city? He'll give me 3 to 4 years and then move on. They're all the same.

In a crunch, I need support. I need people who listen to me, obey me, don't argue. These so-called pros are constantly second-guessing me, arguing. Sure, they make their point sometimes. Meanwhile, I get defeated.

Specialization is overdone. I can take a good manager and put him at the head of public works, or parks and recreation, or the library system. He'll crack heads, dump a few bums, and get the show on the road in a matter of months. The imported professional wants a year to study the situation.

I conducted a mail survey of some 200 recreation chief executives in large American cities in 1977. One of the questions asked was: "What was the political event, development, or pressure that most disturbed you in your recreation work?" The answers were so varied that they defied categorization, but a few were repeated often enough to form a pattern. Mentioned most often were:

1. Prevention from hiring the best qualified person for a key recreation post, after a wide and successful search
2. Pressure to accept and employ an inadequate person in an important job
3. Pressure to accommodate the unreasonable recreation or park demands of a person or group who offered the chief executive (mayor, county executive, etc.) some political advantage

Post election developments on national and local levels will show, even in 1980,

that the "new broom" philosophy is still widespread. Commissioners, superintendents, and directors still work with resumes in their pockets. Postdated letters of resignation still nestle in mayors' locked desk drawers, while commissioners wait to see if they are playing "musical department heads" as newer, politically friendlier persons are named to replace the old.

In many large cities, the "sponsor" system is still in use. This enables the mayor, city council president, county executive, or other political officer to maintain a rather tight control over the disposition of attractive government jobs at various levels. The job-seeker, regardless of professional or academic credentials, must visit some recognized functionary of the majority political party. This could be a congressman, state official, or city leader. After being cleared by that person, the applicant receives a special identifying token, be it letterhead, signed note, stamped yellow card, green ticket, or other symbol. Possession of this token, presumably, means that the applicant's registration and voting record have been checked and cleared by the sponsor. Also weighed is the applicant's record for voluntarism, campaign work, and a voiced willingness to "actively support the policies and the re-election of the party and leaders in power." This sponsor card clears the way for the more conventional screening and hiring procedures of the personnel department. Possession of the sponsor card does not guarantee the getting of a job; lack of the card, however, practically guarantees that the applicant will not even get past the receptionist.

Funding of special programs and projects. When funds arrive locally or are promised from state or federal sources, the mayor, chief executive, or director of the agency must make choices. Will the special Creative Arts Workshop for Developmentally

Disabled Children receive the grant or will the Physical Fitness Project for Former Drug Users receive it? Every program and project has its aficionados, one group more zealous and dedicated than another. A small cyclone of pressures and counter-pressures swirls about the issue, and basic values are sometimes obscured or ignored.

In one large midwestern city where I was visiting as a temporary consultant, such a storm was raging. At stake was the location of a new recreation center for physically and mentally handicapped children, totally funded by a combined federal and state grant. The logical location was in a certain neighborhood devoid of existing recreation facilities. Instead, efforts by civic authorities were aimed at placing it close to an existing private youth-serving agency, a choice influenced by strong political and ethnic pressures. Turmoil, acrimony, and delay resulted, ending in the total loss of the grant. The center was never built, an administrative tragedy for that city.

There is another side to this subject, however. A rare and nameless attribute or sixth sense is enjoyed by certain urban leaders in matters public, an attribute rarely shared by their appointed commissioners and department heads. Ed Costikyan of New York City is one of these gifted politicians; another is Kevin H. White, mayor of Boston. I recall an incident while serving as Commissioner of Parks and Recreation for Boston. Seated in the mayor's office overlooking Faneuil Hall, we had been arguing for some time over a playground rehabilitation program. The city had received a substantial grant, enabling Boston to totally redesign and reconstruct 20 neighborhood parks and playgrounds. I had been arguing for 20 specific locations based solely on demographics, need, deteriorated physical plant, and the like. The mayor was opting for 20 locations based partly on need, but

partly on potential political advantage. "Curtis," said the mayor, a man I believe to be one of the most astute and energetic mayors in the history of our nation, "you're a great parks man, but a lousy politician!" Well, we did it the mayor's way. I was chagrined. Months later, at a series of neighborhood meetings, I was to hear the mayor cheered and applauded for his excellent playground rehabilitation program and locations. It is doubtful that my locations would have elicited such response.

A few big city mayors have displayed this same acumen for things recreational-political, including John V. Lindsay of New York, Moon Landrieau of New Orleans, Joseph Lee of New Haven, Sam Yorty of Los Angeles, Carl Stokes of Cleveland, and Kenneth Gibson of Newark.

Distribution of part-time recreation jobs. This can be an endless pit of community pressures, demands, intrigue, and political influence. Such jobs represent one of the few remaining areas for traditional political favors since today's legal machinery and public awareness have eliminated most of the old-time pork barrel opportunities. Each summer, from mid-June to mid-September, some three million persons are employed by villages, towns, cities, counties, and private agencies in recreation and park positions for a gross payroll of $1 billion. In addition, another one million persons are employed year-round in a variety of part-time situations such as swimming pool lifeguards, playground leaders, crafts instructors, tennis coaches, and others. This work has become a way of life for college students earning tuition money and for school teachers who use their summer vacations and weekends for additional income.

Pressure for these summer jobs begins in late January, with parents inquiring and enterprising college students visiting recreation offices early. Most departments and private agencies endeavor to professionalize this process by setting and announcing standards and insisting on interview schedules. Were this procedure adhered to, playgrounds everywhere would be staffed by the best people available.

Unfortunately, it breaks down. In April, just as the process appears to be working well, the calls, the notes, and the visits begin to come in, anxiously. Special treatment is requested for a "wonderful kid" whose overseas educational trip has been cancelled by poor grades and by a need for summer school, so a job is now essential; "the outstanding athlete" who doesn't want too heavy a summer work schedule that would interfere with his sports practice; or "A friend of _____ (fill in with one: mayor; city councilman; superintendent of schools; president, Chamber of Commerce; city manager; minister; priest; chairman, recreation commission; etc.); she really needs the work and she is an excellent baby sitter!" Add to these the voices of Urban League, Hispanic Alliance, N.A.A.C.P., Italo-American Benevolent Society, Community Action Agencies, Knights of Columbus, Temple Brotherhood, and others warning against the apparent absence of minorities within the ranks of summer workers.

Invariably, the larger the city, the more difficult the struggle by the recreation administrator to be objective and professional in his or her hiring. In a small town of 25,000, the level of professional selection can be kept high, with interference low. In cities the size of Detroit, Kansas City, or Sacramento, on the other hand, it is more likely that the recreation department or agency will receive a long list of names and be told peremptorily, "Hire them!" A few may be rejected on grounds of blatant disqualification such as the holding of two jobs or total

absence from all interview and training sessions. By and large, however, these summer personnel, ill-selected and ill-trained as they may be, frequently end up as the contact leaders who will deal face-to-face with the public in the recreation program. This is a chronic weakness of urban public recreation that requires correction. Private agencies rarely are guilty of such subprofessional hiring practices.

Robert Moses, greatest urban park builder of modern times, puts the point of view of the battered veteran administrator thusly:

The more I see of reformers, the more I value and admire the old-time political leaders who liked their friends, talked straight and kept their word. Their humanity was simply incorrigible. They were mentally honest and not too much concerned with conflict of interest. At the final trump, as in the case of Bunyan's Pilgrim, bugles will welcome them from the other side.[3]

Prestigious board and commission appointments. The selection and appointment of outstanding citizens to nonsalaried leadership and policy-making posts is one of the most important functions of a mayor, governor, or county executive. These people, once invested, create the fabric of philosophy and policy under which a whole city or county operates, be it in recreation, city management, industrial development, urban planning, or community health care.

With the reservoir of idealistic and highly motivated people who, in varying numbers, reside in every American community, one would expect that appointing officers would select only the best. Political expediency, unfortunately, does rear its head, and one still sees appointments that include narrow viewpoint, limited experience and ability, partisanship, and even a total ignorance of recreation theory and philosophy.

This matter of appointments and their quality becomes very important when administrative power plays come into action. Suddenly, after a period of quiescence, a board of directors or a recreation commission is thrust by circumstances into direct conflict with a mayor, county executive, or town board. Now the lay appointees must do research, interview their paid staff, and search their consciences for the solid facts and philosophies on which some final decisions are to be based. A good board made up of men and women who think, do their homework, and have rich personal life experiences to draw on will probably comport themselves nobly and serve the public well. A board or commission, permeated with weak wills, prejudices, narrow minds, and outright ignorance will probably not only fail to find a solution, but will exacerbate the situation with noise, controversy, and open hostility. Elected officials must be made to realize the long-term consequences of a capricious or misguided appointment.

Publicity and ego trips. This is an almost humorous, but highly sensitive area. Early in their careers, recreation administrators should learn the emotional significance attached to the ''right photograph,'' radio voice, or television appearance, especially when it involves elected officials. In the planning of events such as program openings, facility dedications, award ceremonies, and banquets, the recreation professional must be certain that key elected officials and chairpersons of boards or commissions are present at the right time to be interviewed and photographed. The road to administrative disaster is paved with the bones of well-intended recreation professionals who let themselves be quoted as the ''originator of this new park idea'' or ''the creator of that new recreation program,'' thus eclipsing the image of the governor, mayor, or chairperson of the park commission.

Photographs seem so casual when they appear in the local newspaper or on the 6 o'clock television news. If the person in the front row is the reigning political leader or the president of the YMCA, fine! The public is still going to get its park, its new swimming pool, or its expanded bathing beach. The fact that the supportive role of the recreation professionals is played down or that their faces are left out of the picture has to be of small consequence in this setting. This is a psychopolitical ground rule that must be respected everywhere. The pecking order for recreation publicity and photography should be: (1) top elected official (city, village, state, county, etc.), (2) secondary elected officials, (3) top appointed lay and volunteer officials, (4) outstanding volunteer workers, (5) hardest working (and best liked) paid staff member, no matter how low the rank, and (6) the recreation administrator.

Caution: Violation of this rule may be dangerous to your professional health!

GENERAL ADVICE

Recreation professionals cannot ignore the political facts of life if they are to succeed in their career. Whether employed by city, county, Boys' Club, YMCA, or hospital, the professional will be subjected to an endless barrage of political and psychopolitical storms and controversies. Knowledge of them and a basic method of operation are essential for survival and success. The following items should be included in that method.

1. Remain politically quiet while in service. This does not mean political nonaction. Voting is a precious American right and should be exercised. It does mean, however, that vigorous activity and identification by the recreator with one or another specific political party may stimulate situations and discussions embarras-

sing to the local top elected official. It is a very rare recreation professional who can openly and stridently ally himself or herself with one political party and remain in a recreation leadership post for more than a few years. I have been registered with one political party for over 25 years in several different municipalities and have never missed a chance to vote. Service has included locations with single parties and mixtures of both major parties in power. Thankfully, no one has directed that I change party registration for career reasons.

2. Project forward the image of the top elected official or the top board commission member whenever publicity is involved. There will be denials, refusals, and indignant statements such as ''You're the one running this department; *you* should be the one interviewed!'' Don't believe it. Sincere or not, the mayor or board chairperson really needs and wants that publicity; you don't. Accept no argument—force them to the front and retreat to the rear. Never, never get in front of them. Few of them ever forgive or forget. There will be sufficient opportunity to show off your face and talents at conferences and professional meetings where no elected officials are present. Leave the home stage exclusively to them.

3. Develop and exercise a well-rounded philosophy of recreation, its sources, purposes, and goals. Live by this as closely and conscientiously as possible. Without it, you will drift from one political crisis and decision to the next, never certain whether you are doing right or wrong.

4. Accept the aberrations and unpredictables of a public recreation career, including that of leadership in a private agency or institution. Decisions and directions come too fast and too frequently these days for everyone to be completely quality tested for purity, accuracy, and morality. A high percentage of good is all you can shoot for, and it *is* worth shooting for. When mayors, councils, and so forth demand swift response to requests for action, apply your recreation philosophy and then do the best you can. No one is perfect, especially in recreation administration.

5. Always be loyal to your superiors!

RACE

Race and ethnicity, increasingly, enter the realm of recreation planning and administration. The emerging Black, Chicano, Oriental-American, American Indian, and Hispanic groups have become highly visible and articulate as they move into the society that formerly ignored them.

It would be naive for the recreation professional to expect the wide variety of American heritages to fuse together beautifully, simply because they all join the YMCA or register in the same community recreation basketball league. Metropolitan regions such as Seattle, Buffalo, Los Angeles, Denver, San Antonio, Miami, Kansas City, Philadelphia, New York, and Boston have their own unique mixtures of ethnic and heritage groups. These mixtures rarely result from a pleasant, socially desirable pattern of immigration. More often, they reflect some traumatic or catastrophic event that resulted in painful and uneasy coexistence of the cultures. Such bitterness often continues through several generations.

The long resentment of the disenfranchised American Indian, the ''wetback'' image of the Mexican-American, the Castro-motivated Cuban mass immigration to Florida, and the struggle of Black Americans for real equality are complex sociological phenomena that may take decades to resolve. And yet, all people have a deep affinity for recreation, no matter what or where their roots.

RIOTS

On July 27, 1967, President Lyndon B. Johnson appointed the Commission on Civil Disorders to investigate the series of riotous demonstrations that devastated scores of American cities during the preceding 4 years. Hardest hit were Birmingham, Cambridge, Chicago, Philadelphia, Tampa, Cincinnati, Atlanta, Newark, Detroit, Los Angeles, Boston, Hartford, New York, and Washington D.C. Many other cities suffered in varying degrees.

On March 1, 1968, the committee (named the Kerner Commission after its chairman, Governor Otto Kerner of Illinois) made its report to President Johnson and the nation after extensive questioning, data gathering, and analysis in every stricken city. Of the twelve most repeated complaints, a strong fifth was, *poor recreation facilities and programs.* Complaints in every one of the 15 largest cities included inadequate facilities (parks, playgrounds, athletic fields, gymnasiums, and pools), lack of organized programs, complaints and demands on supplies, maintenance, workers' attitudes, hours of operation, and others.

The demands, complaints, and criticisms regarding recreation were only slightly less than those in the following four areas: (1) police practices, (2) unemployment and underemployment, (3) inadequate housing, and (4) inadequate education.

Sunday, February 26, 1978, the *New York Times* reviewed the 10 year old findings of the Kerner Commission and Report. Significant comments from that article include:

The division between white and black Americans still exists, and the prospects of healing the rift may be more dismal today than they were ten years ago. . . . Scars of the riots are still visible in Washington, Detroit, Newark and other cities.

The article also notes that the troubled areas still include desolate expanses of New York, Newark, Chicago, Washington, Philadelphia, Cleveland, Detroit, St. Louis, Gary, Buffalo, Los Angeles, Houston, Memphis, and New Orleans. Together, they add up to several thousand square miles of rubble-strewn streets and vacant lots, abandoned stores, stripped-down automobiles, bleak and bulky housing projects, and, of most significance to our profession, dreary, glass-filled, overgrown park after dismal park. "It is still mostly a segregated society," according to George S. Sternlieb, Director of the Center for Urban Policy Research at Rutgers University, in the *New York Times* article.

Such findings are not surprising to anyone who has ever looked at the recreational settings of any American ghetto, regardless of the ethnic group involved. Glass-strewn playgrounds, basketball backboards without hoops, broken park benches, graffiti-emblazoned walls, boarded-up windows, weedy park areas, and a generally dismal prospect are everywhere. One school of thought prevalent among maintenance personnel working for both municipalities and private agencies in such neighborhoods is, "What do you expect? They're savages, they did it, let them live in it!" The vicious cycle of such thinking should be obvious, and the more frequently employees express themselves so, the more frequently will vandalism and rebellious attitudes be manifested.

Many, although not all, of the administrators questioned, perceived the entire area of service to Negro residents as one that posed a number of difficult problems. However, the problems were perceived in different ways. When pressed as to the major source of their difficulties, recreation directors in suburban communities tended to blame the behavior of Negro youth, making frequent references to "aggressive behavior," "vandalism," "racial antagonism," etc.[4]

In the most enlightening work on this subject, Kraus[2] does an extensive analysis of riot facts, vandalism, and maintenance problems, as well as interviews with recreation administrators, leaders, and participants. Several major cities are involved, and personnel include urban and suburban types of several ethnic backgrounds. His findings include the following:

1. Although recreation, that is, constructive and pleasurable use of leisure time, is regarded as a right of all people, it has in effect been denied to large masses of the urban minority populations. An increasing number of public recreation facilities today are being operated on a fee basis or with an annual charge for membership. Those who are incapable of paying the fee, whether white, Black, or other minority, are excluded from participation. But because Black, Chicano, Indian, and Hispanic groups represent a disproportionately large segment of the American population that is regarded as being below the poverty level, it is obvious that minorities suffer this exclusion acutely.

2. In crowded urban settings, the terms leisure and recreation are ambiguous to minority youths. A staggeringly high rate of youth unemployment makes these middle-class terms meaningless to people who rarely or never work. It is another manifestation of "the beachcomber never gets a vacation" phenomenon. Add to this the fact that corruptive and illegal pastimes such as gambling, vice, and narcotics are far more prevalent in crowded slums of major cities than anywhere else. The difficulty in communicating and explaining ideas such as "wholesome recreation," and "healthful leisure" should be evident in such settings.

3. The shattered family structure of so many poverty level families excludes the most important base for community recreation—the family-oriented activity. Suburban recreation leaders who operate teen centers, Little League baseball, kite flying festivals, and father-son and mother-daughter banquets would be frustrated attempting these programs in urban slums. Nearly half the youngsters involved would have great difficulty getting one parent to participate, let alone both parents.

4. Current efforts of people to restore pride in their roots become, in themselves, a segregating force. In a Black neighborhood, the increasing emphasis on African heritage, foods, dance, music, dress, and language may be strengthening the Black's self-esteem, but it is simultaneously driving the Caucasian out of that particular recreation program and out of the center. Tables are turned, and the low-income, uneducated white youths see themselves as the rejected minority.

The exasperating irony of racial problems occurring in recreation is that, by and large, the recreation setting still comes closest to providing the common ground on which people of sharply different backgrounds can meet and mingle comfortably. Rich and poor, white and Black, brilliant and average all can and do blend successfully on a basketball team, a track team, in a stage production, at an overnight camp, or as part of a fund-raising project. "Blend successfully," of course, does not mean "mix perfectly," for no combination of human beings anywhere has yet been able to do that. The Israelites under Moses, the Apostles under Christ, the sailors under Columbus, the Americans under Washington and Lincoln, all found differences sufficient to argue about, and even kill over.

Further findings of recreation-race studies indicate:

1. Many recreation directors believe that racial minorities in their communities have different patterns of participation as groups than do groups that are not a minority, both in terms of activities in which they participate and their involvement by age groupings.

2. Recreation directors report certain problems related to the provision of services for racial minorities. The problems stem particularly from what the directors regard as antisocial behavior by Black and Hispanic teenagers and from resistance toward Blacks or withdrawal on the part of whites.

3. Sports tend to be heavily racially segregated among teens and adults and are characterized by sharp hostility and racial antagonism.

4. Recreation directors and staff, for the most part, maintain only superficial relationships with antipoverty agencies serving economically disadvantaged persons in the community, and particularly the Black poor.

5. Recreation is not used intelligently or creatively as a means of developing positive intergroup relationships. It is used in a simple, primitive manner by professionals who should know better. Goals often are the burning up of time and energy, rather than the setting of objectives for better understanding and relationships, with recreation providing the transition vehicle.

Race in recreation is not an easy situation. Anyone who has patrolled a dimly lit school locker room as two racially different teams dress after a basketball game senses the tensions that can explode at the slightest provocation. A sneer, a giggle, or a derogatory word can set off a skirmish that will send a dozen injured persons to the hospital. Playground leaders who have labored diligently to guide the residents of a ghetto neighborhood through a hot and tense summer know the vibrations. Still, it is here, it is a fact of life, and the very tautness and threat of racial unrest can make it one of the strongest potentials for good in the hands of the creative urban recreator. Nobody, but nobody, can say "No" to a recreation program aimed at reducing racial tensions.

SOME SUGGESTIONS

America's racial wounds may take generations to heal. Well-planned recreation programs, led by dedicated personnel, can, in their small way, help the situation.

Community analysis

Without a careful study of populations, locations, job situations, family trends, and cultural profiles, a recreation program is strictly hit-or-miss or a time-killer at best. Information and knowledge represent one benefit from such an analysis. A second benefit can be some direct involvement of local people in the study and in the program planning that follows the study.

Staff structure

Often repeated, but frequently violated, is the rule that a local, ethnically oriented program must include some leaders of the same race and background as the potential participants. All of the philosophical utterances are of no value if a Black audience sees only white actors, if an Hispanic or Chicano dance group must sell their ideas to a staff totally made up of Caucasian "Anglos" or "Gringos," or if an Indian committee must present its youth leadership plan to a bureaucrat who does not know a Seminole from an Arapaho. Staffs must be integrated and must reflect as closely as possible the racial mix of the population to be served.

Expand and vary the program

Blacks do have a capacity for things beyond basketball and rock music; Hispanic people are interested in more than bongos, guitars, and maracas; American Indians do need experiences not necessarily connected with moccasins, deerskin, and rain dances. The challenge before the recreation leader in a racial situation is to expand, to diversify, and to seek out new interests and new areas for positive experience. The idea of introducing fly-tieing, opera, stamp collecting, winemaking, model car racing, accordion playing, mountain climbing, and play writing in settings in which basketball, juke boxes, and pinball machines reign supreme may seem audacious, but it is precisely the kind of program expansion and diversification that is needed.

Broaden the participation base

One of the chronic weaknesses of recreation programs in racially oriented locations is the automatic focus on teenagers, almost to the exclusion of all others. This can be self-defeating, since the other age groups and, frequently, the other invisible teenagers who do not attend, represent large power potentials for accomplishment. Working early with the most articulate and mobile teen set is wise, true, because to ignore them is to invite explosions. What is suggested, however, is that as soon as some semblance of teen activities is underway, steps should be taken to reach and involve preschoolers with their parents, mobile elderly persons, young adults, single persons, middle-aged persons, and other groups.

Develop a philosophy

Whatever the rank of the recreation person, be it director or lowly worker, it is important that philosophy and perspective on race and people be constantly broadened and enriched. The work should never be permitted to deteriorate to simply putting in hours. It should be fed and refreshed constantly with the findings and teachings of those who have gone before and those who have demonstrated a real awareness of what makes people function. This is not to suggest a monastic study nor a self-denigration effort. It does suggest that interracial recreation work is important, demanding, and not easily accomplished, and that it needs all the emotional, psychological, and philosophical help it can get.

DISCUSSION QUESTIONS

1. As the new street recreation worker in the crowded inner city of a large city, list people and places you would search out and visit during your first 2 weeks of work.
2. The mayor of a large city contacts you, the director of recreation for a local YMCA. He complains that his superintendent of recreation is inadequate for the job and the city's recreation program is poor. He wants you to step in on an interim basis and improve the situation. You are a woman. What steps would you take to meet the mayor's request?
3. Search through your own experiences in job seeking and/or promotion. Describe two instances in which you obtained or missed out on an attractive position mainly because of an action you would characterize as "political."
4. As the newly appointed commissioner of recreation and parks in a city of 100,000, you are having your first policy talk with the mayor who appointed you. No one else is present. What are the four or five ground rules you would set down for the mayor so that you could do your most effective professional job, but also could be of most value to him?
5. You are the director of recreation in a large private hospital and have been rated "very good" at your job for the past 5 years. A new director of administration summarily dismisses you in a so-called austerity move, then proceeds to install an inexperienced friend in the new title of "Coordinator of Leisure Activities." Outline fully the steps you would take to be reinstated or to receive compensation for damages.

BIBLIOGRAPHY

Banfield, E. C.: The unheavenly city, Boston, 1970, Little, Brown & Co.

Berne, E.: Games people play, New York, 1964, Grove Press Inc.

Bone, H. A.: American politics and the party system, New York, 1955, McGraw-Hill Book Co.

Caro, R. A.: The power broker, New York, 1975, Random House.

Costikyan, E. N.: Behind closed doors, New York, 1966, Harcourt Brace Jovanovich.

de Grazia, A.: Politics for better or worse, Glenview, Ill., 1973, Scott, Foresman and Co.

Eldridge, H. W.: Taming megalopolis, Vol. II, New York, 1967, Doubleday & Co.

Felker, C.: The power game, New York, 1969, Simon & Schuster.

Gottman, J.: Megalopolis, Cambridge, Mass., 1964, MIT Press.

Hansen, N. M.: Rural poverty and the urban crisis,

Bloomington, Ind., 1970, Indiana University Press.

Hauser, P. M., and Schnore, L. F.: The study of urbanization, New York, 1965, John Wiley & Sons, Inc.

Herring, P.: The politics of democracy, New York, 1940, W. W. Norton & Co., Inc.

Key, V. O., Jr.: Politics, parties and pressure groups, ed. 5, New York, 1968, Thomas Y. Crowell Co.

Kirkpatrick, J. J.: Political woman, New York, 1974, Basic Books, Inc.

Liston, R. A.: Politics from precinct to president, New York, 1968, Delacorte Press.

Lowe, J. R.: Cities in a race with time, New York, 1967, Random House.

Lubell, S.: The hidden crisis in American politics, New York, 1970, W. W. Norton & Co., Inc.

Millet, K.: Sexual politics, New York, 1970, Doubleday & Co.

Moorachian, R.: What is a city? Boston, 1969, Boston Public Library.

New York Times: U.S. Riot Commission Report: Report of the National Advisory Commission on Civil Disorders, New York, 1968, Bantam Books.

Perry, J. M.: The new politics, New York, 1968, Clarkson N. Potter, Inc.

Reich, C. A.: The greening of America, New York, 1970, Random House.

Toffler, A.: Future shock, New York, 1970, Random House.

REFERENCES

1. Gregory, D.: Dick Gregory's political primer, New York, 1972, Harper & Row.
2. Kraus, R. G.: Public recreation and the Negro—a study of participation and administrative practices (monograph), New York, 1968, Center for Urban Education.
3. Moses, R.: Public works—a dangerous trade, New York, 1970, McGraw-Hill Book Co.
4. Nesbitt, J. A., Brown, P. D., and Murphy, J. F.: Recreation and leisure service for the disadvantaged, Philadelphia, 1970, Lea & Febiger.

15
MONEY AND RECREATION

Money and its management are as essential to successful recreation operations as are nourishing food and drink to a healthy, vigorous body. The recreation administrator, after researching the history, philosophy, programs, and ideals of the profession, comes face-to-face with inescapably pragmatic reality, the fiscal facts of recreation administration. This is applicable uniformly, whether the agency is a private organization, municipal department, hospital, nursing home, military base, or prison. One does not accomplish noble goals by going broke!

This chapter examines funding sources and needs, budgets, fees and charges, fiscal procedures, and the mechanics of bonds and bonding. But first, there is a look at money itself—what it is and how it works. This should be helpful to both administrators and students. Experience and research indicate that many recreation executives and leaders do not possess the knowledge and skills in money fundamentals important to today's operations. This lack of money knowledge, in fact, is not limited to recreation people, but is suffered by most Americans. Keith Funston, former President of the New York Stock Exchange, remarked in 1960 that the American economy is the eighth wonder of the world, while the ninth wonder is the economic ignorance of the American people. I would like to change that, at least for recreation professionals.

WHAT IS MONEY?

Before money, prehistoric peoples used a form of barter in which no coin was involved. Goods were given for goods, a handful of potatoes for a tooth extraction, a fresh fish for a shiny necklace. This was awkward, however, since some commodities were difficult to move and store. Also, there was no way to build up a reservoir of value for future use. Money was the answer.

Money, legal tender, or coin-of-the realm of one kind or another has since been a basic part of modern man's culture. Gold, silver, jewels, stone wheels, wampum, and seashells are some of the "hard money" used as media of exchange in various parts of the world. In every case, the "money" was widely accepted as a basic measure of value and was regarded as a common means for negotiating valuable energies and commodities. Robertson[7] says: "Money is anything which is widely accepted in discharge of obligations, or in payment for goods."

Modern people give various names to these basic units of exchange, or money, depending on their nationality. Kroner, rubles, yen, piastres, guilden, francs, marks, lira, pesos, and pounds sterling are but a few of the labels. Their equivalency to the American dollar also varies by nationality as well as by current international values. Today the Japanese yen may be the equivalent to 1/200 of a dollar, while a British pound may equal two American dollars. Tomorrow market fluctuations can cause the pound to rise in value and thus equal $2.10 American, while the yen drops to the level of one yen equaling 1/220 of a dollar. All currencies fluctuate in similar fashion though, normally, daily fluctuation remains within small margins. When a currency fluctuates widely and loses considerably, it is called a "weak" or "soft" currency.

Thus, money is simply a means for measuring the value of goods and services and permitting the flexible interchange of those goods and services from human to human, the process being called "buying, selling, hiring, and paying for." Note carefully, money is a means, a measure, a storehouse of value. Money itself is valueless.

Money is more

But, money is more. Money is power, gifts, drive, influence, motivation, stimulation, opportunity, intimidation. It is deeply psychological, and its presence warps the judgment of otherwise objective, intelligent men and women. Most recreation professionals think of money as piles of greenbacks, folding money. They try to envision how much can be stacked on a counter, put into a handbag, a briefcase, a trunk, a carton. No matter how hard they try, however, this kind of thinking has to remain limited to small figures, to ''chicken feed'' levels of money power. Sums of money large enough to change our life styles, to change our cultures, to bring into play new agencies, new major programs on a vast scale, are never reckoned in single piles of dollar bills.

Money, as seen through its health index, the Stock Market, is highly susceptible to psychological ups and downs. In a single day, the Market indicators may rise and fall many points because of announcements such as: ''The President promises to cut taxes if re-elected,'' ''General Motors has new device for saving gasoline,'' ''Kodak will challenge Polaroid with new camera,'' ''Detroit tools up for cheaper, smaller cars using kerosene,'' ''New York's financial picture brightens,'' and ''Egypt and Israel conclude pact.''

Each of these statements can set off enormous chain reactions that influence businesses and industries remote from the headline. These are the beginning of ''trends,'' so-called by money managers and analysts. The Chairman of Merrill Lynch, Pierce, Fenner & Smith, Inc. stated recently at a money seminar in New-

ton, Mass.: ''Once a trend is started, either upward or down, it tends to continue in that direction until another force is brought to bear on it.'' These trends eventually have a bone-crunching impact on all the things we buy, including recreation goods and services.

That the American economy experienced an unprecedented growth after World War II is beyond question. A pent-up appetite for goods and services had been curbed by 10 years of depression and 5 years of world war austerity. This flood broke forth in the late 1940s and early 1950s, and despite several recessions, some of our most violent social upheavals, and two expensive wars, the momentum is continuing into the 1980s. John Kenneth Galbraith,[2] internationally famous economist puts it this way:

The twenty years from 1948 through 1967 may well be celebrated by historians as the most benign era in the history of the industrial economy, as also of economics. The two decades were without panic, crisis, depression or more than minor recession. In only two years, 1954 and 1958, did output fail to expand in the United States. It was during these decades that the new term, gross national product, or GNP, entered the language.

Truly, the 1950s, 1960s, and early 1970s saw fabulous, unprecedented financial and economic growth, expansion, and diversification. Successful hamburger chains bought soft drink companies and book publishers; electronics firms bought aircraft and speedboat manufacturing plants; rapid cash flow and seemingly endless credit stimulated big deal after big deal, which were swallowed by superdeals. All this superspending, superdeals, and superdebt for almost a quarter of a century have brought us up against some money problem situations.

Credit and debt

Our financial system functions on credit. The theory is that people can enjoy trips, cars, beach resorts, and fine clothes while they are young and pay for them later. This supposedly avoids the frustration experienced by people of earlier generations who struggled during their early and middle years only to find themselves wealthy old people, too sick to enjoy their fortunes. This gave rise to the "enjoy now—pay later" theory.

Used wisely, a calculated credit enables people to enjoy the benefits of soundly planned recreation facilities and construction projects such as swimming pools and golf courses *while* we pay for them, rather than requiring the long wait until they are *fully paid* for. What is disturbing, however, about credit and debt is the frightening dynamics of the thing, the way it mushrooms and grows almost without control. Hendrickson[3] states:

Money as cash is a conspicuous presence in the life of contemporary society. There is more coin and paper money in circulation than ever before. For Americans, and people in other Western countries, there is also more money as credit and debt outstanding than there ever has been before, and the *credit and debt overtop the cash by more than ten to one.*

High-pressure selling, installment buying, credit cards, and the easiest bank borrowing systems in history have had a mammoth impact on the American debt picture. Hobart Rowan, syndicated columnist in the *New York Times,* warned in 1976 that the U.S. national debt was heading for the $600 billion mark shortly. He was right, and it continues to rise today, encouraged by frequent raising of the national debt limit. The National Taxpayers Union of Washington, D.C., has estimated that the grand total of federal debt; separate state debts; county, special district, city, town, and village debt; corporate and personal debt; plus all charges, surcharges, interest, and hidden costs, if assembled, would exceed $2¹/₂ trillion. This is $25 thousand billon and breaks down to $114,818.00 of debt for each of 212,000,000 living Americans! Every penny of this debt must be repaid.

This fact should be recalled by recreation administrators when voices nearby tell them "Don't worry, we can float a loan to pay for the new ice rink," "Easy, we'll sell bonds to get the money for construction of the proposed marina," or "Our city's credit is good, the banks will lend us the money for the planned recreation center." This massive pileup of debt leads to a second danger, inflation.

Inflation

Inflation, simply put, means too many dollars chasing too few goods. When national productivity or, for example, the number of shoes one worker produces per working day annually does not rise but costs do, the basic ingredients of inflation are present. When inflation continues to rise every year by 5%, 6%, or sometimes even 8%, it is called *runaway inflation.*

Inflation has been gnawing away at our dollar's value for 10 to 15 years, eroding its purchasing power. The answer to inflation is not artificial controls, ceilings, or gimmicks. The answer is productivity—the manufacture of more and better goods and services at lower unit costs than before. Anything else is pure procrastination, sleight of hand, fiscal gimmickry.

Prices in recreation have been climbing steadily for years. In 1968, one maintenance worker, one full day, cost a department approximately $42.00; in 1978, the cost is $75.00. An artificial ice skating rink,

---

100 feet by 200 feet, with roof, in 1968 cost $600,000, the 1978 cost is $1,300,000, give or take $100,000. The Zamboni ice rink resurfacer cost $11,500 in 1968 and costs $20,000 in 1978. I have purchased all of these goods and services firsthand and have seen these price increases. Coping with inflation is a major administrative challenge for today's recreation professionals.

THE RECREATION INDUSTRY

During this period of unprecedented expansion, the recreation and leisure services industry has not dawdled. Boats, recreation centers, backyard pools, airplanes, dune buggies—a vast array of hardware and services has been and is being produced and consumed. Kraus[4] says:

How has national affluence affected spending for leisure and recreation? Obviously, there has been a tremendous upsurge in leisure spending. . . . The Statistical Abstract of the United States, reported in 1967 that personal consumption for recreation for 1965 (the most recent year then available) was $26 billion. If one were to bring this figure up to a more recent year, 1968, by extrapolating at the most recent rate of growth, it comes to $32 billion per year. Even this impressive sum, however, represents a gross underestimation of actual leisure spending.

In 1967, Merrill Lynch, Pierce, Fenner & Smith, Inc. estimated the field of recreation and leisure at $150 billion annually, and growing. In 1972, the firm estimated that the comprehensive leisure market would reach $250 billion by 1975.

This complex of leisure America includes foods, sports clothes, trips abroad, community swimming pools, city parks, golf courses, Little League uniforms, second homes, third cars, imported cameras, and handcrafted crossbows. Firms such as Winnebago, General Motors, Grumman, Bendix, Black & Decker, Disney Productions, Greyhound, Pepsi-Cola, and Sears Roebuck are all part of the recreation production industry. All produce highly sophisticated leisure products and services.

Recently, the chairman of the board of Warner Communications told me, "We're in recreation—we make movies, comic books, toys, playclothes, we own the New York Cosmos and the soccer legend Pelé—we're a big part of American recreation." And he is right. The perfume industry, enjoying a massive comeback from the primitive dress styles of the 1960s, is grossing over $1 billion in sales annually. Perfume is fun, sex, sociability—it is a form of recreation.

MONEY MANAGEMENT

Funds are needed to conduct recreation programs and activities and to build and operate recreation facilities. To explain this is to belabor the obvious. In its infancy, recreation was borne on the shoulders of dedicated volunteers. Facilities and equipment were borrowed or contrived from inexpensive castoff materials.

A vast professional recreation movement is currently in action, led by tens of thousands of trained professionals, utilizing a broad array of expensive recreation and park facilities, and serving a clientele of 100 million persons or more. Latest total expenditure figures from the National Recreation and Park Association indicate that federal, regional, state, county, city, and village recreation agencies represent a gross annual figure of over $6 billion.

Where once public recreation, as recently as the 1940s, was considered encompassing little more than children's playgrounds, recreation services today include parks, playfields, regional forests, zoos, botanical gardens, museums, beaches, pools, speedways, golf courses, small airports, hotels, craft centers, park police, and environmental training centers. In fact, every phase of recreation service has been improved and expanded.

Sources of funds

Public recreation on village, town, city, and county levels is financed by revenues drawn from property taxes, millage taxes, fees and charges, concessions, sales taxes, federal revenue sharing funds, bond sales, grants, and gifts. Grants are not a regular, predictable source of funding and can be very irregular. Grants will not be discussed as a standard source of funds. Gifts, on the other hand, are discussed in Chapter 12.

Property taxes. This is the primary source of income on the local level, not only for recreation, but for most municipal services. A tax is levied on the assessed valuation of a piece of property (house, acreage, farm, and so forth) as determined by the city or town assessor. The tax levy is shown in terms of mills (tenths of a cent) on the dollar, in cents on each hundred dollars, or in dollars on each thousand dollars of assessed valuation. A tax bill is computed annually, semiannually, or quarterly by the municipality and mailed out to homeowners and businesses for payment. Money so raised is available for all municipal uses, including police, fire, recreation, sanitation, and others.

Millage taxes. The municipality, by law, sets a certain number of mills (tenths of a cent) on each dollar of assessed valuation. This tax is levied annually and is designated specifically for recreation. Normally, this tax ranges between 0.1 mill to 1 mill (equivalent to 1 to 10 cents per $100 of assessed valuation). The reason for this, usually, is a belief that the new and struggling field of recreation services should not have to compete with all other municipal services for its financial subsistence. Further, it makes the needs and expenditures of the recreation operation dramatically visible to the taxpayers.

Fees and charges. These are the monies raised by entrance fees to zoos, skating rinks, swimming pools, rifle ranges, and similar facilities. They also include league and team registration charges, forfeit fees, bus fares, and a wide range of similar revenues. In most municipalities, law requires that these monies be immediately deposited in the general fund rather than be isolated for payment of expenses. Advance arrangements can be made, however, so that finance departments will permit additional expenditures that match these revenues and accomplish the same purpose.

Fees and charges are two of the most widely debated issues in recreation management. Opponents of fees believe that:

1. Everyone needs recreation, the poor in particular. Fees and charges exclude those who need it most.
2. Recreation is basic to humanity, like air, freedom, dignity. Fees on such are inhumane.
3. Charging fees stimulates a sophisticated, profit-making psychology in recreation management.
4. Fees and charges make an agency or municipality more vulnerable to legal suit than when recreation services are free.

Supporters of fees and charges believe that:

1. Fees and charges place the heaviest tax on the heaviest users, the lightest tax on nonusers.
2. A system of fees and charges makes for good gate control and discipline.
3. Such fees enable the recreation system to expand and diversify.
4. Fees and charges are a hedge against inflation and reduce resistance on budgets by governing authorities.

The arguments tend to balance each other, leaving the question open. Experience indicates that fees and charges are not, per se, evil, and they do provide an element of growth potential. The danger, of course, lies in ruthless and insensitive fee structures and the way they are applied. Accommodation for poor, handicapped, disenfranchised people must be included in any fee structure, and the recreation administrator is ultimately responsible for seeing that the fee structure is an asset, not a deterrent, to broad citizen participation in programs.

Concessions. Concessions are legally approved contracts made between the municipality and such recreation and park business operations as park restaurants, rowboat docks, bus lines, marinas, and ice skating rinks. These contracts are generally given to legitimate business firms that bid on opportunities to conduct such operations. When handled well, such concessions can bring in substantial revenues. New York City's Department of Parks and Recreation realizes several millions of dollars annually from such sources.

The preceding revenue sources are considered appropriate for funds to meet operating budget needs, that is, salaries, insurance, fuel, supplies, repairs, vehicles, trees, shrubs, athletic equipment, and so forth. The following three sources are generally used to finance capital items, that is, land acquisition, construction, major rehabilitation, and the purchase of vehicles such as large trucks and bulldozers. Where the items and services purchased for *operating* purposes are expected to have only a 1-year life expectancy, those purchased for *capital* purposes are expected to last 10 to 15 and sometimes 25 years.

Sales Taxes. Many municipalities levy sales taxes on all commercial and business transactions within those particular jurisdictions. These range from 2% and 3% in

some communities to as high as 8% and 9% in others. They are assessed at the time of purchase by the merchant on the total base price of the commodity. In a city with a 5% sales tax, the purchase of a $1.00 book would cost the consumer $1.05, with the $.05 tax receipt going to the city. Such taxes can return substantial sums, frequently in the tens of millions annually in cities of 100,000 population or more.

Traditionally, sales tax revenues are designated for major capital projects such as new street paving, a new public library, or similar construction project. Unless prohibited by local law, however, these revenues may be used for any legitimate use by the municipality, including recreation and park purposes.

Federal revenue sharing funds. In 1972, the Nixon administration introduced a new fiscal program called *revenue sharing*. The purpose was to meet a long-standing criticism made by states that they regularly send far more money to Washington in tax receipts than they ever receive back in services and benefits. Further, the states wanted to make some rapid, dramatic physical improvements locally, and it was often very difficult and time-consuming to involve the federal government in financing these long-term projects.

Based on a complex formula that included the state's population, unemployment rate, industrial-commercial makeup, and annual federal tax contribution, each state is allocated a specific, annual sum of money from the federal government's budget. This sum is available to the local state and to its municipalities, with no strings or provisions attached, and is usually delivered in two installments, each in a check handed over by a federal representative to the governor, mayor, or county executive. The municipality is permitted to use these funds in any legitimate way it wishes—to reduce taxes, hire police officers, build street lights, rehabilitate parks, or any similar endeavor.

Bonds. Bonds represent a primary source of funds for capital purchases and improvements. Some municipalities have the freedom to sell their bonds at will, up to their legal limit, while other communities are required to obtain the taxpayers' approval through a referendum.

A bond is a kind of IOU or loan of money to a government or agency by outside interests (banks or citizens). The bond represents a form of deferred payment by which the cost of the capital project or purchase can be spread over a period of years rather than be incorporated totally into the budget of any one fiscal year. This is particularly important when a city might be operating on a normal annual comprehensive budget of $10 million and is considering a $10 million land acquisition and park development plan. Without the bonding procedure, or similar borrowing, the city would have to double its budget in 1 year to finance the acquisition and development program. With bonds, this money can be borrowed, the project undertaken, and the bonds retired (debt paid off) in 30 years at a modest 5% or 6% interest.

Municipal bonds, or bonds issued by governments for capital improvements, can be placed in three general classifications.

Term bonds are such that the entire amount of the issue, or the principal, comes due at the end of a specific period of time.

Serial bonds differ from the term bonds in that serial bonds provide for payment each year of a specified amount of the principal and interest of the total debt for the life of the bond issue. This plan is similar to that of a person paying off a loan on a home or an automobile. A certain amount of the debt is reduced through regular payments of approximately equal amounts.

Callable bonds may be called in by the issuer for payment at any time or at some specified time before maturity. If bonds were sold at high interest rates, recreation authorities could make substantial savings by calling in the bonds and reissuing them at lower interest rates. Because of this callable feature, such bonds are less attractive to buyers and must carry higher interest rates to induce purchasers.

Average expenditures

The question is often asked in community recreation, "How much should this city (or village or town) spend on its public recreation program?" Answering such a question categorically is as difficult as finding answers to: "How many police officers should we have?" or "What is the ideal ratio of teachers to pupils in a high school class?" All are loaded with variables, qualifications, and unique situations that change the formula and the resultant figure.

Efforts in establishing a rule-of-thumb, however, prompted the NRPA in the early 1940s to recommend a $3.00/$3.00 formula as a per capita base. This meant that, for every person residing in the municipality being studied, the city or town should spend $3.00 for programs and leadership and $3.00 for parks, playgrounds, and facilities maintenance. This meant a total recreation and parks investment of $6.00 per person per year. This figure has had to be increased substantially with the rise of costs in the 1960s and 1970s, until today's gross figure would be more like $10.00 to $12.00 per capita.

Using the above formula may help, but the wise recreation administrator realizes the ambiguity of such a device and its wide margin for inaccuracy. A suburb of prosperous families with many private resources for individual, group, and family recreation may not need to spend as much per capita for community recreation as an industrial community of the same size, but ironically, it may be better able to meet the cost of such needed services. Costs for identical facilities and services vary in different parts of the country. Also, easy and cheap access to facilities furnished by county, state, or federal agencies may relieve some cities of the expense of providing similar facilities. Doell[1] says:

A community should pay for community recreation as much as the citizens are willing to spend—and this depends upon how well informed they may be as to its values and how well satisfied they are with the amount and quality they have already purchased in competition with other values in the community budget.

Although this original formula, and the other comments, were meant to guide community recreation and municipalities, the basic per capita figure and concept are also applicable to large hospitals, mental institutions, prisons, industrial complexes, and military bases. The same strengths and weaknesses of the per capita formula are applicable.

Budget

The budget is the basic instrument for fiscal control and effectiveness, not only in recreation but in every sphere of business and economic activity. The lack of a budget and the skill to utilize that budget means no plan, no objectives, no security; financial disaster may arrive at any moment.

A budget for recreation services is a financial plan prepared by the professional administrator, board, or finance committee. The plan sets specific program goals and the financial resources to attain those goals within a specified period. Most budgets are set up on an annual basis or, less frequently, on a biannual basis. Kraus and Curtis[5] offer four points that a sound budget should encompass:

1. Provide a general statement of the financial needs, resources, and plans of the department, including an outline of all program elements and their costs and allocations for facilities and personnel.
2. Inform taxpayers and government officials of the amounts of money to be spent, the sources of revenues, and the costs of achieving department goals.
3. Help in promoting standardized and simplified operational procedures by classifying all expenditures and requiring systematic procedures for approving them.
4. Serve as a means of evaluating the success of the program and ensuring that its objectives are met.

The budget should be thought of as a management tool and not simply a "laundry list" of needs. For too long, recreation administrators have approached their budget-making chores with a mixture of anxiety and repugnance. They are anxious because they fear that their budget needs will mark them as spendthrifts and poor managers, and they experience a distaste for the repetitious annual paperwork and hearings, reciting item after item, using the same old justifications of previous years.

Properly prepared, a budget is a sound and helpful management tool and is fully in step with modern financial and economic theory. Because of the steps and information collection that are involved, the budget process can accomplish the following for the recreation administrator:

1. It will provide unit costs for leadership and programs for both past and future years.
2. It identifies those geographical areas, demographic groupings, and program sections that consume the most and the least dollars.
3. It provides a current cost-control device for ongoing programs.
4. It enables the administrator to project

anticipated costs and revenues for 5 or 10 years in the future.

Budget preparation is based on the widest collection of valid information possible and a systematic digestion of that information. The resultant data is then converted into a language of costs and is equated with the financial limits of the agency or department. Out of this comes the budget. Steps for budget preparation may be outlined as follows:

1. Set specific time schedule for entire budget preparation process. For example: Interviews—August 1-31; Staff studies—September 15-30; First draft budget—October 15; Review—October 16-31; Final draft by November 15; Formal submission to board (or city council, recreation commission, etc.) by December 1; Review during December, pass officially by January 1. Such a budget timetable must be strictly adhered to or the entire process can collapse.

2. Select rough parameters and major new program ideas from key staff personnel. Discuss.

3. Elicit budget ideas and input from public, or general membership, constituency. Discuss.

4. Produce rough draft, discuss with staff.

5. Inform board or governing body of general outlines that budget appears to be assuming. Invite their comments and guidance.

6. Return to design process. Reshape the budget to bring it into line with 5.

7. Prepare final draft. Discuss with staff.

8. Submit budget formally to board or commission.

Operating budget and capital budget. The operating budget is the fiscal instrument of a department or agency that includes projections, details and costs of all goods, services and commodities to cover a specific period of operation, usually 1 year, sometimes 2 years. It includes salaries, insurance, utility costs, supplies, auto fuel, travel expenses, and all other items regarded as consumable within the year. The operating budget is divided into categories such as salaries, administration, athletic supplies, utilities, and so forth for more efficient record keeping and management.

The capital budget differs from the operating budget in that the capital budget concentrates on major, large-figure, long-term expenditures and purchases. Such items include land acquisition, buildings, park construction, ball fields, ice skating rinks, swimming pools, golf courses, and the purchase of trucks, tractors, and automobiles. No salaries, administrative costs, or operating expenses are permissible in a tight, well-organized capital budget. Items purchased under a capital budget generally have a life expectancy of 15 to 25 years at least, as compared with the 1-year life expectancy of those items in the operating budget.

Program budget. The program budget is a management tool developed during the past 25 years that suggests a continuing evolution of the budgetary process. Unlike the conventional line-item budget that lists item after item, each with its individual cost, the program budget clusters items and their costs into large groups. Each group represents a major program complex or area, for example aquatics, senior citizens activities, or teen center programs. Each of these program groups is then developed with its own rationale, objectives, past history and successes, and a cost analysis that will attain these objectives. The master program budget then becomes an aggregate of the 10 to 15 major program clusters. This is a decidedly more difficult budget to prepare and requires skill in management. On the other hand, it is far more readable and understandable to the uninitiated citizen than is the older "shopping list" type of line-item budget.

Zero-based budget (ZBB). This is a relatively new term, promoted by the highly sophisticated management divisions of IBM, National Cash Register Co., and the Digital Corporation. It is an advanced version of the program budget in which clusters or program groups are further assembled into larger groupings called *decision packages.* A major difference between the ZBB and other budget techniques is that the ZBB starts out assuming no cash budget whatsoever. In other words, the ZBB that is strictly enforced compels the recreation administrator to justify every single dollar proposed. This process demands considerable research, data collection, and digestion.

THINGS TO KNOW AND UNDERSTAND

All recreation professionals should expand their knowledge of money and financial management. Although it is not necessary to be an expert economist, the recreation administrator should be familiar with terms and procedures relating to everyday financial practices. Each of these has some effect on the job, the finances, and the future of the professional's career.

Bonds

A bond is a contract in "debt financing" and is really nothing but an IOU. It is an obligation by a corporation or government to pay back the entire original sum on a specified date plus a specified rate of interest. It is issued or sold to borrow money, and it is sold on the open market like any other commodity. If no one buys your bonds because your credit is poor, you have no money with which to construct that pool,

park, or tennis court. The cost of bonds, that is, their interest rate, is set by the prime interest rate, a function of the Federal Reserve Bank.

Stocks

The issuing of stock is "equity financing." This means that a business or corporation that seeks money to grow, expand to new areas, and build new factories will sell a *piece* or *share* of itself to anyone who wants to buy it for a specific price. *Preferred stock,* a minority of higher priced, elite stock, recieves its annual dividend before the lower priced stock, called *common stock,* receives its dividend. Holders of both types of stock are paid dividends, only *after* the bondholders have received theirs.

Dow-Jones industrial average

This is a kind of combined daily thermometer, blood pressure gauge, and electrocardiogram of the stock market. The Dow-Jones is the oldest of the financial averages or indicators, dating back to 1884. Originally, 11 representative stocks, it has expanded to 30 carefully selected industrial stocks regarded as stable pacemakers for the entire financial world. These 30 stocks account for nearly one fourth of the market value of the more than 1400 common stocks listed on the New York Stock Exchange. The point score at the end of each business day ("Dow-Jones is up today 4 points," or "the Dow-Jones average today is down 2.5 points") is simply the *average* of all gains and losses of the 30 specific stocks during that particular business day.

Gross national product

This is the U.S. government's estimate of the total value of all goods and services we make, perform, buy, or sell during the year. The assembly of an automobile, the teaching of a child by a schoolteacher, the driving of a bus, a doctor's medical services, the work of a waiter in a bar, refunds on your insurance, along with billions more transactions are measured in current market value dollars and added up. The gross national product for the U.S. in 1974 was $1.125 trillion. (Remember, a trillion is one thousand billion!) We are expected to be well past the $2 trillion GNP mark by the early 1980s.

Prime interest rate

This is the interest rate set by banks and lending institutions on loans to their best customers. It can be changed from day to day by the banks, up or down, although they generally limit their changes to one per week. It serves as a control valve on current interest rates generally, hence on business loans, hence on business expansion. If the interest rate is lowered, the loan business becomes brisk and business expands and grows. Prior to our current inflationary fever, prime interest rates ranged from 5% to 8%, moving up and down a quarter of a point at a time. During the late 1970s, they have ranged as high as 12%.

Bulls and bears

This is jargon long used by stock market people. A "bull market" is a situation when stock brokers are buying, with everyone else resisting sales. Prices are rising and optimism prevails. Things are said to be "bullish." For example, the brokerage firm of Merrill Lynch, Pierce, Fenner & Smith, Inc. has been saying for years, "Merrill Lynch is bullish on America," meaning they see a bright, optimistic financial future for the United States.

The "bear market" is exactly the opposite. Brokers are selling, businesses are worried, prices are dropping, no one seems to want to buy, everyone is anxious to sell. An air of pessimism, of impending doom, prevails.

Of course, these situations do not always project so clearly and precisely. There are spurts in both directions, brief dips, rises, rumors, and surprises. This is what makes the brokerage profession so tense and so demanding.

Municipal bonds

These bonds are the backbone of cities' and other municipalities' major financing efforts. Badly buffeted and discredited in the mid-1970s, they are making a strong recovery. "Today, municipal bonds are one of the best and most popular investments Wall Street has to offer.[6] Bonds are sold by municipalities to pay for major capital construction and purchases such as land acquisition, road and park construction, and the purchase of trucks, buses, tractors, and bulldozers.

THINGS TO DO

With this brief look at what money is and how it works, following are a few suggestions by which parks and recreation professional can become more familiar with the day-to-day financial world. This will be helpful in the administration of a department and for getting the most out of the budget dollar.

Meet bankers and brokers. Even tiny communities have at least one bank, savings and loan association, or investment firm. Meet the key people, tell them about the recreation profession, and ask them to talk to you about their work. Ask them for banking literature and for a good financial text to study. Their work is not as remote and mysterious as it may seem.

Read the financial pages. Your local daily newspaper has a financial page, and most are quite readable if you read the columns and articles, not the stock quotations. Sylvia Porter, Edson Smith, Eliot Janeway, Hobart Rowen, and William Brown are a few of the syndicated columnists, but there are dozens more. It will take some persistence to understand their language, terms such as margin, puts and calls, profit-taking, over-the-counter, in-the-box, shells, conglomerates, leverage, arbitrage, and odd-lots. The *New York Times* and the *Wall Street Journal* should be read carefully by the parks and recreation financial student at least once a week. *The Washington Post, Boston Globe,* and major newspapers in San Francisco, Chicago, Philadelphia, Dallas, and Los Angeles give excellent coverage of the stock market and are quite readable.

Occasional reading of *Time, Newsweek, Business Week, U.S. News and World Report,* especially the financial sections and their comments on the leisure industry market, will help immensely in understanding the situation. Other interesting and informative magazines are *Money, Forbes,* and *Finance.*

Collect and read annual reports. This means reports from corporations, not the "whipped cream" reports put out by parks and recreation agencies. A good annual report put out by General Foods Corp. gives much valuable statistical and financial data and gives the reader a sense of "bullishness" or "bearishness" for the year ahead. Most major corporations in America will send their annual report just for the asking. Read and study them.

Seek a financial advisor for your agency or department. In a municipality, it may be your treasurer or commissioner of finance. In private agencies, it may be necessary to seek outside financial counsel. Select an ally or advisor from business, from a school of business, or from the staff of a mortgage and finance company, bank, or savings and loan corporation. No department of any size should be without alert, imaginative financial counsel. Large departments, in cities of 100,000 persons or more, should have a regular, paid financial advisor.

Attend schools of business and finance. This can be adult education/continuing education or the seeking of a degree in business administration. Large banks such as Bank of America, Manufacturers-Hanover, Chase Manhattan, First National City of N.Y., First National Bank of Boston, hold a wide variety of symposia and special training sessions on banks and banking.

Learn buying cycles that are most advantageous to your department. Do not always buy solely when the "Sale" sign goes up, or when the salesman says, "Bargain." Study your budget and buying practices over a 2 to 3 year period. Look at your needs from paper clips to bulldozers and decide when it is most advantageous to you to buy, not necessarily advantageous to the salesperson. Develop a 3-year buying schedule and demonstrate to the mayor or other policy-making official the great advantage accruing to your buying schedule versus the time-worn conventional one. This will take work and help from talented advisors, but be assured that it works and pays off.

View the budget and budget process as aids for creativity and not as dreary, annual exercises. The budget should be under preparation at least two thirds of the year. By the time one budget officially goes into effect, the succeeding budget should be roughed out and the first planning stages begun. Consider the following suggestions.

1. Print up the budget in an attractive, colorful, readable form. Even you, the administrator, will be induced to read and consult it more often.

2. Use the *WAR* technique. When budget ceilings inhibit you and you want to do something new and innovative that costs money, do this: *w*ithdraw, step back and view the large, bulky money lumps you traditionally write into your budget. *a*ppraise the "sacred cows," and pluck them out.

*r*eallocate the money saved to more valuable and high-potential projects.

3. Ask colleagues in other professions to read and digest your budget document. Ask them to make it more understandable and then follow their advice.

Experiment on the stock market for yourself. This can be done on as little as $500 per year if you join a stock club or investment club. Your danger of loss is minimized, but it gives a feel of the market and the entire process becomes much clearer. If funds permit, and after a few successful years, you will be ready to invest more substantially.

DISCUSSION QUESTIONS

1. A wealthy donor offers $1 million to the local YMCA, of which you are the director. The conditions are: (1) that you raise a matching sum in 5 years and (2) that the entire $2 million be invested in *one* major project for recreation and sports, not scattered over several projects. Briefly outline an action plan that you would present to the potential donor within 2 weeks of the offer.

2. You are the superintendent of recreation and parks in an industrial city of 250,000. The mayor has ordered that all department heads change their budget presentations from "line-item" to "program budget" style. He has given you 2 weeks to prepare a general layout. How would you begin?

3. Sometimes it is very difficult to expand recreation budgets or obtain approval for recreation construction bonds in very high-income, highly educated communities. But it is sometimes very easy to promote such moves in low-income, slightly depressed areas. Explain this from a financial point of view.

4. To check your present knowledge of the financial structure of your community, answer the following questions without aid.
   a. What is the annual gross operating budget of your city/town/village?
   b. What is your city's legal bonding limit?
   c. Name five banks or savings and loan companies in your community. Do you know the president of any of them?
   d. What is the total annual operating and capital recreation and parks budget for the municipality in which you live?

5. A major resort firm announces that it may build a multimillion dollar complex in your community including a hotel, golf course, marina, health center, tennis courts, and associated facilities. You are the local director of recreation, and your daily newspaper asks you to assess the financial impact of such an installation on your operations.

BIBLIOGRAPHY

Artz, R. M.: Foundation-trust-endowment gift programs for parks and recreation, Bulletin No. 84, Management Aids, Arlington Va., 1970, National Recreation and Park Association.

Butler, G. D.: Introduction to community recreation, New York, 1959, McGraw-Hill Book Co.

Haas, A., and Jackson, D. D.: Bulls, bears and Dr. Freud, New York, 1967, World Publishing Co.

Hoyt, M.: The young investor's guide to the stock market, New York, 1972, J. B. Lippincott Co.

Kaplan, G. G., and Welles, C., eds.: The money managers, New York, 1969, Random House.

Kemmon, T.: Official guide of U.S. paper money, New York, 1968, HC Publishers.

Kraus, R. G., and Curtis, J. E.: Creative administration in recreation and parks, ed. 2, St. Louis, 1977, The C. V. Mosby Co.

Low, J.: Understanding the stock market, Boston, 1968, Little, Brown & Co.

Manual of practical fund raising, raising funds for projects, Boston, 1972, Boston Municipal Research Corp.

Maxwell, J. A.: Financing state and local government, Washington, D.C., 1965, The Brookings Institute.

Merrill Lynch, Pierce, Fenner & Smith, Inc.: Investing in municipal bonds for tax-free income, New York, 1975.

Merrill Lynch, Pierce, Fenner & Smith, Inc.: Investment opportunities—changing leisure markets, New York, 1972.

Merrill Lynch, Pierce, Fenner & Smith, Inc.: Investment opportunities, the leisure market, New York, 1967.

Meyer, H. D., and Brightbill, C. K.: Recreation administration, Englewood Cliffs, N.J., 1956, Prentice-Hall, Inc.

Milton, A.: How to get a dollar's value for a dollar spent, New York, 1964, Bell Publishing Co.

Money guide to family finance, 1976, Money.

Moore, C.: How women can make money in the stock market, New York, 1972, Doubleday & Co.

Ney, R.: Wall Street jungle, New York, 1970, Grove Press.

New York State Parks and Recreation: Federal and state aid for parks, recreation and historic preservation, Albany, N.Y., 1977.

Newspaper Enterprise Association, Inc.: The world almanac 1975, New York, 1975, The Association. (See sections on Economics, Gold, Corporations, and Stocks.)

Personal money management, 1976, Money.

Report of Commission on Money and Credit: Money & credit, Englewood Cliffs, N.J., 1961, Prentice-Hall, Inc.

Rodney, L. S.: Administration of public recreation, New York, 1964, The Ronald Press.

Rubel, S. M., and Novotny, E. G.: How to raise and invest venture capital, New York, 1971, Presidents Publishing Co.

Rutberg, S.: Ten cents on the dollar, New York, 1973, Simon & Schuster. (A most revealing essay on bankruptcies under chapter 11 of the Banking Laws, a most convenient escape hatch for financial wheelers and dealers.)

Smith, A.: The money game, New York, 1969, Random House.

Tennis Foundation of North America: A manual for financing public tennis playing facilities, Chicago, 1975, The Foundation.

U.S. Department of Commerce: The American economic system . . . and your part in it, Pueblo, Colo., 1975.

Wiltsee, J. L.: Guide to personal business, Business Week, 1974.

REFERENCES

1. Doell, C. E.: How much money should be spent on community recreation? Recreation **46**(3): 174, June 1953.
2. Galbraith, J. K.: Money—whence it came, where it went, Boston, 1975, Houghton Mifflin Co.
3. Hendrickson, R. A.: The cashless society, New York, 1972, Dodd, Mead & Co.
4. Kraus, R. G.: Recreation and leisure in modern society, New York, 1971 Appleton-Century-Crofts.
5. Kraus, R. G., and Curtis, J. E.: Creative administration in parks and recreation, ed. 2, St. Louis, 1977, The C. V. Mosby Co.
6. New York Times **127**:43, 807, January 1, 1978.
7. Robertson, D. H.: Money, Chicago, 1962, University of Chicago Press.

16

PUBLICITY AND PUBLIC RELATIONS

Courtesy Boston Parks and Recreation Dept.

Publicity and public relations are the communications and message-bearing aspects of recreation work. Interestingly enough, most texts on recreation administration place the discussion of public relations very late in the book; some even make it the last chapter. This would seem to indicate two things: (1) recreation professionals do not see publicity and public relations as warranting the same importance given finance or personnel and, (2) recreation professionals are slightly self-conscious about making much of publicity because it is cheapening or demeaning—publicity is associated with commercialism and advertising people. Both of these opinions are erroneous. In fact, one school of thought believes that if recreation administrators were convinced of the importance and effectiveness of good public relations and acted accordingly, the entire recreation movement might be on a considerably stronger financial and political basis than it presently is. Here is one measure of the investment made in public relations by American business people:

Businesses in the United States currently spend more than $5 billion a year on public relations. By any yardstick, it's big business; some 100,000 people are engaged in it and its principal trade association ranks high in the nation with a membership of some 6,000 practitioners in 63 cities, Puerto Rico and 28 countries.[2]

At times elusive and difficult to define in an exact manner, public relations is certainly an extensive, extroverted, tactile form of communication. Appley[1] writes: "Whatever an organization does that affects the opinions of its various publics toward it is public relations." And that, very simply, is it. Public relations is everything a recreation agency or department does that touches or influences peoples' attitudes to-

ward that agency. It may be good, it may be bad. Note that the quote from Appley refers to "publics," not one public. Whether in a remote community of 5000 oil pipeline workers in northern Alaska or a large city such as Philadelphia, recreation people serve many different constituencies or publics, always within the very same community. These subpublics include elderly persons, female adolescents, retired workers, World War II veterans (as distinquished from Viet Nam veterans), college graduates, and drug users among others. The number is infinite. Messages and impacts received differ according to which constituency is involved.

Butler[3] says: "Public relations is good performance publicly appreciated because it is adequately communicated." The area of recreation management has advanced too far to be disturbed by self-guilt over effective publicity and public relations campaigns. The taxpaying and dues-paying publics deserve nothing less than the latest and most accurate information, schedules, locations, future plans, and fiscal outlines.

Basic aims and objectives of a sound and effective publicity–public relations program should be:

1. To inform the general public of dates, times, places, and full particulars of all programs and facilities available.
2. To impress on constituents the philosophy and underlying motives that motivate the department or agency.
3. To advise of future plans for programs and facilities.
4. To encourage involvement in all sectors.
5. To stimulate other programs and activities within other groups, clubs, and agencies through the department's example.

6. To invite that unusual public gift, volunteer, or offer of help that can vastly enrich the recreation program.

7. To spotlight and publicize those unique incidents and personalities that can make urban life more delightful, more surprising, and more rewarding to otherwise bored, disenchanted citizens.

8. To demonstrate to the general public the professional competence of the recreation agency or department and its desire to constantly improve its delivery of leisure services to its various publics.

Good taste is a rare but precious characteristic in public relations work. Cheap, exploitive, repititious, low-grade material pollutes the communications channels in most cities, and recréation agencies sometimes contribute to this. Far better that fewer, finer messages come forth than a constant flow of dull, ineffective pamphlets, books, articles, and radio and newspaper blurbs. A touch of class can give a 3-line message the impact of a nuclear bomb, if handled professionally.

PUBLICITY

Publicity is the direct action aspect of the publicity—public relations effort. Publicity has a very temporal quality about it. It is expected to have effects now or in the immediate future. The Random House Dictionary of the English Language[5] defines publicity as:

1. public notice resulting from mention in the press, on the radio, or through any other medium or means of communications, including word of mouth. 2. the measures, process or business of securing public notice. 3. information, articles etc., issued to secure public notice or attention. 4. public notice or attention resulting from advertising. 5. the state of being public, or open to general observation or knowledge.

Because "public relations is everything," it is a difficult field to encompass. Emphasis, therefore, will be placed on several specific areas of publicity opportunity for recreation administrators: staff, media, cameras, graphics, special items, reports, booklets, and brochures.

Staff

The recreation staff can make or break the publicity effort. Unless each key member of the leadership team sees the need for good publicity and grasps every opportunity, the recreation chief will be frustrated by a very limited return. Staff members must first be made to realize that a steady supply of quality publicity information and special features is essential to maintain contact with the public. Second, they should become familiar with techniques for spotting and taking advantage of publicity opportunities. Third, it is essential that staff members be instructed in the various skills and techniques necessary for transmitting publicity efforts successfully.

Media

The media consist of daily and weekly newspapers, radio, television, in-house newsletters, trade journals, and a variety of special interest and closed circuit radio and television systems. Many recreation personnel assume that commercial media are a captive audience, waiting anxiously for red-hot recreation news. This is not true. No matter how small the radio station or newspaper, its professional staff observes a code of ethics and will insist on quality material. This is to their credit and must be respected. A good rule-of-thumb is to treat every newspaper and its staff as if it were *The New York Times* and every broadcaster as if he or she were from NBC, CBS, or ABC. Such a rule is burdensome, but it will never cause the recreation agency embarrassment.

Newspapers. These have been the primary publicity resource for recreation announcements since the birth of the movement. The recreation program directly affects and interests so many readers that the press readily gives it good coverage. The preparation of news material for the press, however, calls for more than passing skill. The basic news release format (who, what, when, where, why) applies here, but additional touches are needed. The item must be typed clearly, double-spaced, and error free. It should be edited and proofread carefully if the writer hopes to see it published. Above all, it must be early. A minimum of 3 days arrival before the desired publication date is a must, a full week is preferable. Dull, childishly prepared material is doomed before it arrives and is really a waste of time and paper. The news release should be as carefully planned and prepared as a letter to the governor or to a foundation requesting a financial grant.

In addition to conventional news stories, the recreation administrator should seek opportunities for feature articles, picture stories, columns, and special analytical pieces. These enable the recreation department to keep the public informed on the philosophy, problems, future plans, and visions of the agency.

A technique that almost guarantees success is periodic appointments with the publisher or editor of the daily newspaper to discuss past successes and failures and to indicate any projects in the planning stages. This gives the newspaper person the opportunity to make suggestions and to become part of the plan.

It is also wise to have articles published in weekly, ethnic, and special interest publications because each serves a different public or publics.

Radio. The radio was declared dead, or close to it, with television's ascendancy in the 1950s. Mark Twain's pungent comment, "The reports of my demise are premature," is equally applicable to radio's reported departure. Radio bounded back amazingly, and over 100 million radios are in operation daily, roughly one radio for every two Americans.

Free radio time is not hard to come by, no matter how small or remote the community. Most tiny villages and remote open spaces are serviced by at least two or more local stations, while cities such as Boston and New York have at least a dozen stations each. Putting radio time to good use, however, is much more of a challenge than getting it.

The public will not listen to boring amateur radio presentations. The recreation department must work through professional radio personnel to be effective. Spot announcements, special features, surprise broadcasts, local personalities, and requests for listener feedback are some of the more successful techniques. Sports scores, leader personalities, award winners, new construction projects, and an occasional "bad news" report on vandalism or facility abuse represent items suited to good listening. Occasional human interest features are excellent in bringing a familiar intimacy to the show. The Minneapolis Park District has featured the winners in a Halloween costume contest, while Baltimore citizens enjoyed hearing why certain young people had entered the field of recreation. Radio station WEEI in Boston presented a most successful feature on vandalism prevention in the city's parks, including interviews with young people who had been apprehended committing the acts. The audience was substantial. The commissioner of recreation and parks in one city makes spot announcements warning parents of dangerous ice skating and swimming conditions at various times of the year and advising where children should be prohibited from taking risks.

The rules of preparation—neatness, clarity, full details, timeliness—that apply to material intended for the newspaper are equally applicable to material destined for the radio news office.

Television. Since both radio and television are required by federal law to provide substantial blocks of free public service time, the door is open, the space is there. As with radio, the effective utilization of that time is the challenge.

Television brings a need for higher skill in planning than radio because of its two-dimensional quality. Again, the recreation administrator needs the advice and assistance of the television professional in planning and staging the announcement or show. Many a clever idea by the recreator fails because it was not carefully worked out and edited before presentation.

Unparalleled as a means for bringing to mass audiences the thrills and delights of live sports, contests, shows, demonstrations, and training programs, television can be shaped and molded into many directions. The playground pageant, circus, festival, community Christmas display, final point in a championship basketball game—the drama and immediacy of the television screen are incomparable.

Special features, however, should not be overlooked. A scholarly, detailed analysis of a beach erosion problem; a study of Dutch elm disease, or a demonstration of new tree-digging and planting machines can each be an exciting feature for a recreation agency if prepared well and presented skillfully. Two of the most interesting recreation television features in recent years were the full birth sequence of an African Gem Bok (deer) in the San Diego Zoo and a training sequence on street youth workers in cellar clubs in New York City.

Cameras

The skillful use of cameras, tape recorders, slide projectors, and associated equipment is a high-impact feature of an effective publicity campaign. Such a campaign without cameras and audiovisuals is doomed from the start.

Still cameras. A wide range of still cameras is available today, such as the Graflex press, 35mm, instamatic, reflex, and others. Color and black-and-white film can provide varied effects for varied purposes. This makes strategic use of photography a must in the publicity effort.

If a department is large and sufficiently affluent, a regular staff photographer is ideal. Smaller budgets may require that an arrangement be made with a professional free-lance photographer who will cover photo assignments on an agreed on rate, for example, $5.00 per delivered 8″ × 10″ glossy black-and-white print, or on an hours-worked basis. A third, and very helpful arrangement, is to train several members of the staff or the entire staff in the routine use of several different cameras. Although this does not produce many prize-winning photos, it does provide a steady and convenient supply of program photographs at a modest cost. Probably the best overall arrangement would be a combination of the last two elements. This has worked well for hundreds of private agencies and recreation departments.

Movie cameras. Films of recreation activities, if made of carefully selected subjects and accompanied by appropriate sound captions, are quite effective in interpreting the work of the department or agency to neighborhood audiences and community groups. The use of sophisticated equipment and rainbow colors of film has given this medium greater impact than ever before. Not only can activity programs, construction projects, and training sequences be put on film for staff and community use, but original scenarios and film projects have been made into programs themselves. School children, teenagers, and senior citizens have written, staged, directed, and acted in a variety of films on health, fun, fitness, antivandalism, gangs, and other exciting subjects. These films are then often used as integral parts of the publicity effort.

A caution or two is appropriate, however. Quality movie cameras are expensive and delicate and do require some skill and much care. Only 16 mm or larger is practical, and film for these types is very costly to buy and develop, far more than for still photos. Finally, a completed film takes time to make and, on completion, is immediately dated. It cannot be edited, rearranged, updated the way a photo album or a slide talk can. The movie is valuable, but it *is* costly and rather inflexible. Use it sparingly.

Closed circuit television. This relatively recent invention is now available for rental, lease, or purchase. A good working system (one camera, one television monitor, and associated gear) costs from $800 to $1,300. It is as simple to operate as a conventional movie camera, a tape deck, or a home television. Excellent effects can be obtained, however, when used for training, lectures, gatherings within a small area, and any situation when short pieces and events are desired for repetition, later to be discarded. The television camera offers three advantages over the movie camera—it is cheaper to operate, it is extremely flexible, and it provides a sense of immediacy. The tapes are reusable, and no developing is involved. It does not have the polish, however, of a carefully planned and executed motion picture.

Audiovisual equipment. Add to the above equipment, the various other devices on the market—opaque projectors, slide projectors, tape recorders, stereos, transistor radios, movie projectors, screens—and the recreation agency has an expensive but extremely versatile publicity battery. Today's slide projectors are light in weight, but powerful in image. Clever combinations of two or more slide projectors hitting a large, highly visible white wall can be most effective. Combined with skillful taping, stereo, sound systems, and auxiliary movies, the total effect at a high school assembly, church congregation, or city council meeting can be massive.

Most of this equipment is too costly for instant purchase by the average recreation department or private agency. It has been my experience, however, that much of this equipment is already available through local public schools and libraries (both richly endowed with audiovisual equipment), newspaper offices, radio stations, police and fire departments, and large hospitals. For additional equipment, visit the local camera store and/or the local stereo, record, or television shop. Each of these stores, after an explanation by the agency or department, could be the source of loans and advice on sophisticated equipment, even on the slight possibility that a later purchase may be made. A final source of free loans of equipment is YMCA's, YWCA's, Boys' Clubs, and the like in surrounding communities.

The use of such electronic equipment and the execution of a comprehensive publicity campaign involving such equipment requires talent, time, and organization. The agency or department planning such an ambitious use of audiovisual materials and equipment should designate one staff member or hire someone to work exclusively on the subject. Anything less will be an ineffective jumble of useless bits and pieces.

Graphics

A certain amount of basic bread-and-butter printed material is essential to every successful publicity and communications effort by a recreation agency. These should be crisp, informative, and attractive. They represent some opportunities for creativity but not a great deal. It is the occasional special issue, the unusual poster, logo, photo montage that captures the eye and evokes the favorable comment. Here is where the recreation agency should concentrate its talent.

The exhibit or display is an excellent means for making a point dramatically but inexpensively. Drawing on the talents of leaders and participants is perfectly legitimate. This makes available the separate and the combined delights of plaster, posters, rope, metal, sculpture, soap, paper, macrame, wood, bamboo, batik, oil and water paints, and a host of others. Types of displays on exhibits include:

1. Outdoor art shows, photography, dioramas, panel displays
2. Special events such as miniplays or pageants with a message
3. Poster layouts in malls, schools, hospitals, shop windows, and on sidewalks
4. Action demonstrations—nothing, but nothing, has such an impact as the lively speaker or performer, explaining and demonstrating the very message before the eyes of the viewers. Uniformed lifeguards announce the opening of the beaches; firefighters display equipment and remind all viewers about Fire Prevention Week.

As one of the most widely used publicity devices, posters should be designed carefully, not simply slapped together. Making ten messy, overdone posters may have less impact than one excellent poster. Use good, substantial tagboard (24″ × 16″). Each poster should be thought out, reduced to its minimum elements, then painted clearly. A common error is to fill the poster with text, mostly unreadable. If the posters are to be mass-produced by a printer, all the work should go into an excellent mold, the rest is just reproduction.

Placing posters is important. Unusual, highly visible sites should be sought in stores, schools, churches, and gathering places. If the site is already glutted with cheap, gaudy posters, go elsewhere—a poster at such a visually polluted site is completely wasted.

Reports

Annual and seasonal reports on programs and accomplishments of the recreation department are important parts of the overall publicity plan. Reports should not be pumped out as mere aggregates of facts, numbers, and data. They should contain all necessary data, but in special reference sections, available when wanted. The main body of reports, on the other hand, should be readable messages that show problems, opportunities, and the future of the recreation program. Such reports become valuable publicity items because people read them, rather than toss them aside to gather dust.

Special items

Awards. One of the most infallible publicity-getters is the award and the award ceremony. Given periodically, the awards going to "Greatest Volunteer," "Oldest–Longest-Term Leader," "Athlete of the Month," "Most Improved Dancer," and others are naturals to bring interesting headlines. The banquet, dance, tournament, school assembly, or city council meeting where these awards are presented will overflow with guests, parents, and relatives of the person being honored. Rarely will the press and radio fail to cover such an event, and should the award be given to a stage star, professional athlete, or nationally known politician, the event may rate television coverage as well.

Special days, weeks, and months. The NRPA has for years declared June "National Recreation Month" and has received a great deal of positive publicity from the hundreds of activities and special events that occur during the month. New Rochelle, New York declared the first week in June "New Rochelle Tennis Week," and the mayor signed a proclamation so stating. In a ceremony before lunchtime crowds, the mayor himself presented the proclamation to the city Tennis Committee. The ceremony was followed by demonstrations of Tennis-on-the-Street and a variety of tennis clinics and small contests. Hundreds of people watched, and the Department of Parks and Recreation was able to publicize its entire summer tennis program and schedule. The event was given much coverage by the local daily newspaper and two radio stations.

Special days, weeks, and months offer endless possibilities: "Frankfurter Week," "Playground Opening Day," "National Frog Day," "Elmville Grandpa's Day," "Golf Week," "Visit your Park Week," and others.

Tours and open houses. These events offer delightful opportunities for showing public officials, board members, parents, PTAs, local residents, service clubs, and other interested groups exactly what is going on in the recreation department. Guided tours or open houses are usually scheduled at the time of dedication of a new facility, the beginning of a seasonal program, or any other occasion that shows the department in a favorable light. They should be carefully planned, including the following:

1. Travel the route beforehand, checking for errors, oversights, hazards.
2. Set up guides, fixed points, route, and so forth.
3. Keep the operation on schedule or embarrassing backups and confusion will occur.
4. Anticipate latecomers, some very, very late.
5. Assemble at the end of the tour for a general question and answer session.
6. Gather the involved staff together for a critique or evaluation immediately after the event is over.

Kraus and Curtis[4] recommended a publicity kit that could be very helpful, especially to the small recreation department or agency. This kit should include items such as:

1. Public address system: a portable amplifier and speakers (at least 30 watt output) that is light enough to be handled by one person, either man or woman, phonograph or tape deck, and suitable albums.
2. Cameras: 35mm still camera, Graflex press, 16mm movie camera, and instamatic camera.
3. Poster materials: colored ink markers, pens, rulers, and plastic letter stencils and guides; mimeograph and construction paper; drawing boards and tagboard; uniform poster, made in quantity, with about one fifth of its space devoted to a colorful department heading and the remainder clear for special announcements, photographs, and the like.
4. Display complex: a homemade or purchased portable display complex consisting of folding tables, hanging panels, and lights that may easily be disassembled, moved, and set up for display purposes at city hall, banks, restaurants, shopping cen-

ters, or conferences and training meetings.

5. Work table and hardware: a sturdy work table, 4 feet by 6 feet, with scissors, paper-cutting blade, stapler, and similar office tools, along with an adjacent steel filing cabinet offering organized storage of papers, booklets, and department public relations materials.

PUBLIC RELATIONS

Public relations, faced squarely, is not a stunt, a picture-taking campaign, a publicity coup that has momentary explosive impact, but fades quickly from mind and memory. Public relations, if effective, is continuous, all-pervading, in the operations of a recreation department or agency. Public relations is the sum of voices, letters, and the receipt and handling of queries, complaints, and suggestions. It is the prompt and reasoned response on the part of the recreation director to ideas, criticisms, and suggestions from the participants. Public relations is the working uniforms, schedules, and attitudes of staff personnel toward the public, the cleanliness of vehicles, and meeting places. Encouraging good relationships with the general public and with surrounding agencies such as other city departments, schools, churches, and YMCA's are just two ways in which the recreation agency can improve the effectiveness of its public relations.

Public schools

Probably the most vital area for good relationships is between the recreation agency and the local public school system. Use of buildings, pools, gymnasiums, classrooms, and grounds; cooperation between personnel of both facilities; full participation by students and parents are all goals of such a relationship, one that is so easily disrupted by administrative error or discourtesy.

Schools and recreation activities are closely related in their philosophies and their work. It is essential that there be very close understanding and cooperation between the personnel of both facilities. Some of the devices that can strengthen this relationship are:

School board member on the recreation board or commission. This technique maintains close communications and helps keep both facilities aware of each other's problems.

Joint acquisition and development of areas and facilities. This very sound and economic approach to new and rehabilitated facilities was pioneered in the 1950s by Hubert I. Snyder, Director of Parks and Recreation for Baltimore County, Md. It compels an opening of the mind to the needs and concerns of the other agency, and it results in a facility and use plan that accommodates the best of both spheres of activity.

Joint use of facilities. To duplicate many of the very costly facilities used by both agencies would be financially prohibitive. The economics of the situation compels cooperation, which necessarily results in concessions and compromises for the needs of the other facility.

Joint program planning. Nothing is more exasperating than to find a school program in open competition with an agency recreation program in the same community. Joint planning precludes most of this. First aid, swimming lessons, community soccer, Halloween window painting, holiday and vacation programs, day camps are but a few of the activities and programs that flourish under cooperative arrangements, but frequently fail when attempted in a competitive setting.

Other city departments

A warm and friendly relationship with the many other units of city government is most helpful to a municipal recreation department. If the police commissioner is aware of long-range recreation plans and efforts, and if the police department can expect early notice, full information, and courteous response when problems arise, there is a very good chance that the police department will be very helpful. The absence of these cooperative efforts by the recreation staff may result in a truculent, uncooperative police department that characterizes the recreation agency with comments such as: "wacky," "careless," "disrespectful to police officers," or "They never tell us what's going on!"

Similar communication should be encouraged with the law department, the departments of public works, finance, and transportation, the public library, and other branches and divisions of the municipal government. One recreation department in Florida annually holds an open house to which it invites only the officials and staffs of its neighbor departments and divisions of city government. Over refreshments and small talk, the staff of the recreation departments shows films and slides and gives a brief but comprehensive report on the past, present, and future for local recreation. A question and answer session concludes the evening.

Private agencies

It would be a shortsighted recreation department that failed to perceive the major recreational contributions of such voluntary and privately funded agencies as the YMCA, YWCA, Boy and Girl Scouts, Campfire Girls, Catholic Youth Organization, YMHA, Boys' Clubs, and similar community organizations. Warm, open, and cooperative relationships between the recreation department and these units will unlock and lubricate many avenues of cooperation and cosponsorship. For example, a local YMCA may be planning a large outdoor boxing show on a summer evening

at exactly the same time the recreation department is planning a judo-karate street demonstration nearby. If good relations exist, both will soon learn of the conflict and a compromise will be worked out. Either one will reschedule its event, or both will combine their efforts in one single boxing and judo-karate exhibition. The public is the beneficiary, since people can now see both events, and the two agencies will feel a sense of having worked together. Periodic meetings and exchanges of information will help to enhance this sense of cooperation.

Community service agencies

Ethnic, economic, and special interest committees, task forces, and action groups are an integral part of today's leisure activity scene. Community action agencies, Urban League, Hispanic Alliance, First Americans, Asiatics in America, Welfare Mothers, Parents Without Partners are but a few. To maintain direct and active relationships with all of them would demand the full time and attention of staffs far larger than those of the typical community recreation department. On the other hand, it is important to know which are the most alert, the most articulate, the most aggressive, the most active, and then devise a plan for staying in touch and maintaining good communications and rapport. These are the citizens, the taxpayers, the recreation constituency—they expect to be kept informed and involved, and they deserve nothing less.

GENERAL COMMENTS

If public and private recreation departments and agencies are to be fully successful in their mission, they must expand and strengthen their public relations efforts. Publicity and effective communications materials are also important so that timely details, rates, schedules, locations, and plans are available at all times to the citizens who finance such programs and who deserve convenient access to them.

Public relations programs of recreation departments should originate in honesty, self-confidence, and a genuine desire to be of service to the public. To be successful, that same public relations program must be based on the premise that wholesome recreation thrives in an atmosphere of cooperation among other service agencies. The public relations program that does not encompass this cooperative stance is not really public relations at all, but only a self-serving propaganda device.

DISCUSSION QUESTIONS

1. As director of recreation for a medium-sized city, you are told that your department's public relations image is poor. Outline a series of steps that might rectify that rumor.
2. Two agencies in the same city, the YMCA and the Boys' Club, are in a heated battle over which agency should receive a $250,000 United Way grant toward a new indoor swimming pool. As director of the local YWCA, you are asked to intercede. Outline a public relations plan that could bring these two agencies back into a spirit of cooperation. Be sure to involve the public.
3. An advertising agency informs you, the public relations director of the recreation department of a large city, that it will deliver to you 2 days hence for 2 full hours the most outstanding professional quarterback of the National Football League. He can be used in any legitimate way as speaker, clinic instructor, visitor to centers, and so forth. Outline exactly how you would use those 2 hours and show all the preparations you would make.
4. The annual NFL Super Bowl is regarded as one of the greatest publicity packages of all time. Give several features of its planning and execution that you like and some that could be improved. Does the Super Bowl image help local recreation? Explain.
5. The recent advent of women's liberation, National Organization for Women (NOW), Equal Rights Amendment (ERA), Affirmative Action, and simi-

lar movements has had a substantial impact on male-female relationships. Identify and explain several ways in which these movements will make contemporary recreation publicity campaigns different from those of 10 to 15 years ago.

BIBLIOGRAPHY

Adams, A. B.: Handbook of practical public relations, New York, 1965, Thomas Y. Crowell Co.

Butler, G. D.: Playgrounds: their administration and operation, ed. 3, New York, 1950, The Ronald Press.

Funk & Wagnall's standard reference encyclopedia, vol. 20, New York, 1962, Standard Reference Works Publishing Co., Inc.

Hjelte, G.: The administration of public recreation, New York, 1947, The Macmillan Co.

The International City Managers Association: Municipal recreation administration, ed. 4, Chicago, 1960, The Association.

Lutzin, S. G., and Storey, E. H.: Managing municipal leisure services, Chicago, 1973, The International City Managers Association.

Meyer, H. D., and Brightbill, C. K.: Recreation administration, Englewood Cliffs, N.J., 1956, Prentice-Hall, Inc.

Sternloff, R. E., and Warren, R.: Park and recreation maintenance management, Boston, 1977, Holbrook Press Inc.

The 1971 World Book Year Book, Chicago, 1971, Field Enterprises Educational Corp.

The 1974 World Book Year Book, Chicago, 1974, Field Enterprises Educational Corp.

REFERENCES

1. Appley, L. A.: Management in action, New York, 1956, American Management Association.
2. Budd, J. F., Jr.: An executive's primer on public relations, Philadelphia, 1969, Clinton Book Co.
3. Butler, G. D.: Introduction to community recreation, New York, 1959, McGraw-Hill Book Co.
4. Kraus, R. G., and Curtis, J. E.: Creative administration in recreation and parks, ed. 2, St. Louis, 1977, The C. V. Mosby Co.
5. Random House Dictionary of the English language (unabridged edition), New York, 1966, Random House.

17
CAREERS IN RECREATION

So you want to work in recreation? Sounds almost contradictory, doesn't it, *work* in *recreation?* Well, recreation has become a challenging and exciting professional field in which apprentices, interns, leaders, supervisors, and executives actually do work at helping other people to enjoy their valuable recreation hours and leisure pursuits.

This was not always so. Until very recently, the vast majority of leisure activities were spontaneous, homespun, part of a cultural ritual at just about every age and level of civilization. Leadership was voluntary, and much of the instruction in leisure skills such as dance, song, painting, hunting, fishing, and weaving was provided by parents, older siblings, or grandparents. Only since World War I and the early 1920s have we seen the growth of a professional, salaried leadership cadre in recreation.

A career in recreation will bring a mixture of experiences to the professional— love, frustration, anticipation, knowledge, confusion, curiosity, nervousness, satisfaction, and sometimes, overwhelming exhaustion. Recreation work is intimately related to people, and it must be based on a real appreciation for human needs, wants, desires, and learning capacities. Further, it must accept, to a great extent, the foibles and fickle tastes of even the most stable participants.

In 1950, there were 6784 full-time professional recreation leaders nationwide, in 1960 there were 9216. In 1966, the number had risen to 65,213 and, in 1975, to 84,105.

IMPACT OF RECREATION CAREER

The impact of a career in recreation work may be described under four headings: (1) social, (2) family, (3) financial, and (4) personal.

Social

The negative aspects of the work are felt most keenly by the young professional. Whether he or she is working in a private agency, a commercial recreation center, a municipal recreation and parks department, or a large hospital, opportunities for a personal social life are limited. The young professional, presumably not hampered by house, large family, and domestic responsibilities, is expected to work many evenings, weekends, and holidays. Often the newest member of a recreation staff is assigned those programs and activities that require only modest skill and planning ability, but demand large investments of time, physical labor, and personal supervision. Sports leagues in basketball, softball, and baseball played during the evenings and on weekends, community tennis tournaments, Saturday night teen centers, weekend ski trips, and holiday family activities are the kind of programs that delight the community or agency but put a heavy demand on the time and energy of the young professional. It is this kind of early pressure, as much as low salaries, that drives many young recreation workers out of the profession shortly after they start.

But some remain, study, and grow in their jobs. These people experience the full social impact of working in the recreation field. They enter new communities and meet the citizens of that community and the patients in its hospitals; they survey playgrounds and work for repairs of existing equipment, fresh designs, and new equipment; they plan teen centers for adolescents; they plan parades, art shows, flea markets, and tennis tournaments. Sometimes they see tears of loneliness, the despairing threat of a person threatening suicide, and, perhaps, too rarely, they hear a community express its appreciation for all their work. There is a unique kind of social dividend to the work.

Family

The family of the new recreation professional can sometimes present a problem when it comes to understanding the work or describing it to others. "What does my son do? Well, he's in recreation or sports or something, a kind of gym teacher" or "He works for a hospital in the wards, he entertains them with bingo and movies—kind of a babysitter I'd guess you'd call him." In an explosive moment when careers are being discussed, an angry father may say to his college-bound daughter "What, 4 years of college to learn recreation? I can teach you all you need to know about sports and games in 4 hours. Why don't you become a teacher or a doctor, so you'll have a decent job when you get out of school?" Despite my 30 years in professional recreation work, my own mother still does not comprehend what my work really is.

The new recreator must be prepared for this family blind spot and not be too impatient with their skepticism. Our profession is still too new and its end products too difficult to perceive quantitatively for our families, friends, and associates to appreciate fully and clearly what we do. Following are a few steps that can help new recreators clarify their job and future work to their families.

1. Show one or two of the several professionally produced films that describe our areas of responsibility. Three of these are *A Chance to Play, Rx Recreation,* and the new *In Search of Balance.* All three are available through the NRPA.

2. Select two or three particularly good back issues of the magazine *Parks and Recreation,* spread them before your family and use the stories and illustrations to dramatize the depth and variety that recreation work encompasses. Almost invariably, members of the group will exclaim, "I never realized the extent of recreation work."

3. Arrange a brief tour by private auto through your community for two or three people you particularly wish to educate. Prepare them with 5 minutes of philosophy of recreation, aims, goals, and the problems faced by recreation planners and workers in any crowded, congested urban area. Then visit the crowded downtown with its movie theatres, bowling alleys, bars, and restaurants (commercial recreation). From there, visit a small park, a medium-sized playground, a sports field, and an enclosed swimming pool or ice skating rink. Include also a visit to a hospital or mental institution if one is nearby, as well as a YMCA, Boy's Club, Jewish Community Center, or settlement house (private, voluntary agency recreation). Mention briefly and point out parking facilities, and litter and garbage control, lighting, uniforms, signs, money and ticket booths, security problems, leaders on duty, supplies and equipment, and the variety of groups and activities that are taking place in each of these facilities.

4. Invite to your home or introduce to your friends a recreation professional who knows his or her field and is articulate in describing the work, goals, and some realistic aspects of the profession.

One or more of these steps should help immensely in clarifying the recreation profession and assist family and friends to better understand the great potential that our work offers. This is particularly helpful when the early stages of career require evening and weekend work, because this is when family and friends become most critical of the field as a lifetime choice.

Financial

In the beginning, the financial picture is bleak. Most beginning recreation positions in cities, counties, hospitals, prisons, and private agencies have an annual salary of from $8,000 to $12,000 depending on the area of the country. Fringe benefits are uniformly good, however, whether one works for a municipality or private institution. Fringe benefits generally include full hospitalization insurance, six to nine personal leave or sick days, 2 weeks paid vacation, full payment into a pension plan, and one or two other factors, depending on the employer. It has been estimated that employers, both public and private, contribute from 45% to 65% beyond the workers' basic salary for their fringe benefits.

Nevertheless, these fringe benefits are not immediately translatable into cash, and the young worker feels the shortage of the modest salary. Further aggravating the picture is the pressure on one's clothing budget and the need to use a private automobile. Although many recreation leaders do their actual work in some form of sports or dance uniform, there are still many situations in which street clothes are worn. They can become covered with paint or decorative materials at a teen center dance, or they can be saturated moving between activity locations during a rainstorm. Good shoes can be damaged tramping through a muddy sports field that is under construction. The recreator's auto may be robbed or its windshield damaged while it is parked in a tough neighborhood or on the edge of a baseball field. There never seem to be enough department vehicles to go around and the top officials of the department or agency usually get to use the few that are available. Clothing allowances or funds for dry cleaning and repairing are still the exception rather than the rule.

Add to this the cost of professional organization dues ($25 to $100), possible union dues, several evening meals out each month, purchase of occasional professional textbooks, and an evening college course or two, and it is easily understood why the early professional years can be financially frustrating.

There is consolation, however. The salary structure of professional recreators has been moving up steadily and not simply to match the inflationary spiral. In 1960, beginning recreation workers or leaders with bachelor degrees received annual salaries of from $5000 to $7000. By 1970, this same beginning salary, nationally, ranged from $6500 to $9000—an increase of approximately 30%, more than the rise in cost of living.

In addition, many departments and agencies reduced their standard workweek from 50 hours to 46, 44, and even to 40 hours. Mileage allowances for business use of privately owned automobiles were raised from 8¢ per mile to 15¢ and 18¢ per mile during the same period. Such fringe benefits as personal or sick leave days, annual vacation, pension contributions by the employer, and medical insurance plans also improved substantially.

This is not to say the recreation profession is high paying. It is not, particularly when one considers the heavy wear and tear on nerves, stomach, social life, pocketbook and personality that the work entails. Even the top salaries earned by men and women holding advanced degrees and two or more decades of professional service rarely exceed $35,000 annually and much more rarely top $45,000. There are perhaps 10 recreation positions in America with annual salaries exceeding $50,000.

Personal

Most important is an assessment of what impact the recreators feel on their personal lives and development. Hours are irregular because recreation professionals are expected to work when their constituents/consumers play. This means late afternoons and evenings on weekdays, and mornings, afternoons, and evenings on weekends and holidays. This is particularly hard on the young, unmarried recreator. Many of the best opportunities for them to seek attractive peer companionship (Saturday mornings on the tennis courts, Saturday afternoons at the football game and cocktail party, Saturday night at the disco or bowling alley) are preempted by recreation duties. Evening meetings in the community, Bingo games in the ward, senior citizen bus trips to downtown theatres, school picnics, and supervisory patrols of beaches and pools during the hottest part of the summer all place heavy demands on the time and attention of young recreation professionals, and they are constantly reminded of the fun, freedom, and diversion that their peer group is enjoying before their very eyes.

The telephone adds to the personal intrusion of recreation work. Phone calls at dinner for information, complaints, sports protests, phone calls late in the evening demanding decisions on weighty program matters, phone calls for advice on ways and means for setting up local activity programs, and phone calls challenging articles and statements in the evening newspaper attributed to recreation workers are among the most irritating calls that tease, criticize, and actually scare. They are probably based on some past negative decision or punishment meted out to the phone caller and are often aimed at innocent bystanders. Recreators may develop a strong dislike for the telephone itself since many of their phone calls are of a problematic nature. The secretary warns, "Mrs. Brown called. She's angry because you didn't give

her son a summer job. The staff at the recreation center phoned and want you to rush over. The pool is leaking. Oh yes, and the Mayor called. He's furious because you left his name out of the story in the newspaper. He wants you to call him right away!" Personal impact is considerable, and intestinal fortitude is required if equilibrium is to be maintained.

Psychological rewards should be considered, however. The thrill of arriving on a new job and knowing you are wanted and needed; the pioneer sensation of opening new avenues for planning and cooperation among groups and individuals who formerly had little or no rapport; the pleasure of seeing prisoners rise from their bitterness and distrust and joyfully particpate in a circus, stage play, or holiday festival; the exhilarating experience of having a mayor or hospital administrator shake your hand before a cheering audience and declare you "the finest recreation leader we have ever known!" These recognitions, coupled with reasonably good salaries and steadily improving fringe benefits, make the recreation profession a rewarding career.

CANDIDATES

What kind of people should seek careers in professional recreation? This question is not easily answered. Chapter 9 covered the technical and mechanical side of personnel work—the recruiting, selecting, training, supervision, titles, duties, specific qualifications, and general administrative personnel practices. Here, the question is not a technical one, but a psychological one—who should become a recreation worker or professional? Through experience and association with thousands of recreation professionals, I believe the following characteristics are desirable for recreators.

Outgoing personality

Successful recreation workers must be interested in people of all kinds and in what they do, their weaknesses as well as their strengths. They must display a willingness to meet people, to chat, to make the first overture when others are reticent, or to reinterest persons who have become disenchanted. Persons who are bitter, withdrawn, overly egocentric, paranoid, or just plain dull will most probably fail as recreation professionals.

Intelligence

A reasonably animated and well-nourished intellect is necessary for recreators to deal with the people, problems, and opportunities they face. A bright, alert mind is a major asset. This does not mean that the top student in the high school graduating class or the student who makes the Dean's list will automatically make a prime recreation leadership candidate. Such a student, brilliant as far as books are concerned, may be a complete failure in working with people. On the other hand, certain potential recreator candidates may already be frantically involved in the high school or college power and action structures. They flit about, demonstrating to both faculty and fellow students that they are planless and shiftless; they join too many groups; they are elected to too many offices they cannot fill; they accept too many tasks they cannot complete; and they are constantly proposing new and complex projects and stunts for their associates and themselves. These campus fireballs are often the bane of their teachers with their nervous energy and lack of conformity. Their very enthusiasm and ubiquitous presence turn off most members of their peer group. These people may, with sound guidance and training, become superb recreation leaders.

Synecticism

A synecticist is a person who, instinctively, is a collector and connector of ideas, concepts, visionary thoughts, and myriad pieces of seemingly insignificant or worthless information and data. The synecticist weaves these disparate bits and pieces into bold and exciting new possibilities.

As an example, a synecticist, visiting a friend's home, observes a pool table in the basement but is told the balls and cues have been lost. Observing a large piece of unused plywood in the garage, the person suggests it be combined with the pool table and be used as a table tennis arrangement or as the surface for a model train. Another example would be the observation of an empty store on Main Street and the recollection that a certain group in town is looking for a teen center site. The synecticist's mind immediately connects the two, resolves the problems that might discourage the project, and suggests the idea to those who can implement it, usually offering personal help.

Articulation

The capacity to communicate effectively by spoken and written word is essential. A brilliant and active mind is useless if the person cannot speak clearly and in a manner appropriate to the setting, be it street corner, storefront, school auditorium, city council meeting, or network television.

Similarly, the tasks of assembling and promoting recreation plans, programs, and new facilities require the skillful preparation of reports, charts, letters, memoranda, training directions, news releases, and annual reports. The ability to write clearly and quickly is most helpful to busy recreation professionals, especially if they become executives. It is not necessary to be an English major, poet, author, or Pulitzer Prize winner. Good sentence structure and simple, clear writing is all that is needed.

Curiosity

A great asset to the recreation education candidate is a curious and searching mind. To compare all recreation aspirants to the legendary Man of all Ages, Leonardo da Vinci, may be overdoing it, but we certainly find some interesting points in MacLeish's[1] description of the man. He says that da Vinci was endlessly curious, impatient, and intense, and that he found a lifetime too short for all his endeavors in art, nature, the sciences, even human rights. He had one of history's greatest intellects. Blending artistic brilliance with scientific curiosity, he relentlessly pursued knowledge—from anatomy to aeronautics, from music to mechanics.

Wherever his imagination led, Leonardo's pen followed. He was always jotting ideas on scraps of paper, inspired by what he saw in foundries and flour mills, what he knew of ancient Greek inventions and contemporary engineering, and what he dreamed. When words failed, Leonardo drew.

He was free, as few humans have ever been free, to become whatever his gifts might make of him.

But the boy also differed from his associates in other, less commendable ways. His master soon discovered that he was capricious, quick to boredom, and conscienceless when it came to completing a job.

Characteristically, Leonardo left his work unfinished.

A gracious person, pleasing if not loving, a singer, versifier, maker of marvelous illusions, he was both performer and showman. He devised puzzles and games, and jokes that made people "roar with laughter." He won the friendship of dukes and kings. Admirers called him "the Divine Leonardo," and said he could do anything.

In his heart, Leonardo felt defeat. He sensed the coming of death with desperation, knowing now he would never finish the works on which he was engaged or, more important, carry out the many fantastic projects that forever filled his extraordinary mind—that his consuming thirst for understanding would never be quenched.

Painter, sculptor, mathematician, engineer, singer, musician, anatomist, writer, astronomer, politician—such a man may have set unreachable standards for most of us, but surely he provides an inspiring model for social science professionals, including those in recreation.

A zest for action, a love of good music, or the thrill of watching a flaming sunset or a soaring glider in the sky are all symptomatic of the curious, appreciative mind. A satisfied feeling at solving a crossword puzzle, at putting the last piece of a jigsaw puzzle into place, at writing a poem that someone admires, or a longing to visit distant places such as remote islands in the Pacific or the fjords of New Zealand are further examples of the experience-hungry, Leonardo-type of personality. This is desirable in the recreation candidate, even on a greatly reduced scale.

SPORTS

Frequently, young people are directed toward recreation careers because they have been outstanding athletes in high school or college. This is particularly true of male stars in football, baseball, or basketball. Some of these young men do have excellent qualifications and eventually become successful recreation workers and administrators. It is wrong, however, to assume that every outstanding athlete is a prime candidate for the recreation field. Young people who excel as football tight ends or basketball guards 3 years in a row may, off the field or court, be shy, introspective people, very ill at ease when asked to speak before a group. High school tennis stars may lack the comprehensive view of recreation and sports as an important part of a well-rounded life. To them, tennis may simply represent the opportunity for all-expense scholarships to college.

Day camps, hospital wards, and recreation centers are replete with the failure stories of brilliant athletes who brought little else to their jobs other than an excellence in one sport. Too often, the professional weaknesses of such young stars are deliberately ignored in the hope that they will somehow acquire the necessary skills and personality factors so important to a recreation professional. Brilliance in one or more sports really has no more direct relevance to leadership excellence than brilliance at music, painting, poetry, or mountain climbing. The odds are the same in all of them.

It must be emphasized that some athletic stars do make excellent recreation leaders and administrators. Bringing to a recreation setting a high skill and, incidentally, a sparkling reputation, can make many otherwise drab programs and centers come alive. Teenagers, critical and cynical at times, will often rise enthusiastically at the arrival of a well-known basketball or soccer star and will listen to his advice and direction in a way that escapes the average staff leader. Nevertheless, the point is that today's recreation administration responsibilities may require the professional to have contact with drama, music, crafts, ballet, playground design, staff training, public relations, finance, and other areas above and beyond sports. For a potential recreation candidate to be limited to a single sports achievement is to limit his or her pro-

fessional growth opportunities for the future.

GUIDANCE

One of the most sensitive contacts along the way to choosing a recreation career is the high school guidance counselor. Most high schools have at least one trained guidance counselor for every 1000 students. In addition, many high schools provide a guidance center consisting of a room or rooms equipped with books, magazines, reference manuals, and college catalogues as well as films and slides related to careers, colleges, and technical schools. Programs include career assemblies and films, visits by college representatives, and individual consultation meetings with students indicating specific interests. All of this is an aid to guiding the right boy or girl in the direction of a career as a professional recreation leader or administrator.

There are basic strengths and weaknesses in such high school guidance programs and they should be identified.

Strengths

The guidance person has access to the full academic and extracurricular record of the student, and personal interviews are easily arranged.

Other faculty and staff may add opinions when requested by a recognized guidance counselor.

Students are comfortable in familiar surroundings and can do considerable career research by themselves within the guidance center. They are not inhibited or embarrassed when asking questions.

In the low-key atmosphere of the career guidance center, students usually select the college or university that offers the best major for them rather than that which provides glamour or social status advantages.

Weaknesses

The high school vocational guidance counselor's time is thinly spread over hundreds of anxious junior and senior students. It is difficult to give more than fleeting attention to any one student's problem.

Often, the image of the recreation profession is oriented toward physical education. Potential candidates are asked whether they want to teach class, be a coach, or be a gym teacher. None of these positions is directly identified with the field of recreation, even though all are indirectly related.

Some guidance counselors are almost totally unaware of the existence of a recreation profession, or else they see it as limited to playground leaders and athletic instructors. Such counselors can give misleading directions and thus eliminate a bright young potential leader from exploring further.

Despite the shortcomings, the high school guidance counselor and center still represent a primary contact point for the student interested in recreation.

COLLEGES AND UNIVERSITIES

Approximately 187 colleges and universities offer full undergraduate curricula in professional recreation leadership. An additional 158 junior and community colleges provide 2-year programs, conferring associate degrees. Some 34,000 students are enrolled in these programs. Of the 187 colleges and universities, about half also provide graduate study leading to master's and doctor's degrees in municipal park and recreation administration, leisure services administration, and others.

Of the remaining 3000 higher educational schools, colleges, and universities, more than half offer some classes, colloquia, seminars, and symposia in the field of recreation, leisure, psychology of play, recreation for elderly persons, recreation for handicapped persons, and a wide range of courses in cultural arts recreation. These courses can be of great help to the aspiring social workers, school teacher, psychologist, medical administrator, and industrial engineer. It is a mistake, however, and a gross underestimate of the depth and complexity of leisure motivation to assume that one or two of these minor courses in recreation will sufficiently prepare a recreation professional. Substantially more training and experience are needed to produce the complete recreator.

There are some 300 colleges and universities in America that offer degree programs in professional recreation leadership and administration. These include 2-year programs leading to associate degrees, 4-year programs leading to bachelor degrees, and graduate programs leading to master and doctor degrees. A representative list of these campuses includes:

North Carolina State University
Department of Recreation Resources Administration
Raleigh, North Carolina

New York University
Department of Leisure Studies, School of Education and the Dance
New York, New York

Grambling University
Department of Recreation and Leisure Studies
Grambling, Louisiana

Adelphi University
Department of Health, Physical Education and Recreation
Hempstead, New York

Brooklyn College
City University of New York
Department of Physical Education, Health and Recreation
Brooklyn, New York

University of Iowa
Department of Leisure Studies and Recreation
Iowa City, Iowa

Herbert H. Lehman College
City University of New York
Department of Health, Physical Education and
    Recreation
Bronx, New York

State University at Brockport
State University of New York
Department of Recreation and Leisure Studies
Brockport, New York

University of Massachusetts
Department of Landscape Architecture and Re-
    gional Planning
Division of Leisure Studies
Amherst, Massachusetts

State University at Cortland
State University of New York
Department of Health, Physical Education and
    Recreation
Cortland, New York

University of Michigan
Department of Health, Physical Education and
    Recreation
Lansing, Michigan

University of Indiana
Department of Leisure Studies and Recreation
Bloomington, Indiana

University of Illinois
Department of Health, Physical Education and
    Leisure Studies
Urbana, Illinois

Pennsylvania State University
Department of Physical Education and Recre-
    ation
State College, Pennsylvania

University of Maryland
Department of Health, Physical Education and
    Leisure Studies
University Park, Maryland

University of Oregon
Department of Leisure Studies and Administra-
    tion
Eugene, Oregon

University of Minnesota
Department of Health, Physical Education and
    Recreation
Minneapolis, Minnesota

California State University
Department of Physical Education and Recre-
    ation
Fresno, California

University of Missouri
Department of Recreation and Park Administra-
    tion
Columbia, Missouri

Idaho State University
Department of Park and Recreation Administra-
    tion
Pocatello, Idaho

Ohio State University
Division of Parks and Recreation Administration
School of Natural Resources
Columbus, Ohio

North Texas State University
Division of Recreation and Leisure Studies
Denton, Texas

Northeastern University
Department of Health, Physical Education and
    Recreation
Boston, Massachusetts

University of New Hampshire
School of Health, Physical Education and Rec-
    reation
Durham, New Hampshire

Springfield College
Department of Recreation Administration
Springfield, Massachusetts

Transfers within the same college

Obviously, a person already enrolled in
an undergraduate program for recreation
and park majors at an accredited college
or university is committed to a career
in recreation. With others, it may not
be so clear. The students may be on a
campus that provides a recreation undergraduate curriculum but may be enrolled
in a different department or course of

study. If the student has thoughts of transferring, a few preparatory steps should be taken.

1. The student should do a self-study as to personality traits, living habits, degree of empathy for people, long-range career plans, and status of personal health. The aim here is to ascertain whether the new interest in a possible recreation career is more than a passing fancy and whether a substantial personality and experience base exists on which to build. Sometimes, a very promising young chemistry student has a desire to lead people, speak out, design living areas, build parks, and purify rivers. His background in high school and college, however, may show strong leanings toward science and mathematics. Everyone concerned with this person's decisions must make sure that he does not become a mediocre and disenchanted recreation worker rather than a brilliant and happy scientist.

2. It is wise for the curious student to speak to other undergraduates who are already in the recreation curriculum. These people will usually give honest, candid answers on the type of training and classes that they receive and the nature of the work, faculty, texts, job opportunities, field work requirements, and so forth.

3. Faculty members and the chairperson of the recreation curriculum or department should be met and interviewed by the prospective student to accumulate more information and to hear the faculty side of the story. It helps to submit high school and college academic transcripts to the department interviewer so that the applying student's background and preparation may be appraised.

4. If after these steps, the interest persists, the student should ask faculty help in arranging a transfer into the recreation educational curriculum.

Transfers to other colleges

If the interested student is enrolled in a college that has no undergraduate program in recreation education, the following steps may be taken:

1. Locate a campus nearby that has such a recreation undergraduate program, visit the campus, and follow the steps for transferring to a recreation department in the same college.

2. If no recreation campus is nearby, write to the National Recreation and Park Association, 1601 North Kent St., Arlington, Va. 22209 and describe the problem and information desired. Several advisory booklets have been prepared by the educational branch of the NRPA and the Society of Professional Recreation Educators (SPRE), and these can be very helpful to the undergraduate seeking guidance.

3. Visit the nearest municipal recreation and park department, be it on the village, town, city, or county level. Most such departments are supervised by persons who have completed some college training in the field, and they can give useful advice and direction on careers.

4. Attend one or more professional meetings of the local or state recreation society. This organization consists of professional and paraprofessional workers and administrators in departments of recreation and parks, hospitals, industrial centers, convalescent homes, and public schools. These people are receptive to the queries of young college students and can give substantial advice and direction. For information on the date, time, and place of the nearest professional recreation society meeting, contact the National Recreation and Park Association, 1601 North Kent Street, Arlington, Va. 22209.

The annual national convention of the recreation and park profession, called the Parks and Recreation Congress, is held in a different major city each year, usually in the fall. NRPA can provide the schedule of conferences for 5 years in advance. In addition, most state recreation societies hold their own state recreation conferences each year so that people who cannot travel long distances will be able to attend a professional conference.

INTERNSHIP

One of the most significant stages in the development of the recreation professional is the intern period. Variously entitled fieldwork, field assignment, student teaching, and apprenticing, this is the first realistic job experience to which the new professional-to-be is exposed. Its value cannot be overestimated, yet it is still not completely accepted by the practitioners in the field.

If any one practitioner has led the way in establishing the value and dignity of the intern position, it is Recreation Commissioner Robert Crawford of Philadelphia. In the mid-1950s, the recreation field was growing rapidly, but most professionals were so absorbed in their day-to-day problems and in their own ambitious moves up the job ladder that they had no time to look back and offer a helping hand to new and inexperienced novices. Commissioner Crawford was an exception. In 1956 he established Philadelphia's first recreation intern position and, with the cooperation of the National Recreation Association, filled it with a hopeful young recreation worker. The intern period was 1 year, and a small stipend was included, considerably below that of the lowest ranked regular civil service worker in the Philadelphia Recreation Department. This financial structure averted the otherwise abrasive situation that would have occurred had this noncompetitive, non–civil service worker moved in above the regular ranks of workers.

The stipend was small but the tasks were huge. Under Commissioner Crawford's watchful eye, the intern learned by doing—cleaning parks and planning of special events, driving maintenance machinery, interviewing new employees, writing news releases, and leading roller skating sessions. No phase of this huge department's operations escaped him.

Periodically, Commissioner Crawford or a staff member would interview the intern and evaluate his work. This prevented his being completely absorbed by the daily routine and all objectivity and perspective being lost.

The initial intern project was so successful that the first candidate was later employed by the Philadelphia Recreation Department and never left. He was followed in quick succession by many other bright, enthusiastic, young men and women. A resume that included the item, "Intern, Philadelphia Recreation Department," was usually well-received by prospective employers.

Commissioner Crawford wrote about his intern project and its success, and the NRPA conducted meetings and published pamphlets on it. Gradually, it caught on and has since been emulated by hundreds of departments, hospitals, centers, and private agencies.

In 1964, the Topeka, Kansas, Recreation Commission established its first summer recreation internship program in cooperation with seven other local and state agencies. This had the advantage over the Philadelphia plan in that it involved a shorter period of time, 2 months, and a smaller cash figure. While functioning as part of the summer playground staff, the summer interns were given extra research and development assignments, were regularly interviewed by supervisors, and were evaluated in written records.

Nonsalaried interns

Much more common today is the plan by which recreation education students, in their junior or senior years of college, select fieldwork or temporary intern position for the purpose of training and experience. This practice not only receives the full endorsement of the college or university the student attends, it is actually planned and administered by that institution. The steps in establishing such assignments are as follows:

1. By their junior year of college, recreation students usually have selected their area of concentration, be it public recreation, therapeutic recreation, outdoor recreation, camping, or other. They so notify their faculty advisor.

2. The students then choose two locations for fieldwork or internship assignment. Ideally, these two sites should be different from each other and offer a wide variety of work experiences. For example, a therapeutic recreation major might choose a large Veterans Administration hospital in a rural setting for one location and a small convalescent home for elderly persons in an urban neighborhood as the second site. Plainly, the staff size, budget, equipment, schedule, activities, and type of supervision would vary considerably between these two assignments. Similarly, a public recreation student might choose a job with a large county park and recreation department for the first assignment and a small suburban YMCA center for the second one. Most of these assignments are for about 8 weeks each.

3. The students write formal business letters to the administrator of each of their choices, requesting permission to intern there and including full background material on themselves and their recreation education curriculum. These letters should be sent sufficiently early (2 to 3 months) so

that in the event of a refusal by the administrator, sufficient time will remain in which to arrange alternate sites.

4. On acceptance, the student prepares for the coming assignments by obtaining and studying all possible material describing the training sites. This material might include annual reports, activity brochures, maps, financial statements, news releases, organizational charts, and so forth.

5. Students arrive at the sites and begin the period of internship.

During the internship period, regularly scheduled conferences are held between the intern, the immediate on-site supervisor, and the executive of the agency or department. This is essential to the success of the internship concept, and any carelessness here can damage the students and their chances for productive experience.

Work experience should be broad and varied. Of primary importance is the exposure and growth of the intern. Any work performed or projects accomplished for the agency must be regarded as secondary in importance and a bonus to the agency. This point is often overlooked by the student's recreation supervisor. Anxious to have as much as possible accomplished, the supervisor may use every available bit of time and energy of the intern, totally ignoring the need for planning, variety, observation, conferences, and evaluation. The intern might, under such conditions, be used as a cost-free recreation center worker or director, putting in 4 or 5 nights a week running programs. Or if he had mechanical abilities he may be used as an extra repairman in the department's motor shop, fixing another vehicle each working day. Both of these examples are fatal to the intern concept, since the intern is immediately placed in a job rut with no variety and is being used as a source of cost-free labor by the agency or department. Samples of valuable, productive work for the recreation intern are:

1. Three-day assignment in hospital ward to move about, observing recreation leaders at work and assisting where possible. Evaluation conference to follow.
2. Assigned to lay out a full-day program for prison wing, 50 people, utilizing specified budget and equipment available.
3. Assignment to serve as announcer at teenage amateur show in local teen center. Evaluation later.
4. One-week assignment to travel about city with superintendent of park maintenance, observing repair problems, vandalism, vehicle dispatch, manpower disposition, and so forth.

It is important to note that none of the above precludes the assignment of hard work or substantial responsibility to an intern. It does say, however, that work and study assignments for recreation interns should be: (1) significant and dignified, (2) carefully planned in advance, (3) scheduled appropriately, (4) timed for 3- to 5-day duration and no more, (5) commensurate with the intern's ability, and (6) followed by discussion and evaluation. The whole point of the intern period it to provide a transition from the student world to the world of day-to-day professional work and administration.

Practitioner's responsibility

Very important to the success of the intern program is the attitude of the professional recreator, the person under whom the intern serves. If he or she believes there is a genuine need for such fieldwork and maintains a close and conscientious contact with the intern throughout the training period, the intern experience holds every promise of being successful and rewarding. On the other hand, if the professional recreator sees little of value in the process, except for a windfall of free or low-cost labor, the intern period will hold little professional growth for the student and may actually embitter him or her against the recreation field.

I have found many successful park and recreation executives who speak enthusiastically about the values of interning, both to the student and to the agency. However, some department heads and agency executives still do not accept interns when offered by colleges and continue to speak negatively about the process when discussed at conferences and meetings. Some reasons for their negative attitudes follow.

1. *Ignorance of the process:* The executive has never seen the intern in action, nor has anyone thoughtfully explained the many advantages the program offers to all concerned. Without such knowledge, that particular agency rarely moves to obtain an intern.

2. *Bad experience:* The agency or executive experienced something unpleasant in the past, involving a recreation intern, and condemned the whole mechanism as a result. Drinking, partying, tardiness on schedules, petty pilferage, too much social life, financial problems—one or more of these could certainly turn the supervising executive into an enemy of the intern process, unfair as the judgment may be.

3. *Faculty ineptitude:* The person or persons handling liaison between the student intern and potential training sites perform in a careless or inadequate manner. Paperwork is not exchanged early or on schedule. The intern arrives unexpectedly. During the intern period, the person on campus either requires an excessive number of reports and supervisory confer-

ences or totally ignores the intern and makes no response to urgent queries by the supervising professional. At the conclusion of the intern period, the person on campus fails to thank the agency and conclude the project gracefully. These situations can easily alienate the recreation agency.

The intern process has been accepted, generally, by the executive, the teacher, and the student. Appreciation for its early success goes to practitioners such as Bob Crawford, to many fine educational personnel, and to the Society of Professional Recreation Educators (SPRE). As a teaching device, it is no less valuable to the recreation profession than it is to teaching, medicine, law, or other established professions.

AREAS OF CONCENTRATION
Primary areas

The five main areas of concentration or specialized training for those interested in professional recreation careers are community recreation, therapeutic recreation, outdoor recreation, private agency recreation, and commercial/industrial recreation.

Community recreation. This area pertains to the offices, departments, and divisions of government that hire people and expend budgets to provide recreation facilities and programs for the general public. All levels of government are included—village, town, city, county, state, and federal, as well as special park and recreation districts, commissions, and other unique governmental creations. Typically, it means the department of recreation that functions under a city mayor, a county executive, or similar elected official. Municipal and state parks, beaches, tennis courts, playgrounds, ice skating rinks, and outdoor swimming pools are the types of facilities that are most often identified with municipal recreation. The primary source of budget funds is the municipal or state tax levy. Most of the jobs in community recreation are of civil service status.

Therapeutic recreation. This area includes professional recreation work done within hospitals, mental institutions, homes for elderly persons, convalescent centers, and similar health centers. By extension, it also includes the work done with recreation techniques in any large institution that encloses or concentrates people such as a prison, detention center, drug addiction education center, internment camp, or refugee center.

Unlike community recreation, in which the recreational fun, thrill, skill, or satisfaction is generally regarded as an end in itself, therapeutic recreation sees its work and techniques as a means toward a further end. That end may be the rehabilitation of a convicted criminal so that he can face future release more stably, or the recreation program may assist in bringing back to equilibrium a wildly distorted and physically ailing drug overdose victim. Therapeutic recreation has much in common with occupational therapy and physical therapy, two terms commonly used in medical and physical rehabilitation centers. Relationships between worker and participant here are numerically smaller and more intimate than those of community recreation. Because of the confining nature of such institutions, much of the recreation activity occurs within the walls or compound of the hospital or prison.

Some therapeutic recreation occurs outside institutions in the case of homebound patients or in instances in which a person is able to travel to a recreation center for activity despite an illness or handicap. It is this latter area, recreation for the developmentally disabled, that is experiencing great expansion and diversity throughout the country. Brain damage, autism, hyperactivity, mental retardation, heart problems, diabetes, partial sight, and paraplegia are some of the illnesses and handicaps that are being helped substantially by professionally prescribed, planned, and operated programs of therapeutic recreation. This area of concentration is fully described in Chapter 4.

Outdoor recreation. The person choosing a career in outdoor recreation is usually one who derives great pleasure and satisfaction from activities that are simple and close to nature itself. Hiking, snowshoeing, cross-country skiing, fishing, camping, bicycling, and survival courses are the kinds of activities involved in outdoor recreation. Also included in this category are many environmental and ecological interests such as organic farming, forestry, fishery operation, land management, and general improvement of the biosphere.

There is a group of outdoor recreation activities that border on the resort/commercial side but, because of their vigorous setting and tremendous popularity, should be mentioned here. These include trap and skeet shooting, deep-sea fishing, hunting with gun and bow, sportsmen's centers, spinning and casting, water skiing, and hang gliding.

Generally, however, the professional in outdoor recreation deals with relatively simple, ageless forms of activity in a way that ensures there will be opportunities for enjoyment of similar activities for generations to follow. Earth, sky, water, forest, sand, mountain, river, plain, desert, and swamp are the locales that excite and motivate the outdoor recreation leader.

The federal government and many countries and states employ outdoor recreation leaders and administrators. Most of these work in large regional, state, and national parks, but even municipalities today use outdoor recreation staff to bring the skills, techniques, and nature lore of the great outdoors to the crowded schools and recreation centers of the inner cities. Still other outdoor recreation workers serve as interpretive nature educators in camps, outdoor demonstration areas, and trailside museums. Many of the skills and crafts traditionally identified with the Boy Scouts and Girl Scouts are basic to outdoor recreation, namely, tracking, knot-tying, primitive cooking and nourishment, animal and plant identification, campsite sanitation, and pollution prevention.

Private agency recreation. Recreation activities have been a basic part of most private youth-serving and community-serving institutions. YMCA's, YWCA's, YM-YWHA's, settlement houses, Boys' Clubs, Girls' Clubs, police athletic leagues, B'nai B'rith, CYO's, and other such agencies have incorporated sports and recreation programs as a major incentive for youths to join and participate.

A slightly different emphasis, however, has been placed on these programs and activities in the private, youth-serving or family-oriented institutions. Where the satisfaction and pleasure of the recreational activity is generally regarded in community recreation as an end or objective in itself, private agencies use recreation for further ends or goals. Membership growth, character building, family strengthening, and leading young people in the direction of moral growth have been destinations, while recreation serves as an inducer and vehicle. Regular activities may be interspersed with Bible and scripture reading, staff and lay boards may include clergy as advisors and spiritual counselors, and campaigns and fund-raising drives are frequently tied in with local churches and temples, their clerical staffs, and their congregations.

Recently, in an effort to keep up with the times and to bolster sagging membership, private agencies have expanded their recreation programs and some have de-emphasized the spiritual and moral growth goals. This is not to say their interest and concern for character building and spiritual strength has diminished. Rather, the private agencies have accepted the need to provide rich and varied recreation programs if they are to attract today's youth.

In private agency recreation, programs are heavily building-oriented. Most operations center around a central "Y," Boy's Club, settlement house, or a chain of decentralized "Y's" located in suburban settings. Gymnasiums, swimming pools, billiard and game rooms, weight training and physical fitness rooms, and club facilities constitute the central core of the typical private agency program. Some institutions, located on more spacious suburban sites, may also include outdoor baseball, softball, and basketball facilities. These are the exception, however, since most private agencies attempt to locate themselves near the crowded, low-income downtown areas of a city or town.

Nationwide, some 10,000 recreation professionals are employed in private agencies. The majority have been professionally trained and hold associate or bachelor degrees. Most such organizations place heavy emphasis on in-service training. One-day, week-long, and extended training periods are part of the year's planning for professional personnel in Y's, Boys Clubs, and similar organizations.

Commercial and industrial recreation. Grouped together here are two subareas that have substantial relationship to each other. The existence of a profit-making motive separates commercial and industrial recreation from community, therapeutic, outdoor, and private agency recreation.

Commercial recreation is that segment of the total recreation picture that is primarily profit-oriented. It pertains to amusement parks, movie theaters, ski lodges, sightseeing boats, circuses, vacation travel, commercial resorts and beaches, dinner theatres, theme parks, and similar enterprises. Walt Disney World is probably the best known of these huge fun and recreation complexes. Others include Knott's Berry Farm, Six Flags over Texas, King's Dominion, Lion Safari Country, Great Adventure, Busch Gardens, and the ski slopes in Aspen and Vail, Colorado. These complex businesses are laid out with the same thought and precision as any large commercial investment. Included are market analyses, engineering and architectural studies and plans, community relations campaigns, environmental impact studies, financial plans, personnel talent searches, and strategic timetables that compare with the opening of an International Olympics or an amphibious military landing in wartime. Recreation leadership in these leisure complexes provides an ongoing, dynamic relationship with the anticipated customers and users of the facility. Until recently, work of this type was rarely open to professionally trained recreation college graduates. With the improved and broadened curricula now available, however, more of these quality students are finding careers in the commercial area.

Industrial recreation includes those persons who work within large business-government-industrial concentrations and who provide programs of wholesome recreation and sports for the employees. Such staffing and programs are usually limited to firms or offices with 500 or more employees at one specific location, since smaller companies are considered insufficient to justify the expense of a full-time recreation worker and office. Nevertheless, there are in America some 800 firms and business locations employing over 1200 recreation, physical fitness, and social directors for their executives and employees.

In some areas, several firms with individual employee populations of less than 500 workers, such as in an industrial park, will combine to employ a full-time industrial recreation leader. This recreator will prepare schedules, talks, instructions, and special events so that all are served well and no one firm receives less than its fair share of activity. Common locations, staggered schedules, mobile equipment, interfirm competition, and exchanges of personnel are all methods by which a recreation leader may extend the program to all concerned. This a boon to the small business firm.

Program content of such industrial recreation schedules usually includes softball and basketball leagues, holiday celebrations, group travel abroad, dramatic groups, arts and crafts classes, musical instrument groups, horseshoe pitching, fishing, hobby meetings, and dances. In many such settings the alert recreation leader will ask the participants for ideas, suggestions, and offers for help so that the activity program truly reflects their tastes and needs.

Miscellaneous areas

These areas of recreation employment include career opportunities in the armed forces, resorts, schools, state and federal parks, and travel agencies.

Armed forces. Recreation personnel in the armed forces, almost all professionally trained and prepared, provide leisure counseling and organized recreation programs for off-duty personnel of the Army, Air Force, Navy, Coast Guard, and Marine Corps. In addition, they work closely with the families of the service personnel, especially at large overseas bases. They attempt to involve military personnel and their families in the cultures and activity patterns of the surrounding civilian communities, thus avoiding the negative stereotype of two sharply segregated societies. In peacetime, the work of the armed forces recreation professional is very similar to that of the community recreation professional serving a municipality of from 10,000 to 25,000 people. Some 900 recreation professionals are now employed in this sector, and a special branch of the NRPA is the Armed Forces Recreation Society (AFRS).

Resorts. Recreation personnel in this category serve as social activity organizers and directors at places such as the Concord Hotel in the Catskills, the MGM Grand Hotel in Las Vegas, at Playboy Resorts, at Sun Valley, Idaho, or on board luxury liners during ocean cruises. Some 500 to 600 persons are currently employed in this area. Some have professional recreation degrees, but many lack any formal recreation training. Rather, they have great enthusiasm, exceptional sociability, considerable knowledge of game and party skills and, quite often, are young and attractive. It is very demanding work, particularly because the clientele is almost always anxious for escape, change, release, or endless fun activity. It places great pressure on the activities leader and, for this reason, relatively few persons make lifetime careers of it. Pressures notwithstanding, it can provide an exciting period in the life of the young recreation professional.

Schools. In communities in which municipal recreation programs are inadequate or nonexistent, the school board or school department may employ professionally trained and certified recreation teachers or directors. An estimated 5000 recreation professionals are employed by American school systems. These people work closely with local teachers, administrators, and youths, developing after-school, evening, and weekend sports, games, and recreation activities. Closely tied to the school system, their emphasis is on activity for boys and girls from first grade through high school, with the greatest attention given to the third through tenth grades. All other age groups receive varying degrees of attention and programming. Facilities utilized are almost entirely those of the local school system. This type of work is steady, predictable, and interesting, but, by nature, does not lend itself particularly to wide age spreads or the inclusion of varied segments of the community. Many school systems are conservative in their policies, and the recreation program planning is similarly conservative. Outstanding exceptions include Long Beach, Calif.; Flint, Mich.; Milwaukee, Wis.; and Hewlett-Woodmere, N.Y.

State and federal parks. Despite the vastness of state and federal parks, reservations, and forests, the actual recreation staffs connected with such agencies are small. Nationwide, less than 7000 recreation persons are so employed on a full-time basis, although this number is augmented by at least 150,000 part-time personnel. The greatest number of personnel are employed during the busy summer months. Activities include nature hunts, bird-watching, trail rides, forest zoology, picnics, camping activities, white-water boat trips, evening bonfire parties, songfests, square dancing, and star identification. This type of recreation work is especially attractive to men and women who like the outdoors, great spaces and distances, and a simple, primitive life style.

Travel agencies. A modest number of recreation personnel are utilized as tour guides and social recreation directors by travel and tour agencies. These persons are usually assigned a specific group of clients, from 20 to 50 in number, and remain with these same people for the 3- to 30-day duration of the tour. Unlike the conventional tour guide whose duties are limited to punctual appointments, safe passage, and comfortable accomodations, the traveling recreation person includes fun and leisure time activities in the schedule. Providing songs on board bus, train, or plane and books, games, and special events enroute are part of their jobs. Parties, side trips, birthday celebrations, souvenir collecting, and the meeting of exciting celebrities along the way are all considered the responsibility of the touring recreation leader. Like the resort hotel recreation leader, this job is a demanding and tiring one. Although it enables the professional leader to see places and people otherwise not accessible, it also leaves the leader exhausted at the conclusion of a tour. With some exceptions, this type of recreation work appeals to young people and rarely do people make a lifetime career of it.

BIBLIOGRAPHY

Frye, V., and Peters, M.: Therapeutic recreation: its theory, philosophy and practice, National Recreation and Parks Association, Arlington, Va., 1976, Burgess Publishing Co.

Henkel, D. D., and Godbey, G. C.: Parks, recreation and leisure services, employment in the public sector, status and trends, Arlington, Va., 1977, National Recreation and Parks Association.

Kraus, R. G.: Recreation and leisure in modern society, New York, 1971, Appleton-Century-Crofts.

Lutzin, S. G., and Storey, E. H.: Managing municipal leisure services, Chicago, 1973, The International City Managers Association.

Madow, P.: Recreation in America, New York, 1965, The H. W. Wilson Co.

National League of Cities: Nation's cities, Washington, D.C., 1977, The League.

Public Works Journal, Ridgewood N.J., 1977, Public Works Journal Corp.

REFERENCE

1. MacLeish, K.: Leonardo da Vinci: a man for all ages, National Geographic **152:**296, September 1977.

18
POTPOURRI*

*This chapter consists of several articles and monographs on various phases of recreation and leisure services that I have written.

PRAGMAESTHETICS

The customary description of a trip abroad, even an educational trip by a professional, can make dreary reading. Comments such as "the lovely beaches," "the warmth of our host—the governor," "they are such a happy, friendly people," and "Spring is a riot of color here," leave me cold. Such saccharine descriptions depict every country outside America a veritable paradise, a Shangri-la of beauty and idyllic living. The world is not that simple. A research trip abroad can be a challenging and exciting experience for recreation or urban planning professionals if they prepare themselves in advance with motives, areas of concentration, and a kit of search techniques that will dig beneath the surface of the society they are observing. Only then will the real essentials, the fascinating idiosyncrasies and oddities of alien philosophies come to light. Only then will they bring home something fresh, intriguing, and productive from those far-off lands.

A few years ago, I joined a group of 32 zealous travelers heading for a 17-day tour of major cities in Holland, Germany, Finland, Sweden, and Denmark. Labeled the "Urban Design Odyssey," the group included recreators, architects, city planners, urban renewal specialists, business people, elected officials, and interested homemakers. It was my privilege to serve as tour director, though many of the group knew Europe far better than I. We met months in advance of the trip and discussed in detail things for which we would search. It was an intense and dedicated assembly, and a finely detailed planning and observation schedule was forged.

An absolute minimum of wandering and conventional sight-seeing was included, while a maximum of significant stops, visits, and educational side trips was plotted. Advance arrangements were completed with chief gardeners, planners, consultants, parks directors, museum officials, conservationists, and expert guides in each of the major cities to be visited. Each member of our group contacted friends who had already visited the target cities and inquired about details and tips that would help us in our quest.

The painstaking efforts paid off. An enormous amount of productive visiting, interviewing, questioning, and sampling occurred. Large quantities of demonstration materials and thousands of photographs were collected. During the trip, frequent brainstorming periods were held to digest what had already been acquired and to sharpen our senses for the targets ahead. Ideas were cross-pollinated en route, and revised editions of these ideas were restudied every few days. Keen self-analysis and constructive criticism characterized these sessions.

The result was a rich crop of ideas, impressions, concepts, and philosophic gems that our group brought back to our home cities. These ideas have been under further study since then and several have been implemented. Aside from the broad, clearly defined urban patterns of each city, we discerned second magnitude, less defined characteristics, syndromes, and impressions. Acquired subconsciously through our sharpened sensitivities, these ideas saturated our thinking after we returned home and will always color our permanent images, perhaps more than the earlier, heavier, more obvious impressions. Following are a few of these concepts.

The word, *pragmaesthetics,* a word devised from *pragmatic* and *aesthetic,* aptly describes a delightful characteristic of European urban planning, particularly in the smaller details of decor.

In the magnificent City Theater of Helsinki, Finland, we viewed a stunning piece of bronze wall sculpture that was 30 feet in length, hung from the low ceiling, parallel to one long wall of the lobby, and suspended at shoulder height from the floor. It appeared to be a great wavy bronze snake with hooked barbs coming out of its body. Only as we looked, did it dawn on us that it was a magnificent coatrack and each of the hooks would accommodate several garments. We oohed and ahed, but it was only the beginning of countless illustrations of this quaint European eccentricity.

I entered a tiny men's rest room in Solvang, Germany, through a beaded doorway curtain, suggestive of Somerset Maugham's *Rain,* and approached a commode over which hung a beautiful, small crystal chandelier. Pragmaesthetics!

In Amsterdam and Copenhagen the variety of street bicycle racks was endless. They appeared as circular drums, metal fountains, cuts in the sidewalk, and tree-shaped racks supporting bicycles from above. Nowhere did I see the conventional American straight-pipe bicycle rack.

Stockholm marks its parking slots in small city parking areas with outlines of raised Belgian Block, contrasted against the flat surface of the red brick paving. No ragged painted white lines are used. Amsterdam's gaily painted houseboats form inner linings along the retaining walls of many of its centrally located canals. These charmingly adorned vessels are houseboats of the old-fashioned barge type and have little in common with our new fiberglass style. They add a medieval touch to already charming waterways.

In Hanover, Germany, I observed my first deikvagenlarums, 5 feet-high, grass-covered dirt walls that, if sliced through the middle, would present triangular cross sections about 8 feet wide at the bottom and tapering to the top. These lined both sides of the roads that traverse the mid-city

forests in this German industrial center. The walls insulate the nearby picnic groves and campsites from noise, headlights, and noxious fumes to a surprising degree. In addition, they heighten the feeling of remoteness and primitiveness for the campers, even though they are only a few feet from a main road.

In the lobby of a Stockholm restaurant, we observed a tapestry-like item, about 3 feet wide and 9 feet long, hanging on a wall. It was made entirely of scrap pieces of heavy metallic embroidered and brocaded materials, cut in square, overlapping swatches. The pattern was casual but repetitious, and it contained fluted effects, overlaps, and a variety of tones. We nicknamed it a "scrapestry," and it epitomized the European imaginative treatment of commonplace things to produce an esthetic effect.

On the floor of the City Council Chamber of Hanover, Germany, is a vast maplike depiction of this city of 500,000 and its land-use masterplan. Made of terrazzo, inserted stone blocks, and long thin strips of bronze, this living map enables councillors and city officials to literally walk across and through various discussion items that happen to be on the city's business agenda. At intervals of 3 to 5 years, craftsmen are brought in and any significant revisions are made to bring the design up to date. The result is a striking image in miniature of a growing city for visitors to view, and a practical, working device for city officials to study in their municipal ruminations.

"Banners, banners everywhere" is a message we brought home from northern Europe. Gay, colorful banners, long slender streamers, and huge city flags are lavishly displayed throughout the downtown areas. Wherever a small plaza or open plot is available, cities and private businesses install towering poles and hang a variety of colorful and interesting banners from them. Depicted are Boy Scout Week, National Wine Week, national holidays, birthdays of celebrities, and in many cases, no special event at all. As one strolls the main streets and sees the undulating banners and all their colors, one is mindful of an international world's fair.

Stockholm, suffering from the writings and scribblings on its walls and buildings that all cities endure, erected a huge, public graffiti wall, measuring 8 feet high and 100 feet long, in the heart of its busiest public plaza. Painted white, this surface is available for all writers, markers, defacers, or protestors to inscribe their messages in paint, ink, lipstick, or other medium. One warning is printed at the top of the graffiti wall: "Write anything you like, but remember that you are responsible for what you write." During my visits to that wall, I was impressed by the antipodal points of view, the cute cartoons, and the clever humor. Relatively little smut appeared. At the end of each week, Park Department employees paint the entire length of the wall in white paint, providing a vast new tablet for the writings of the next week. It was one of the most interesting ideas that I brought back from Europe.

During the trip, we were impressed by the apparent disinclination of Europeans to pound home their public relations points, as we might have expected. Rather than tell us, "This is the way you Americans should do it," they would simply lead us to these sights and subject us to experiences without the Madison Avenue commentary. Frequently, at the end of a busy day, my companions and I would be discussing aspects of the day's tour over a leisurely drink. Only then would certain subtle movements and exposures of the day surface for us, and we would be all the more stunned by their delayed impact. Illustrations of this would

include the "allotment gardens," so prevalent in the Netherlands and Germany. These small squares of open-space land at the edge of major cities lay side by side over hundreds of acres. Each square measured about 30 feet by 30 feet and was carefully tilled by a fee-paying urban weekend farmer or gardener. Some squares produced corn and vegetables, while their immediate neighbors might glow in a splash of chrysanthemums. The next two squares might have carefully cultivated ginkgo trees, with the following spaces returning to vegetable production. These thousands of patchwork minigardens are relatively unheralded throughout the world, and regardless of which city we were in at the time, our guide would pay them only the slightest attention.

Invariably, group members would ask, "What about vandalism?" and just as invariably our guide would shrug the question off as hardly worthy of reply. Readers should consider carefully the significance of this urban confidence in people's self-discipline.

The existence of flower carts, pushcarts, and fresh fruit wagons on countless corners, the strategic location of downtown "forests" in the very heart of built-up urban cities, and other pleasant surprises were treated casually by our guides and hosts. The cumulative effect of these sights and of this low-key unmerchandising we summed up in another homemade term, *osmoculture* (osmosis and culture).

As I admired a particularly stunning fabric-covered living room set in the Scandinavian Trade Center of Copenhagen, Denmark, I asked the director of the Center if the material was a plastic. "Plastic?" he asked. "We use no plastics in our furniture. In fact, we use no substitutes at all. That furniture is covered with genuine Danish red cowhide!" If this were an isolated case, it would hardly deserve mention, but time after time I found that Europeans, wherever the economy permitted, demanded the real thing and decried substitutes. In a small restaurant in Solvang, Germany, I again innocently questioned whether a series of paintings on the wall were "prints." The restaurant manager, with mild indignation, pointed out that he would have no prints in his restaurant and that these particular originals had been done by an elderly gentleman who lived upstairs above the restaurant. Wood carvings, ivory, inlaid work, even pencil drawings were invariably originals rather than copies or substitutes. This has deep significance for our American culture when one considers our enormous productive machinery that creates and distributes substitutes and synthetics in all types of handicraft, and in many cases, mass-produces things that purport to be custom-made.

Northern Europe can boast of its share of tall buildings, great bridges, large industrial plants, and many of the frustrating rushes, jams, confusions and congestions indigenous to major cities of the world. Nevertheless, these same Germans, Dutch, and Scandinavians have retained and cultivated a delightfully cozy, scaled-down-to-human-size quality in much of their urban design, planning, and street appointment.

Stockholm maintains over 400 human-scale sophisticatedly comic sculptured pieces on its streets and in its parks. A young, pregnant lady, a workman arising from a manhole, two overweight professional boxers squaring off in a ring, and other quaint, earthy, and human-sized figures are strategically located throughout the park system and on the busy downtown streets of Stockholm. Each figure is mounted on a 3-foot cubic granite block.

Small squares and parklets dominate the urban scene in Europe. The very smallness and the neatness of these parklets lend a quaint, lilliputian charm to many ancient neighborhoods. Attention to the finest detail is an obsession. The pupils of eyes are carefully drawn in on figures placed in parks and open spaces. The ornamental scrollwork of garden furniture is carefully etched. Intricate details in such things as bicycle racks, drinking fountains, and park benches make them appear as furniture on the lawn of a wealthy man, rather than apparatus installed in public parks.

The presence of large numbers of bicyclists, in close contact with heavy downtown traffic, reduces the scale of urban transportation to one more tolerable by people. There is something very intimate and social about a bicycle passing by, pedalled vigorously by a gray-haired grandmother with two bags of groceries in her rear basket. The human scale, repeated in an infinite number and variety of ways in the downtown scene of Europe, provides much of the intimacy and quaintness that American tourists hungrily absorb and for which they seek despairingly in their own home cities.

A trip abroad for the professional person can be simply a "Baedeker," a travel talk, a sojourn, a vacation. I find no fault with these. On the other hand, a recreation professional on an educational trip abroad should seek those subsurface signals, connotations, movements, and vibrations that no book, film, lecture, or record album can transmit. It was the discovery of these precious subtleties that made the Urban Design Odyssey so significant for me.

PURPLE RECREATION

The young executive in trim business suit, briefcase in hand, arrives home from a busy day at the office. Carefully locking his apartment door, he retires to his bedroom, removes his masculine clothing, and slowly and daintily dresses and makes up as a young woman. He tingles with excitement as he sets forth for his evening of delight. The man is a transvestite, one of tens of thousands who derive pleasure and satisfaction from temporarily donning the garments, the mannerisms, and the life patterns of the opposite sex. When his excursion in transvestism is over for the evening, he will return to his apartment, undress and retire, to rise in the morning and assume his role of an apparently normal young businessman.

Transvestism is part of what I call *purple recreation*. These activities lie in the shadowy half-light, half-dark zone between what society normally calls "good" or "wholesome" and that which most of society condemns as "bad," "foul," or "evil." This penumbral area of purple recreation includes acts and pursuits that bring a degree of pleasure or escape to the participants, but which suggest gross self-indulgence, greed, immorality, or cruelty and arouse repugnance in most of the remainder of society. Some purple recreation ventures may result in only mild harm to the short-term participant. Others can cause major physical or mental damage, financial loss, or death, if indulged in heavily or for long periods. Kando[1] says:

Another area of leisure and culture on which the counterculture has put its permanent imprint is sex . . . the rock movement and the counterculture took it upon themselves to subvert the sexually repressive society and the value system upon which it has been based. . . . The movement freed the libidinal, that which could be potentially disruptive.

Excursions into drugs of all kinds have characterized the past 15 years and the explorations continue. Marijuana, heroin, cocaine, and opium were only ingredients from Warner Brothers movies and oriental bazaars until 1965. Now they are used by military service personnel and students at most colleges, as are hashish, LSD, mesca-line, glue, amphetamines, and angel dust. Magazines such as *High Times, Recreation Drugs,* and *Smoke* circulate freely in student unions and in many local recreation centers.

Books and box office hits during this period of liberation have included the keystone of soap operas, *Peyton Place,* followed by *The Exhibitionist. The Voyeur,* a novel about the sex magazine publishing business was generously laced with peeping devices, pornography production, and blackmail. *Mrs. Portnoy's Complaint, The Adventurers,* and *The Valley of the Dolls* followed the same theme of explicit sex, lascivious self-indulgence, and total lack of inhibition. "Let it all hang out" and "Do your own thing" have been mottos and rallying cries of the movement. David Slavitt of White Plains, New York, who writes under the pseudonym, Henry Sutton, says, "Women who read my books tend to be suburban matrons, married to very busy husbands. We all like to hear what's going on over the backyard fence. People read my books because they get the whole story without any mixups, and nobody really gets hurt."

"Chicken fanciers," males who enjoy sexual relationships with very young boys and girls, have been an expanding street phenomenon during the 1970s, especially in the Times Square area of New York City. Over 3000 boys and girls were picked up in Times Square by New York City police for vagrancy, soliciting, and disorderly conduct during 1977, and most of them admitted to some form of prostitution for money, food, or shelter. It does not appear that many of these youngsters were so behaving for their own pleasure, but the adult males who took advantage of them apparently were.

Every large city has its bars that cater exclusively to homosexuals or lesbians. They range from the tiny spots to the lavish, semiprivate clubs with posh cocktail lounges and private rooms.

The provocative stage play, the burlesque, the girlie shows, topless waitresses, and the "bump and grind" girls of the discotheque all provide a brimming supply of sensuous performance for pay in every major city of the United States. One Westchester, New York, night club features a show in which men dress up as chorus girls and bills it the "Powder Puff Review." This show regularly plays to packed houses of both sexes.

The hottest item in the motion pictures and television today is the "art film," featuring homosexuality, lesbianism, sadomasochism and spicy mixtures of the three. The viewers include all types of interested parties from the academically curious to those who giggle and jiggle in motel rooms as they participate vicariously in the events on the screen. Movie critic for the *New York Times,* Richard Schickel, says that the male is the voyeur of the species. He sees the screen as a large lighted window, through which we observe sex anonymously, under cover of darkness and in a condition of psychological aloneness. What males see through that window is, of course, very intimate behavior, according to Schickel. To that male, Schickel states, pursuit of this kind of intimacy is irresistible, and it is not the art spirit that is driving him. According to Schickel, it is perfectly alright for males to slip, somewhat furtively perhaps, into seats in a decaying downtown movie house, even during business hours, and conveniently and painlessly reestablish their connections, if not with life, with a reasonable facsimile. He sees it as an easy way to assuage the peculiar loneliness of urban existence and to enrich one's fantasy life.

Even the movie house entry is rapidly becoming unnecessary with the burgeoning porn film cassette industry. Now, favorites like *Deep Throat* and *The Devil and Miss Jones* are available for a fee on motel television, or they can be purchased for from $50 to $200 a copy and played on home television cassette consoles.

More than 100 million comic books, luridly illustrated with pornography and geared to adolescent sales, are printed and distributed monthly in the United States. According to *Morality in Media,* a monthly newsletter published by the New York Catholic Archdiocese, the U.S. Postal Service has announced that dealers have cast aside all restraint and are indiscriminately flooding the mail with "offensive, sexually oriented materials by means of mailing lists, to millions of young and old alike." More than 500 pornographic and salacious magazines flood the American newstand, drugstore, candy store, bus, or airport terminal. *Playboy, Playgirl, Hustler, Cheri, Penthouse, Oui,* and *Screw* are among the most popular.

Gambling, whether it be a mild investment in chance for fun or an obsessive sinking of the family's fortune on a roll of the dice, is an established purple recreation. Las Vegas represents a $1.4 billion handle annually at the gaming tables and their auxiliary services; Atlantic City is girding furiously to become the new "Las Vegas East." When one tallies the action at Reno, Los Angeles, Miami Beach, New Orleans, New York, and Puerto Rico and throws in the betting take from dozens of other cities, the dimensions of recreational gambling begin to emerge. Kraus[2] indicates that pari-mutuel betting on thoroughbred and trotting horse racing annually during the late 1960s exceeded $5 billion. Dog racing adds another billion to this gross. Kraus also says that: "Each year, for example, the Mafia exploits the human urge to gamble to the extent of handling $20 billion in illegal bets on racing and a variety of other major sports events, of which it keeps $7 billion in profits.'' These figures give us a rough total, legal and illegal, of $25 billion, in the late 1960s. With the inflationary surge of the period, these figures would today have reached an annual gross of $40 to $50 billion, even if no actual increase in betting activity took place.

An interesting news item in the *New York Daily News,* January 25, 1978, was headlined: ''Judge Rules 'Recreation Sex' is Legal.'' Judge Margaret Taylor, in a case charging a 14-year-old girl with prostitution for $10.00, declared the law against female prostitution unconstitutional and dismissed the charges saying: ''However offensive it may be, recreation commercial sex threatens no harm to the public health, safety or welfare, and therefore may not be proscribed.'' How many other Americans see prostitution as simply another form of commercial recreation?

Witchcraft is thriving. This strange alchemy of eroticism, animalism, and antireligion may be difficult to identify with recreation but, in hundreds of covens (witch gatherings), thousands of amateur warlocks assemble for their weekly rituals amid black candles, motherwort, tinkling bells, and pentagrams. In the October 30, 1977 *Westchester-Rockland Newspaper,* Jim Cavanaugh described the thriving witch cultures in New York and Los Angeles, including shops and stalls selling books, nostrums, and paraphernalia of witchcraft. He sees it as a growth industry. Summers[3] observes:

''Satanism is alive today. It is a power in the land. Mysterious, unseen, wholly evil . . . there is hardly a village without a witch. In our great cities, our larger towns, our seats of learning, Satanists abound and are organized (as of old) into covens of wickedness.''

Once upon a time, the family game manufacturing leaders, Parker Brothers and Milton Bradley, sold only moral uplift games such as Mansion of Happiness, Checkered Game of Life, Parcheesi, Chinese Checkers, and The Game of Christian Endeavor. With the overwhelming success of Monopoly, the pattern changed.

On display are Parker Brothers and Milton Bradley names like, ''Outwit,'' ''Instant Counterattack,'' and ''Lie, Cheat and Steal,'' whose very names indicate how they're played. The ''Instant Counterattack,'' package which promises ''a game that brings out all the trickery and dastardly behavior that's been lurking in you,'' says it all.[4]

The game of Counterstrike has a bold box cover that states: ''A game of methodical defense and sudden, slashing attack. A game of skill and the cold, cold chance of dice. A game that brings out the worst instincts in you, from avarice through downright treachery.''

Purple recreation is difficult to assess because it ranges from the innocuous and off-color to the brazenly amoral. Conditions vary with each person. An innocent poker game in the kitchen is a mild cousin to the compulsive betting of the family fortune at Las Vegas; a mild highball before dinner is made of the same ingredients that reduce men and women to sodden hulks when their drinking escalates.

The Curtis scale

To depict a spectrum over which recreation activities, and purple recreation in particular, range, the Curtis scale was devised. The extreme left on the scale represents ''Bad'' in the generic, at its generally accepted worst. The most evil, corruptive, universally negative acts or pastimes imaginable by the reader should characterize this left pole. Premeditated murder, rape, torture, and theft from the most helpless people are a few illustrations. The other extreme, at the right-hand pole, represents the totally innocent, guileless, brotherly, sis-

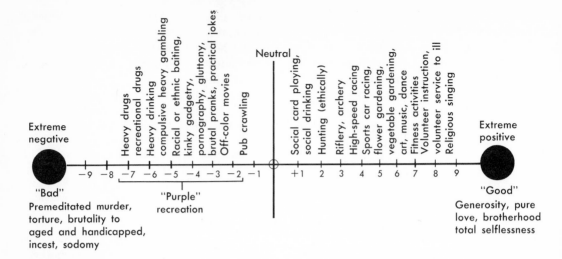

terly, unselfish, satisfying, and edifying acts, whatever such may be in the reader's mind. Selfless love, good samaritanism, deepest loyalty, and neighborliness exemplify this right-hand pole.

Next, a straight line between left and right poles is bisected. The center is the cusp, where "goodness" and "badness" divide, only a hair's breadth apart, of course. By placing zero at the center, and advancing +1, +2, +3, and so forth from center to right end, a positive or "good" scale is produced. Similarly, beginning at center and moving left, the line is marked −1, −2, −3, and so forth to the left, or "bad" extreme.

On the completed scale, most conventional "wholesome" recreation activities fall between −3 and +6, with average to heavy drinking and gambling, at the −3 mark, and square dancing and mountain climbing at the +6 point. Purple recreation activities would fall between −2 and −7. Overlapping takes place at all edges of areas and makes sharp distinctions impossible. In addition, these scorings are personal and quite subjective.

Purple recreation is part of our culture,

though it borders on the warped, the deviate, and the corruptive. Most of us have occasionally succumbed to it when we visit a race track or titter over a saucy photograph. From here, the outer dimensions are beyond measure.

As professional recreators, we must study this shadowy territory carefully, objectively, and analytically. We are peering inexpertly into the labyrinth of people's minds and motivations. If we are to deal more effectively with today's complex leisure needs and desires of all people, we must learn more of this off-beat zone of purple recreation, this compulsive preoccupation of so many Americans.

ON PROBATION

Increasingly, public recreation departments are relying on the use of school buildings, grounds, and facilities to provide part or all of the physical plant needed to accommodate their programs and activities. The community school movement of the 1970s accelerated this development. This is good because it represents cooperation, expanded use of publicly purchased facilities, and a coordinated effort for wholesome use of leisure time. However, in working with public school systems and their administrators, recreation professionals face certain problems such as differing philosophies, limited accessibility, conflicts in scheduling, damage, and shared materials. No problem, though, looms larger than what may be labeled the "on probation" kind of thinking.

This is the line of thinking by which school administrators, from assistant principals up through superintendents, regard recreation activities and programs in their facilities as temporary, transient, and directly dependent on continued "good behavior." A total absence of inconvenience to school administration is a requisite for the continuation of the program. Such an "on probation" clause is never written and is rarely spoken, but it is implied in relationships. Implicit is the warning that the recreation program had better be careful and not permit any damage or other nuisance or it will be chastised. Such chastisement may involve a warning, followed by a summary action such as expulsion from the facility in which the program has been functioning.

If the recreation activity or program were sponsored by a group of irresponsible individuals, such thinking might be justifiable. It is unreasonable, however, that a responsible department of local government, in this case the recreation commission or department, should be so treated. This arrangement can create a feeling of suspicion between the staffs of both departments, discourage novel programs or new experimental techniques, and prevent stimulating exchanges of ideas and assistance between the two staffs. Loyalty to superiors compels both agency staffs to watch and check up on the other. Eventually, this reaches all program participants and puts them in a defensive state of mind. The net result is a cat-and-mouse game that has no reason for existence in a situation in which mutual trust and good faith should prevail.

Under such a system, certain recreation activities will operate successfully and effectively for weeks, months, and sometimes years with little or nothing to disturb the smoothness of the operation. Then if an incident occurs that creates a problem or results in physical damage or breach of discipline, peremptory action usually results. Instead of a cooperative joining of forces by school and recreation personnel to solve such problems, frequently an attack is made on the program, on the *symptoms,* and on the department sponsoring the program as being the *cause*. The school administrator issues warnings, and if the situation is not corrected quickly, the programs are suspended and use of school facilities withdrawn. Rarely do we find school systems and their top officials who, when faced with such problems, will join with recreation officials in a mutual attitude of "this is important to both of us and to the community, so let's work it out together."

Significant to all this is the prestige of education. In most communities the status and influence of the board of education, and particularly the superintendent and staff, is enormous. This is understandable and justified by the grave responsibilities involved and the dedicated job traditionally done by professional educators. This tremendous influence, however, makes even the candid comments and unofficial attitudes of the top administration most significant. Herein lies the injustice and danger of damage when school administrators do not take a positive stand on the question of community recreation and use of facilities. A vague, dubious, raised-eyebrow attitude toward public recreation on the part of the school administration can only result in erosive doubts, concern, and confusion on the part of teachers, PTA members, and other local groups. In such an atmosphere, any untoward event or incident related to the recreation program will assume the dimensions of a calamity, will confirm everyone's previously held fears, and will often force all nonrecreation groups to join in a loosely united antirecreation front. This is especially true in such volatile and vulnerable programs as teen centers and activities involving trouble-prone youth.

Suppose we look at the other side of the situation for a moment. If negative thinking were as characteristic of recreation personnel as it is of so many school personnel, there is adequate material on which recreators can focus. They (and note that I would deplore such thinking) might urge the need to close some schools because of the following shortcomings suffered by a considerable number of school districts:

1. The significant number of mediocre or woefully inadequate school teachers who are employed.
2. The displayed weakness of the physical education programs in many school systems in meeting the challenge of national physical fitness among elementary children.
3. The widespread practice of holding two jobs, not only by school teachers but by some deputy administrators. This moonlighting leaves little time for reflective thinking on major education problems or for generating special projects with youth.
4. The theory of "graduate school work at all costs," wherein school teachers have little time beyond their daily schedules to spend in their local communities because of attendance at nearby colleges pursuing advanced degrees.
5. The ill-planned and sadly neglected outdoor play facilities of many school districts.
6. The demonstrated inadequacies of school personnel when confronted by gangs, lack of discipline, thefts, and extortion by youth.
7. The sluggishness with which school systems and their curricula have attempted to adapt themselves to the dynamic changes of the past 15 years.
8. The shocking drop-out rate of American high school students and the disappointing academic performance of so many college freshmen.

It would be ridiculous to propose that recreation people start feuds with school systems over these weaknesses. In most cases a conscientious effort is being made by school systems to improve and to attain the highest standards possible. The point being made here is that the negative and persistently critical analysis of public recreation, indulged in by so many school administrators, has no place in modern public administration.

Most school administrators vehemently deny such negative attitudes and are sincere in such denials. They state that, "We believe in what you are doing and want to help"; "We know you will agree that our high standards will have to be carried over into the recreation program or we'll have chaos in schools"; We're for your recreation program, *after* we take care of all our school needs." Such statements, sincere or not, fail to reduce "on probation." The true sentiments of the school administrator are spotlighted when an unpleasant incident occurs that makes the use of school facilities an issue. If the school personnel join with the recreation personnel in a concerted attack on the problem, they are forward-thinking pioneers to be treasured. If they lay the problem in the lap of the recreation personnel, wrapped in dire warnings and lectures, the recreation personnel know their operation is on probation.

I would recommend that school administrators assess the importance, significance, and desirability of having *any* kind of community recreation programs in their areas and using their facilities. If they do not believe there is justification for these programs or merit in their operation, they should honestly and courageously say so. On the other hand, if they believe there are legitimate reasons for such programs and if they believe they represent a gain toward both the school's aims and recreation's aims, I suggest they courageously and honestly place their firm support and assistance where they will help in making these programs successful.

No program, be it recreation or other, can survive a prolonged period of being on probation or on trial. Failure is only a matter of time, and the public is the loser.

POLICE-SPONSORED RECREATION

Wholesome recreation, properly planned and administered, can aid in deterring juvenile crime and waywardness, although recreation is no cure-all for this complex problem involving so many factors in our modern society. Nevertheless, experience has shown that young people are less inclined toward delinquent behavior when they are participating in recreation activities than when they are left to spend their leisure time aimlessly. Since the function of the police department in American society is as much to prevent crime as to apprehend criminals, it would appear that police are justified in utilizing the recreation method in crime prevention, particularly among young people.

The question, then, is not whether or not police should use this method, but rather how it should be done. Should police departments establish and operate their own separate recreation programs and facilities, or should they depend on the programs and facilities of existing private and public recreation agencies? The following analysis of police-sponsored recreation should aid in resolving this question.

The use of the recreation method by individual police officers in their work with youth is not new. Examples of its have occurred since the formation of the first organized law enforcement agencies. The night watchman or constable of colonial times who attempted to straighten out a wayward boy by introducing him to the town athlete was using it. Likewise, the modern policewoman who persuades a confused teenaged girl to join a local girls' club rather than solicit on street corners is utilizing, to an extent, the recreation method in crime and delinquency prevention.

In recent years, however, the value of the recreation method has become widely recognized by police and social work agencies, and its utilization is rarely left to chance or the individual police officer's imagination. This is particularly true in large cities. Hundreds of police departments in this country and abroad use recreation on a planned and organized basis. Their devices range from the forming of a single athletic team or club by an individual police officer in a small community to such large-scale operations as the Police Boys' Club of Baltimore, the Junior Police of Los Angeles, and the Police Athletic League of New York City.

In most instances, the size of the community or municipality has governed the size and extent of the police-sponsored recreation program. In some small communities the police have simply entered a team or two in a local sports program, while in larger cities, the police-sponsored recreation unit operates a full-scale athletic program of leagues, games, and championship tournaments for large numbers of teams. Likewise, in most small communities the police have used local public or private recreation facilities, while in larger cities, they use separate recreation centers, fields, playgrounds, and other facilities.

Sports is the program activity most frequently utilized, but some of the larger police-sponsored recreation programs include dramatics, dancing, arts and crafts, music, and even outdoor camping. Boys' activities have traditionally been emphasized over those of girls, but this is changing with the times. A notable exception to this is the track and field program operated by the New York City Police Athletic League. This city-wide program has reached many thousands of youngsters, and the participation of girls in terms of numbers and achievement has rivaled that of boys. In fact, several Olympic female athletes have been graduates of the N.Y.C. Police Athletic League.

The success to date of these varied devices and techniques of police-sponsored recreation would be difficult to appraise. Police recreation, as a field, is still too heterogeneous in aims, techniques, and scope for an objective appraisal. In some cities, a high participation figure might be interpreted as success. However, if closer inspection indicated that the majority of participants were not those in whom the police should be interested or if large numbers of those youngsters situated in subnormal environments were being missed or ignored, then success would be dubious. Similarly, the acquisition of additional sports and recreation facilities, increased staffs and budgets, better publicity and public relations should not in themselves be construed as clear evidence of a successful

operation. Police-sponsored recreation is based on the premise that it will help to prevent crime by working with youth. Only accurate long-range studies of large numbers of cases and situations in which recreation is used by police as a crime-prevention device will establish with some certitude the success or failure of the police-sponsored recreation program.

Frequently, at professional recreation conferences and meetings, a public or private recreation executive or worker may be heard saying: "Why don't those cops stick to their police work and leave recreation work to recreation people?" or "Things were fine in our town until the police chief decided to start a P.A.L. Then he moved in, took over the best facilities, and started competing with everyone else." At the same meetings, however, there are just as many reports of wise use of the recreation method by a police officer or department or of excellent cooperation between police and local recreation authorities on a joint recreation project. In a small New Jersey town, for example, the one-man Police Athletic League staff of the local police department is doing an outstanding job. Instead of competing with local recreation authorities, this police officer works with them. He uses their facilities and programs, feeding his troublesome gangs or individuals into the public recreation activities. In reciprocation, he provides police cooperation to the public and private agencies by expediting the procurement of parade permits, permits for use of fire hydrants, and permits for other recreation projects. He helps with the coaching of teams and officiating at games and assists the recreation workers in a number of other ways. Cooperation is the key to the smooth-working system in this town.

A consideration of some advantages and disadvantages involved when the community police sponsor and operate recreation programs should be helpful.

Advantages

The traditional hero worship in boys and girls for the uniformed policeman still exists. The cop who can box, hit a homer in softball, sink a long shot in basketball, or run a fast mile is twice the hero he would be in civilian clothes. This may serve as a bridge between youth and the law.

Police are extremely close to the grass roots of communities everywhere. They come into daily contact with the infinite number of groups, organizations, nationalities, and individuals that make up communities. This is particularly true in crowded, underprivileged sections of large cities. These contacts can be invaluable in organizing an indigenous recreation program for youth in such areas.

Much of police officers' daily work is with youth. Whether they are checking on cases of truancy, youthful drinking, ball games in streets, teenage hot-rodding, or simply returning a lost or runaway child, police officers are developing an awareness and firsthand understanding of the psychological problems and recreation needs of children and youth.

Frequently, the authority connected with the police officer's position may be needed to open up a tight situation. For example, he may pressure a street gang into visiting a local agency so that members may at least be introduced to the many recreation activities and facilities available to them. Some persons may question the value of this authoritarian approach to the promotion of recreation interests. These critics must realize, however, that the finest program and facilities are of no avail if the youths do not enter the building or program for so much as a look. If this method encourages no more than one in ten to join the program and return regularly, its use has been more than justified. Note that this point refers chiefly to police and recreation in highly delinquent areas.

The age and background of today's police officers must not be overlooked. Today's police officers are, generally, a younger group than those of 25 years ago. Among them are a high percentage of war veterans, athletes, and persons who have attended some college. Their personalities, former occupations, war experiences, and widely varied backgrounds represent a bridge useful in reaching and working with wayward youngsters who might scorn the conventional community recreation approach.

Disadvantages

Prevention of crime and maintenance of the public peace constitute the primary functions of police departments. This does not include providing recreation programs and facilities for youth. Consequently, all the difficulties involved in attempting to carry out a strange additional duty are inherent in this situation.

Most police department budgets are trimmed to a minimum on even the most orthodox police equipment and activities. Rarely, if ever, is any sizable fund provided for police-sponsored recreation programs. Therefore, finances must be augmented by donations through ticket sales, fund drives, and so on. Frequently, this places the uniformed police officer in the role of ticket or "ad" salesman or gift solicitor. Public reaction is generally good financially but poor psychologically. Police officers dislike this task even more than those approached. In addition, it puts an exorbitant value on publicity for the program since it must be kept constantly before the public eye to ensure continued contributions. It is a short step to the highly touted tournaments and champions, the endless pictures of politicians and celebrities donating cash or presenting trophies, and the consequent neglect of the youths who are lost somewhere along the way.

Owing to their small operating budgets and the informal manner in which many police-sponsored recreation programs are established and operated, little regard has been shown for the professional training and background of the operating personnel. This is true particularly in the police-sponsored recreation activities of towns and small cities. In the larger cities greater concern has been evidenced regarding professional preparation. By and large, however, the general pattern in selecting staff is to choose young police officers, frequently former athletes, who have some college background, physical training in the armed forces, or work in youth camps or in boys' activities. Rarely are any professional requirements beyond these established or observed. There has been an increase in in-service training, but a great deal more of this is needed.

Police departments and their methods of operation have evolved slowly over the years and many of the old-time philosophies and techniques still linger. Steeped in tradition as it is, the modern police department may still, on occasion, be guilty of an anachronistic philosophy or technique, and this can thwart the efforts of the police recreation program or unit. For example, a police officer doing an excellent job in youth work may be returned to pounding a beat in uniform on relatively short notice for any number of reasons. This could discourage an ambitious officer from laying too extensive plans or programs in a temporary recreation assignment. The officer may further be discouraged by the attitude of fellow police officers who frequently regard the officer doing youth or recrea-

tion work as having "pull" or being in a "soft" detail.

Police officers are some of the starkest realists alive; their work makes them so. Consequently, they often question the values of social work techniques used in delinquency prevention and treatment. True, the esoteric aims and motives of some social workers in handling juvenile delinquents have frequently justified this skepticism on the part of the uniformed officer who must cope daily with the problems on the street. Nevertheless, this has created a situation wherein little rapport exists between the working police officers and the social and recreation workers in their locales. Many police departments operate a juvenile or youth bureau, one of the functions of which is to maintain this liaison between police and public and private youth and recreation agencies. However, this arrangement has the drawback of placing a third party between the private social or recreation worker and the police officer on the street who is in closest contact with the actual situation.

There are additional advantages and disadvantages of police-sponsored recreation, but the ones listed here should give a good indication of the breadth of the problem.

General recommendations

For those who may be planning to institute programs of police-sponsored recreation, a few recommendations follow:

1. *Determine the need for recreation.* Study the specific problem, condition, or community closely from several angles. There should be ample reason to believe that a recreation program will help the situation or else the program is not worth considering. Sound professional recreation and social work advice should be solicited to aid in determining this need.

2. *Search for an existing agency to meet*

the need. Whatever the condition or problem, it is quite possible that an organization or agency already exists locally that can meet this need for recreation. Is there a municipal recreation department? Search the area for a club house, settlement house, youth agency, group work agency, church or school group, or any other existing unit that may be equipped to meet the need or that may, in fact, already be attempting to meet the need. Upon finding such an agency, enlist its help in doing the job.

3. *Help the agency.* After enlisting the aid of the local agency to meet the need for recreation, throw all the help and support you can muster into assisting the agency to do the job. Work as closely as possible with agency personnel who are attempting to meet the particular need. For example, if a group of wayward boys has been entered in a local youth club's program by a police officer interested in their case, the police officer can assist the club staff by being present when possible at meetings and involving the boys, by participating occasionally in sports events with them, by encouraging them to participate more and more in the recreation program, and by keeping the agency personnel posted on any new outside developments that might affect the boys' behavior. Occasionally, the officer may provide the authority needed to keep the boys in the program long enough for it to have some perceptible effect. The officer's continued interest in these cases can have a very definite effect on the results of the agency's work with them.

4. *Establish police-sponsored programs.* When the search fails to disclose a local agency capable of meeting the determined recreation need, a police-sponsored recreation program should be established to do the job. This may mean anything from the formation of an individual athletic team, league, or boxing club, to building and staffing police-sponsored playgrounds and youth centers.

If, however, at a later date, a private agency is located or a new agency is instituted that can adequately meet the need for which the police-sponsored recreation unit was established, the police officers should give all their support to the agency assuming the task. This is consistent with the policy that police-sponsored recreation is established and operated only where there is no public or private agency capable of meeting the specific recreation need concerned.

Additional suggestions for police-sponsored recreation units already in operation follow.

Confine activities to definite trouble spots or areas. Concentrate on these. To provide broad, city-wide programs of community recreation for all children is, after all, not within the scope of the average police department. This is the job of the public and private recreation agencies established specifically for this purpose.

Keep overhead and operating procedures to a minimum. Avoid duplicating the work of other recreation agencies or competing with them.

Obtain professionally qualified personnel, whether they be police officers or civilian employees. Beware of entrusting this recreation program to just anyone.

Cooperate closely with other recreation and youth-oriented agencies. Wherever possible, transfer participants and projects into these outside agencies, thus leaving the maximum of your personnel and facilities for work in the critical problem areas.

Avoid overstressing publicity on the programs or twisting the activities into mere publicity material. This tendency can become chronic with agencies totally dependent on fund-raising for finances, and it can seriously hamper the effectiveness of the program. Overemphasis on the membership theme and boasting of tremendous participation figures should also be avoided.

Be professional. Subscribe to all accredited publications and information sources in the field. Maintain regular contact with the NRPA and be represented at all professional recreation conferences within geographic reach of the location. Make use of the wealth of useful information available, and provide other recreation agencies with up-to-date accounts of what you are doing.

As a means toward crime prevention among youth, the recreation method can be a useful device in the hands of a soundly organized and operated police recreation unit. Competition with, or overlapping of, public and private recreation agencies by the police-sponsored unit is wasteful and unjustifiable. Cooperation with other agencies by the police-sponsored unit is the key to its ultimate success in meeting recreation needs and thus helping to prevent crime.

LET'S DE-SOPHISTICATE

Is your program "all nylon, neon, and chrome?" This is an appeal to recreation departments all over the country to take a hard, objective look at their activities and operating policies with an eye to reducing their rich program fare. Perhaps it can be blamed in part on television, on our accelerating life style, on technology, and on a lot of other things, but the net result is a mild stampede to soup-up or apply "slick-em" to many of our programs and activities. Many recreation executives have liberally sprinkled their schedules with sports car gymkhanas, social dance classes for small children, holiday parades of flashy convertibles loaded with glamour girls, beauty contests, fashion shows for youngsters, and some herculean efforts to bring as much of the equipment, techniques, lingo, and expense of adult professional sports into the work of children's games.

What do we hope to achieve? We may transform the community recreation program from a dusty, tousle-haired, patched-in-the-seat kind of thing into something of nylon, neon, and chrome. Let's de-sophisticate! Let's keep our enthusiasm high, stimulating people to participate, rather than merely to watch, but let's stress more of the wholesome and less of the gaudy and flashy program ideas.

Making men and women out of our youngsters too soon, with heavy emphasis on social and ballroom dancing when they are 9 to 12 years of age, is one specific demonstration of this salute to glamour. The tendency of boys and girls to prefer rough, outdoor activities to dancing and parlor games is often thwarted by well-intentioned social directors, professional and lay, who cajole the sheepish 10 year olds with "but you *must* learn to dance!" Then when resistance melts to the extent that they have learned a few stiff steps, they are literally shoved into social dance situations and encouraged to place this type of recreation high on their "must-do" list. Needless to say, the youngsters either brave the next few years, uncomfortably tolerating these dance situations, or they become genuinely preoccupied in them to the extent that interest in the more robust, outdoor activities may wane.

If this type of social pressure were left to individuals, damage might remain small, but of late many recreation departments have aided and abetted this movement to make our youngsters old before their time. Dance classes are meticulously organized and operated for pint-sized participants. The old-fashioned waltz and fox trot take a back seat to rock, the mambo, the cha-cha, the hustle, disco, and the merengue. Recently, some departments have teamed up with large retail stores and have staged children's fashion shows in conjunction with these dances. Do the children model in conventional children's clothes? No! They model scaled-down versions of what glamorous adults wear, from strapless evening gowns and high heels for the girls to tuxedos, homburgs, and *Saturday Night Fever* styles for diminutive "men." Why can't this age group be encouraged to add new sports and skills to its repertoire and utilize square and folk dancing, roller skating, musical games, and vigorous party games?

Putting parades together used to mean ranks of marchers, decorated floats, colorful signs, live bands, and forests of flags and banners. Most readers, however, have seen recent parades, some put on with recreation department assistance, that consist of a half dozen late-model convertibles borrowed from local car dealers (and labeled with advertising signs) and a truck or two, scantily decorated with a few strands of crepe paper and mounted with a raucous public-address system, playing taped music.

It is a fact of life that the automobile has become a big factor in the life of the modern American teenager. However, must we, as professionals, encourage this almost fanatic interest in cars and riding by sponsoring hot-rod shows, driving gymkhanas, sportscar shows, and motorcades to and from places? Isn't it a part of our responsibility, as fitness-minded people, to counter some of the lazy, car-riding habits of today by encouraging interest in walking, hiking, bicycling? Let's chip away some of the golden aura that surrounds the car in the teenager's mind and replace it with an affection for fast, strong legs and trim figures. Needless to say, there is little to justify the recent establishment of midget-racing car clubs using tiny, powered racers, piloted by drivers as young as 5 and 6 years of age. After hours behind the wheel of a powerful lit-

tle racing car, what charm could remain for a child in a slow bicycle or a pair of roller skates? The advent of the inexpensive Moped (gasoline-powered bicycle) has made powered wheels even cheaper and easier to obtain.

When it comes to the sports waterways, a similar intoxication exists with the outboard motor. Sheltered waterways are crammed with youths of all ages driving every conceivable type and size of powerboat, the faster the better. Rowboats and canoes are few and far between. Recreation departments can do much to bring back their popularity. And here I have a complaint with water skiing. For the time, expense, fuel, and heavy equipment involved, it serves very few people. It is pure fun, of course, but offers little in the way of body development or carryover skills for other sports. The chance of water skiing being included in the Olympics is dim, to say the least. Meanwhile, this activity needs fast, powerful boats, and large portions of water area become too dangerous for other activities while someone is skiing.

Little League has done a fantastic job for over a quarter of a century in reviving interest in baseball and providing vigorous sport for millions of boys. However, there is little need for much of the lingo and paraphernalia many individuals bring into their youth sports programs. Miniature ball parks include public address systems, for instance, that announce the name of each player coming to bat as though he were a World Series star. In Pop Warner Football, expensive equipment, such as heavy football helmets, have ponderous plastic chin guards for 8 year olds who are exposed to little or no risk of the serious chin injuries that might occur among older, bigger players. Unnecessarily gaudy uniforms, warm-up jackets, and sweatshirts might well be replaced by less expensive but serviceable baseball suits or uniform T-shirts. These items would reduce the glamour elements that presently embellish our children's sports. A happy exception to this is the rapidly growing and very popular youth soccer program. Here, the expense and equipment have been kept minimal, and participation maximized.

You can lop off much of this artificiality, this Madison Avenue chrome, from your programs without doing serious harm. Trim the glamour from your activities. The positive results from your program will, in time, show a marked increase in interest and attendance. Stress, instead, the simpler, less expensive, and more basic types of activities. Hiking, running events, bicycling, throwing, community singing, acting, square dancing, constructing, simple camping, swimming, and rowing are the things that should be emphasized. Santa Claus' arrival on an old fashioned sled may not make as hot news copy as would his arrival by sports car, jeep, army tank, helicopter, or jet, but it makes better traditional community recreation for the kids, the kind they can understand and cherish for years to come. Ease up on the garish, the artificial, the "quick, easy, and big." Feature the human, the handcraft way, the live band, the warm, full voices (off-key included), the foot-travel way, the intimate, the small-town way. Three simple goals should guide your choice of activities: (1) fitness through fun, (2) family recreation and (3) community spirit.

Fitness through fun means getting the point across to youth and young adults that it's fun to box, to lift weights, to run, to hike, to swim, and that a fitter, trimmer body will be a by-product. Family recreation, a "must" for any sound-thinking recreation department, means skating parties, picnics, outings, shows, trips, and countless other events, all with a family flavor. Community spirit implies events such as parades, municipal birthdays, celebrations to kindle and nourish a genuine feeling of affection and identity with your town.

The jet-atomic-rocket age is here and we stand on the threshold of outer space. However, even on the moon there will be room for a square dance, a minstrel show, a volleyball game, and other old-fashioned leisure time diversions. In fact, the hunger for such "earthy" activities may be greater than ever.

REFERENCES

1. Kando, T. M.: Leisure and popular culture in transition, St. Louis, 1975, The C. V. Mosby Co.
2. Kraus, R. G.: Recreation and leisure in modern society, New York, 1971, Appleton-Centure-Crofts.
3. Summers, M.: A popular history of witchcraft, New York, 1973, Causeway Books.
4. Sunday News p. 9, March 5, 1978.

19
TOMORROW'S LEISURE

Looking into the future has always fascinated humans and sometimes frightened them. Such peering forward can draw criticism and scorn and the labels of "dreamer," "starry-eyed," or "spaced-out." But without such straining to look over the horizon, we are next to helpless in the face of rapidly changing events. We might be better able to cope with these changes if we have some inkling of what tomorrow may bring. As Toffler[3] puts it: "In dealing with the future, at least for the purposes at hand, it is more important to be imaginative and insightful than to be one hundred percent 'right.' Theories do not have to be 'right' to be enormously useful."

No crystal ball is needed. A glance at today's newspapers, professional journals, recreation publications, and scientific news items provides volumes in the way of signals, directions, and guideposts to tomorrow's life and tomorrow's leisure. Guaranteed to be accurate? Of course not, simply a series of guidelines and indicators that, when translated and extrapolated, provide a tantalizingly fuzzy outline of things to come. Even these fuzzy outline images are subject to further influence and change as new trends and new factors come to bear. Nevertheless, here we go.

HEALTH, MEDICINE, AND DEATH

The American annual health, hospital, and medicine bill is approaching $200 billion. People are unhappy with it; everyone is convinced there must be a better way, a cheaper way to be healthier and happier in this affluent society.

Medicines and therapeutic drugs are proliferating and are being used in countless new settings—to alter behavior, to help marriages, to ease pain, to produce greater Olympic performances, and to induce greater sexual potency.

Mechanical aids and prosthetic devices are becoming more sophisticated and more effective. Cardiac pacemakers, electronic eyes, plastic valves for the heart, organ transplants and replacements, teeth, ears, bones, and hips are all being manufactured and installed in humans with increasing degrees of success. Organ banks and transplants are rapidly becoming standard procedure in many surgical centers.

Our knowledge of food, nutrition, and our own bodies is advancing. Dr. John Knowles, Director of the Rockefeller Foundation and former Administrator of the Massachusetts General Hospital, has stated that the next big advance in American health will be getting people to take care of themselves, improving their own health.

Finally, the formerly guarded subject of death and dying is opening up and is being discussed candidly by television, press, radio, and the public.

These changes in health and medicine have some significant possibilities for the future of recreation. Therapeutic recreators must prepare for convalescent patients who live to be 85, 90, and 100 years old, assisted by electronic and pharmaceutical aids. Arms and legs, once regarded as hopeless, will be restored or replaced. With greater use of substitute limbs and organs, it will be difficult to identify who is "whole," or "normal," as compared with those with all types of replacement parts. More mechanical aids will emerge and multiply. A recent ad in the *New York Times* for Hammacher-Schlemmer, America's most famous housewares shop, extolled the virtues of the "Environmental Sound-X." This 8 inch by 10 inch by 10 inch box, a solid state electronic sound conditioner, "promotes sleep, relaxation, and concentration." It can simulate "white sound" (nonidentifiable), single waves breaking on a beach, a rough, random surf sound, or a variety of night rain sounds—all for $129.95.

Behavior modification, the intensive psychological effort to alter personalities, will be widely used. Recreation specialists must learn the skills and effects of this process, as well as biofeedback.

Recreation and fitness activities will become increasingly popular, especially if they generate self-confidence and self-sufficiency. Judo, karate, hiking, swimming, parcourse skills, rope climbing, dancing, wrestling, weight lifting, boxing, and gymnastics can anticipate considerable growth.

The gap between high-skill professional athletes and formerly low-skill amateur athletes will narrow. Amateurs in recreational sports will utilize the latest training techniques and devices, the finest playing gear, films, books, and so forth so that they will be ready to challenge professionals in tennis, golf, wrestling, sailing, boxing, and a host of other activities.

Increasingly, recreation will be thought of less as "fun" and more as "therapy." Clinical as this may sound, it will enable a much greater professionalization and a far greater budgetary investment than today. There will be more documentary evidence to corroborate recreation's real contribution to physical and mental health. It will then assume its deserved professional role alongside law, surgery, finance, psychiatry, and education.

Home health care will expand tremendously. Dr. B. Leslie Huffman, Jr.,[1] President of the American Academy of Family Physicians, says: "Over and over, we have found that patients do best at home. At home they keep involved, they feel needed, they feel independent. And they are happier

among their own belongings." This will mean a far greater decentralization of patients, more home visits by recreation therapists, and a decreasing amount of large hospital ward recreation.

A whole new psychology of life/death/the hereafter will develop. Formerly, where recreation interests were difficult to arouse in persons with terminal cancer, paralysis, pneumonia, and leukemia, this may change with a broadening horizon of life after death. A new kind of optimism on the part of patients may enable the recreator to bring some happiness and joy into otherwise morbid lives. It is conceivable that recreation leaders will convince patients with terminal diseases that they should utilize their remaining time to learn recreational skills for use in the "great beyond."

FAMILY GROUPS

The traditional family unit in America continues to experience unprecedented change. Birth rates are at record lows; divorces and separations at record highs. The appetite for sex has not abated, but the variety of philosophies, techniques, and devices aimed at preventing childbirth is wide and deep. The following news item is indicative:

Aside from total abstinence, there's no more effective form of birth control than sterilization. It now rivals the pill as the leading contraceptive methods used by married couples in the U.S., according to a recent study for the National Institutes of Health. Vasectomies—the universal operation for men—accounted for about half the 6.8 million sterilizations for contraceptive purposes reported in the survey. They are fairly minor operations that are usually done on an outpatient basis.[2]

I am disturbed by the finality of this process and the awesome possibility for the human future implicit in it. We are told that such operations are "easily undone" or reversed at any time, but the practice is too new and the history too short for anyone to be certain of its ultimate impact on the procreation of people.

Meanwhile, all family structures and family relations are being buffeted by constantly shifting social winds. Many households today consist of one person. Residences of two males, two females, several individual young people, and a man and woman living together without formal marriage are relatively common. In others, one adult lives with someone else's children, or one parent lives alone with his or her children. The traditional household of working Dad, homemaking Mom, and their own three or four children is not nearly as prevalent as it was just 10 years ago. More than half of today's wives/mothers are in some kind of full- or part-time paid employment.

Some additional forces have an impact on the quality and pattern of American family life. Early social sophistication of children; women's liberation; heavy television viewing; technological equipment in elementary schools; wide mobility through cars, cycles, trucks, and vans; and a highly charged advertising atmosphere are just a few. The result is a fragmented family life and a tendency toward erratic choice of leisure places and things. Unfortunately, this can also bring on tension, stomach trouble, headaches, and emotional breakdowns.

These changes in the traditional family group have significant possibilities for the future of recreation. There will be an increasing need for family recreation that is cheaper, more exciting, and more convenient to urban neighborhoods. Family swimming, picnicking, bicycling, camping, and even competitive activities such as judo, wrestling, fencing, and boxing will be encouraged for family participation.

Family rates at restaurants, motels, parks, resorts, theaters, and arenas will make it far more attractive to go family style rather than solo. Further, it will be more advantageous for groups of families to combine for trips, theatre, restaurants, amusement parks, and resort reservations. Entrepreneurs will realize that such price concessions are more than recovered through regular patronage and in savings on security, insurance, and vandalism repair.

New homes will include radical changes to accommodate leisure life styles, home sports, games, gardening, hobbies, crafts, and physical fitness activities. There is a strong possibility that such leisure innovations may return the family unit to its former popularity.

The recreator must prepare for and accommodate a much broader spectrum of household units than was characteristic in the 1980s. A more permissive society and an increasing national mobility connected with jobs, research, college, family units, religion, and health will bring about widely scattered and mixed living units, each of which moves between and among many of the others. This represents a substantial challenge to the recreator.

MONEY, CREDIT, AND WEALTH

Dollar figures continue to spiral upward, and it is not entirely the result of inflation. Individual earnings are increasing, and the sums of money involved in corporate giving, executive fitness and health, and industrial and commercial recreation are astronomical. The Ford Foundation, with permanent assets of over $3 billion, contributes $250 million annually to projects and charities, including human services and education.

Meanwhile, a rather disturbing mass of credit and debt continues in America and throughout the world. Thousands of new millionaires are being created, many of them founded on paper and hopes for business success in the future. The competitive banks of today provide "instant loans," "redi-credit," "phone loans," and other attractive devices that put almost unlimited credit spending directly into the hands of depositors. Inevitably, such open systems invite abuse. This combination of continued expansion of leisure services and a tidal wave of credit buying should provoke the following:

Many agencies and municipalities will do less bonding of large capital projects and more pay-as-you-go financing. This is aimed at avoiding high interest payments and remaining attractive on the municipal bond market, just in case a bond issue becomes inevitable. Major construction projects will be fewer and much more carefully selected.

Many conventional recreation activities will be linked up with credit card systems so that there will be very little cash handled at recreation centers, YMCA's, and community schools. This will substantially increase memberships and participation but will ultimately complicate the collecting of fees, and will bring recreators a new problem—collecting bad debts.

A teaming up of community recreation and commercial recreation is inevitable. The community recreator has the experience, expertise, and close contact with local people; the commercial recreator has the money, designers, and publicity potential. This could mean public parks and beaches taken over, improved, and operated by Howard Johnson, Inc., Holiday Inns, or Hilton Hotels. Pools, ski lodges, horseback riding stables, and ice rinks are all adaptable to this new team effort. The bold designs, dramatic presentations, and attention-getting programs of the commercial sector will be introduced into large urban parks such as Griffith's Park, Los

Angeles; Lincoln Park, Chicago; Fairmount Park, Philadelphia; and Central and Prospect Parks, New York City.

TRAVEL, ENERGY, AND TRIPS

Energy will never again be cheap, at least not before the year 2000. Ways and means must be found to combine efforts to bring recreation closer to people (counter to the trend of the 1950s and 1960s when leisure and recreation facilities were moved farther and farther away from urban population centers). Consumption of energy will be curtailed, and new commercial recreation ventures must bear this carefully in mind. Some of the effects of this conservationism include the following.

Fewer new artificial ice rinks will be built without roofing and insulation to withstand changes in temperature and atmosphere. No new uncovered rinks will be built south of Boston or Sacramento.

Growth will be in technically sound, sealed malls or giant buildings where all facilities will be protected against the elements. Thus, the facility will be assured 12 months of operation compared with just the summer months that were considered adequate in the past.

Car pooling and bus transportation will increasingly become part of recreation planning. Long trips will be less frequent. Short, in-city trips will be encouraged. This could be a boon to older northeastern cities that have seen their constituents moving farther into the suburbs for 25 years. It could also be a stimulus to bring many of them back to the city as residents.

We may have seen the last of the gigantic enclosed stadiums to be built. These mammoth buildings are so expensive to plan, build, and operate, and so many sports franchises have perished, that such growth appears ended. The energy consumption of these massive sports and entertainment facilities is enormous. Not only is the energy expensive, but it may shortly be reduced in supply and it is not possible to operate these great installations on half power. Smaller, old-fashioned ball parks and stadia will flourish because of their traveling convenience and their relatively low cost of operation, a very important factor in the future plans of public recreation departments. Ancient Fenway Park in downtown Boston, with its modest 30,000 capacity, suddenly looks quaint and homey, and may never be replaced by a big new stadium.

SCIENCE AND TECHNOLOGY

Toffler warns us repeatedly of the awesome technological and scientific marvels already available to us and the geometric rate by which these marvels grow. Aviation, medicine, surgery, psychiatry, radio, electronics, construction, space-propulsion, food research—each of these and dozens more continue to produce engineering miracles faster and faster. The recreator works within this, an accelerated inventive culture, and must be alert to its incredible potential. Let us look at what some of these scientific and technical advances can mean to recreation.

Electronics are unbelievable. A recent Consumer Electronics Show at Las Vegas brought together 43,000 manufacturers, buyers, and distributors of electronic devices. "It was an excellent year in every product category. We ran out of everything," stated Edward J. Garland, Vice President of Toshiba America, Inc., one of the largest electronics manufacturers in the world. In 1977, 5 million electronic television games were sold, along with record sales in television sets, sound systems, calculators, and digital watches. Now, intrafamily "marriages" are taking place in which the television set is teamed up with

clock, sound system, and calculator; the television game moves up to new levels of sophistication; electronic memories store unlimited amounts of information and entertainment for future replay—there is no ceiling in sight for these hybrid developments.

The American public, and for that matter the publics of every nation, are technology minded. This invites a vast expansion of electronic recreation. Golf-o-rama, the electronically simulated indoor 18-hole golf game is extremely popular with bona fide golfers, especially during inclement weather and the winter months. This suggests possibilities for instruction in fencing, crafts, gymnastics, body building, musical instruments, and other high skill areas. The recreation center of the future, be it located in apartment house complex, military base, hospital, or prison, may be only a small suite of activity rooms built around a television console with unlimited tapes and casettes. A great portion of the learners and participants may never come to the center but may take their direction and instruction by way of closed circuit television monitors in their apartments, wards, or cells.

Nathan Cobb, staff writer for the *Boston Globe,* believes that by the early 1980s, American television-watching will have reached a science fiction level of sophistication and complexity. The viewing area will now be a fine-grained 5 feet by 5 feet screen dominating the entertainment room. Cobb notes that the A. C. Nielson Co., internationally renowned rating master, finds the typical home television set turned on 6 hours and 19 minutes daily. This is a total of 2260 hours per year or 200 hours more than most of us work during the same year. Only sleep time tops television time, and not by much.

There will be a new television equipment explosion, matching and outdoing the stereo explosion of the 1960s. Variety, flexibility, and interconnections will be featured. Some $10 billion will be spent on items such as Sony's Betamax, Quasar's Great Time Machine, and Sanyo's Vcord II, with RCA, Magnavox, Sylvania, JVC, Panasonic, Toshiba, and Pioneer right behind them. Recreation skills, recreation philosophies, body facts, knowledge about sex, love, fear, birth, and death will pour from these devices in undreamed of quantities.

The great amount of knowledge and technology deriving from NASA and the space projects will have its impact on recreation and sports. Experiments on human beings have already begun with raised and lowered atmospheric pressures, gravities, temperatures, whirling speeds, and so forth. Variations of these concepts will likely be converted into Coney Island–like parks, resorts, and gadgetry so that ordinary citizens may experience the thrills and physical sensations of space travel. Medical and educational possibilities of these technologies will also be researched in hopes of producing fitness through adaptability. The potential here for recreational therapy is vast.

America's present industrial plant is considered obsolete by Japanese and German standards. These two countries, devastated by World War II bombings, started from scratch in the 1950s and built everything new. Ours is still a patched-up version of a 1920-1940 model. The next giant step by industrial America may overtake and surpass Japan and Germany in a year 2000 version of automation. This could eclipse anything we see now and could change the work week and life-style of America on an unprecedented scale. The size, quality, and depth of this challenge to the recreator is frightening. The 4-day week may become the 2-day week, the work day a mere 3 hours. People

will search for leisure pursuits as never before, and while they search, they may have to be on their guard avoiding the ominous social predictions of George Orwell's *1984*.

OPEN SPACE

A curious dichotomy appears to have become a permanent fixture in the modern image of the ideal living environment. As people become more technologically sophisticated and skilled, their appetites for the simple, the homespun, and the primitive become more insatiable. Camping, hiking, log cabins, seashore cottages, bicycling, and vegetable gardens have been growing phenomenally as popular leisure diversions. All indications are for continued growth into the next century, with nostalgia becoming a way of life in itself.

This means a militant public campaign to secure and expand forests, prairies, national parks, wilderness areas, and other special preserves. Regional and state parks are important, but nothing can replace, electronically or psychologically, the vastness of the mountaintop, the sweep of the open surfing beach, or the hills of America's Great Plains. Even those who rarely visit the national parks and forests derive a reassurance and security from the fact that they are there in their enormous solitude. Primitive open space will take on a value beyond today's appreciation.

The variety of recreation gear will multiply and subdivide. Special devices for snow skiing, water skiing, surfing, snorkeling, hang gliding, gymnastics, flying, fencing, mountain climbing, and sailing will reflect the effects of new inventions, new engineering, and new electronics. Simulation, the computer-controlled process by which students can be installed and instructed in the most complex, exciting, and potentially dangerous situations with absolutely no danger, will open unlimited new learning opportunities. Skills and techniques for an infinite number of hobbies, crafts, sports, and diversions will be made instantly available through the new technology. One of the most serious problems facing people in the 1980s may well be what Toffler calls "overchoice," the frustration of facing an overwhelming glut of new, quick, exciting, cheap, and instant skills, hobbies, and study areas. We may all suffer the agony of the small child turned loose in F.A.O. Schwartz's main toy shop and told, "Go ahead, play with anything; it's all yours!"

SUMMARY

Tommorrow's recreation and leisure is already here, in part. It is discarding many of the earlier, primitive captions of "fun," "play," and "happiness," and adopting such prestigious labels as "therapeutic," "cathartic," "developmental," and "behavior modificational." Professionals will learn to document their efforts and justify their budget demands through hard facts and sound research. The methodology of educational research will become much more a part of recreation operations, as will systems analysis and cost/benefit ratios. The era of planning, budgeting, and acting recreationally for the "general good of the public" is past. The era of zero-based budgeting, backed by flawless research and evidence, is here.

Merrill Lynch, Pierce, Fenner and Smith, the world's largest brokerage house, has declared the areas of leisure services and health care to be two of the greatest investment fields of tomorrow.

Our work will enjoy an increased sophistication and, most important, an elevated dignity and respect in the eyes of medical, legal, engineering, education, and governmental professionals. The profession will expand and change and it will continue to offer challenging and satisfying careers.

REFERENCES

1. Huffman, B. L., Jr.: Money p. 118, October 1977.
2. Money p. 46, September 1977.
3. Toffler, A.: Future shock, New York, 1970, Random House.

INDEX